RETRIEVING THE AMERICAN PAST

A CUSTOMIZED U.S. HISTORY READER

EDITED BY

Instructor Gregory Gordon
College of Lake County
U.S. History 1876 to present

PEARSON CUSTOM PUBLISHING

Director of Database Publishing: Michael Payne
Sponsoring Editor: Natalie Danner
Development Editor: Katherine Gretz
Editorial Assistant: Samantha A. Goodman
Marketing Manager: Nathan L. Wilbur
Operations Manager: Eric M. Kenney
Database Project Specialist: Christopher Milot

Printed in the United States of America

10 9 8 7 6 5 4 3 2 1

0-536-61173-4
BA 5567

PEARSON CUSTOM PUBLISHING
75 Arlington Street, Suite #300/Boston, MA 02116
Pearson Education Group

CONTRIBUTORS

Senior Editor
Saul Cornell

Managing Editor
John Day Tully

Copy Editor
Ann Heiss

Assistant Managing Editor
Douglas M. Paul

Contributing Editors

Tyler Anbinder
Kenneth J. Andrien
Jean Harvey Baker
Michael Les Benedict
Mansel Blackford
Paul C. Bowers
Rowland Brucken
John D. Buenker
John C. Burnham
Joan E. Cashin
William R. Childs
Albert J. Churella
Steven Conn
Saul Cornell
Nick Cullather
Jeanette Davis
Merton L. Dillon
Daniel Feller
Charles Coleman Finlay
Emily Greenwald
Mark Grimsley
Bernard N. Grindel
Peter L. Hahn
James Hansen
Susan M. Hartmann
Mary Ann Heiss
Earl J. Hess
Michael J. Hogan
R. Douglas Hurt

Bruce Karhoff
Michael Kazin
Terence Kehoe
K. Austin Kerr
Frank Lambert
Valerie Mendoza
James McCaffrey
Allan R. Millett
Pamela J. Mills
Daniel Nelson
Margaret E. Newell
Josef Ostyn
Carla Gardina Pestana
Patrick D. Reagan
Randolph A. Roth
Hal K. Rothman
John A. M. Rothney
Leila J. Rupp
Richard D. Shiels
David Sicilia
C. Edward Skeen
Amy L. S. Staples
David L. Stebenne
David Steigerwald
Marshall F. Stevenson, Jr.
Warren R. Van Tine
Christopher Waldrep
J. Samuel Walker

Contents

The Rise of the Gay and Lesbian Movement

Transformation, Endurance, and Rejuvenation of American Indian Societies, 1870–1995

Jeanette Davis and Warren Van Tine

INTRODUCTION

Despite America's propensity to amuse its children with toy toma-hawks and feather bonnets and a current surplus of plastic soda cups embellished with the smiling face of Disney's Pocahontas, most Americans have little understanding of Native American history and culture. They have little knowledge of the legacy of the Indians' struggles to survive beside (or within) an ever-encroach-ing white world. What little comprehension most people have of historic Indians, they received from sentimental portrayals of the child-like "noble savage" or from fierce renditions of the "blood-thirsty heathen." Many modern Americans form their opinions of contemporary Indians from rumors of apathetic urban Indians surviving on welfare, or from accusations about drunken reserva-tion natives partying on profits from tourists' high-stakes bingo games.

Aware of the need to reassess the Native Americans' place in this country's historical record, and motivated in part by parallel concerns about black history, scholars of the 1960s–70s began to face the problem head on. Continuing attempts to incorporate Indian experiences into the pages of American history are produc-ing an ever-accumulating stack of published scholarship by histo-rians, anthropologists, and ethnographers. While today there is still a shortage of works on Indians by Indians, academic acknowledgement of this deficiency has stimulated efforts both to encourage Native Americans to write Indian interpretations of their own past and to find examples of "Native American voice" in the written record.

Part of the problem of incorporating the Indians' story into the general history of America is that there is no one Indian experi-

ence. While sharing an awareness of their corporate "Indianness," American Indians, known to scholars as "Native Americans," are composed of a growing number of individuals, each with differing perspectives and agendas. Some Indians are members of organized tribes; others are "urban Indians" or non-reservation Indians who may or may not have tribal affiliation. Some are "fuller-bloods" who can trace their Indian ancestry for numerous generations; others genetically have more white blood. (This factor is periodically made important by certain state/federal laws and regulations; the question of Indians with even traces of black blood only increases the legal and social implications in a racist society.) Some Indians are traditionalists who actively promote cultural continuity. Other Indians are eager to participate more fully in the white man's world, and, thus, accept varied levels of assimilation. This diversity is not a modern phenomenon. Too often, by depicting Indians as one monolithic entity with limited hopes and dreams, historical accounts of Native Americans have encouraged, or at least not discouraged, stereotypical images that are lifeless and colorless when compared to the vibrant humanity that composed the Native American peoples of the past, and that exist as the Indian community of the present. The documents that follow provide a tiny glimpse of the larger, more complicated, more enriched modern American Indian experience.

THIS LAND IS MY LAND! . . . OR IS IT YOURS?: THE UNITED STATES AND ITS "INDIAN PROBLEM"

The dramatic appeal of tragic symbolism may be partly responsible for America's tendency to bring the Indian narrative into mainstream history by simply inserting cameo roles for the likes of Geronimo or Sitting Bull. This makes for exciting history, but it tends to distort the reality of the past by limiting Indian participation to battles against white aggressors. This focus often portrays Indian peoples as passive victims or brutal savages who have no place in mainstream history after the last battle on the Great Plains. While Native Americans' ongoing struggle to retain smaller and smaller portions of a land they once enjoyed with impunity must be told, the story did not end with the closing of the nineteenth century. The readings provided here follow the ongoing historical struggle that Indians wage for control over their land, their lives, and their future; these selections also provide an opportunity to compare two different approaches to writing about the historical experiences of Native Americans.

As author of The Patriot Chiefs: A Chronicle of American Indian Resistance, *historian Alvin M. Josephy, Jr., chose to narrate the stories of nine renowned American Indians in order to record the long struggle between the white and red man as the embryonic nation of America slowly spread across the North American continent. The abridged selections included here reveal a dramatic glimpse at two historic Native American heroes, Crazy Horse and Chief Joseph. Originally copyrighted in 1958, almost annual reprintings necessitated a renewal of the copyright in 1989, perhaps testifying to the popularity of the "cameo" approach to Indian history.*

Vine Deloria, Jr., and Clifford M. Lytle in The Nations Within: The Past and Future of American Indian Sovereignty, *incorporate*

5

the experiences of Native Americans into the historical context of main-stream America by highlighting the basic problem of sovereignty. The selected reading follows the struggles of American Indian nations trying to deal with assimilation while being tossed back and forth like a legal football between state and federal authorities.

The "Indian Problem": Crazy Horse, Sioux Warrior

The end of the Civil War left many Americans bewildered, restless, or impoverished. Thousands of white and black Americans trekked through "Indian country" on their way west, lured by the hopes of striking gold or optimistically seeking a fresh start in a less violated part of America. This steady invasion aggravated the fears of the Indians who recognized the white travelers as only the advance guard of an encroaching army of traders, miners, soldiers, and settlers. For several decades, Crazy Horse was one of many Indian warriors who sparred in a series of bloody battles with U.S. soldiers. He was among several Sioux war chiefs who led their people into battle at the Little Bighorn River in 1876, rather than acquiesce to the white man's lust for the red man's homeland. While his valor won him the esteem of his people, his actions only fueled the anger of the American populace, calling for an ultimate conclusion to the "Indian problem."

Seeking retribution, the U.S. government forced peaceful factions of the Sioux to sign away the lands of the hostiles, despite an 1868 treaty that specifically required all treaty changes be approved by three-fourths of all of the adult males of the tribe. One Sioux band crossed over into Canada with Sitting Bull, remaining in exile until 1881. Crazy Horse's band evaded the soldiers by wintering in the Tongue River canyons until they ran out of food and ammunition. With the spring of 1877, Crazy Horse triumphantly led his undefeated band into the enemy fort to try to come to peaceful terms, an act that quickly led to his imprisonment. After Crazy Horse met his death at the hands of his military guards, his people performed one last act of valiant resistance as a memorial to their fallen leader. While on a forced march to their recently mandated new reservation, Crazy Horse's band swiftly turned their horses toward Canada, leaving their surprised and outnumbered federal escort to continue west-

ward with a reduced number of soon to be "reservation Indians" under redoubled surveillance. Thus, even in death, Crazy Horse's bravery and determination served as a model for his people in their continued efforts to resist oppression. From an Indian perspective, Crazy Horse's bravery and dignity under stress earned him a revered place in the pantheon of Native American heroes. But, amid the violent confrontations during the era of expanding frontier settlement, white Americans considered Crazy Horse one of the most savage and frightening of all their Indian enemies. In the following selection, Alvin M. Josephy, Jr., provides a brief account of Crazy Horse's best known exploit. Excerpted from Alvin M. Josephy, Jr., The Patriot Chiefs: A Chronicle of American Indian Resistance (New York, 1989), 257-59.

It was a little before three in the afternoon, June 25, 1876, the centennial year of the United States and the climactic day in the long history of warfare between the North American Indians and the white men. From a grassy ridge overlooking the valley of Montana's Little Bighorn River, Lieutenant Colonel George Armstrong Custer . . . started his five troops of the 7th Cavalry, some two hundred and twenty-five men, down the slope toward a huge encampment of Sioux and Cheyenne villages that lay along the river.

The American commander's impulsive action and the savage resistance of the Indians who swarmed out to meet him ended in a sensational massacre that shocked the nation. It was not the greatest triumph ever scored by Indians. . . . But the victory of the Sioux and their Cheyenne allies came when the industrialized American nation reached from coast to coast, when great armies and great generals had proved the might and power of the United States in a four-year Civil War, and when hostile natives were no longer a menace but a nuisance. The scalped and mutilated bodies on the bluffs above the Little Bighorn shamed and angered the American people. They smarted under the whipping, searched for scapegoats, attacked the Army, the government, and the so-called "peace element" that had pleaded for patience with the Indians, and demanded speedy retribution and a policy that would end further problems with "hostiles." . . . [T]he Sioux were the biggest and strongest unsubdued nation left in the United States, and the day had arrived to crush them.

. . . As in many Indian wars, the natives—wild and cruel as they had been made to seem—were not the aggressors. Ringed ever more tightly by growing numbers of white men, they had struggled desperately to maintain their freedom and way of life. Their battles were wild thrashings to escape the whites, to drive them away, and to keep enough of the huge plains country free of civilization for themselves and the herds of buffalo on which they lived.

Nor had they been united in their trials. Like many tribes before them, they had their weaklings and turncoats. . . . They also had their patriots, men who counseled freedom or death and who died on battlefields or in irons, shouting defiantly, "Come on, Lakotas [Teton Sioux name for "allies"], it's a good day to die!" American military leaders and war correspondents in the West, seeking a native genius behind the Custer massacre, singled out one of the Sioux for recognition, . . . [a] war leader named Sitting Bull, and after the wars Buffalo Bill and others promoted the obliging but still unchastened Sitting Bull as the greatest of all the Sioux warriors. But to the Indians themselves the title was misplaced. In the loneliness of a guardhouse at Fort Robinson, Nebraska, on September 5, 1877, their noblest hero, a shy, brooding young chief named Crazy Horse, only thirty-five years old, fighting wildly to free himself from imprisonment, died under the furious lunges of a sentry's bayonet. . . . When Crazy Horse died, tears and a bitter stirring for revenge swept his followers among the Sioux nation, and agency officials feared a new uprising. Today, on the Sioux reservations of the West, his name is enshrined in the memories of his people, who are proud of their relationship to him. He never signed a treaty with white men, and resisted them all his life. To the Sioux he is the greatest of all their leaders.

The "Indian Problem":
Chief Joseph, Nez Perce Peacemaker

The Nez Perce, composed of several wandering bands, were devoted to their home territory in the northwest. In 1855, Nez Perce leaders signed a treaty with the U.S. government that defined a large reservation for the tribe. In the 1860s, increased white encroachment on Nez Perce lands prompted the government to attempt to force a new treaty on the peaceful Indians. Joseph, as chief of one of the bands, shared the responsibility for helping his people to decide how to respond to the white man's continued demands. The tension mounted as increased numbers of whites criss-crossed native lands searching for gold and homesteads. Thus, violence may have been inevitable. Young hotheads, both white and Indian, committed rash acts that rebounded on their people. Amid the bloodshed, Joseph and several other Nez Perce chiefs decided to lead their people to safer country; they were soon chased by contingents of armed soldiers.

Unknowingly foiled when their progress was telegraphed ahead to the appropriate military post, the Nez Perce camped for the night within a day's march of the Canadian border. During a brief lull in the soldiers' surprise attack, Chief Joseph made a personal decision that enough blood had been spilt. Joseph's dignity, even in the face of bloody defeat, aston-ished his captors. Whereas the massacre at the Little Bighorn aroused public anger against the Indians, Joseph's eloquence had the opposite effect. It caused a public outcry for an end to frontier violence and a peaceful solution to the "Indian problem." Chief Joseph's speech is in-cluded in the narrative below, abridged from Alvin M. Josephy, Jr., The Patriot Chiefs: A Chronicle of American Indian Resistance *(New York, 1989), 313-24, 326-32, 336-40.*

In June 1877, just one year after the Custer debacle, an unex-pected Indian outbreak flared in the West. To an American public wearied and disgusted with a governmental policy, or lack of policy, that seemed to breed Indian wars, this one, an uprising by formerly peaceful Nez Percés of Oregon and Idaho, was drama-tized by what appeared to be superb Indian generalship. One army detachment after another, officered by veterans of the Civil War, floundered in battle with the hostiles. Western correspondents telegraphed the progress of a great thirteen-hundred-mile fighting retreat by the Indians, swaying popular imagination in behalf of the valiant Nez Percés and their leader, Chief Joseph, who . . . became something of a combined national hero and military genius.

The government received no laurels, either, as the long trail of bitter injustices that had originally driven the Nez Percés to hostility became known. The war, like most Indian troubles, had stemmed from a conflict over land. For centuries the Nez Percés had occupied the high, grassy hills and canyon-scarred plateau land where Washington, Oregon, and Idaho come together. A strong and intelligent people, they had lived in peace with the whites since the coming of Lewis and Clark in 1805, and it was their proud boast that no member of the tribe had ever killed a white man.

Joseph was the leader of only one of the Nez Percé bands, a group of some sixty males and perhaps twice that number of women and children, who lived in the Wallowa Valley in the northeastern corner of Oregon. . . . [They] had lived there in security and peace for generations. . . . At the time there were some four to six thousand Nez Percés; most of them lived in small fishing villages . . . widely spread over a vast expanse of territory. . . . [D]uring his youth Joseph visited most of the settlements with his father, learning the tribal lore that held them all together as a single nation. . . .

From their earliest days, the Nez Percés were known to be a traveling people, and at various periods of the year journeyed far and wide from their home settlements. . . . Sometime about 1730 the Nez Percés first saw horses. . . . [T]he Nez Percés learned to practice selective breeding and developed a strong and beautiful type of spotted horse [Appaloosa] that became known for its speed and endurance. . . . By the end of the eighteenth century many of the Nez Percés had become essentially plains Indians, though they continued to return regularly to their home villages on the Columbia River tributaries. . . .

. . . [In 1805,] the members of the Lewis and Clark Expedition . . . emerged in the Nez Percé country. It was an exciting event for the villagers, who had never seen whites before. . . . [T]he Indians welcomed them into their settlements and gave them food. . . . In

1812, American traders of John Jacob Astor's company finally reached the Northwest and opened trade . . . and the Nez Percés received a growing supply of guns and trade goods. . . . The Indians liked the wild, free fur men, who helped them fight their mutual enemies the Blackfeet, and who lived with them in their camps as equals. . . . [S]ome of the mountain men took Nez Percé women as their wives. . . .

. . . [V]arious churches were soon racing one another to Oregon to save the Indians' souls. . . . A few of the leading men were converted. . . . [In] time many of the natives became disillusioned with the white man's medicine [religion], which did not seem to give them the new power in war and hunting that they expected. . . . [After neighboring Cayuse Indians, panicked by a measles epidemic, massacred a group of missionaries, Joseph's father took his band back to the Wallowa Valley to avoid further bloodshed.]

In 1855, after peace had returned to the country, . . . [Joseph's father] and the other Nez Percé leaders signed a treaty that defined a large reservation for the tribe. . . . But in 1860, when white trespassers found gold on Nez Percé land and . . . [w]hite men cheated, bullied, and murdered Nez Percés in their own country . . . there was no redress. . . . [In] 1863 commissioners arrived from the East to try to end the turmoil by gathering the Indians into a new and smaller reservation. For a while the Nez Percé chiefs at the council were united in opposition to the Americans' proposal, but finally, after secret night meetings with individual chiefs, in which the commissioners apparently gave promises of private favors, some of the leaders, headed by Lawyer, agreed to accept the new reservation. . . . [Joseph's father,] with some two-thirds of the tribal leaders, refused to sign the document. . . . [T]he aging chief is said to have returned to the Wallowa in anger from the council and to have torn up the Bible the missionaries had given him, exclaiming that he wanted nothing more to do with the white men or their civilization. . . .

. . . [In 1871, after burying his father within the disputed boundaries of their sacred homeland, Joseph] protested to the Indian agent on the reservation, and an investigation was undertaken by the Bureau of Indian Affairs to determine whether the Treaty of 1863 affected Joseph's band, which had not agreed to it. The inquiry resulted in a decision that the Wallowa still belonged legally to the Indians, and on June 16, 1873, President Grant formally set aside the Wallowa "as a reservation for the roaming Nez Percé Indians" and ordered the white intruders to withdraw.

. . . The settlers, refusing to move, threatened to exterminate Joseph's people if they did not leave the valley. In defiance of the presidential order, more whites rolled in by the wagonload. . . . In 1875 a new and confusing presidential edict reopened the Wallowa to white homesteaders.

The Nez Percés were dismayed. Young Joseph, called by the Indians Heinmot Tooyalakekt, meaning "thunder traveling to loftier mountain heights," counseled patience. He moved the Indian camps from the neighborhood of the settlers and again appealed to the federal authorities. . . . [A] new commission of five members was appointed to meet with the Nez Percés in November 1876 with authority to make a final settlement of the matter for "the welfare of both whites and Indians.". . .

[When the commission insisted that Lawyer had signed away the Nez Percé homeland in 1863,] Joseph had a ready reply that embarrassed them. "I believe the old treaty has never been correctly reported," he said. "If we ever owned the land we own it still, for we never sold it. In the treaty councils the commissioners have claimed that our country has been sold to the government. Suppose a white man should come to me and say, 'Joseph, I like your horses, and I want to buy them.' I say to him, 'No, my horses suit me, I will not sell them.' Then he goes to my neighbor, and says to him, 'Joseph has some good horses. I want to buy them but he refuses to sell.' My neighbor answers, 'Pay me the money, and I will sell you Joseph's horses.' The white man returns to me and says, 'Joseph, I have bought your horses and you must let me have them.' If we sold our lands to the government, this is the way they were bought.". . .

[With tensions mounting between whites and Indians, the commissioners were left to render a decision.] . . . [T]hey rendered it: Unless, within a reasonable time, all the non-treaty Nez Percés (the other bands that had not signed in 1863, as well as Joseph's people in the Wallowa) voluntarily came onto the reservation, they should be placed there by force. . . .

Immediately after the decision the Indian Bureau defined the "reasonable time" and ordered the Indians to come onto the reservation by April 1, 1877. It was almost an exact repetition of the order of a year before that had started the hostilities with the Sioux. . . . [T]he Indians pleaded in proud but pitiable terms to be allowed to remain in the lands where their fathers were buried . . . . [After humiliating attempts to negotiate with the whites,

Joseph finally realized that his little band had no choice. Ordered to relocate on a much smaller reservation, the Indians were granted a short grace period to gather their horses. It was during this respite that violence broke out when an infuriated young Indian brave sought revenge for the previous murder of his father by a white man. Certain of war, but hoping to retreat in peace, the non-treaty bands stole away. The U.S. military soon followed.]

Alert Indian spies warned the Nez Percés of the troops' approach. . . . The chiefs were uncertain whether to resist and detailed six men to take a flag of truce forward and try to arrange a peaceful meeting with the officers. . . . Behind the men with the white flag were other Nez Percés, sitting on their horses waiting. . . . Then a volunteer [with the U.S. Army] raised his rifle and shot at the truce team . . . and the fight was on. . . . In a few minutes the entire [army] command was cut into small groups fighting desperately for their lives. . . . [The Indians' victory] spread alarm throughout the settlements of the Northwest and angered the rest of the nation, to whom the Custer massacre was still fresh. . . . Within a week [General O. O.] Howard himself took the field. . . .

From the beginning it had been assumed by the whites that Joseph, spokesman for the non-treaties in peacetime, had also been leading them in war. . . . In addition, the Nez Percés had been conducting themselves in an unusual manner for Indians "on the warpath," refraining from scalping or mutilating bodies, treating white women and noncombatants with humanity and even friendliness, and otherwise adhering to what was considered the white man's code of war. This too was credited to Joseph. . . .

The truth was that Nez Percé successes were resulting from a combination of overconfidence and mistakes on the part of the whites, the rugged terrain that made pursuit difficult, and, to a very great extent, the Indians' intense courage and patriotic determination to fight for their rights and protect their people. Indian strategy and tactics had also played a role, but at each step of the way these were agreed upon in councils of all the chiefs and were carried out on the field by the younger war leaders and their warriors. . . . [The Nez Percé, at times outnumbered almost six to one, fought a series of bloody battles against U.S. Army troops as the Indians worked their way east and north from Washington and Idaho toward the Montana-Canada border and safety.] They had had enough of Howard and thought that if they left Idaho and went somewhere else the general . . . would leave them alone. . . .

[This] meant the final abandonment of their homeland, but with the people's safety weighing heavily on them Joseph and the other chiefs reluctantly agreed to the exodus. . . .

Smarting under increasing criticism from Washington, . . . Howard once more took after the Indians, doggedly following their trail up through the thick and tangled forest growth of mountain slopes to the high, ridge-top route that led from Idaho to Montana. . . . [W]ord of the Indian flight had been telegraphed ahead to Montana. . . . On and on the Indians hurried. . . .

. . . About thirty miles short of the Canadian line, exhausted by the long flight, they paused to rest, confident that they had outdistanced all pursuers. . . . The assault caught the Nez Percés in three groups. Some, including women and children, were on the distant side of the camp and were able to mount and flee to the north, where they scattered on the broken plains, to die from hunger and exposure or eventually to reach Canada in small, pitiful groups. Others, including Joseph, were trapped with the horses at some distance from the camp. A third group, at the village, found protection behind a low-lying ridge. These warriors, hidden behind rocks, opened a deadly fire on the attackers. . . .

The siege went on amid cold and snow flurries, and on October 4 Howard reached the battlefield with a small advance party that included two treaty Nez Percés. The appearance of their old enemy [Howard was the driving force behind the treaty/relocation struggle.], heralding the arrival of reinforcements for [Colonel Nelson] Miles, finally took the heart out of the suffering Nez Percés. . . . The chiefs held a final council. White Bird and Looking Glass still opposed surrender. Joseph pointed to the starving women and children in the shelter pits and to the babies that were crying around them. "For myself I do not care," he said. "It is for them I am going to surrender."

As the council broke up, Looking Glass was suddenly struck in the forehead by a stray bullet and killed. As the surviving warriors gathered around the slain chief, Joseph mounted a horse and, followed by several men on foot, rode slowly up the hill from the camp and across to the army lines where Howard and Miles awaited him. As he reached the officers, he dismounted and handed Miles his rifle. . . .

"Tell General Howard I know his heart," he said. "What he told me before I have in my heart. I am tired of fighting. Our chiefs are killed. Looking Glass is dead. Toohoolhoolzote is dead. The old men are all dead. It is the young men who say yes or no. He who led the young men is dead [Joseph's brother, Ollokot]. It is cold and we have no blankets. The little children are freezing to death. My people, some of them, have run away to the hills, and have no blankets, no food; no one knows where they are—perhaps freezing to death. I want to have time to look for my children and see how many I can find. Maybe I shall find them among the dead. Hear me, my chiefs. I am tired; my heart is sick and sad. From where the sun now stands, I will fight no more forever."

. . . At first the Indians were shipped by flatboats and boxcars to unfamiliar, hot country in the Indian Territory, where many of them sickened and died. But friendly whites and sympathetic societies in the East continued to work for them, and public sentiment finally forced approval of their return to the Northwest. In 1885 Joseph and most of his band were sent to the Colville Reservation in Washington. Joseph made many attempts to be allowed to resettle in the Wallowa but each time was rebuffed. In 1904 he died, broken-hearted, an exile from the beautiful valley he still considered home.

Attempts to Tidy Up After the "Indian Problem"

The closing decades of the nineteenth century witnessed a number of episodes of recalcitrant Indians refusing to bow to the wishes of the white man's government. But, finally most Native American groups were rounded up and confined. While many Americans were content to leave the Indians out of sight and out of mind, on ever-shrinking reservations, well-meaning but misguided reformers insisted that Native Americans had to be educated, forced to conform, and assimilated into white society.

Over the years the federal government has vacillated between extreme assimilationist policies and other policies, that on the surface appear to grant the Indians themselves a measure of control over their own destiny. In the 1960s-70s, many Native Americans, fed up with ineffective federal policies that often took the Indians two steps forward and three steps backward, began to speak out in militant protests.

In February 1973, members of the American Indian Movement (AIM) occupied Wounded Knee, South Dakota, the site of an 1890 massacre of Sioux Indians by U.S. soldiers. AIM's purpose was to draw attention to the United States's record of almost four hundred broken treaties with the Indians and to emphasize the harsh conditions (widespread poverty, extreme unemployment, alcoholism) on the reservations. Federal officials, still mad over AIM's six-day occupation of the Bureau of Indian Affairs in Washington, D.C. four months before, quickly surrounded the protestors. Witnesses differ on what happened next, but when the smoke cleared one Indian had been killed and another wounded in a battle with FBI agents. The seventy-one day siege finally ended with the government once again promising to reassess the treaty rights of Indians.

In the following selection, professor and author Vine Deloria, Jr., a Standing Rock Sioux and former executive director of the National Congress of American Indians, along with his co-author, Clifford M. Lytle, look back to the events at Wounded Knee and explain that the basic problem undermining U.S. Indian policy is the government's lack of understanding of the Indians' historical concept of sovereignty. Abridged from Vine Deloria, Jr., and Clifford M. Lytle, The Nations Within: The Past and Future of American Indian Sovereignty *(New York, 1984), 1–4, 7–15.*

It is not difficult to see that although Indians are poor and generally live in isolated places in rural America, they are not in most respects radically different from other Americans living in the same circumstances. In fact, one might observe, most Indians are not distinguishable from other Americans except on those occasions when they shed working clothes and perform dances in fancy costumes. . . . [W]hy do Indians believe they are different? And why does the United States government treat them differently?

Modern social reality and historical political reality are rarely consonant with each other. Contemporary Indian communities, both reservation and urban, represent the continuing existence of a particular group of people who have traditionally had a moral and legal claim against the United States. The fact that many Indian tribes continue to exist unassimilated is not due to the practice of traditional ceremonies as much as it testifies to the complex of legal and political ideas that have surrounded Indians for two centuries and made them understand the world in much different terms from any other group of American citizens.

American Indians are unique in the world in that they represent the only aboriginal peoples still practicing a form of self-government in the midst of a wholly new and modern civilization that has been transported to their lands. . . . The United States, after successfully revolting against the king of England, claimed to inherit Great Britain's right to buy the lands of the Indians [based on the Doctrine of Discovery articulated for the Christian kings much earlier by the pope], and this doctrine, modified to fit the internal, domestic law of the United States, has been the primary conceptual focus for all subsequent federal Indian law. . . .

Under the Constitution, Congress is given exclusive power to regulate commerce with foreign nations, among the several states, and with the Indian tribes. . . . There is no inherent power in any of the fifty states to deal with Indians at all. . . . [T]he Indian Citizenship Act of 1924 . . . gives all Indians born within the territorial limits of the United States full citizenship but adds that such status does not infringe upon the rights to tribal and other property that Indians enjoy as members of their tribes. A dual citizenship exists here . . . [;] Indians are not to lose civil rights because of their status as members of a tribe, and members of a tribe are not to be denied their tribal rights because of their American citizenship. Unfortunately, this distinction has not often been preserved, and in the 1920s, and again in the 1950s, Congress attempted to sever unilaterally the political relationship between Indian tribes and the United States, using the citizenship of individual Indians as its excuse. . . .

When we look back at the treaty negotiations between the United States and the respective Indian tribes, there is little mention of the complex of ideas that constitutes nationhood. . . . In almost every treaty, however, the concern of the Indians was the preservation of the people, and it is in this concept of the people that we find both the psychological and the political keys that unlock the puzzling dilemma of the present and enable us to understand why American Indians view the world as they do today. When we understand the idea of the people, we can also learn how the idea of the treaty became so sacred to Indians that even today, more than a century after most of the treaties were made, Indians still refer to the provisions as if the agreement were made last week. The treaty, for most tribes, was a sacred pledge made by one people to another and required no more than the integrity of each party for enforcement. That the United States quickly insisted that the treaties should be interpreted rigidly as strictly legal documents has galled succeeding generations of Indians and made permanent peace between Indians and the federal government impossible.

The idea of the people is primarily a religious conception, and with most American Indian tribes it begins somewhere in the primordial mists. . . . Tribal names generally reflect the basic idea that these particular people have been chosen from among the various peoples of the universe . . . to hold a special relationship with the higher powers. . . . Because the tribes understood their place in the universe as one given specifically to them, they had no need to evolve special political institutions to shape and order their society. A council at which everyone could speak, a council to remind the people of their sacred obligations to the cosmos and to themselves, was sufficient for most purposes. . . . Indians had no awareness of the complexity that plagued the lives of other peoples, in particular the Europeans.

. . . The Indians watched without understanding as the residents in the European settlements [in colonial America], bowed before arbitrary authority with a meekness that the Indians loathed. . . . Many Indian nicknames spoke derisively of the whites as "people who take orders," or "people who march in a straight line." . . .

To the Europeans, Indians appeared as the lowest form of man. No formal institutions were apparent. Leaders seemed to come and go almost whimsically. . . . No one seemed to be in charge of anything. . . . Most important social/political positions of leadership in tribes depended upon the personal prestige and charisma of the individual . . . [;] respect rather than popularity was the criterion by which Indians selected who would lead them. . . .

This kind of leadership and these kinds of informal governing institutions existed long ago, when Indian tribes were free to live as they wished. The substance of those days remained in Indian memories, but the political institutions and social customs changed quite rapidly as more contact with whites occurred, so that we can speak of these things now as the spiritual but not the practical heritage of Indians. . . . With respect to the lands they lived on, many Indians felt a strong religious duty to protect their territory. Future generations would need the lands to live on, many previous generations had migrated long distances to arrive finally at the place were the people were intended to live. One could sell neither the future nor the past, and land cessions represented the loss of both future and past to most Indians. . . .

[Faced with ever-expanding militant white settlers, many Indians were forced to relocate, often repeatedly.] Although Indians surrendered the physical occupation and ownership of their ancestral lands, they did not abandon the spiritual possession that had been a part of them. Even today most Indians regard their homeland as the area where their tribe originally lived. . . .

Today a terrible divisiveness exists in many Indian tribes. After almost a century of regarding their reservations as a place to live, Indians are discovering that they are being prodded into leasing large portions of their lands so that others can exploit the mineral wealth that lies underneath the ground. . . . Sacredness and utility confront each other within the tribal psyche, and it is not at all certain how Indians will decide the issue. Most Indians are so desperately poor that any kind of income seems a godsend. . . . [Yet,] as land is alienated, all other forms of social cohesion also begin to erode, land having been the context in which the other forms have been created. In such ideas lie the conceptual keys to understanding how the Indian experiences the world today.

With such understanding, we can see that the occupation of Wounded Knee in 1973 was far more traumatic for Indians than it was for whites, who might have felt a little disturbed at the idea of Indian militants taking up arms against the United States. Wounded Knee is symbolic of the conflict that is raging in Indian hearts everywhere. It arose basically over the question of how the Sioux, and by extension other Indians, should deal with the untenable situation created by the federal government in their communities. The tribes faced seemingly insoluble problems involving the form of tribal government [with the United States often imposing forms contrary to Indian traditions, forms that usually benefited the more acculturated Indians while placing the traditionalists at a disadvantage]; the claims filed against the United States that were not moving toward resolution; the use of land, tribal and individual, on the reservation; and the nature of education that Indians were receiving. Above all was the perennial dilemma of how Indians could pursue their own religious traditions in a world that refused to recognize the essential spiritual nature of life.

Politically the Wounded Knee occupation pitted traditional Indians and militants against the established tribal government, which had adopted a constitution and bylaws during the New Deal under somewhat less than promising circumstances. . . . [Sioux traditionalists had often voiced opposition, but] since the tribal government was the only form of political participation that the United States government would recognize and deal with, the traditionals had little choice except to boycott the tribal government and then hope that some crumbs would fall from the table of government largess . . . —an uncomfortable dilemma, to be sure.

From the perspective of the protestors, the point at issue in Wounded Knee was the *form of government* that the Sioux would use to direct their own destiny. From the perspective of the established tribal government—and, by extension, the federal government—the point at issue was *the direction that the existing tribal government would take.* . . .

Supporters of the tribal government argued that only through the Indian Reorganization Act [1934] did the Indians have self-government and that attacking the existing tribal government was in essence advocating anarchy, a condition that the United States could not allow under any circumstances. The response of those people who supported the traditionals and militants was that self-government was a delusion, because the existing tribal government had been created by the United States simply to serve its own purposes, supplanting the traditional government and customs with an alien institution and its rules and regulations. Where, one Sunday during the seventy-one-day occupation, the Indian protestors announced that they constituted the "independent Oglala Nation" and declared that a state of war existed between that nation and the United States, few Americans realized that it represented deep and persistent conviction among the Oglalas.

Wounded Knee, in the end, represented the philosophical divisions within all Indian tribes, the collision between the political dilemma of nationhood and the adoption of self-government within the existing federal structure. The traditionals certainly focused on the morality of the case, but the incumbent tribal government, for all its faults, spoke with a bitter contemporary pragmatism that could not be ignored. Wounded Knee could have happened on any Indian reservation, and while the occupation was dragging out to its final spasms, even many a conservative Indian suggested that maybe such activities were necessary to awaken the bureau and the president to their responsibilities.

When we distinguish between nationhood and self-government, we speak of two entirely different positions in the world. *Nationhood* implies a process of decision making that is free and uninhibited within the community. . . . *Self-government,* on the other hand, implies a recognition by the superior political power that some measure of local decision making is necessary but that this process must be monitored very carefully so that its products are compatible with the goals and policies of the larger political power . . . [in which] the larger moral issues that affect a *people's* relationship with other people are presumed to be included within the responsibilities of the larger nation.

The postwar generation of Indians had been enthusiastic about self-government because it has represented a step forward from the absolute prostration the tribes suffered when the federal bureaucracy preempted all social and political functions on the reservations after the passage of the General Allotment Act [Dawes Act, 1887]. Thus, having a tribal government that did have minimum respect accorded it by the federal agencies . . . did help Indians regain a measure of self-respect that had been lacking for several generations. . . . Indian tribes exercise in some respects more governing powers than local non-Indian municipalities and in other respects more important powers than the states themselves.

But such privileges do not assuage the needs of a spiritual tradition that remains very strong within most tribes and that needs to express itself in ways familiar to the people. Thus, Wounded Knee was the inevitable product of the experiment in self-government because it represented the first effort to establish the dignity of the tribe in a manner consonant with the people's memories of their older way of life. . . . Self-government was not wrong; it was simply inadequate. It was limited in a fundamental way because it circumscribed the area in which the people's aspirations could express themselves. . . .

Self-government is not an Indian idea. It originates in the minds of non-Indians who have reduced the traditional ways to dust, or believe they have, and now wish to give, as a gift, a limited measure of local control and responsibility. . . . Since it will never supplant the intangible, spiritual, and emotional aspirations of American Indians, it cannot be regarded as the final solution to Indian problems.

Questions

1. *Both Crazy Horse and Chief Joseph fought and killed U.S. soldiers in battle and eventually surrendered to the military with dignity. They both aroused intense feelings among their enemies and among their own people. What were the various reactions to each man—from the American populace? from the U.S. government? from the Sioux or Nez Perce? Why do you think these two heroic leaders elicited such differing responses?*

2. *Public opinion can have a powerful, if sometimes slow-acting, effect on governmental policy. Reactions to Crazy Horse and Chief Joseph influenced Indian policy in the late nineteenth century, and public gratitude for the wartime service of Native Americans in World War I is believed to have contributed to the passage of legislation in 1924 that finally declared American Indians to be citizens of the United States. With the sometimes illusive, sometimes effective, power of public opinion in mind, what are your views on how the experiences of Native Americans should be included in modern history texts and classes?*

3. *Based upon Deloria and Lytle's explanation of Native American concepts of sovereignty and nationhood, consider how, if you were a Native American living in 1924, you might have felt about being declared a United States citizen. What do you perceive might have been the advantages and disadvantages of U.S. citizenship?*

VISION QUEST:
ASSIMILATION OR TRADITION?

After the bloody battles on the Great Plains at the close of the nineteenth century, the United States government rounded up as many Native Americans as could be found in the canyons, mountains, and deserts across America. The government tried to confine the Indians to reservations—whenever possible on lands considered undesirable for white habitation. Over the years, many methods were devised to try to deal with the "Indian problem," but one overriding theme permeated each attempted solution—assimilation, ongoing attempts to force the Indian to remake himself in the white man's image. These redundant efforts continued with little regard for centuries-old Indian political and cultural traditions. Seldom were the Indians themselves seriously consulted as to their thoughts on the matter of their own future.

Tribal factionalism increased with the mounting tensions created by the shifting punitive, remedial, and paternalistic governmental policies. These changing policies were often complicated by state and federal jurisdictional and policy disputes. As two world wars and the increased popularity of the automobile and television ended the possibility that the Indians could just be hidden and forgotten on isolated pockets of reservation land, blood quantum (percentage of Indian blood) became a test of each Indian's eligibility to participate in many state and federal programs and certain tribal functions. Representative tribal governments were often imposed on groups who were more comfortable with traditional practices, such as consensual self-determination through nonbinding council debates. Some tribes, like the Navajo, who formally declared themselves the Navajo Nation in 1969, developed a strong sense of corporate allegiance to their reservation group. Others, like the Iroquois, who issue their own national passports and separately declared war against Germany during World War II, cite ancient treaties to reassert levels of affiliation and sovereignty unrecognized by the U.S. government.

Even when Native Americans were consulted about their own future, they were seldom listened to—but listened to or not, they were seldom quiet. In the 1960s-70s, with America's increased awareness of minority rights, Indian protests became louder and more militant. Cries of "Red Power" mirrored contemporary calls for Black Power, even as tragedy unfolded once more at Wounded Knee and a meaningful opportunity was lost at Alcatraz Island. Today, nearing the turn of the twenty-first century, America's Indian people still suffer (more than their statistically proportionate share) from conditions of poverty, sickness, and underemployment. Alcoholism and apathy are undeniable problems. But, including the story of the struggles against these formidable foes must not be allowed to undervalue the successes and the tenacity and courage of generations of Indians who faced the white man's demands of surrender but refused to break the bonds that tied them to each other and their collective identity as Indians.

Letters Home

As part of the assimilationist policy instituted by the passage of the Dawes Act in 1887, more and more Indian children from various reservations across America were transported to boarding schools far away from the influence of their parents. At some of the schools, children were punished for "acting Indian" and forced to speak only the English language. At the Indian Industrial School at Carlisle, Pennsylvania, students were allowed to write home as many times as they desired, but were required to write home at least once a month. This mandated letter (allegedly only this letter) was opened, inspected, and often published in the school's monthly newspaper and circulated among the white population. The following letters were excerpted from The Morning Star, *the monthly newspaper of the Indian Industrial School.*

Selected letters published January 1886

"Here I am trying to get education for our life time. I think the education is the greatest thing in the world. If I get education I will make use of it. I am not going to give up as long as I live in this world. When I go home out over the west I will try to work my way out of the reservation and try to be a citizen. If I get no education I *just feel like* the *deaf and dumb.*"

" . . . I thought how this country looked two or three hundred years ago, how it used to be woods, no cities, no villages, except Indian villages: but what was the use of calling them villages? for they were moving around all the time, and there were no farm, no railroad, but now there are farm-houses along the roads. . . . Why didn't the Indians think of this work instead of hunting or doing nothing? It was because they had no knowledge of things. Why didn't they cultivate their lands?

That debating club, (composed of our boys and girls) said, let the Indians alone and let them work for themselves. Why didn't they work for themselves before the white settlers came to this country. . . . Our lands were wasting because we did not know how to work! If Indian Territory were left for the Indians they would not know how to care for their grounds. They need the white people to show them. . . . I am very sorry for my people, (the Apaches [at the time of Geronimo's uprising]) because of the trouble they are doing now. . . ."

"We must learn how to work before the white people come to settle in the reservation, if you don't know how to work, then the white people should get in to reservation you won't have any land. . . ."

Selected letters, February 1886

"If I have not died when I get home I will succor you."

"I wish you all could understand about this wonderful Christian life."

"If you could only read my letters I could then tell you all about my thoughts."

"We discussed in our Debating Club whether the Indians should become citizens now or not. It was a tough question."

"I am awakened to a realizing sense to relate something to you. I almost desire to be with you. In looking far back over my life, I never saw any other Indians but Sioux, at this school I see so many Indians from different tribes and when they first came here they all talked different languages but now it is one great language with great news in it and a power every where."

"I am doubtful if I go back, if I can get any thing to do to earn my living. I have worked on the farm for two summers out among the farmers in this state, and gave as good satisfaction as any white boy of my age and I can do it yet. Some of the boys who went home are hardly doing anything because the Agent hasn't anything for them to do. I fear if I should go out there and find no employment I might lose my learning."

Selected letters, March 1886
"I am doing well about the obedience."

"I am trying hard to look forward and not backward."

"I hear that you have again given away every thing. This makes me feel dreadful. Can't you come over on the civilized side?"

"We shall all be glad to return to you when we get through this noble education and show you something better than the old customs."

Selected letters, April 1886
"Last Saturday a week ago the record for English speaking was "No Indian," "No chewing," and "No smoking." The week before two boys were reported as having spoken Indian during the week. There are about thirty eight different tribes here but they all speak one great language. . . ."

Selected letters, June 1886
"Sometimes I don't want to obey when I look backward, that way is not right so I am sorry then and look forward and not backward and I look in and not out and I look up and not down.". . .

"I am glad to hear from the Crows. I hear they are doing well and making money, raising sheep, horses, cattle, vegetables, that is good. . . . I have forgotten my language because we speak nothing but English at this school all the time."

Selected letters, July 1886
"You must work hard, for the white people say we are too lazy to work, I am not lazy to work.". . .

"You want me home but how can I help you if you are going to have me stay at home and lay around doing nothing. After I have been here six years, would I be foolish enough to wear the same old Indian clothes again? No, oh no! catch me wearing Indian clothes again after being six years in school and having good teachers around me and going to school among civilized people. . . ."

Wounded Knee, 1890

The winter of 1890 was an extremely harsh one for the Sioux of the Nevada/South Dakota region. The Indians were no longer allowed to hunt the rapidly diminishing buffalo, and even the Sioux's own cattle were rationed by the white soldiers. With the coming of winter, lines of Indian women waited anxiously for the government handouts of flour, cornmeal, and coffee. It is no wonder that many Sioux were drawn to the visionary prophesies of Wovoka, a Paiute shaman, as the message of the Ghost Dance religion spread. Based on traditional beliefs, but infused with a Christian-like promise of rebirth of dead ancestors, the "pan-Indian" religious revival message foretold of the return of the buffalo and the demise of the white man. Local whites quickly became frightened by the vigorous movements of the Ghost Dance. Rumors of Indians preparing for war were fueled by the Lakota Sioux belief that special Ghost Dance shirts were bulletproof. As the federal government flooded the area with heavily-armed troops, reporters inflamed the situation with flashy headlines and both "staged" and real pictures. On December 29, 1890, the tinderbox finally ignited. One gunshot, perhaps accidently fired, and the "wild gestures" of the dancers precipitated a massacre at Wounded Knee Creek, South Dakota.

In 1991, a group of historians working at the Nebraska Historical Society gathered together the society's collection of photographs of the Ghost Dance incident. Together with other relevant pictures from other collections, these photos provided the basis for a unique historical narrative—a picture book of the event at Wounded Knee as seen by eyewitnesses. Some of the photographs are reproduced below, along with captions and quotes that accompany the published collection. Taken from Richard E. Jensen, R. Eli Paul, and John E. Carter, eds., Eyewitness at Wounded Knee *(Lincoln, Nebraska, 1991), 8, 10, 27, 22, 45, 47, 64, 73, 76, 85, 91–92, 105–6, 116–17, 125, 131–32, 163, 162, 171, 176.*

Excerpts reprinted from *Eyewitness at Wounded Knee*, Richard E. Jensen, R. Eli Paul, and John E. Carter, eds., published by the University of Nebraska Press, 1991. Copyright © 1991 by the University of Nebraska Press.

December 3, 1890, Sergeant George B. DuBois, stationed at Fort Yates, wrote in a letter:

"I have not seen the famous ghost dance and I dont believe any one els has if the press does say so. The dance of Sitting Bull is 38 miles from here and they will not allow any one within five hundred yards of it[.] an associated press reporter was the closest that any one has been here and he was about five hundred yards and took a snap shot with a Kodac for our photographer here [George Scott]. I saw the negative and will try and get one of the pictures if I can as I believe it is the only one taken of any of the dancers. It shows them dancing in a circle around a pole and one lonley teepy about forty yards from the circle. The medicine teepy I suppose and old [Sitting] Bull and two or three others are standing about half way between the teepy and the dancers. The Indians did not know that they were being taken in with a Kodac[;] if they did it would have went hard with the poor fellow."

Ghost shirts and dresses were specially prepared garments worn by adherents of the new religion. This example from the W. H. Over Museum has the [blue] painted *V*-shaped neck, fringes, and feathers typical of Lakota shirts. Only the Lakotas believed them to be bulletproof. Whites viewed this as evidence of the Lakotas' warlike intentions, choosing to ignore the primarily defensive character of a bulletproof garment. Although many Indi-

Photograph courtesy of the W.H. Over State Museum, (Vermillion, SD).

ans owned weapons, they would not be needed for an offensive war since the whites would disappear through supernatural means. Songs sung at the ceremonies included one about the Messiah's, or Father's, gift of the garments to the believers.

Telegram from newly-appointed Indian agent for the Pine Ridge Reservation, Daniel F. Royer, to General Brooke, November 16, 1890:

"Indians are wild and crazy over the ghost dance. . . . We are at the mercy of these crazy demons. We need the military and need them at once."

Dispatch from Major General Nelson A. Miles to Brigadier General John R. Brooke, November 17, 1890:

"You are directed to send each of the Rosebud and Pine Ridge agencies two companies of infantry and one troop of cavalry. . . . As the Indians would not remain at the agencies in case of outbreak, the remainder of your command should be prepared to intercept any body of hostiles if they move west or south, taking advantage of the use of telegraph and railway."

Upon arriving at one of the Sioux encampments, Colonel A. E. Sheldon, editor of the Chadron, Nebraska Advocate, *commented on November 27, 1890:*

"There was peace at Pine Ridge, . . . whatever might be in the homes of frightened settlers and in the great newspaper offices."

Carl Smith, the Omaha World-Herald *correspondent at Pine Ridge observed:*

"The situation is just this, the troops are here, having marched up the hill like the army of the king of France, and now it seems that there is nothing to do but to march down again. . . ."

The Chadron Democrat *agreed, responding:*

"The situation seems to be that something must be done to excuse the coming of the troops here."

On ration day Indians came to the agency to receive rations of bacon, cornmeal, flour, coffee, and sugar. Up to six hundred women waited patiently in line while the issue agent checked ration cards and doled out the allotted amounts based on the size of the family. The rations were intended to assist the Lakotas while they made the transition from an economy based on buffalo hunting to one of subsistence farming. In 1890 the rations were

Photograph courtesy of the Nebraska State Historical Society.

reduced about 20 percent. When this reduction combined with a crop failure, the Lakotas undoubtedly did suffer. . . . The lack of food was often cited as a major cause of the Ghost Dance's popularity. Although privation undoubtedly contributed to the spread of the religion, a more fundamental cause lay in the Lakotas' desire to reclaim control of their own destiny.

Although only about one-third of the Lakotas became Ghost Dancers, many others, like Red Cloud, gave their tacit support. The aging but still influential Oglala chief denied any connection with the religion, but Agent Royer's assessment of the chief's position was probably more accurate. In an October 30, 1890 letter, he wrote, "While Red Cloud is not a prominent man in the dance, he is quietly encouraging his people to keep it going."

Question posed to reporters of the Omaha World-Herald *by Red Cloud's son, Jack Red Cloud, November 23, 1890:*
    "White men had religions and religious celebrations. Why shouldn't an Indian be treated just the same?"

After the army occupied the Pine Ridge Reservation, General Brooke ordered the Indians to abandon their homes and Ghost Dance camps and move to the agency. He hoped to separate the "friendly" from the "hostile" Indians so he could deal with the latter more effectively.

Schoolteachers described the situation at the Pine Ridge Indian school during the winter of 1890–91:

Elaine Goodale Eastman:

"The doors of the large Oglala boarding school were kept locked by day as well as by night and the grounds, surrounded by a high fence of barbed wire, constantly patrolled by armed guards. These boys and girls, held partly as hostages for the good behavior of their parents, in part for their own protection, must be fed, taught, and kept in order."

Thisba Hutson Morgan:

"It was the noon hour and the children were scattered over the grounds at work and at play, awaiting their call to dinner, when the first runners from the battlefield reached the Agency. The children were the first to get the news and report it to us, because they could interpret the sign language of the runners as they reached the knoll behind the school house, outstripping the Army couriers, swift though they were. The children were panic stricken as more news came in for many of them knew that their parents must have been in the fray. A few of them escaped in their excitement. . . . We hurried them into the house . . . [and] tried to soothe and comfort the best we could the wailing, hysterical, fainting children. . . ."

Reporter Charles W. Allen, an eyewitness to the battle at Wounded Knee, recalled:
"We rode past what but recently had been the site of a far-flung camp of white and brown army tents and the grimy old canvas of torn tepees; now marked only, here and there, by the bended willow frames and shattered poles of what so lately were shelters for the living."

Peter McFarland, a government employee present at the battle, reported:
"The Hotchkiss guns on the hill fired into an Indian wagon. . . . Several Indians were firing on the soldiers from behind this wagon. The shell sent into it knocked it to pieces and killed a number of warriors."

Dewey Beard, a Miniconjou, described the battle from his position in a ravine:

"I was badly wounded and pretty weak too. While I was lying on my back, I looked down the ravine and saw a lot of women coming up and crying. When I saw these women, girls and little girls and boys coming up, I saw soldiers on both sides of the ravine shoot at them until they had killed every one of them."

Photograph courtesy of the Nebraska State Historical Society.

One hundred forty-six bodies were interred in a mass grave on the small hill where the Hotchkiss guns had been positioned.

Theodore Ragnar, a soldier in the cavalry, later remembered the Seventh Cavalry leaving Wounded Knee for Pine Ridge Agency after the battle:

"Slowly, for the sake of the wounded, the long column left the battleground where the reds were lying as dark spots in the winter night and their sign of peace, the white flag, was moving gently with the wind."

Susette LaFlesche Tibbles remembers talking to a young Indian girl being treated at the local Episcopal church:

"[She was a] young girl, who had a ghost shirt on underneath her clothes [who] said, 'They told me if I put this on the bullets would not go through, and I believed them. Now see where we are.'"

Addison E. Sheldon, editor of the Chadron Advocate, *recalled seeing some of the survivors who escaped during the fighting. They were later reunited with kinsmen when the dancers surrendered in January 1891:*

"I still see them, the defeated, dejected Big Foot Sioux who were prisoners at Pine Ridge, December 31, 1890. . . . A band of men, women and children (mostly women and children) occupied the center of that yard. Some of them were prostrate on the ground. Some were sitting cross-legged, rocking to and fro in silent suffering. Some sat upon their ponies stiff and straight, but yet suffering."

Photograph courtesy of the Library of Congress.

On January 7 Plenty Horses (center) shot Lieutenant Casey while the latter was in one of the Ghost Dance camps, trying to initiate peace talks. After his arrest, he was incarcerated at Fort Meade and brought to trial in Sioux Falls, South Dakota. Plenty Horses explained his actions: "I am an Indian. Five years I attended Carlisle and was educated in the ways of the white man. When I returned to my people, I was an outcast among them. I was no longer an Indian. I was not a white man. I was lonely. I shot the lieutenant so I might make a place for myself among my people. Now I am one of them. I shall be hung, and the Indians will bury me as a warrior. They will be proud of me. I am satisfied." . . . Plenty Horses's lawyer successfully argued that the shooting was an act of war, for which he [Plenty Horses] could not be punished in a civil court. He was sent home to Rosebud [Reservation Agency].

After the final surrender, twenty-seven Ghost Dancers were imprisoned at Fort Sheridan, Illinois, by order of [General] Miles. The general believed that this group might lead a revival of the religion in the spring. They left Pine Ridge on January 26, expecting to spend six months at the army post near Chicago. Buffalo Bill Cody realized that such a group could become a feature attraction. Despite their imprisonment and the Bureau of Indian Affairs' ban on the employment of Indians by wild west shows, Cody used his considerable influence to secure their release. On March 30 twenty-three prisoners were placed in Cody's custody and they joined the show for a yearlong tour of Europe.

Four troops of the Ninth Cavalry [black buffalo soldiers] finally left Pine Ridge Agency on March 24. One trooper, W. A. Prather, the regimental poet, set their plight to verse:

> The rest have gone home,
> And to meet the blizzard's wintry blast,
> The Ninth, the willing Ninth,
> Is camped here till the last.
>
> We were the first to come,
> Will be the last to leave,
> Why are we compelled to stay,
> Why this reward receive?
>
> In warm barracks
> Our recent comrades take their ease,
> While we, poor devils,
> And the Sioux are left to freeze.
>
> And cuss our luck
> And wait till some one pulls the string,
> And starts Short Bull
> With another ghost dance in the spring.

The Ninth's eagerness to leave probably matched the wishes of the Sioux. A trooper wrote: "The Indians complained that some colored troops came to their camp, so they are objecting to our color and prefer the whites. This shows what civilization is doing."

Senator Dawes Reviews "Indian Problem"

The U.S. government instituted various policies in its attempts to find a solution to its "Indian problem." In an 1886 speech before the Indian Rights Association, Senator Dawes tries to find a more promising solution. Taken from The Morning Star, *vol. 6, no. 6 (January 1886); 1–2.*

There is a good deal in the Indian that is revolting, and that must be condemned. There is a great deal, however, about him that is intensely interesting. . . . White men came over here with the idea that the land belonged to civilization and that their duty was to convert the Indians. But those who came made little progress. The Indian remained the same. And we find the Indian tribes today an insoluble substance in the body politic, refusing to assimilate with the civilization around them.

. . . The Indian is leaving the last acre of his heritage. In times past he had land enough in his rear and game enough to sustain him. He cared little for the pressure in his front, and he retreated like the game, with little complaint. But, with the pressure from the West as well as the East, his means of subsistence began fast to disappear. . . . The cattlemen can make so much out of their ranches that they are driving the Indian rapidly to bay. Yet he is here as numerous—probably more numerous than when our ancestors landed on these shores. Something must be done with him. . . . They are idle, rambling and predatory. 300,000 tramps smarting under wrongs, real or fancied, no element exists in this country, and none can be conceived of so fraught with danger to life or property as this. . . . For 250 years he has been buffetted, starved, frozen, shot down by the hundred and has survived it all. The spirit of the Indian, so resolutely heroic, will make in the future the best specimen of the man and woman of America. How is the work to be done? It is easier to suggest a plan than to make it practically successful. . . . We have treated them as independent nations within the States. . . . That did not last but a few years. The State of Georgia was the first to resist having an independent sovereignty within its limits. It drove the Indians out in the face of the solemn guarantees of treaties with the national government, and the government could not help it. Then the United States bought out the Indians, and gave them the deed of the land in the

Indian country. . . . We established what is called the reservation system. We ran lines around country that the white man did not happen to want that very day, and put the Indian inside them and told him to make the best of it. That system had to be abandoned, because there was nothing for the Indian to live on. . . .

. . . [P]ublic sentiment was so aroused that the policy of forcing Indians into the Indian Territory [Oklahoma] was abandoned. Then the same administration thought it would be a good idea to increase the power of the chiefs, and they tried that. . . . There are now numbers of scholars in schools. . . . But when these children come out of the schools, what is to be done with them? . . . Unless some one takes care of them and provides work nine tenths of them will return to their old ways and be lost. The United States has adopted the plan of giving lands in severalty, but it can be applied to so few that the idea that it is going to solve the problem is a delusion. . . .

But, whatever you do, keep your faith with the Indian. . . . Gen. Sherman says we have made 1000 treaties with the Indian and broken every one of them; and yet we wonder that he does not trust us!

Vietnam Vet Issues
Modern Battle Cry for Treaty Rights

American Indians have accumulated quite an outstanding record as loyal servicemen in America's wars. Not only have Indians repeatedly served as valuable scouts, since before the American Revolution, but in several modern wars Native Americans served beside white and black servicemen in numbers far greater than the Indians' proportionate share of the population. In the selection that follows, a Native American Vietnam veteran explains why he can no longer risk his life abroad for a country that allows his Indian brothers and sisters to be unjustly jailed and murdered at home over treaty-guaranteed fishing rights. Taken from a statement by Sidney Mills in Alvin M. Josephy, Jr., Red Power: The American Indians' Fight for Freedom *(Lincoln, Nebraska, 1971), 81–85.*

October 13, 1968

I am Yakima and Cherokee Indian, and a man. For two years and four months, I've been a soldier in the United States Army. I served in combat in Vietnam—until critically wounded. I recently made a decision and publicly declare it today—a decision of conscience, of commitment and allegiance.

I owe and swear first allegiance to Indian people in the sovereign rights of our many Tribes. . . . I HEREBY RENOUNCE FURTHER OBLIGATION IN SERVICE OR DUTY TO THE UNITED STATES ARMY.

My first obligation now lies with the Indian people fighting for the lawful Treaty Right to fish in usual and accustomed waters of the Nisqually, Columbia and other Rivers of the Pacific Northwest, and in serving them in this fight in any way possible. . . .

This fight is real—as is the threat to Indian existence under the enforced policy objectives of the State of Washington, as permitted by the compromised position and abdication of responsibilities by the U.S. Government. The defense of Indian people and a chosen way of life in this fight for unrelinquished fishing rights is more compelling and more demanding of my time and commitment than any duty to the U.S. military. . . .

. . . The U.S. would have accepted sacrifice of my life in Vietnam in a less legitimate cause—in fact, nearly secured such sacrifice and would have honored such death. Yet I have my life and am now prepared to stand in another battle. . . . I have given enough to the U.S. Army—I choose now to serve my people.

My decision is influenced by the fact that we have already buried Indian fishermen returned dead from Vietnam, while Indian fishermen live here without protection and under steady attack from the power processes of this Nation and the States of Washington and Oregon. . . . Just three years ago today, on October 13, 1965, 19 women and children were brutalized by more than 45 armed agents of the State of Washington at Frank's Landing . . . in a vicious, unwarranted attack. It is not that this is the anniversary of that occasion that brings us here or which prompts my declaration on this day—but rather the fact that such actions

Excerpts from " 'I am a Yakima and Cherokee Indian, and a Man': Statement of Sidney Mills, October 13, 1968" reprinted from *Red Power: The American Indians' Fight for Freedom* by Alvin M. Josephy, Jr., published by University of Nebraska Press, 1971. Copyright © 1971 by Alvin M. Josephy, Jr. Reprinted by permission of IMG — Julian Bach Literary Agency, Inc.

... have come to be an everyday expectation in their lives. . . . I will not be among those who draw pride from a past in which I had no part nor from a proud heritage I will not uphold. We must give of ourselves today—and I will not be content to have women or children fighting in my stead. At the least, I will be among them—at the least, they will not be alone.

The disturbing question is, "Why must our Indian people fight?". . .

Citizenship for the Indian has too frequently been used as a convenience of government for deprivation of rights and property held owing to our being Indians. We did not generally become citizens of this Nation nor lawful residents of its States until June 2, 1924—and not when all other people gained nationality and citizenship under the Fourteenth Amendment in 1868 . . . [because] it was immediately held in the U.S. Supreme Court that Indians were born unto the allegiance of their Tribes and not unto the allegiance of the United States. The granting of citizenship was not to act negatively upon Indian allegiance nor rights. It is such first Allegiance that I now declare. . . . We will fight for these Rights and we will live our life!

Indian Invasion

In 1963, the U.S. government transferred the last prisoner from the maximum security prison at Alcatraz, leaving the island a white elephant in the midst of San Francisco Bay. In 1964, a handful of Sioux ceremoniously took over the island of Alcatraz for four hours, setting the stage for a longer occupation by a motley assemblage of mostly urban Indians in 1969. The 1960s was a decade of protests, demonstrations, high hopes, and unlimited dreams. In the selection below, Adam Fortunate Eagle, born Adam Nordwall on the Chippewa reservation in Red Lake, Minnesota but later renamed and adopted into the Whistling Water Clan of the Crow Nation, retells the event for his children, his people, and the white world. Abridged from Adam Fortunate Eagle, Alcatraz! Alcatraz!: The Indian Occupation of 1969–1971 *(Berkeley, 1992), 14–16, 18–23, 26, 44–48, 71, 151.*

The dramatic Indian occupation of Alcatraz, which got so much national and international attention in 1969, actually began five years earlier, in 1964. About a year after the prison closed, a handful of Sioux landed on the island and staked out claims under a 100-year-old treaty permitting non-reservation Indians to claim land the government had once taken for forts and other uses and had later abandoned.

The Sioux "takeover" lasted only four hours. . . . All the papers ran stories. The handful of Bay Area Sioux, born on a reservation in South Dakota, had chartered a boat, landed on Alcatraz on the blustery Sunday morning of March 8, 1964, and driven claim stakes into the ground under the Sioux Treaty of 1868 . . . to test the validity of the 1868 treaty and remind people of the more than 600 treaties which had been broken and other injustices which were still being committed against Native Americans by the federal government. . . .

A lot of readers probably did think of the takeover as a comic opera or a stunt. Of course it was a stunt. . . . Dumping tea into Boston Harbor was a stunt, and those guys didn't even have the courage to own up to their real identity. They dressed up as Indians instead, but that subterfuge didn't stop the history books from making heroes out of them. Our men really were Indians, real-life Dakota Sioux, and they wanted the world to know it. . . .

Actually, the provision permitting Indians to stake claims on unused government land had been revoked by Congress in 1934, but because of the 1868 treaty a specific exception was made for the Sioux, who had been forced to cede much of their land for the construction of a string of forts. So it all sounded perfectly reasonable. . . .

Of course, the 1964 action was never meant to be an occupation, and it wasn't. Exactly four hours after the landing the U.S. Government forced the Sioux to leave under threat of arrest and prosecution . . . , and the ball began rolling in the direction of the much bigger and longer-lasting Indian occupation of 1969. What those Sioux really did was begin a dream. . . .

We felt that if Alcatraz became Indian country it would, almost by magic, solve all sorts of problems of being Indian in the Bay Area and serve as a beacon of hope and pride for Indian people all over the country. . . . In 1968, a Senate subcommittee stated that "50,000 Indian families live in unsanitary, dilapidated dwellings, many in huts, shanties, even abandoned automobiles." The report went on to state that the average annual Indian income was $1500, 25% of the national average; the unemployment rate among Indians was 40%, more than ten times the national average . . . and thousands of Indians had migrated or been relocated into cities only to find themselves untrained for jobs and unprepared for urban life. Many returned to their reservations more disillusioned and defeated than when they left. . . .

. . . [In 1953,] when the government began to look at closing down the reservations, they ran into an interesting problem: the Indian reservations were full of Indians! . . . So by 1958 the decision had been made to establish eight relocation centers in major U.S. cities. Four of those centers were set up in California cities. . . . The Indians that signed up for the program were given bus tickets to whichever center they had chosen. . . . When the BIA [Bureau of Indian Affairs] found a job for their Indian "client," he was cut off from BIA services after his first paycheck. Many of the jobs were temporary. It didn't take long for the Indian to realize he had been trapped. . . . Needy urban Indians found themselves in a new type of entrapment—too poor to go back to the reservation and too "Indian" to receive the benefits of society. . . .

Indians began to find each other, partially out of a sense of loneliness and confusion in their new urban surroundings and partially out of an urge to share a cultural identity. . . . The Bay Area Indian community continued to grow as Indians kept pouring into the area, and the United Council gradually took on a more "activist" orientation until finally in 1969 it became the driving force behind the occupation of Alcatraz. . . .

Proclamation of the Indians of All Tribes:

To the Great White Father and All His People:

We, the native Americans, re-claim the land known as Alcatraz Island in the name of all American Indians by right of discovery. We wish to be fair and honorable in our dealings with the Caucasian inhabitants of this land, and hereby offer the following treaty: We will purchase said Alcatraz Island for 24 dollars ($24) in glass beads and red cloth, a precedent set by the white man's purchase of a similar island about 300 years ago. We know that $24 in trade goods for these sixteen acres is more than was paid when Manhattan Island was sold, but we know that land values have risen over the years. Our offer of $1.24 per acre is greater than the 47¢ per acre the white men are now paying the California Indians for their land. We will give to the inhabitants of this land a portion of that land for their own, to be held in trust by the American Indian Government—for as long as the sun shall rise and the rivers go down to the sea—to be administered by the Bureau of Caucasian Affairs (BCA). We will further guide the inhabitants in the proper way of living. We will offer them our religion, our education, our life-ways, in order to help them achieve our level of civilization and thus raise them and all their white brothers up from their savage and unhappy state. We offer this treaty in good faith and wish to be fair and honorable in our dealings with all white men. . . . We feel that this so-called Alcatraz Island is more than suitable as an Indian Reservation, as determined by the white man's own standards. By this we mean that this place resembles most Indian reservations, in that:

1. It is isolated from modern facilities, and without adequate means of transportation.
2. It has no fresh running water.
3. The sanitation facilities are inadequate.
4. There are no oil or mineral rights.
5. There is no industry and so unemployment is very great.
6. There are no health care facilities.
7. The soil is rocky and non-productive and the land does not support game.
8. There are no educational facilities.
9. The population has always been held as prisoners and kept dependent upon others.

Further, it would be fitting and symbolic that ships from all over the world, entering the Golden Gate, would first see Indian land, and thus be reminded of the true history of this nation. This tiny island would be a symbol of the great lands once ruled by free and noble Indians. . . .

Use To Be Made of Alcatraz Island . . .

1. A Center for Native American Studies will be developed . . .
2. An American Indian Spiritual Center will be developed . . .
3. An Indian Center of Ecology will be built . . .
4. A Great Indian Training School will be developed . . .
5. Some of the present buildings will be taken over to develop an American Indian Museum . . .

INDIANS OF ALL TRIBES
November 1969, San Francisco, California

. . . This occupation lasted for nineteen months. . . . One of our original goals for Alcatraz had been to set up an institute of higher learning, an Indian college. I think that in ways we were successful beyond our wildest dreams. We educated an entire country about Indian life, and the experience of the occupation educated many Indians who went on to become leaders and spokespeople in the Indian movement. The spirit and the lessons of Alcatraz became part of history and can never be lost. We lost the island itself, but Indian loss of land is nothing new in this country. I mourn our loss—the loss of the land, the loss of the dream. But I also rejoice, and I am fiercely proud of what we won.

American Report Card

The following selection, written by Sherman Alexie, an award-winning author and enrolled Spokane/Coeur d'Alene Indian from Wellpinit, Washington, on the Spokane Indian Reservation, is but a sample of Alexie's deeply symbolic and often ironic work. Alexie speaks for the largely invisible majority of Indians who live on reservations as enrolled members of federally recognized tribes. Excerpted from Sherman Alexie, Old Shirts & New Skins *(Los Angeles, 1993), 27.*

VISION (2)

No money for lunch so I rode an elevator to the top of the ONB Building, highest elevation in Spokane, where I stood at a window and witnessed 500 years of America: *Over 1 Billion Illusions Served.*

There is so much of this country I love, its supermarkets and bad television, the insane demands of a dollar bill in my pocket, fireworks celebrating the smallest occasions.

I am happy I can find a cup of hot coffee 24 hours a day.

But, America, in *my* country, there are no supermarkets and television is a way of never opening the front door. The fields here are green and there are no monuments celebrating the invasion of Christopher Columbus.

Here, I imagine 1492 and 1992 are two snakes entwined, climbing up the pole some call good medicine, while others name it progress or Manifest Destiny. Maybe it's economics or an extra-inning baseball game. Maybe it's Cotton Mather and Andrew Jackson looking for rescue. Maybe it's a smallpox blanket wrapped around our shoulders in the coldest winter.

Then again, who am I to talk? In the local newspaper I read this morning that my tribe escaped many of the hardships other Native Americans suffered. By the time the 20th century reached this far west, the war was over. Crazy Horse was gone and the Ghost Dancers were only ghosts. Christopher Columbus was 500 years and 3,000 miles away, fresh from a starring role in the Great American Movie.

I've seen that film at the reservation drive-in. If you look closely, you can see an Indian leaning against the back wall. You won't find his name among the end credits; you can't hear his voice or his song.

Extras, we're all extras.

"Vision (2)" by Sherman Alexie reprinted with permission from the *North Dakota Quarterly,* Vol. 59, No. 4 (Fall 1991).

Questions

1. Study the letters that the students at Carlisle Industrial School wrote to their families on the reservation. What attitudes do you find displayed? Do you perceive any underlying tensions that might have influenced the statements made by Plenty Horses to explain his attempt on Lieutenant Casey's life after the Wounded Knee incident in 1890? Do you think the court was correct in judging the attempt to have been an act of war? Explain.

2. Compare the feelings expressed by Plenty Horses with those revealed in the statement by the Vietnam vet, Sidney Mills. Do you think Mills was justified in his actions? Would or should Mills have received the same judgment as Plenty Horses? Explain.

3. The Dawes Act of 1887 divided reservation land, formerly held in common, into individual allotments that often passed quickly into white hands, usually leaving a legacy of poor Indians, both landed and landless. Traditionalists (often fuller bloods) faced ongoing pressure to assimilate, and acculturated Indians (often mixed bloods more adept at dealing with whites) assumed many of the positions in the tribal governments instituted by New Deal policies. During the New Deal the process of allotment was halted, and attempts still continue to consolidate Indian lands. Then, in the 1950s, the U.S. government instituted a program to relocate reservation Indians in urban industrial settings. Focusing on Adam Fortunate Eagle's story of the invasion of Alcatraz, an invasion he explains in part by urban Indians' need to consolidate their roots, and Sherman Alexie's poetry commenting on how a reservation Indian feels when traveling off the reservation, discuss how federal government policies might have added to factionalism within the Indian community.

FURTHER READING

For more information on modern American Indian perspectives, see Vine Deloria, Jr., Custer Died For Your Sins: An Indian Manifesto *(New York, 1969). There are numerous books available that focus on specific Indian tribes/nations. For example, see John R. Finger,* Cherokee Americans: The Eastern Band of Cherokees in the Twentieth Century *(Lincoln, Nebraska, 1991), a study of the eastern Cherokee and their battle to overcome the legacy of the Trail of Tears. For more on the Iroquois's fight to assert their treaty-guaranteed sovereignty, read Laurence M. Hauptman,* The Iroquois and the New Deal *(Syracuse, New York, 1981). Dee Brown,* Bury My Heart at Wounded Knee *(New York, 1981) retains it high authoritative status on the subject. For the perspective of Native American women, consider Mary Crow Dog and Richard Erdoes,* Lakota Woman *(New York, 1990); and Wilma Pearl Mankiller and Michael Wallis,* Mankiller: A Chief and Her People *(New York, 1993). For more thought-provoking poetry, peruse Sherman Alexie,* The Business of Fancydancing: Stories and Poems *(Brooklyn, New York, 1992) or* The Lone Ranger and Tonto Fistfight in Heaven *(New York, 1993).*

The Rise of Big Business and the Persistence of Small Business in American Industry, 1850–1920

Mansel G. Blackford

INTRODUCTION

In 1901, J. P. Morgan, America's best-known and most powerful investment banker, combined Carnegie Steel with other firms to form United States Steel, capitalized at over $1.4 billion. The establishment of the world's first billion-dollar corporation was a signal that big business had achieved a permanent institutional status on the American scene. Morgan organized United States Steel from firms that had earlier competed in the marketplace. Now those firms could cooperate; and through their combined size, control of iron ore, and efficiencies of production, Morgan expected that they would dominate the nation's steel industry, reducing price competition. A key element in modern America had been created: in 1860 no single American company was valued at $10 million, but by 1904 some three hundred were.

Giant firms clustered in just a few fields. Nearly all were in industry. Of the 278 American companies with assets of $20 million or more, in 1917, some 236 were manufacturing companies. By way of contrast, only five were agricultural firms (one each in ranching, the growing of sugar cane, and the harvesting of crude rubber, and two diversified multinationals, the United Fruit Company and its competitor, the Atlantic Fruit and Sugar Company). Of the manufacturing businesses, 171 firms, or nearly three-quarters, were in just six groups: 39 in primary metals, 34 in food processing, 29 in transportation equipment, 24 in manufacturing machinery, 24 in oil refining, and 21 in chemicals. These companies shared certain characteristics. Most had combined production with distribution—previously, these two business functions had been carried out by separate companies—by the time of World War I. Nearly all were multi-unit enterprises with factories spread across the United States.

The share of America's industrial output coming from small businesses dropped as large manufacturing ventures rose to prominence. Corporations—the legal form assumed by most big businesses, but relatively few small businesses (most small firms were single-owner proprietorships or partnerships)—accounted for three-quarters of America's industrial production by 1904. Small businesses also became less important as employers. By 1914, nearly a third of all industrial workers found employment in plants with 500 or more in their labor forces, and another third in those with 100 to 499. As large companies arose in manufacturing, a growing share of industrial workers found employment in companies operating more than one plant; at least a third of the nation's workers did so by 1923.

Small businesses did not, however, disappear from the industrial scene in the United States. The same set of census statistics alluded to above show that in 1914 a third of America's industrial workforce found employment in firms with 100 or fewer laborers. If small businesses are defined as those with 250 or fewer workers, 54 percent of those employed by manufacturing concerns worked for small firms. Moreover, some fifty-four thousand little businesses, those with six to twenty workers, were still in operation on the eve of the First World War. Those small businesses that survived and prospered in manufacturing did so by following several strategies. In some fields—such as leather working, furniture making, and lumber milling—few economies of scale existed, and big businesses did not develop. That is, the cost of production per number of goods made did not decline as the number of products turned out increased. In these areas, small manufacturers continued to make goods much as they had in earlier years. In those realms in which big businesses did emerge, small industrialists had to adapt to the presence of their larger counterparts, and many small firms were quite successful in doing so. [Portions of this introduction have been previously published in Mansel G. Blackford, A History of Small Business in America (New York, 1991), 28–37.]

RAILROADS:
PIONEERS IN BIG BUSINESS

As business historian Alfred D. Chandler, Jr., wrote, railroads were "pioneers in big business" in America. Railroads developed new management techniques later used by a wide variety of industrial firms. By uniting America economically, railroads created a national market for industrial goods, setting the stage for the more general growth of big business in the United States.

Railroads: The First Big Businesses

As the first emerging big business, railroads faced management challenges unknown by previous, much smaller enterprises; they, however, also could generate much larger profits, if those challenges could be met. In solving their problems, railroads developed basic management techniques still used in the United States and abroad. Excerpted from Mansel G. Blackford and K. Austin Kerr, Business Enterprise in American History, *3d ed. (Boston, 1994), 126–35, 137–39, 141–42, 147–48, 165.*

By the 1850s, individual railroads had become the biggest businesses of their day. Even before the Civil War, the trunk-line railroads [major routes handling long distance through traffic] controlled about 500 miles of track each and employed hundreds,

Excerpts reprinted from *Business Enterprise in American History* by Mansel G. Blackford and K. Austin Kerr, published by Houghton Mifflin Company, 1994. Copyright © 1994 by Houghton Mifflin Company.

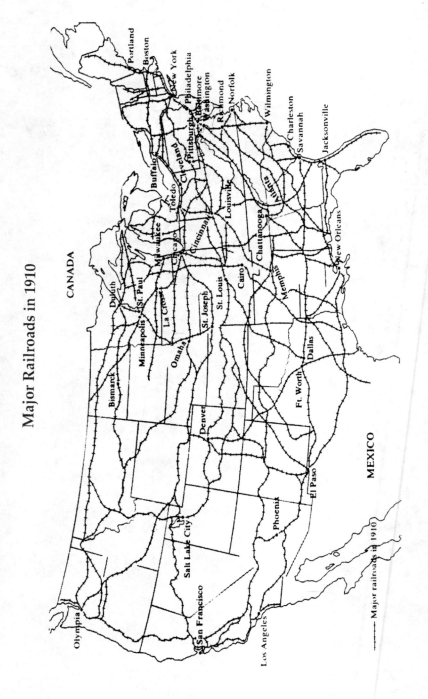

Major Railroads in 1910

Major railroads in 1910

sometimes thousands, of workers. During the late 1860s and early 1870s, trunk-line railroads such as the New York Central and the Pennsylvania established control over through routes to the West, and entrepreneurs completed America's first transcontinental lines. Building these lines was an expensive task; the trunk-line railroads connecting the East with the Midwest were capitalized at from $17 million to $35 million each. Other pre-Civil War businesses paled by comparison. Even the largest textile mills employed fewer than a thousand people, and only a handful were capitalized at more than $1 million.

Railroads continued to grow in size and complexity after the Civil War. Hungry for capital before the war, they [the railroads] became voracious after it. . . . In the 1880s, Americans built an annual average of 8,000 miles of track, so that by 1890, the nation had 166,000 miles of track, and a growing number of large cities were linked by a national transportation network. The construction of more than 254,000 miles of track finished the system by 1916, but even by the end of the 1880s, an integrated, nationwide railroad network was available to farmers, manufacturers, merchants, and passengers. . . .

Because of their rapid expansion, railroads faced unprecedented managerial problems. They were much larger in terms of people employed, regions served, and capital invested than any other companies of the period, even the biggest textile mills. Moreover, their operations were more complex and much faster than those of other businesses. . . . Decisions that affected the lives of people over ever-larger regions needed to be made quickly and accurately in the railroad business, and suitable ways of making such decisions had to be developed. . . . Even more complex were strategic problems: problems of financing expansion and problems in meeting competition. . . .

Clearly, business executives could not run railroads in haphazard ways and hope to survive very long. The complexities of both the operating and the strategic problems called for systematic management methods. Railroad executives solved their problems through the establishment of business bureaucracies, the first in American history. For the most part, railroad officers acted as innovators in setting up new management systems in response to specific business problems. . . .

. . . [Benjamin] Latrobe [chief engineer of the Baltimore & Ohio Railroad] set up an administrative structure that separated the responsibility for activities into two parts: a finance department to handle the internal and external financing of the line and to take care of other matters of grand strategy, and an operations department to run the trains. The operations department was separated into geographic divisions. Each geographic division, in turn, possessed three managers—one in charge of transportation (scheduling and running the trains), a second in charge of constructing and repairing the roadbed, and a third in charge of repairing machinery. All three functional managers reported to their respective functional superiors in the central office, where the railroad's general superintendent coordinated the work of the different managers. . . .

The Pennsylvania Railroad became known as the "standard railroad of the world" because of its good management. Herman Haupt, a West Point graduate, helped develop its bureaucratic organization during the 1840s and 1850s in his position as the railroad's superintendent of transportation and as its general superintendent. This structure was then more fully developed by J. Edgar Thomson, the railroad's president. In 1857, Thomson enlarged the central office of the line by separating the accounting from the treasury department and by creating a secretary's office and a legal department. Thomson also clarified relations between the head office and the railroad's operating divisions and began moving in the direction of fully demarcating the duties of its officers. In the 1860s and 1870s, he completed the task of separating the responsibilities of the executives in the central office from those of the managers in the railroad's three regional divisional offices, and he installed financial controls by which the executives in the central office could monitor and coordinate work throughout all of the divisions.

Three hallmarks of modern business management stand out in the steps taken by these railroad executives. First, they began to separate policy making from operations—that is, they began to divide strategy and tactics. Different groups of executives were in charge of overall planning and of operational details. It came to be the job of top management to plan for the future of the lines and to coordinate the functions of different parts of the lines. Second, and directly related to the first point, the railroads began to build bureaucratic organizations staffed by middle managers. These middle managers were essential to the development of the railroads as big businesses. While the top management in the central office concentrated on grand strategy, the middle management in the divisional offices attended to the operational details. These middle managers received reports from conductors, station managers, and the like, digested them, and then made their own reports to the top management, forming a chain that connected the various levels of the railroad bureaucracy. And if they were the chain, better financial reporting—the third hallmark of modern business management—was one of the major links. Railroad executives developed new types of accounting methods to hold together and analyze the work of their complex business empires. . . .

. . . [Of specific interest,] railroad executives developed _cost accounting_. They divided their companies' costs into various categories of fixed costs (such as those of roadbeds and tracks) and variable costs (such as that of labor). Because their fixed costs were much higher than their variable costs, railroad managers sought to run as many fully laden cars as possible. And they used cost accounting to pinpoint problems in their companies' operations and to aid in setting profitable railroad rates. The men responsible for railroad accounting thus pioneered in administering prices, as opposed to allowing invisible market forces to determine them.

The adoption of bureaucratic methods by railroads marked a fundamental shift in how American business people conducted their affairs. The personal business world of the merchant [in earlier times] gave way to the more highly organized and impersonal world of modern big business, a trend that continued in the late nineteenth and twentieth centuries and that came to characterize many firms beyond the railroad industry.

The changes occurring in railroad management were important not only for the railroad industry but also for a vast array of other businesses and industries in the United States. As their companies grew in size and complexity during the 1870s and 1880s, America's industrialists sought new management methods and structures by which they might control them. They found these methods and structures, in part, in their nation's railroads. The general idea of bureaucratic rather than personal management and specific methods of accounting and statistical controls spread from the railroads to other industrial ventures.

As railroads increased in size [the subsequent rise of big business and] . . . [e]conomic growth created new opportunities for businesses to expand the scope of their operations, and the building of America's railroad network lay at the heart of this business expansion. [This allowed for the exploitation of the resources in America's interior and permitted industrial enterprises to tap the growing domestic market.] . . .

The Spread of Big Business

The growth of the U.S. population and its concentration into cities linked by the railroads [and the telegraph] was an important change that allowed entrepreneurs to construct big businesses. The population of the United States rose from 31 million people in 1860, to 63 million in 1890, to 106 million in 1920, and most of that growth occurred in the cities. . . . The growth in population combined with the railroad system to create unprecedented business opportunities.

Not everyone favored the development of large railroads. Safety problems prompted broadsides like this one condemning the railroads. (Courtesy of The Library of Congress.)

The story of Andrew Carnegie and the steel industry illustrates the importance of railroads and expanding cities to the rise of big business. Carnegie benefited directly from the example of the railroads in organizing his steel business; the railroads and urban construction projects provided significant markets for his steel mills. A Scottish émigré who moved with his family to Pittsburgh in 1848, Carnegie owed much of his success to what he learned in the railroad business. In Pittsburgh,

Carnegie held several low-paying menial jobs, including that of bobbin boy in a textile mill, before becoming one of the city's leading telegraph operators. While he was working as a telegrapher in 1852, Carnegie was hired by Thomas Scott, the superintendent of the western division of the Pennsylvania Railroad, as his personal telegrapher and secretary. When Scott became a vice president of the line seven years later, Carnegie succeeded him as superintendent of the railroad's western division, a position he held until he resigned in 1865 to pursue other business interests. . . .

When Carnegie entered the steel business in 1872, he brought with him several important lessons from his railroad experience. He was aware of the large and expanding market for steel that railroads were creating with their requirements for track, bridges, and locomotives. In fact, one of his first major sales was steel track to the Pennsylvania Railroad. Moreover, in managing his steel company Carnegie took to heart the obsession of railroad executives with low-cost, high-volume operations. Like the railroads, steel was a capital-intensive business, and Carnegie sought always to lower the costs and increase the volume of production of his steel mills. Like the executives of the Pennsylvania Railroad, he installed sophisticated cost-accounting and recordkeeping systems in his company, systems he used both to locate production inefficiencies and to reward (or penalize) his plant managers. Take care of the costs, Carnegie believed, and the profits would take care of themselves.

Carnegie's policies proved successful. He created the largest steel company in the world and, with bankers and other American steelmakers, established the United States as the leading steel-producing nation. By 1900, America's output of pig iron had risen to 15 million tons, surpassing Great Britain's. The output of steel in the United States soared from 70,000 tons in 1870 to more than 4 million tons just twenty years later, as steel went into America's expanding railroad network and into skeletons for the buildings of the nation's growing cities. By 1900 American steel production had leaped to nearly 12 million tons, and in 1920 it reached 47 million tons. By the latter date, the United States was producing about 60 percent of the world's steel. . . .

. . . [As the example of Carnegie Steel shows, mass production was one of the keys to the development of big business.] The opening of the national market enticed manufacturers into boost-

An unlikely combination: steel king Andrew Carnegie, William Jennings Bryan, railroad magnate James J. Hill, and John Mitchell of the UMW. (Courtesy of The Library of Congress.)

ing their production, and the development of new technological processes made increased output feasible.

Mass production first appeared in industries processing liquids, where the application of new heat and chemical processes made it possible to turn out more product in less time with fewer workers. The use of enlarged stills, superheated steam, and catalytic cracking permitted the development of large-batch or continuous-process production in the oil, sugar, fats, and alcohol industries during the 1870s and 1880s.

Breakthroughs in machinery designs brought mass production to a number of mechanical industries at a slightly later date. The use of a machine to make cigarettes transformed that industry in 1881. By the mid-1880s, one machine made 120,000 cigarettes per day, many more than the 3,000 that could be made by hand. The adoption of similar continuous-process machinery also remade the match, soap, and grain-milling industries, bringing mass production to them in the 1880s and 1890s.

Finally, the establishment of mass production in the metalmaking and metalworking industries occurred in several steps. First, more complex and expensive machinery was installed to make and work the metal. Using new steel alloys as cutting edges on machine tools greatly sped metalworking processes. Even more important, entire plants were designed to ensure as continuous a flow as possible from the suppliers of raw materials through the various production processes to the shipment of goods to market. Inefficiencies and bottlenecks in production were eliminated. . . .

As they grew larger, the big businesses of the late nineteenth and early twentieth centuries developed internal structures different from those of most earlier enterprises. These structures evolved in response both to the opportunities of the new national market and to the increasing complexity of manufacturing processes and goods. The national market offered glittering possibilities to American business people, but it also presented them with previously unknown perils. The nationwide transportation network broke down local monopolies, intensifying competition across the United States and demanding changes in business methods. At the same time, the tremendous increase in the output of their factories and the growing complexity of goods their factories produced raised additional difficulties for industrialists, giving rise especially to problems in marketing the increasing numbers of technologically sophisticated products.

In an attempt to reestablish control over their economic destinies, business executives restructured their companies. Vertical integration was one common response to the problems and opportunities of the new national market and became a hallmark of big business in America. In vertical integration a company that initially engages in only one stage of the production and sale of its goods may acquire control of its sources of raw materials and/or the making and sale of its finished products.

Andrew Carnegie's desire to control fully his costs of production while taking advantage of the opportunities offered by the national market for steel led him to construct a self-contained, vertically integrated business empire. Initially, the Carnegie Steel Company depended on other firms for many of its raw materials—iron ore, coking coal, limestone, and the like. This situation displeased Carnegie, because he thought he was being charged too much for the raw materials and, even more important, because he could not always secure enough of them during times of peak production. To lower his costs and ensure adequate supplies, Carnegie moved to control his sources of raw materials. In the 1880s and 1890s, Carnegie gained control of the Frick Coke Company (a producer of coking coal), the Mesabi iron-ore range, and numerous limestone quarries. Moreover, to carry the raw materials to his smelters near Pittsburgh, Carnegie acquired a fleet of Great Lakes ore ships and put together a railroad system of about a thousand miles of track. He also took steps to control the making and sale of finished steel products. In the 1890s, Carnegie began production of a wider variety of finished goods than in early times, and he set up his own sales offices in major cities in the United States and Canada. . . .

Horizontal integration provided a second mechanism by which industrialists tried to restructure their companies. In horizontal integration, a number of companies combined forces to control one step in the production or sale of their products. As in vertical integration, the goal of horizontal integration was to bring order to an unstable, highly competitive business situation. Horizontal integration sought to lessen competition, thus reducing the risks to the capital invested in America's new industrial enterprises. John D. Rockefeller's Standard Oil Company was a classic example of horizontal integration, as Rockefeller and other oil magnates sought to control their rapidly expanding industry.

The growth of the oil industry, like that of the steel industry, was explosive. In Pennsylvania in 1859, E. L. Drake sank the first commercial oil well in America. This strike led to oil booms throughout the East and Midwest during the late nineteenth century, as Americans substituted kerosene for whale oil and candles. Oil discoveries in Oklahoma, Texas, and California in the 1890s and early 1900s further expanded the petroleum industry. In the early twentieth century, oil began gradually supplanting coal as a source of energy for railroad locomotives and some industrial plants. And with the development of the automobile, gasoline emerged as the major oil product in the 1910s and later. . . .

Rockefeller was a pioneer in the oil industry. Born in Richford, New York, in 1839, he had moved to Cleveland, Ohio, by the time he was sixteen years old. There he entered the business world as a bookkeeper in the firm of a commission merchant, earning a salary of fifty cents per day. Using his own savings and a gift from his father, Rockefeller became a jobber of hay, grain, and meat in 1859. Rockefeller took his work very seriously. "Don't be a good fellow," he later warned people. "It is my firm conviction that every downfall is traceable directly or indirectly to the victim's goodfellowship, his good cheer among his friends." Not surprisingly, he was viewed as solemn and humorless. "Oh, young Rockefeller—he's a stick!" noted the son of the Cleveland merchant who first hired Rockefeller. But Rockefeller was successful, and he soon used the earnings made in trade to go into the oil business.

Rockefeller entered oil refining in 1863, just four years after Drake drilled his well. By 1867, he owned a large refinery in the Cleveland area and purchased oil for it from well-owners in Pennsylvania and other eastern states. Needing capital for further growth, he incorporated his company in 1870 as the Standard Oil Company. The anticipated expansion occurred. However, oil refining was a very competitive industry, and Rockefeller and his rivals soon found themselves battling fiercely over the national market for kerosene and other oil products. No one really wanted to engage in this competition, which threatened to disrupt operations and lower profits.

To lessen competition, the owners of the Standard Oil Company and forty other oil-refining companies entered into a trust agreement in 1882. They turned over the common stock in their companies to nine trustees. The nine trustees then operated the companies in ways that avoided competition among them. In return for the stock in their original companies, the shareholders received trust certificates, and each year the nine trustees distributed what they thought were equitable shares in the earnings of the refining companies to the shareholders. By the 1890s, Standard Oil controlled more than 90 percent of the petroleum refining capacity of the United States. . . .

Additional changes soon took place in Standard's structure. In 1889, New Jersey amended its incorporation law to become the first state allowing one company to own stock in another company—to become a "holding company." Many large corporations took advantage of this provision to become holding companies by incorporating in New Jersey. Standard Oil was one of these firms. In 1899, Standard incorporated under New Jersey law and purchased the stock of the other members of the trust. In the early 1900s, Standard emerged as a single operating company. Its management sold or closed inefficient plants and rationalized the work of the corporation by uniting offices, such as sales offices, previously operated separately. Once horizontally integrated,

Standard turned to vertical integration. In the 1880s, Standard had begun securing its own supplies of crude at a reasonable cost. Somewhat later, Standard began operating long-distance pipelines to transport its oil and sales outlets to market it. . . .

As their companies grew in size and became fully integrated enterprises, the decisions of the managers of big businesses played ever-larger roles in determining how the business system of the United States functioned. In those parts of the nation's industrial economy dominated by big businesses, the visible hand of management replaced the invisible hand of market forces in controlling production and distribution of industrial goods and services. Decisions once made in thousands of independent market transactions became concentrated in the hands of managers of relatively few big businesses. By the opening decade of the twentieth century, in fact, key segments of U.S. industry were characterized by oligopoly. That is, in some fields of manufacturing, a handful of companies dominated their markets. Oligopoly was particularly characteristic of the metal, oil, rubber, chemical, tobacco processing, electrical machinery, transportation equipment, and sugar refining industries. As early as 1904, a few major companies controlled at least half the output of seventy-eight industries in the United States. During the opening decade of the twentieth century, the structure of much of American industry assumed its modern form: oligopolist and concentrated.

The emergence of big businesses in some fields, combined with the vigorous persistence of small businesses in other fields, illustrates a key fact about America's business system in this period: it was fast becoming a dual system. The big businesses, "center firms," were at the center of the nation's new business system. Center firms were capital-intensive companies, such as Standard Oil and Carnegie Steel. They often used continuous-processing or large-batch production methods to achieve important economies of scale. Center firms were also usually vertically or horizontally integrated (or both) and frequently exercised some degree of control over their markets. As large ventures in manufacturing, communications, and transportation, the center firms were of tremendous importance to America's emergent industrial economy; the fortunes of a single center firm often had a ripple effect on the nation's economy as a whole. "Peripheral firms," on the other hand, were smaller, for no production efficiencies resulted from increasing their scale of production. They were likely to be labor-intensive rather than capital-intensive and usually had no control over their markets. Small businesses in the aggregate remained very important to the American economy, but what happened to any single peripheral firm had little impact upon the national economy. . . .

Although American business executives may have had a difficult time understanding the economic changes occurring in the late nineteenth and early twentieth centuries, the actions they took to deal with those changes permanently altered the nature of business in the United States. Big businesses with managerial bureaucracies replaced many small businesses run directly by their owners. Vertically and horizontally integrated companies supplanted single-unit firms, thus leading to concentration in industry and to the creation of oligopoly in many fields of manufacturing. These developments, in turn, influenced the nature of economic decision making in the United States. With the rise of big business, decisions about the production and distribution of goods that had previously been made by the free interplay of market forces came to be internalized within the business firm. The visible hand of management replaced the invisible hand of the market in determining the functioning of part of the American economy.

Small Business Persists: Specialty Products and Niche Markets

---

Small manufacturing firms remained an important part of America's economy despite the development of large industrial corporations. Rather than competing head-to-head with their larger counterparts, smaller industrial firms pursued a strategy of developing specialty products for niche markets—a strategy successfully used by textile, steel, and other small industries throughout the twentieth century. Selected from Mansel G. Blackford, A History of Small Business in America *(New York, 1991), 38–43, 45.*

Most small businesses that succeeded in manufacturing . . . succeeded by differentiating their products from those of their larger counterparts. Doing so often meant producing a wide range of goods for rapidly changing regional and seasonal markets. Part of the ability to accomplish this task lay in the possession of intelligent, innovative work forces; another part lay in the flexible use of the most advanced (not primitive) technologies. In short, by carving out market niches, and by developing new production methods, small businesses could remain as independent enterprises in successful coexistence with larger firms. Among the fields in which small firms prospered well into the twentieth century were textiles and metal making.

As the nineteenth century progressed, the textile industry divided into two segments. In Waltham and Lowell in New England, large factories employed unskilled workers to turn out standardized goods for the mass market. The mills quickly became fully integrated in the production of textiles, with all the steps—preparation, spinning, weaving, and dyeing—carried out on different factory floors linked by elevators. These milling companies were among the largest businesses of the antebellum period. As early as 1832, eight of them were capitalized at at least $600,000 apiece. They each employed hundreds of workers, and their physical plants were large. In 1849 one company possessed five mills, each of which was five stories tall, with each story taken up by one room measuring 40 by 151 feet. By the 1830s and 1840s, all the companies had adopted the corporate form of organization, and most were run through rudimentary managerial hierarchies. Few small textile firms developed in Waltham or Lowell, for the large businesses controlled the available plant sites and sources of waterpower, denying access to others. By 1850, 12 corporations employed 12,000 textile workers in Lowell. . . .

The textile business developed differently in Philadelphia. In 1850, 326 firms employed 12,400 textile workers. Two-thirds possessed 25 or fewer workers, and 28 of the largest 32 employed only between 102 and 225 workers. Though employing as many workers in the aggregate as their counterparts in Waltham and Lowell, the Philadelphia firms were capitalized at much less—$4.7 million, about a third of the amount invested in the Lowell and Waltham companies. Most of the Philadelphia companies were organized as single-owner proprietorships. Only about 17% were partnerships, and even fewer—a scant 3%—were corporations.

The Philadelphia firms competed successfully throughout the nineteenth century with the much-larger mills of New England by stressing specialization and flexibility in production and marketing. Few Philadelphia firms tried to master all aspects of textile production; most specialized in one or two steps, which they then did very well indeed, using the most up-to-date machinery and employing skilled workers, often men, at high wages. Their productivity levels were high. In their labor practices as in their management methods, the Philadelphia mills differed from the larger mills in Lowell and Waltham. The Lowell and Waltham mills employed young, unskilled farm women as workers and treated them very paternalistically, housing them in company dormitories and strictly supervising their morals. Turnover rates were probably higher in Lowell and Waltham than in Philadelphia, thus probably making productivity lower in the northern mills. With skilled work forces and modern machinery, the Philadelphia mills could also more rapidly switch to various types of cotton, wool, and other fabrics as needed.

For the most part, the owners of the Philadelphia textile establishments did not become members of their city's social elite—in sharp contrast to the situation in New England, where mill owners became influential figures in cities like Boston. Instead, the Philadelphia mill owners remained close to their work, and a commercial elite of merchants long dominated Philadelphia's affairs. This circumstance paid an unexpected dividend. Although Philadelphia was not immune to labor unrest, disturbances were mitigated by bonds uniting managers and workers. Workers and managers knew each other personally through work on the plant floor and through membership in the same churches and social organizations. Moreover, many mill owners had started as skilled artisans, often renting space for their nascent ventures and only later expanding their enterprises. Workers and owners "talked the same language" and respected each other, even when they disagreed.

The flexibility of the Philadelphia firms served them well during the crises of the 1860s and the 1870s. Most adjusted better than their counterparts in Lowell and Waltham to the cotton shortage and the wartime demands of the Civil War by shifting to the production of woolen goods and other items. Similarly, their flexibility allowed the Philadelphia mills to prosper and expand even during the hard times of the mid-1870s, a period in which many New England mills encountered severe difficulties. By the early 1880s, Philadelphia possessed 849 textile establishments employing 55,000 workers, the largest such concentration of firms and workers in the nation. These were mostly profitable firms. The return on capital in Philadelphia's cotton textile companies averaged 23% in 1890, compared with 6% in the Lowell and Waltham companies and 8% in cotton textile firms nationwide. Most of the Philadelphia companies remained what they had been in the antebellum years—small, family firms in which the owner-manager personally supervised every aspect of his firm's operations. As a spokesman noted with pride, Philadelphia's textile community was "composed almost exclusively of individuals and individual firms . . . no corporations."

Small size and versatility continued to be hallmarks of the Philadelphia textile firms into the twentieth century. Not even the depression of the 1890s, which ushered in merger movements in many industries, led to concentration in Philadelphia's textile industry. Economic factors militated against mergers—the flexible, batch system of production; the ease of entry into the industry; and the near-absence of scale economies—but more important was the character of the men owning the mills. They identified personally with their businesses, which they often viewed as extensions of their families. Philadelphia remained the domain of small firms. In 1905, 728 textile companies capitalized at a total of $100 million employed 60,000 workers within the city of Philadelphia (there were additional firms in the suburbs and nearby areas). As before, these were flexible, specialized companies attuned to making rapid production changes as markets altered (in 1910, for example, a carpet maker celebrated its twenty-fifth anniversary by bringing out its 25,000th pattern). . . .

. . . [I]n America's iron and steel industries . . . large companies, such as Carnegie Steel and later the United States Steel Corporation, did come to dominate important segments of their industries. By using new, large-batch production methods, they turned out vast quantities of homogeneous steel products, mainly rails and structural steel, for America's expanding national market. Nonetheless, smaller iron and steel mills continued to thrive alongside the giants, even in Pittsburgh, the heart of the nation's iron and steel industry, well into the twentieth century.

Pittsburgh's iron and steel industries took form as collections of relatively small businesses. As late as 1870, the typical firm was capitalized at just $210,000, produced 3,000 tons of iron and steel annually, and employed only 119 workers. Like their counterparts elsewhere in America, Pittsburgh's iron and steel mills were unintegrated enterprises. They engaged in only one or two, not all, of the steps involved in turning out iron and steel products. The companies were for the most part family businesses, with about 40 families dominating the industries. The owners lived in Pittsburgh or nearby areas and ran their businesses themselves, eschewing the use of managerial hierarchies.

The switch from iron to steel, and with this change the use of the capital-intensive Bessemer and open-hearth methods, altered the situation in Pittsburgh, but only somewhat. Despite the expansion of new methods of steel making, iron production continued to grow as well, and older methods of steel making, such as the crucible process, continued to enjoy popularity. Many mills did become larger, but few approached the enormous size of the Carnegie operations. By the late 1880s, the average Pittsburgh iron and steel firm was capitalized at $805,000, produced 14,000 tons of iron and steel, and had a work force of 332. Many of these firms continued to be run by well-established Pittsburgh families (Carnegie was considered an outsider). The rise of a few giant firms, such as Carnegie Steel, should not obscure the continuing importance of the many smaller companies, for there remained 58 independent iron and steel mills in Pittsburgh in 1894.

The independent Pittsburgh mills (those not part of the expanding Carnegie empire) survived and indeed prospered by specializing. Rather than compete with Carnegie Steel in the large-batch production of rails and structural steel, most coexisted side by side with the Carnegie enterprises by producing specialized goods for niche markets. In pursuing this strategy Pittsburgh's independent iron and steel producers closely resembled the approach to business taken by Philadelphia's textile makers in their competition with the larger companies of New England. Oliver and Phillips, the Sable Rolling Mill, Vesuvius Iron, Juniata Iron, Crescent Steel, Hussey Wells and Company, and LaBelle Steel were some of the firms that successfully specialized. Oliver and Phillips, for instance, went into the making of nuts and bolts, wagon hardware, and barbed wire, while Vesuvius engaged in the production of bar and sheet iron, rods, hoops, and nails. . . .

Throughout the nineteenth century and into the twentieth, the independent mill owners composed much of the social elite of Pittsburgh, in marked contrast to the lesser social role played by the textile makers in Philadelphia. From the 1840s through the 1890s, 141 families owned and operated iron or steel mills in Pittsburgh. About half of these families were considered to be among the city's upper class. This situation continued into the middle twentieth century, as many iron and steel families entered banking. It was this social elite—based on iron, steel, and finance—that largely controlled Pittsburgh's political and cultural life for many years, losing its hegemony only after World War II.

Their positions as leaders in their community influenced how the independent iron and steel mill owners dealt with their labor forces. Perhaps both because they were close to their workers in relatively small plants and because they cared deeply for the welfare of Pittsburgh, most tended toward a grudging acceptance of unions and a pragmatic willingness to try to work with them. More so than the operators of the much-larger Carnegie mills, the owner-operators of the small independent facilities sought to achieve a harmonious relationship with their workers, especially in the 1870s and 1880s. In the 1890s and later, following the lead of the larger firms, the independent mill owners became less tolerant of labor. As they adopted more capital-intensive equipment and were influenced by the examples of violence against labor at Carnegie Steel, they turned more of their attention to breaking unions. . . .

. . . Common themes run through the successes of those small companies which proved capable of coexisting with big businesses in manufacturing. Consciously or unconsciously, the small manufacturers adopted a growth strategy that would remain one of the keys to success in small business into the late twentieth century: they developed specialty products that they then sold in niche markets, thereby often avoiding direct competition with their larger counterparts. To make this growth strategy work, the firms usually adopted (or developed themselves) the most advanced production technologies available. These small companies were not backward workshops using obsolete equipment but were instead among the most advanced industrial establishments of their day.

Running the companies were managers deeply committed to their success. Most of the companies, even those organized as corporations, continued to be operated as family enterprises. The businesses remained single-unit enterprises devoid for the most part of managerial hierarchies (though some of the independent Pittsburgh mills did develop simple hierarchies in the late nineteenth century). More than a quest for profits animated their owners. A sense of personal satisfaction, almost a sense of craftsmanship, remained a primary motivating factor for their executives and workers.

Questions

1. *Why were railroads so important to the development of big business in America? Why do historians call railroads "pioneers in big business"? What did manufacturing firms learn from railroads in terms of new management methods?*
2. *Why did big businesses develop in American manufacturing in the late nineteenth and early twentieth centuries? What was vertical integration and why was it so important for large manufacturing firms in America?*
3. *How did smaller companies persist in some areas of industry? How did they compete (or coexist) with their larger counterparts? What is meant by "niche markets" and "specialty products"?*

THE SEARCH FOR ORDER,
THE STRUGGLE TO SURVIVE

The selections below offer contemporary perspectives on major trends in American business during the late nineteenth and early twentieth centuries. The first two sources provide first-hand explanations of specific organizational innovations in big business: bureaucratic management, pioneered by the nation's railroads, and vertical integration, exemplified by Andrew Carnegie's steel empire. The concluding documents present contrasting accounts of how smaller companies fared in the era of big business. The first business failed when it attempted to compete directly with the powerful Standard Oil trust. The experience of the second, however, illustrates how some smaller businesses flourished by finding a "niche" in the market, by utilizing advanced technology, and by adopting some of the accounting and managerial techniques perfected by their larger counterparts.

Railroads Change Their Management Methods

The New York & Erie Railroad and the Chicago, Burlington & Quincy were among America's leading trunk-line railroads of the mid- and late-nineteenth century. As they grew in size and complexity, railroads developed modern bureaucratic management methods, as this report from the superintendent of the New York & Erie Railroad illustrates. Selected from The Railroads: The Nation's First Big Business, Sources and Readings, *ed. Alfred D. Chandler, Jr. (New York, 1965), 101–3, 108, 118–20.*

Superintendent's Report

OFFICE GENERAL SUP'T N. Y. & ERIE R. R.
NEW YORK, March 25, 1856

HOMER RAMSDELL, ESQ.

PRESIDENT OF THE NEW YORK AND ERIE RAILROAD COMPANY:

SIR:

. . . *Theoretically*, other things being equal, a long road should be operated for a less cost per mile than a short one. This position is so clearly evident and so generally admitted, that its truth may be assumed without offering any arguments in support of it; and, notwithstanding the reverse so far as *practical* results are considered, has generally been the case, we must look to other causes than the mere difference in length of roads for a solution of the difficulty.

A Superintendent of a road fifty miles in length can give its business his personal attention, and may be almost constantly upon the line engaged in the direction of its details. . . . In the government of a road five hundred miles in length a very different state of things exists. Any system which might be applicable to the business and extent of a short road, would be found entirely inadequate to the wants of a long one; and I am fully convinced, that in the want of a system perfect in its details, properly adapted and vigilantly enforced, lies the true secret of their failure; and that this disparity of cost per mile in operating long and short roads, is not produced by *a difference in length,* but is in proportion to the perfection of the system adopted. . . .

In my opinion a system of operations, to be efficient and successful, should be such as to give to the principal and responsible head of the running department a complete daily history of details in all their minutiae. Without such supervision, the procurement of a satisfactory annual statement must be regarded as extremely problematical. . . . [I]t will scarcely be expected that we can at once adopt any plan of operations which will not require amendment and a reasonable time to prove its worth. A few general principles, however, may be regarded as settled and necessary in its formation, amongst which are:

1. A proper division of responsibilities.
2. Sufficient power conferred to enable the same to be fully carried out. . . .

3. The means of knowing whether such responsibilities are faithfully executed.

4. Great promptness in the report of all derelictions of duty, that evils may be at once corrected.

5. Such information, to be obtained through a system of daily reports and checks that will not embarrass principal officers, nor lessen their influence with their subordinates.

6. The adoption of a system, as a whole, which will not only enable the General Superintendent to detect errors immediately, but will also point out the delinquent.

Organization

The following comprises a list of the principal officers acting directly under the General Superintendent, with powers and duties arranged with reference to obtaining the results proposed.

1. Division and Branch Superintendents.
2. Masters of Engine and Car Repairs.
3. Car Inspectors.
4. General Freight Agent.
5. General Ticket Agent.
6. General Wood Agent.
7. Superintendent of Telegraph.
8. Foreman of Bridge Repairs.

For the more convenient working of the road it is now separated into Divisions. . . . The several Divisions and Branches are in charge of Superintendents, who are held responsible for the successful working of their respective Divisions, and for the maintenance of proper discipline and conduct of all persons employed thereon, except such as are in the employment of other officers acting under directions from this office. . . . They possess all the powers delegated by the organization to the General Superintendent, except in matters pertaining to the duties of General Ticket Agent, General Freight Agent, General Wood Agent, Telegraph management, and Engine and Car Repairs. . . .

All that is required to render the efforts of railroad companies in every respect equal to that of individuals, is a rigid system of personal accountability through every grade of service.

[DANIEL C. McCALLUM]

Organization of Railroads (1885)

[A memorandum from Charles E. Perkins, president of the Chicago, Burlington & Quincy Railroad]

IN DECIDING the question of organization it will be necessary to consider two stages, so to speak, of railroad development. The first stage where the volume of traffic is not sufficient to make necessary or to warrant the highest degree of physical efficiency; and the second stage where the volume of traffic is so great as not only to warrant the expenditure, but also to make it economical to maintain the physical efficiency at the highest point.

Ordinarily the second stage will come only with increased mileage and while there are exceptional cases where roads of small fixed mileage acquire a large business by reason of their forming a link in a through line, or being in direct competition with one or more other roads between two commercial centers, they are so rare that it is best in considering the general question of organization to assume that a road in the second stage will be one of 500 miles or more in length. . . .

The responsible head of the operations of a road in the first stage is usually the general superintendent, a general manager only becoming necessary when the road has grown and business has so increased as to make it desirable to confine the general superintendent to the care of the machine alone. In the first stage he can and will himself look closely after his track and rolling stock as well as the traffic. In the second stage with the increase of traffic he will find his time and mind largely occupied with business questions, and also that he can draw the straight line of perfection to work to, and can safely trust to educated experts most of the questions relating to the efficient maintenance of the machine. The proper economical maintenance of a road in the first stage is not an exact science, while that of a road in the second stage is, and scientific methods which would be unnecessary and extravagant on the one may become necessary and economical on the other.

An organization for the management of a road in the first stage is comparatively simple. The duties of the president will be to advise the chief financial and accounting officer and the chief operating officer and also the purchasing and supply agents, to supervise and execute all important contracts, to conduct the most important negotiations, to specifically approve all expenditures chargeable to capital account before they are incurred, to supervise and direct the most important purchases of material and equipment, and to watch closely the results by means of reports from the heads of the two great departments of accounts and operations. . . .

An organization for the management of a large road in the second stage is on the other hand more complex. Here the duties of the president will be the same as in the first stage of development, but the amount of expenditure, the number of contracts, negotiations, reports, interviews, new schemes, etc., will have so largely increased that the president may require the aid of one vice president to assist him generally and possibly two or three personal assistants with fixed duties besides.

The departments of accounts and finances will also have grown so that a second vice president may be needed to look after the treasurer, the auditor and the secretary, three offices which in the first stage would be so combined as to be held by one, or at the most two, persons.

So of the departments of operation and construction. If the mileage is large it will be found expedient probably to put a third vice president at the head of this great department, which controls so largely the income and outgo. Under him again will be a general manager in direct charge of the daily details and taking the position occupied by the general superintendent in the first stage. The purchasing agent will act under the 3rd vice president and also especially in making large purchases of rails, rolling stock etc. directly under the president.

Andrew Carnegie and Carnegie Steel

Carnegie Steel was the largest industrial enterprise in the world in its day and formed the basis for the establishment of United States Steel. Vertical integration—the linking of all the steps in making steel in one company—gave Carnegie Steel production cost advantages over its less-well-integrated rivals. In his autobiography, Carnegie discussed how he organized his firm and some of the reasons he was successful. He stressed the importance of vertical integration, especially owning his own supplies of raw materials and his own pig iron furnaces (pig iron was then made into steel). Excerpt from Autobiography of Andrew Carnegie *(Boston, 1920), 220–22, 226–27.*

THE one vital lesson in iron and steel that I learned in Britain was the necessity for owning raw materials and finishing the completed article ready for its purpose. Having solved the steel-rail problem at the Edgar Thomson Works, we soon proceeded to the next step. The difficulties and uncertainties of obtaining regular supplies of pig iron compelled us to begin the erection of blast furnaces. Three of these were built. . . .

. . . We were the second firm in the United States to manufacture our own spiegel [a combination of iron, magnesium, and carbon], and the first, and for years the only, firm in America that made ferro-manganese. We had been dependent upon foreigners for a supply of this indispensable article, paying as high as eighty dollars a ton for it. . . .

We continued to develop our blast-furnace plant, every new one being a great improvement upon the preceding, until at last we thought we had arrived at a standard furnace. . . . The blast-furnace department was no sooner added than another step was seen to be essential to our independence and success. The supply of superior coke was a fixed quantity—the Connellsville field being defined. We found that we could not get on without a supply of the fuel essential to the smelting of pig iron; and a very thorough investigation of the question led us to the conclusion that the Frick Coke Company had not only the best coal and coke property, but that it had in Mr. Frick himself a man with a positive genius for its management. He had proved his ability by starting as a poor railway clerk and succeeding. In 1882 we purchased one half of the stock of this company, and by subsequent purchases from other holders we became owners of the great bulk of the shares.

There now remained to be acquired only the supply of iron stone. If we could obtain this we should be in the position occupied by only two or three of the European concerns. We thought at one time we had succeeded in discovering in Pennsylvania this last remaining link in the chain. We were misled, however, in our investment in the Tyrone region, and lost considerable sums as the result of our attempts to mine and use the ores of that section. . . .

To make a ton of steel one and a half tons of iron stone has to be mined, transported by rail a hundred miles to the Lakes, carried by boat hundreds of miles, transferred to cars, transported by rail one hundred and fifty miles to Pittsburgh; one and a half tons of coal must be mined and manufactured into coke and carried fifty-odd miles by rail; and one ton of limestone mined and carried one hundred and fifty miles to Pittsburgh. How then could steel be manufactured and sold without loss at three pounds for two cents? This, I confess, seemed to me incredible, and little less than miraculous, but it was so.

Opposition to Standard Oil

Not all Americans favored the development of big business; many saw large firms as threats to economic and political independence in the United States. Standard Oil, one of the first large industrial concerns, became the butt of much criticism. Independent refiners feared the competition from Standard Oil, whose costs of production were lower, resulting in lower consumer prices for goods such as kerosene. No independent producer was more outspoken than George Rice, who refined crude oil in Marietta, Ohio. Rice believed Standard Oil was using unethical means to destroy his business. In particular, Rice thought railroads colluded with Standard against him—charging less to carry Standard Oil's products than they charged him. Rice also accused Standard of undercutting his prices in an unethical fashion. Selected from "Testimony of George Rice, November 11, 1899" in the Industrial Commission: Preliminary Report on Trusts and Industrial Combinations *(Washington, 1900), 1:687, 704.*

"I am a citizen of the United States, born in the State of Vermont. Producer of petroleum for more than 30 years, and a refiner of same for 20 years, but my refinery has been shut down during the past 3 years, owing to the powerful and all-prevailing machinations of the Standard Oil Trust, in criminal collusion and conspiracy with the railroads to destroy my business of 20 years of patient industry, toil, and money in building up, wholly by and through unlawful freight discriminations. I have been driven from pillar to post, from one railway line to another, for 20 years, in the absolutely vain endeavor to get equal and just freight rates with the Standard Oil Trust, so as to be able to run my refinery at anything approaching a profit, but which I have been utterly unable to do. I have had to consequently shut down, with my business absolutely ruined and my refinery idle. . . .

Outside of rebates or freight discriminations I had no show with the Standard Oil trust, because of their unlawfully acquired monopoly, by which they could temporarily cut only my customers' prices, and below cost, leaving the balance of the town, nine-tenths, uncut. This they can easily do without any appreciable harm to their general trade, and thus effectually wipe out all competition, as fully set forth. Standard Oil prices generally were so high that I could sell my goods 2 to 3 cents a gallon below their prices and make a nice profit, but these savage attacks and cuts upon my customers' goods, and their consequent loss, plainly showed to them their power for evil, and the uselessness to contend against such odds. . . ."

A Smaller Manufacturer:
The Buckeye Steel Castings Company

The success of small firms in the iron and steel industries was not limited to the Pittsburgh region. Buckeye Steel Castings Company of Columbus, Ohio, was formed as a partnership in 1881. It was one of some two hundred companies producing a variety of cast-iron goods for the local market in central Ohio. Buckeye did not produce a specialty product, which might have given it an advantage over its competitors, and it came very close to failing during the hard times of the mid-1880s. Buckeye Steel, however, was saved by the development of a specialty product for a niche market—an automatic railroad car coupler. Originally made out of cast iron in the 1890s, and later out of stronger cast steel, this technologically sophisticated coupler gave Buckeye an edge over its competitors and allowed the company to break into the national market. New management techniques, especially new cost accounting practices, also made Buckeye more competitive.

In his approach to cost accounting, Buckeye's plant superintendent was among the most advanced managers of his day, pioneering in the inclusion of indirect and overhead expenses as part of his costs of produc-

tion, as illustrated by the following April 1905 financial report. Taken from Mansel G. Blackford, A Portrait Cast in Steel: Buckeye International and Columbus, Ohio, 1881–1980 *(Westport, Connecticut, 1982), 56–57.*

Costs of Production for April 1905

Metal in mould	$ 49,266
Moulding	17,730
Core-making	4,873
Annealing and cleaning	3,419
Fitting and finishing	15,725
Patterns and drafting	414
Repairs to plant and equipment	5,266
Locomotive service, heat, light, and power	2,779
Selling expense	2,755
Shipping expense	989
Office expense	698
Superintendence	527
Miscellaneous expenses	2,691
Salary of officers	838
Advertising	250
Insurance and taxes	350
Freight	2,347
Testing	259
Total	$ 111,179
Add for defective castings	2,241

. . . While not engaging in true capital accounting (few businesses had reached this level of sophistication), Buckeye's superintendent was figuring monthly charges for furnace repairs, building repairs, machinery repairs, and building depreciation as production costs as early as 1903. He explained his accounting methods in that year:

> For instance, we produced 18,500 tons of castings from the beginning of operations to Dec. 31, 1903.
> Total cost furnace repairs $12,129 = 70¢ per ton.
> Repairs of buildings about $3,000 = 20¢ per ton.
> Repairs of machinery about $6,000 = 35¢ per ton.
> Depreciation of buildings figures at 3% per year.
> Buildings are worth $200,000. Depreciation is $5,000 or 35¢ per ton.

Depreciation of machinery is figured at 10% per year. Machinery is worth $250,000. So depreciation comes to $25,000 or $1.40 per ton.

Questions

---

1. *What unique problems did managing a large railroad network entail? How did the New York & Erie Railroad attempt to meet these challenges?*
2. *How did Andrew Carnegie pursue vertical integration in his steel empire? In what ways did such a policy bring "order" and "efficiency" to Carnegie's operations?*
3. *Why, according to George Rice, did his oil refining business fail? Do you think his judgment of Standard Oil's business practices is fair? Why or why not? What specific techniques and strategies used by Buckeye Steel Castings allowed that company to survive? Explain.*

FURTHER READING

Alfred D. Chandler, Jr., Visible Hand: The Managerial Revolution in American Business *(Cambridge, 1977), examines the emergence of big businesses. Two good studies of Andrew Carnegie are Harold Livesay,* Andrew Carnegie and the Rise of Big Business *(Boston, 1975); and Joseph Frazier Wall,* Andrew Carnegie *(New York, 1970). Allan Nevins,* John D. Rockefeller: The Heroic Age of American Enterprise *(New York, 1940), and Ralph and Muriel Hidy,* Pioneering in Big Business, 1882–1921 *(New York, 1955), look at the history of Standard Oil. John N. Ingham,* Making Iron and Steel: Independent Mills in Pittsburgh, 1820–1920 *(Columbus, Ohio, 1991), and Philip Scranton,* Proprietary Capitalism: The Textile Manufacture at Philadelphia, 1800–1885 *(Cambridge, 1983), present industry studies emphasizing the roles smaller firms played in manufacturing.*

The Emergence
of the Modern
Labor Movement

Pamela J. Mills and Warren R. Van Tine

INTRODUCTION

The years between the Civil War and World War I witnessed the emergence of the modern American labor movement in response to the explosion of industrialism and the rise of big business. Yet the form and philosophy that the labor movement ultimately took was not preordained. Rather, three different "consciousnesses" competed for dominance during these years.

The first was a "community consciousness" best articulated by the Noble and Holy Order of the Knights of Labor in the 1870s and 1880s. Broadly speaking, the goal of the Knights was to return the worker to a position of equal citizenship and to restore social harmony within the community through a program of education and a range of reforms, the most radical of which was to temper competitive capitalism through the creation of producer cooperatives, in which workers could also be owners.

The second current seeking to represent workers during these years was that of "class consciousness" as articulated by the Socialist Labor Party beginning in the 1870s, the Socialist Party from the turn of the century, and most stridently the Industrial Workers of the World (IWW) from its founding in the 1900s through World War I. Unlike the Knights of Labor, such class-conscious workers thought that no degree of social harmony could exist as long as the capitalist system prevailed. To them, the working class's salvation would come through victory in the class war—either through electoral success at the polls or by physically driving the bosses out of their offices—followed by the creation of a worker-controlled cooperative commonwealth.

In the end, the labor organization that became the dominant voice of workers by 1910, the American Federation of Labor

(AFL), rejected the community vision of the Knights of Labor and the class struggle rhetoric of the IWW for a much more cautious "craft consciousness." The AFL shunned the efforts of the Knights and IWW to organize all workers regardless of race or gender and built a closed structure of largely white, male, skilled craftsmen. Its goal was not community rejuvenation or social revolution, but simply gaining shorter hours, better working conditions, and higher pay for its members. Dubbed "business unionism" or "pure and simple" unionism, the AFL avoided extensive political involvement or entangling links with social reformers. Basically, it accepted the American social and economic system as it was with all of its disparities and simply sought a bigger piece of the pie for those it represented.

ESTABLISHING A PHILOSOPHY
FOR AMERICAN LABOR

The three perspectives about what a labor movement should be or do were not just philosophical speculations, but were deeply rooted in the adherents' own life experiences. John H. M. Laslett links the three forms of unionism competing for dominance in the late nineteenth and early twentieth centuries to the lives of their three most articulate advocates, Terence Powderly of the Knights of Labor, "Big Bill" Haywood of the IWW, and Samuel Gompers of the AFL. Laslett is quick to point out that such an approach, while illuminating the social basis for each outlook, does not explain why the "craft conscious" AFL prevailed over the "community conscious" Knights of Labor or the "class conscious" IWW. For the answer to that question one must turn to the role of the state, the activities of business, and the texture of American culture and society. Abridged from John H. M. Laslett, "Establishing a Philosophy for American Labor," in Men, Women, and Issues in American History, *eds. Howard H. Quint and Milton Cantor (Homewood, Illinois, 1975), 2:67–87.*

Historians have frequently puzzled over just why and when it was that the dominant labor ideology in America, unlike that in most European countries, became limited to the narrow, pragmatic, job-conscious form of trade unionism exemplified in the history of the American Federation of Labor and in the life of its most famous leader, Samuel Gompers, who was President with only one year's interruption from 1886 (the year of its founding) to his death in 1924. They have generally attributed the growth of the AF of L's hegemony to broad national developments that took place in the United States during the last quarter of the 19th century. These developments, which in themselves had little to do with the labor movement, were initially accomplished by a supposed psychology of abundance, induced by widespread opportunities for self-employment and the presence of an open frontier. Later there was a shift to a psychology of scarcity induced by urbanization, mass immigration, and the declining independence of the skilled artisan. Only relatively recently have historians troubled to ask themselves whether any other form of labor ideology existed in America, still less inquired as to its extent or popularity. . . .

. . . [T]he job-conscious philosophy of the American Federation of Labor won out over both that of the Knights of Labor and the IWW [Industrial Workers of the World], at least until the 1930s. The Federation's membership also became much larger than either of its rivals. The Knights of Labor tumbled from its peak of 750,000 in 1886 to relative insignificance by 1900; and the IWW . . . never acquired more than approximately 50,000 members at any one time. The AF of L, on the other hand, had organized two million workers by 1917, four million by 1921; and thereafter its numbers never fell below two and a half or three million, rising rapidly to more than six million in the 1930s under the competitive stimulus of the CIO [Congress of Industrial Organizations]. But these developments had far more to do with specific events taking place both within the labor movement and in American society at particular points in time . . . than they did with any overarching or readily predictable historical design. Neither the individual lives of [Terence V.] Powderly, Gompers, or [William D. "Big Bill"] Haywood, nor even a brief survey of the organizations they led, can of course tell us anything absolutely conclusive about the reasons for these historical developments. Nevertheless, they can point to some highly important trends.

Although the broad, producer-oriented tradition of the Knights of Labor was both older and more deeply embedded in the history of American reform movements than either the revolutionary syndicalism of the IWW or the narrow business unionism of the AF of L, institutionally speaking it was the AF of L that appeared first. . . .

Samuel Gompers, principal founder of the American Federation of Labor, . . . was born on January 27, 1850, in the impoverished Spitafields silk-weaving district of east London. . . . Gompers at the age of ten was apprenticed to his father's own trade of cigarmaking. . . .

. . . [In 1863] the Gompers family, oppressed by poverty and a growing number of children, . . . migrated from London's east end to its equivalent on the lower East Side of New York. . . . For 18 months young Samuel helped his father roll and cut cigars in the combination kitchen, living room and workshop which, aside from a single bedroom, was all that the Gompers family could afford. At the age of 17 Gompers married Sophia Julian, another London-born Jewish immigrant, moved out of his parents' home to start a family of his own, and began to look about him. Employed now in a larger cigar factory instead of in a tenement workshop—and avidly studying history, science, and economics at night school—Gompers attended debates at Cooper Union on the nature and purposes of the labor movement. He sat around the long cigarmaking tables discussing them with his friend Sam Prince and his mentor Ferdinand Laurell, and in the winter of 1874 joined the great Tompkins Square demonstration of the unemployed. Six months later he was elected president of the largest Cigarmakers International Union [CMIU] local in New York City, Local 144.

The ensuing five years were fateful ones for Gompers, for the CMIU and, as it later turned out, for the American labor movement as a whole. During the depression of the mid-1870s, employers in New York's cigar industry had transferred much of their production from the larger shops to tenement houses, which were much more difficult to organize and where near-starvation wages were usually paid. In response Gompers, Adolph Strasser, and Sam Prince among others led a general strike of New York cigarmakers in the fall of 1877. Their goal was to abolish the tenement house system. From seven to ten thousand men walked out, supported by cigarmakers across the country. Gompers, dismissed from his job, pawned everything but Sophie's wedding ring and moved into even cheaper quarters in Brooklyn. But still the strike was lost. Leaders of Local 144 were finally convinced of the need to reform the CMIU along English lines.

Up to this point the union had admitted rollers and bunchers as well as skilled cigarmakers. There was no uniformity in dues or initiation fees, and strike benefits were paid only when there happened to be money available. At the 1879 convention of the CMIU, Gompers with Strasser in support, secured adoption of a wide range of changes designed to transform the union from a confederation of loose, sovereign locals into a tightly knit, financially sound, and stable institution primarily serving the interests of the skilled. The changes were most significant and suggestive: high dues to build a financial reserve during depressions; strike, sick, and death benefits that would provide a financial incentive for permanent membership; centralized control, especially in authorizing strikes; and, perhaps most important of all, the English principle of equalization of funds making money from one local available to others in time of stress. . . .

. . . Most of the craft unions that were later to establish the AF of L had suffered severely during the depression of the mid-1870s. . . . Moreover, in the early 1880s knowledgeable observers of the labor movement were understandably more impressed with the rapidly rising star of the Knights of Labor—already recognized then as a broadly-based national labor federation embracing unskilled workers, small town employees and even some farmers, as well as skilled artisans—than they were with the weak, fragmented Federation of Organized Trades and Labor Unions (the AF of L's immediate predecessor), which could boast the support of only a few, scattered east coast unions. Equally promising, at this early stage at least, was the short, but dignified and scholarly-looking figure of the man who would become the Knights's second and most famous Grand Master Workman, Terence V. Powderly. In three short years he had risen from the obscurity of a blacklisted employee on the Delaware, Lackawanna and Western Railroad to become Mayor of Scranton, Pennsylvania and then, in 1879 at the astonishingly young age of 30, he was chosen national leader of the Knights of Labor.

Although born on January 27, 1849, only 12 months before Samuel Gompers, and experiencing much of the same poverty and deprivation in his early years, this difference of one year symbolized a gap of at least a generation in terms of the overall development of the American labor movement. Gompers'[s] formative years had been spent amid urban craftsmen struggling to defend their skills; and the solutions he advocated to the labor problem, although narrow and ultimately stulifying [stultifying] in their social consequences, appeared essentially modern and forward-looking at the time they were first advocated. Powderly's youth, by contrast, was spent in the rural atmosphere of the small, isolated, railroad town of Carbondale, Pennsylvania. . . .

Land and currency reform, temperance, third-party politics, and a deep but essentially utopian and backward-looking commitment to rescuing the "independent producer" from the onrush of post-Civil War capitalism were thus the dominating influences in Terence V. Powderly's early life. He had left home at the age of 13 to become a railroad machinist, a member of the Machinists and Blacksmiths Union and, in 1877, Corresponding Secretary of District Assembly 5 in the Scranton-Reading area. In varying degree these ideas were also reflected in the national policies of the Knights of Labor. So, too, was a broad ecumenicalism with regard to organizing the great mass of working people, irrespective of race, occupation, and skill. The K of L made far greater efforts to implement ideals of social equality among its members than most American labor organizations, either before or since. . . . Also a far wider variety of occupations—among them farmers and small tradesmen as well as semi-skilled and unskilled laborers—were encouraged to join both the "mixed" and the "trade" Local Assemblies of the Knights. Few of the aforementioned were permitted to enter into the skilled unions of the AF of L. For Powderly, as for many Knights, the slogan "An injury to one is an injury to all" was taken more seriously than either before or since in the American labor movement.

The corollary to this broad, humanitarian approach—and probably the most important ingredient in Powderly's social philosophy—was his hostility toward the wages system. "The aim of the Knights of Labor—properly understood—is to make each man his own employer," Powderly repeatedly stated. But this antipathy toward capitalism had no Marxism in it. Indeed Powderly was contemptuous of most socialists. . . . Unlike Haywood, Powderly was opposed to strikes or revolutionary violence as a means of solving labor disputes. And unlike Gompers (who was also strongly anti-Marxist, although for very different reasons), he had little understanding of or sympathy with a purely economic analysis of society.

Accompanying Powderly's antipathy to class conflict and his belief in education as a panacea for numerous social ills went an abiding faith in both producers' and consumers' cooperation, and this despite repeated practical disappointments. Such cooperation was a means of subverting the wage system and of returning to an economy more consistent with the human scale. . . . Thus at the first General Assembly after his election as Grand Master Workman . . . , Powderly insisted that the delegates eschew such relatively "petty questions" as higher wages and shorter hours, and embark instead "on a system of cooperation, which will make every man his own master, and every man his own employer." Almost none of the cooperatives established by the K of L succeeded. . . . By the end of the decade inefficiency, lack of money, and the strong opposition of many elements in the business community had forced the Knights's leadership to abandon cooperation as the major tool of social reconstruction. Instead, they placed their hopes on organization, education, and third-party politics, and in particular on the program of the People's Party.

. . . The ethos of the Knights prompted resistance to the idea that American workers had become permanent wage earners who needed full-time labor leaders to guide them. Certainly it was no discredit to Powderly that he sought to maintain in his own life a position as an "independent producer." Less easy to condone, however, was his quixotic policy toward strikes. . . . Powderly, it is true, personally disapproved of the use of the strike weapon. . . . But his naive belief in arbitration as the only proper means for settling industrial disputes led him to ignore the fact that employers, then as now, rarely concede anything to the workers unless forced to do [so]. Finally, his extremely ill-timed attempt to discipline the strikers in the middle of the 1886 walkouts brought grass-roots anger and resentment. . . .

In turn, these losses greatly strengthened the hand of those skilled workers in the Order who had never approved the Knights's policy of encouraging Mixed Assemblies (enrolling all of the workers in a given area into one local irrespective of occupation or skill). Having joined the Knights only because their own craft unions had been temporarily overwhelmed by the mid-1870s depression, these skilled workers now seized upon the opportunity presented by the defeat of the Gould and Chicago stockyard strikes to demand the establishment of Trade Assemblies (groups of workers defined occupationally rather than geographically) and to reject the larger organizational philosophy of the Knights. With the sudden rise in K of L membership early in 1886, numerous craft unions . . . accused the Knights of stealing their members. Although accounts of such raiding were undoubtedly exaggerated on both sides, one such incident led to open warfare between them and ultimately to the downfall of the Knights. The main protagonist in the struggle was none other than Samuel Gompers'[s] Cigarmakers Local 144.

. . . In the ensuing fight for control over the labor movement the tide ran quickly against the Knights. Employer hostility, the Order's virtually uniform lack of strike success after 1886, and the attempt by Mixed Assemblies to prevent their members from joining the craft unions alienated many of the skilled. Long-standing organizational weaknesses, the unwarranted assumption by the public that the K of L had supported the Haymarket riot of May 1886, and the depression of the mid-1890s did the rest. By 1895 the once-proud Knights had been reduced to less than 75,000 members, the bulk of them coming from the hard core of small-town mechanics, shop-keepers, petty employers and farmers to whom the organization's all-inclusive producer philosophy had made its first and most forceful appeal.

. . . Faced by rising criticism of his authoritarian handling of the Knights's internal affairs and by his inability or unwillingness to delegate responsibility to other officials, Powderly was forced out of office in 1893 by an alliance of western agrarians and eastern socialists. . . .

With Powderly out of the way and the Knights of Labor in rapid decline, President Gompers of the AF of L . . . proceeded to institutionalize at the national level the principles of high-dues-high-benefits, pure-and-simple, craft unionism that Gompers had first developed during his years with Local 144 in New York. . . .

Soon after Gompers'[s] confirmation as President of the AF of L in 1886, he began that stream of articles, speeches, and addresses to labor conventions that would be reiterated continually over the next 30 years. All upheld the virtues of craft unionism. . . . Gompers accepted the inevitability of conflict between employers and employees owing to their divergent economic interests, and he vigorously upheld the necessity for strikes. Indeed, . . . as a young man he was in many respects a Marxist. . . .

. . . [T]he radical implications in Gompers'[s] class view of American society were progressively whittled down by two basic considerations. The first of these was a growing preoccupation with dividing up control over the terms of employment of the purely urban labor force between the AF of L and the employers. . . . This preoccupation evolved into a view of the labor movement as defensive and job-conscious rather than militant and class-conscious. Such a view not only ignored farmers and other petty-bourgeois elements but also made no attempt to challenge capitalist ownership of the means of production. Gompers'[s] second consideration was based on the changes in technology, which increasingly threatened the position of industry's hand-skill workers. In response to this development, the AF of L limited its interests still further, ignoring not only farmers and petty-bourgeois elements but semi-skilled and unskilled workers as well. The reasons for these changes . . . derive essentially from the fact that the AF of L was born out of a reaction against the broad and inclusive character of the Knights of Labor, which was understandably unwilling to devote more than a limited share of its resources to defending the interests of the skilled worker.

. . . Labor lost one strike after another in the 1890s. These disputes involved both unskilled and semi-skilled workers as well as craftsmen—steelmen at Homestead in 1892, railroad workers at Pullman in 1894, and coal miners nationwide in the same year. Numerous other critics joined Socialists in attacking the AF of L's exclusive preoccupation with the interests of skilled workers as narrow, self-serving, and ultimately futile. The introduction of mass-production techniques, they argued, with its attendant destruction of craft lines, had already placed the unskilled into competition with the skilled for a wide range of jobs. The influx of new immigrants from southern and from eastern Europe that took place in the 1880s simply worsened matters. The proper answer was to open up the unions to the entire labor force and not, incidentally, on the basis of the Mixed Assemblies of the old Knights of Labor. Rather there should be modern industrial unions—with each incorporating all of the wage workers in an industry into a single, coherent, and militant mass union. . . .

It was in this context that a second great labor leader arose to challenge the hegemony of pure-and-simple trade unionism—William D. Haywood of the Industrial Workers of the World. . . . On June 27, 1905, at Brand's Hall in Chicago, the 36-year-old Haywood—a tall, powerful figure of a man, of ample girth but with a handsome face set off by a patch over his right eye (the result of a childhood accident)—brought the IWW's 200 founding delegates to their feet in a ringing denunciation of the labor philosophy of the AF of L. "The American Federation of Labor," he argued, "which presumes to be the labor movement of this country, is not a working class movement." "It includes organizations which prohibit the initiation of a . . . colored man; that prohibit the conferring of the obligation of foreigners." And, he continued, "The Industrial Workers of the World will be formed, based, and founded on the class struggle, having but one object and purpose and that is to bring the workers of this country into the possession of the full value of the product of their toil." Following Haywood's advice the IWW adopted a form of organization . . . in which all American workers—skilled and unskilled, native and immigrant, black and white, and even Orientals, an earlier target of labor's hostility in the western metal mines—were to be grouped into five main "industrial departments," with low dues and free, universal union transfer cards. The whole organization would be under the general aegis of a central IWW administration in Chicago.

Bill Haywood had taken a considerable time to come to this revolutionary position. Born in Salt Lake City, Utah, in 1869—20 years after either of our other two labor leaders and less susceptible, therefore, to labor ideologies that had been fashionable before the Civil War—Haywood's early life nevertheless bore more resemblance to Powderly's than it did to that of Gompers. . . .[He] acquired his first knowledge of the labor movement from Pat Reynolds, an Irish fellow-worker who had earlier been a member of the Knights. Like Powderly, Haywood was a brilliant orator, while at the same time being more direct in his language and much more forceful. Although well-read, Haywood was in many respects anti-intellectual. Essentially a man of action, he was at his best when addressing a crowd, debating with opponents, or leading a strike demonstration, as in the famous Lawrence textile strike of 1913. There was no air of the effete intellectual about him, still less that of the pompous labor bureaucrat.

And yet, like Gompers, Haywood was also a good administrator. The period between 1914 and 1917, when he was working full time for the IWW, was one of the few in which the organization achieved a modicum of stability. To be sure, he also had qualities that would have shocked the Victorian moral code of his elders in the labor movement. An unhappy marriage to Nevada Jane, a crippled, care-worn, frontier woman, frequently drove him to the solace offered by saloons and brothels. Indeed, in January 1906, when he was arrested—along with President Charles A.

Moyer and Charles A. Pettibone of the Western Federation of Miners [WFM]—on trumped-up charges of murdering ex-Governor Steunenberg of Idaho, Pinkerton detectives found him in a Denver house of prostitution, virtually within walking distance of his family home. Despite these lapses as well as an often-exaggerated reputation as a no-good layabout and as a sinister subversive, Haywood at his best was a hero to ordinary working people in a way that Powderly and Gompers never were. . . .

. . . [I]t is paradoxical that he first came to the fore as an efficient trade union administrator. . . . What in fact turned the moderate Socialist reformer into a militant and a rebel was the ruthless, bitter, and—from the WFM point of view—disastrous 1903-1904 Cripple Creek strike. Before walking out, over a matter that in its origin was nothing more alarming than the eight-hour day, the WFM locals had offered to negotiate with the gold mine owners. But the Colorado Mine Owners Association, in conjunction with state Governor James H. Peabody and numerous Citizens Alliances, were determined not only to categorize the WFM as an un-American, seditious and even as a criminal organization but also to smash it. In a naked display of power the State sent in militia, made illegal searches and seizures, and forcibly deported over 400 miners from Colorado. Deputies openly attacked Haywood himself on the streets of Cripple Creek. He wounded one of them severely, but was freed soon afterward since the deputies were clearly to blame.

The Cripple Creek strike represented the culmination of a long series of bitterly fought struggles that had all the characteristics of class war. It was a turning point in Haywood's career just as the 1877 general strike of cigarmakers in New York City had been for Samuel Gompers. . . . Cripple Creek prompted Haywood to reject conventional labor tactics in favor of militant industrial unionism as the only proper form of labor organization. . . . It also caused him—and many of those who would join him in founding the IWW 18 months later—to doubt even the value of Socialist political action as a means of affording protection to the worker. Again, interestingly enough, Haywood, like Gompers, rejected Socialist politics. . . . [Haywood] had come to see the union not as providing a substitute for the liberal state, but as offering the means for fashioning a revolutionary alternative to it. The only direct experience of state power for many Wobblies [nickname of the IWW] had been at the receiving end of a policeman's club; but they nonetheless feared that even members of their own class, if elected to political office would become corrupted by participation in capitalist politics. Hence direct action in the form of strikes, demonstrations, sit-downs, and even sabotage (although the degree to which the IWW actually practiced violence was predictably exaggerated by the press) was preferred to voting as the only sure means of asserting economic control over the means of production. In theory at least, the culmination was the general social strike.

The character of its membership influenced the IWW's hostility towards political action. Before 1908 its members were largely western metal miners or disaffected AF of L members working in industrial occupations. Following the withdrawal of the WFM from the IWW in 1908, IWW membership came to be drawn, with some exceptions, from a sub-proletariat of lumbermen, wheat farmers, migratory fruit pickers, unnaturalized immigrants or southern Negroes. Since many of these workers could not vote, the IWW's ideological move towards syndicalism was thereby reinforced and encouraged.

. . . President Gompers and other AF of L leaders . . . denounced the IWW as a dual union. . . . The IWW's goal, they charged, was not to promote industrial unionism, but "to direct, pervert and disrupt the whole labor movement." If the trade union movement were to be based on the fatuous "scheme" of industrial organization, Gompers told a Pittsburgh audience in August 1905, "the tinker, tailor, and the candlestick maker would legislate upon every minute detail affecting the interests of the workers." In other words, the labor movement would revert back to nothing more than "the old K of L idea." . . .

Gompers'[s] assertion . . . that success for the IWW would have simply meant a reversion to the "old K of L idea" was wide of the mark. True, the IWW reasserted the Knights's old spirit of solidarity among all the workers, its antipathy towards craft-union exclusiveness, and its hostility toward capitalism as an institution. But it looked forward to a revolutionary general strike as the ultimate means of changing capitalist society and not backward to the recreation of a pre-industrial order. It upheld direct action and even violence as the catalysts of change, rather than arbitration and political action. And although its membership was organized into general unions that were more like the Mixed Assemblies of the K of L than the industrial unions later organized by the CIO, it accepted fundamental Marxist notions concerning the inevitability both of industrialization and of revolution. It did *not* seek to resurrect utopian ideas of a cooperative universe.

Bill Haywood's leadership may be measured by his degree of responsibility for the IWW's progressive retreat into the fringes of the labor force. . . . Nonetheless, it is less easy to assess the role of leadership in contributing to the IWW successes and failures than it is about either the Federation or the Knights. First of all, it was far more of a grass-roots kind of organization than either of the other two, thus tending to reduce the role of national leaders. Moreover, the IWW, almost from the first, was subject to such hostility from the press, from employers, from state agencies, and from Gompers and the AF of L itself (the AF of L willingly joined in the federal government's wartime persecution of the organization as subversive), that it is dubious whether any leader could have significantly altered the IWW's place in history.

And yet in Haywood's very first speech to the 1905 founding convention, he himself appeared to reflect the Wobblies' ambivalence about their role which was to dog the IWW in its subsequent development. "We are here for the purpose of organizing . . . an organization broad enough to take in all the working class," he asserted, a purpose which, had the IWW been allowed to carry it out successfully, might perhaps have generated a mass labor movement of industrial unionists two generations before the CIO appeared. "What I want to see from this organization," however, Bill Haywood added, "is an uplifting of the fellow that is down in the gutter." Organizing fellows down in the gutter is what the IWW came largely to be remembered for. It was a noble ideal, but it certainly did not make for organizational stability.

. . . Biographical sketches such as these can illuminate the movements out of which the dominant labor ideology in America ultimately came. But they do not, of course, tell why the conservative AF of L officials, despite the increasingly anachronistic character of many of their views, managed to retain control of the labor movement of this country until the 1930s. History after all, especially the history of social movements, is more than a record of the actions of great men. . . .

. . . [P]rofound internal developments in the nature of American society also determined labor's choices. The creation and preservation of a form of labor aristocracy was central to Gompers'[s] efforts. . . . [Organized challenges from common workers] did not succeed in America—at least insofar as such can be seen in the efforts of the leaders of the Knights of Labor and the IWW. This failure can be attributed partly to Gompers'[s] own good fortune and astuteness, and partly to weaknesses of leadership displayed by Powderly and Haywood. But it was due more to the presence of other factors—government and big business preference for AF of L unionism; the suppression of left-wing alternatives; and, perhaps most importantly of all, the ethnic and racial fragmentation of the labor force.

Questions

1. *How did the differing backgrounds of Gompers, Powderly, and Haywood shape their consciousness about what a labor movement should be?*
2. *Which approach to unionism—community, class, or craft—do you think would have best met the workers' needs? Why?*
3. *What reasons does Laslett give for the AFL becoming the dominant voice of the American labor movement by World War I?*

Three Approaches to Unionism

In the late nineteenth and early twentieth centuries, workers in America's mines, mills, and shops sought ways to protect themselves from the forces unleashed by the rise of industrial capitalism. On the job, they found their skills diluted, their work routinized, the workplace impersonalized, their security ravaged by frequent layoffs and unemployment, and themselves alienated from the products of their own labor. In the community, workers confronted poor housing, sanitation, and recreational facilities. They also experienced increased marginalization as a solidifying class structure transferred an even greater share of political, economic, and social power to the hands of the upper class and its middle-class allies.

Workers responded to these changes in a myriad of ways. Many took individualistic action, most notably moving from job to job or place to place hoping to find a better situation. Thus, the rates of both job turnover and geographic mobility were every bit as high for working-class people in the Gilded Age and Progressive Era as they are today. At times, individualistic-minded workers would temporarily band together out of frustration and strike an employer. (Most strikes before the 1930s were not initiated by labor unions.) Far more often than not, however, such efforts would fail. Any nascent organization would collapse, leaders would face employer blacklists, and the followers would as likely as not move on to another job in another place.

A small but significant minority of workers, however, recognized that the only meaningful way to improve their lot was to form permanent labor unions. (Until the 1930s, union members never represented more than ten percent of the nation's workforce.) Yet these workers were not united on what the focus and purpose of unions should be. Broadly speaking, three perspectives on unionism competed for dominance from the 1870s to the 1920s, each nominally represented by a national organization.

The Noble and Holy Order of the Knights of Labor, founded in 1869, was the most significant organization of workers until the 1890s. The order clearly sought to perpetuate the more egalitarian, producer-oriented society that supposedly existed in the pre-Civil War era. To do this, it sought to change the hearts and minds of the people—to establish a counterculture to the emerging material culture linked to the rise of industrial capitalism. The Knights sought to replace competitiveness with cooperation, strife with harmony, denigration with character (thus its emphasis on temperance). Believing that "An injury to one is the concern of all," it opened its doors to all producers—skilled as well as unskilled, black as well as white, women as well as men. The Knights' vision of a cooperative alternative to competitive capitalism and the Knights' inclusiveness, however, were not accepted by all who flocked into their ranks, particularly during the turbulent times of the mid-1880s. Whereas the Knights offered a dream of a better world, many members only wanted better conditions in this one and abandoned the organization and resumed their individualistic strategy when higher pay, shorter hours, and improvements on the job were not forthcoming.

Skilled workers, particularly in the building and printing trades but also in other crafts such as cigarmaking, were never very comfortable with the Knights' inclusiveness or idealistic vision. Skilled workers had been among the first workers to form unions for the purpose of addressing specific issues—wages, hours, working conditions—rather than broad social reform. In 1886, this approach gained a national forum when several national craft unions formed the American Federation of Labor as an umbrella organization to challenge the Knights' intrusive recruitment of skilled workers.

Under the leadership of Samuel Gompers, the AFL sought to advance the interests of skilled craftsmen, both against technological changes and de-skilling brought on by industrial capitalism and against competition from less-skilled workers whose ranks were surging because of the forces of immigration and urbanization. Gompers accepted industrialization as a given and simply wanted to gain a larger share of the benefits from that system for the AFL's membership. He had no desire to restructure society, to reach out to the truly marginalized and dispossessed. Indeed, he tried to keep the AFL from getting too tied to various reform movements or politics. Such an approach has been labeled "job conscious unionism," "pure-and-simple unionism," and even "business unionism." In 1893, quizzed by a congressional committee over what labor wanted, Gompers's answer was simply, "More!" This was a vision held by most skilled workers (and probably most workers not even *affiliated with the AFL), thus, providing a framework that allowed the American Federation of Labor to survive.*

Just as the idealism and inclusiveness of the Knights brought the AFL forward as a challenger, the pragmatism and exclusiveness of the AFL also brought forth the challenge of the Industrial Workers of the World. The IWW was born in the Rocky Mountain West in the midst of an era in which silver, copper, and lead miners were reduced to working for giant industrial concerns. It was nurtured in the East among unskilled immigrant steel, textile, and rubber workers. The IWW matured amidst the western lumber and agricultural laborers, as an inclusive organization that shunned the pretenses of skilled craftsmen and sought to organize all workers as a class.

Sparked to life by employer violence such as the Coeur d'Alene strike and the Colorado Labor Wars, the IWW saw workers trapped in a class conflict with industrial capitalists. Only when workers united as a class, took control of the factories and mines from the capitalists, and instituted a cooperative commonwealth would a truly egalitarian society be established. Like the Knights, the IWW was both visionary and inclusive, opening membership to anyone regardless of their sex, ethnicity, or job. Unlike the Knights, however, the IWW advocated confrontation and strife (and walked a hazy line around the issue of violence). The IWW rejected the idea that conditions could be changed through electoral politics, not only because so many of its members were disenfranchised but also because it saw the political process as firmly controlled by the hidden hand of capitalism. Rather, it advocated that workers directly confront the boss at the job site and in the pocketbook, through strikes and sabotage. Such militant rhetoric—which far exceeded the IWW's actual deeds—provided the justification needed for both private business and local, state, and federal repression, particularly during World War I and its immediate aftermath. Moreover, the radical rhetoric and the general disapproval by mainstream society of the IWW deterred most workers from joining the organization or staying with it too long. Although the IWW lingered on after 1920, its importance to the American labor movement, like that of the Knights of Labor, which faded from the scene after 1900, had ended. The main organization claiming to speak for American workers during the 1920s was the least representative of all, the American Federation of Labor.

Different Visions:
The "Rule of Perfect Equality Among Men"—The Knights of Labor

Terence V. Powderly was the Grand Master Workman of the Knights of Labor during its heyday in the 1880s and early 1890s. As leader of the Knights, he felt his primary task was to educate the membership on the true purpose of the Order. In his autobiography, Powderly discusses some of the practices and rituals of the Knights, hinting at the broader religious and social values that underlay the Knights's perspective. Abridged from The Path I Trod: The Autobiography of Terence V. Powderly, *ed. Harry J. Carman, Henry David and Paul N. Guthrie. (New York, 1940) 47, 49–57, 59–60.*

From 1869 up to 1878, the Knights of Labor had no platform, preamble or declaration of principles, and the extreme secrecy surrounding its movements gave to organizers a latitude of expression in explaining the purposes of the order that was limited only by the imagination of the organizer.... [The early organizers' goal was to establish] the "rule of perfect equality among men" when that organization became strong enough to successfully champion the cause of oppressed humanity....

To the Knights of Labor, all who toiled might find entrance and a welcome. The scavenger doing his work on the street was admitted on exactly the same terms of equality as the highest priced or most skilled artisan. The name of the Order was never printed and seldom spoken. Only in the assembly was it mentioned and then only that the newly initiated might know the name of the Order he had joined....

When a candidate was presented for initiation, he was asked three questions. First: "Do you believe in God, the Creator and Universal Father of all?" Second: "Do you obey the Universal Ordinance of God, in gaining your bread by the sweat of your brow?" Third: "Are you willing to take a solemn vow binding you to secrecy, obedience, and mutual assistance?" ...

The Worthy Foreman [presiding officer of the local assembly] when the candidate came before him would say:

> In the beginning God ordained that man should labor, not as a curse, but as a blessing; not as a punishment, but as a means of development, physically, mentally, morally, and has set thereunto his seal of approval in the rich increase and reward. By labor is brought forth the kindly fruits of the earth in rich abundance for our sustenance and comfort; by labor (not exhaustive) is promoted health of body and strength of mind, labor garners the priceless stores of wisdom and knowledge. . . .
>
> In all the multifarious branches of trade, capital has its combinations, and whether intended or not, it crushes the manly hopes of labor and tramples poor humanity in the dust. We mean no conflict with legitimate enterprise, no antagonism to necessary capital, but men in their haste and greed, blinded by self-interest, overlook the interests of others and sometimes even violate the rights of those they deem helpless. We mean to uphold the dignity of labor, to affirm the nobility of all who live in accordance with the ordinance of God, "in the sweat of thy brow shalt thou eat bread." We mean to create a healthy public opinion on the subject of labor (the only creator of values or capital), and the justice of its receiving a full, just share of the values or capital it has created. We shall with all our strength support laws made to harmonize the interests of labor and capital for labor alone gives life and value to capital, and also those laws which tend to lighten the exhaustiveness of toil. We shall use every lawful and honorable means to procure and retain employ for one another, coupled with just and fair remuneration, and should accident or misfortune befall one of our number, render such aid as lies within our power to give without inquiring his country or his creed. Without approving of general strikes among artisans, yet should it become justly necessary to enjoin an oppressor, we will protect and aid any of our number who thereby may suffer loss and as opportunity offers, extend a helping hand to all branches of honorable toil. . . .

It was one of the aims of the Order to cause every member to know how to "write his name in full" [on a membership card] . . . instead of being obliged to make his mark in the presence of witnesses who might deceive him as to the purport of the instrument he signed. I had the evidence of over one hundred men in Scranton that the lesson taught by that card, one of the first card systems, influenced them to take a course in writing so that they could not only write but read their names and other things beside.

. . . [I]n this organization we were to understand that while we had rights to battle for, we owed duties to our fellow men as well. We could claim no right for self that did not carry with it an obligation and a call to do our duty by and to others.

. . . We admitted all men and taught them the significance and value of organized, coöperative effort. Workers who up to that time dreamed that their callings could not be classed as skilled were taught to know that there is no unskilled labor. . . . All trades, all callings came into the Knights of Labor, and, catching the inspiration born of touching elbows in a common cause, they called their fellow toilers together to meet with them at the dawn of the day of specialty. We believed one man to be as good as another and entitled to the same "rights, privileges, and benefits" in life. Maybe we placed a too implicit faith in what the Declaration of Independence held out to us. Perhaps some lingering, belated wind from the scenes of the early days of the French Revolution carried to our minds the thought that equality could be won, so far as rights and duties went, without reddening our record with a single drop of human blood. . . .

When we vitalized and gave to the world the declaration of principles of our old Industrial Brotherhood we held out the chart of truth as we saw it. For doing so we were derided, sneered at, ridiculed, laughed at, and when we caused this nation to stop and think, those who were aiming at making everything subservient to wealth and corporate power changed their attitude and began to abuse us.

. . . We had no organizers, paid or otherwise. Every member carried a message to his fellows, and in a short time assemblies began to grow and flourish. . . .

I tell you of this happening [a railroad strike in 1877] that you may know something about the hardships endured by the pioneers of the labor movement. We walked, daylight and dark. We ate, not when we were hungry, but when and where we could get it. We shared our homes, tables, and beds with each other. I often had two or three Knights of Labor with me over night. We slept in shanties, ash pits, freight cars, or wherever night caught us after our work. Why did we do it? Because it was necessary and we wanted to be of use. . . .

We have been compared to the early crusaders, but I cannot think of a comparison less fitting. A crusader is, or was, a fellow who dressed himself up in a suit of sheet iron clothing, pulled an iron skillet over his head, drew on a pair of steel, knuckle-jointed gloves, climbed up on a horse that always looked too fat to run, set a crowbar-looking thing called a lance into a metal-lined pocket in the saddle, and, in company with a lot of other animated hardware stores rode out of town "on their gaily caparisoned steeds" in the direction of the Holy Land to rescue the tomb of the Saviour. . . .

The Knights of Labor aimed at rescuing man himself from a tomb, the tomb of ignorance. The aim was to roll away the stone from that tomb that he might know that moral worth and not wealth should constitute individual and national greatness.

. . . The great strike of 1877 in Pennsylvania made victims of hundreds of Knights of Labor, who left the state and went in all directions carrying with them no murderous lance; neither were they dressed in garments of steel. They were clothed in righteousness, and bore in their hearts and minds God's high and holy command: "Love your neighbor." Perhaps we did not always give the public to understand that love of neighbor was our aim for we had to strike, boycott, and do other things not supposed to be in accord with the Ten Commandments. But remember that for the first time in human history labor, in the last quarter of the nineteenth century, stood at least partially solidified, partially organized, and partially united in opposition to a power that had its origin in the first lockout, on the day that Adam and Eve were locked out of that rather exclusive garden in which fruit was grown with apples a specialty. That power was greed, century-fortified, steel-armored greed, and you must not blame us for striking against it now and then or for using other harsh methods.

Different Visions:
"A Permanent Constructive and Conserving Force"—The American Federation of Labor

Samuel Gompers was president and the leading publicist of the American Federation of Labor from the organization's founding in 1886 to his death in 1924. Gompers offers a brief description of the philosophy of "pure-and-simple" unionism and the social values underlying it. Abridged from Samuel Gompers, Seventy Years of Life and Labor: An Autobiography, *ed. Nick Salvatore (Ithaca, New York, 1984), 53–54, 103, 105.*

Our union was a great deal more than a militant organization. As we studied our trade problems and tried out policies for bettering conditions for cigarmakers, we soon found that we had to understand our industry as a whole. Trade agreements were made early in the cigar industry. The procedure was very simple. Our union drew up a bill of prices and submitted it to the employer. If he accepted, the transaction was complete; if he refused, we undertook to negotiate an agreement. If we failed, a strike or lockout resulted.

A problem which demanded our thought from the beginning was how to stabilize the union and retain progress achieved. I saw clearly that we had to do something to make it worthwhile to maintain continuous membership, for a union that could hold members only during a strike period could not be a permanent constructive and conserving force in industrial life. The union must develop within itself cohesive forces that would make for continuous effort. I gathered all the information I could get on the benefits provided by the British trade unions. I saw that our problem was different from that with which the English had to deal, in that militancy must dominate until we established our right to represent the workers of our craft in making trade agreements. An out-of-work benefit, provisions for sickness and death appealed to me. Participation in such beneficent undertakings would undoubtedly hold members even when payment of dues might be a hardship.

. . . I proposed that we consider providing for uniform dues and benefits for all members. These motions were referred to the Committee on Constitution of which I was the chairman. Our Committee recommended to the convention constitutional changes providing uniform dues of ten cents a week and initiation fee, traveling benefits, annual equalization of funds among all unions, a sinking fund on the basis of fifteen cents for each member and twenty-five cents for each newly initiated member, a traveling loan system. . . .

My job as the president of the A. F. of L. was coveted by no one in the early days. There was much work, little pay, and very little honor. Though the Federation had been created by agreement, it had to be given reality by making it a force in industrial affairs. The necessary first step was to win for the Federation the good will of the wage-earners. The Federation was the unified activity of the trade union men. It was dependent upon good will and understanding of economic power. So I became a seeker of men. I wanted to win them for a labor movement which was sound philosophically, competent economically, and inspiring spiritually. At times I was well-nigh consumed with zeal, so that I gave little thought to anything else. My work was my life. So in recording the events of my life the labor movement is the controlling purpose.

. . . The nineties brought no spectacular growth for the A. F. of L. There was steady progress, but it seemed painfully slow to my ardent hopes and boundless aspiration. Between 1890 and 1900, obviously the primary thing to do first was sustained effort to gather into the folds of the Federation national labor organizations that were eligible to membership.

Different Visions:
"Abolition of the Wage System"—
The Industrial Workers of the World

A number of prominent radicals were associated with the Industrial Workers of the World, but unlike the Knights of Labor or the American Federation of Labor, the IWW had a much more diffuse leadership structure. While speeches and pamphlets played a role in getting the IWW's message out, far more important were the popular art forms used to educate an often illiterate—at least in English—audience. In 1908, the IWW issued one of the most revolutionary statements ever made in its "Preamble of the Industrial Workers of the World." To popularize their message and motivate the masses, the IWW also utilized songs, such as, "Workers of the World, Awaken!" by Joe Hill (who wrote hundreds of such pieces, mostly to familiar religious music), and artwork that graphically drove home their point. Taken from Rebel Voices: An I.W.W. Anthology, *ed. Joyce L. Kornbluh (Ann Arbor, Michigan, 1964), 12–13, 143, 25, 33.*

PREAMBLE
of the Industrial Workers of the World

The working class and the employing class have nothing in common. There can be no peace so long as hunger and want are found among millions of working people and the few, who make up the employing class, have all the good things of life.

Between these two classes a struggle must go on until the workers of the world organize as a class, take possession of the earth and the machinery of production, and abolish the wage system.

We find that the centering of management of the industries into fewer and fewer hands makes the trade unions unable to cope with the ever growing power of the employing class. The trade unions foster a state of affairs which allows one set of workers to be pitted against another set of workers in the same industry, thereby helping defeat one another in wage wars. Moreover, the trade unions aid the employing class to mislead the workers into the belief that the working class have interests in common with their employers.

These conditions can be changed and the interest of the working class upheld only by an organization formed in such a way that all its members in any one industry, or in all industries if necessary, cease work whenever a strike or lockout is on in any department thereof, thus making an injury to one an injury to all.

Instead of the conservative motto, "A fair day's wage for a fair day's work," we must inscribe on our banner the revolutionary watchword, "Abolition of the wage system."

It is the historic mission of the working class to do away with capitalism. The army of production must be organized, not only for the every-day struggle with capitalists, but also to carry on production when capitalism shall have been overthrown. By organizing industrially we are forming the structure of the new society within the shell of the old.

Joe Hill composed the words and the music to this song, which appeared in the ninth edition of the I.W.W. songbook.

WORKERS OF THE WORLD, AWAKEN!

By Joe Hill

Workers of the world, awaken!
Break your chains, demand your rights.
All the wealth you make is taken
By exploiting parasites.
Shall you kneel in deep submission
From your cradles to your graves?
Is the height of your ambition
To be good and willing slaves?

Refrain:
Arise, ye prisoners of starvation!
Fight for your own emancipation;
Arise, ye slaves of every nation
In One Union Grand.
Our little ones for bread are crying,
And millions are from hunger dying;
The means the end is justifying,
'Tis the final stand.

If the workers take a notion,
They can stop all speeding trains;
Every ship upon the ocean
They can tie with mighty chains;
Every wheel in the creation,
Every mine and every mill,
Fleets and armies of the nation
Will at their command stand still.

Join the union, fellow workers,
Men and women, side by side;
We will crush the greedy shirkers
Like a sweeping, surging tide.
For united we are standing,
But divided we will fall;
Let this be our understanding—
"All for one and one for all."

Workers of the world, awaken!
Rise in all your splendid might;
Take the wealth that you are making,
It belongs to you by right.
No one will for bread be crying,
We'll have freedom, love and health
When the grand red flag is flying
In the Workers' Commonwealth.

[*The following appeared in* Solidarity, *June 30, 1917.*]

The Hand That Will Rule the World—One Big Union

[*This illustration of the Wobblies' belief that only the IWW could save the workers from the woes of industrial capitalism was printed in* One Big Union Monthly *in July 1920.*]

Union Inclusiveness—
Attitudes Toward Women
Paternalism: Samuel Gompers and the AFL

One approach to a better understanding of the various currents of unionism is to look at the treatment of subgroups of marginalized workers, such as women. Samuel Gompers and the AFL were rather reluctant recruiters of women. Heading an organization composed overwhelmingly of skilled, white male workers who were interested in limiting access to a discrete number of high-paying jobs, Gompers did little to open up to women the trades covered by his organization. Rather, he dealt with the women's question in broad, posturing generalizations, as examples from his self-serving autobiography illustrate. Selected from Samuel Gompers, Seventy Years of Life and Labor: An Autobiography, *ed. Nick Salvatore (Ithaca, New York, 1985), 126–29.*

I have known a number of remarkable women both within and without the labor movement. Nothing has been more essential to the sustained progress of the labor movement than the conscious and unconscious co-operation of the womenfolk of union men. My daily observation taught me the meaning of the sacrifices made by the wives of men who have devoted themselves to the labor movement. Not only did the wife share privations and actual want, but she lived the spiritual sacrifice of being helpmate to a man who gives an absorbing cause first demand on his life. . . .

There have been within the labor movement, in addition to those who sustained this sort of auxiliary relationship to the labor movement, wonderful women trade unionists, for the labor movement, like all primary human movements, is neither male nor female—it is the instrumentality of unity. So I have never felt that there was properly a sex phase to the fundamentals of trade unionism. Trade unionism is to protect all who work for wages, whether male or female.

Devotion to trade unionism leads to interest in movements for freedom in all relations of life; consequently, I was early interested in the movement for equal suffrage. Equal rights for all brought me logically to endorse the women's struggle for equal political and legal rights. At that early day, the cause was at the height of its greatest unpopularity. I was one of the early advocates of woman's suffrage. . . .

While the large number of women were advocating equal suffrage, but few of them devoted any attention or activity to a movement in which I was deeply interested—that is, the movement to secure to women and girls equal pay with men and boys who were engaged in the same work. It was one of the principles for which I strongly contended within the labor movement. I believed, and as time goes on, I have become more fully convinced, that political equality without some degree of industrial independence would be more of a fantasy than a practical reality. . . .

It was the beginning of the twentieth century when the Women's Trade Union League was launched—a somewhat different type of working-women's organization—for the purpose of organizing women into trade unions. . . . [T]he leaders in this movement were largely social workers. I was in sympathy with the movement and gave it my cordial co-operation because I hoped it would lead to genuine trade union work.

. . . Some of the staunchest workers in the labor movement have been women. Some few of them . . . have been rewarded by official position in unions whose membership is composed of both men and women.

Union Inclusiveness—
Attitudes Toward Women Romanticization:
The Industrial Workers of the World

The IWW actively recruited women and had a number of notable female leaders, including Elizabeth Gurley Flynn and Mary "Mother" Jones. Still, its depiction of women in its pamphlets, songs, and pictures was highly idealized—replacing a very popular bourgeois stereotype of the

"True Woman" with one of the "Rebel Girl." This vision is revealed in the song "The Rebel Girl," written by the IWW's most famous songster, Joe Hill, in 1915. Taken from Songs of the Workers: To Fan the Flames of Discontent *(Popularly known as The Little Red Songbook.), 34th ed. (Chicago, n.d.), 38–39.*

THE REBEL GIRL

(words and music written by Joe Hill in jail, February 1915)

la - dy Is the Reb - - el Girl. - - - -
la - dy Is the Reb - - el Girl. - - - -

CHORUS

That's the Reb - el Girl, That's the Reb - el Girl, To the

work - ing class she's a pre - cious pearl She brings cour - age

pride and joy - - - To the fight - ing Reb - el Boy - - We've had

girls be - fore but we need some more in the In - dust - rial

Work - ers of the World - - - For it's great to fight for free - dom

With a Reb - - el Girl. - - - - -

Union Inclusiveness—
Attitudes Toward Women
Separatism: The Knights of Labor

In the area of recruiting women, the Knights of Labor were far more progressive than the AFL and far more successful than the IWW. Estimates are that ten percent or more of the Knights' membership was female. Some organized in mixed assemblies with men, but many more organized in separate women's assemblies, which numbered 113 at the Knights' high point in 1886. The Knights established a Women's Department headed by Leonora Barry to coordinate the Order's work with women. While her appointment and the accomplishments of the Knights were a milestone for the labor movement, in the end she was frustrated with the results. As the following passages from her annual reports reveal, Barry found the policy of separatism and its underlying male attitudes to be barriers to true equality for women within the movement. Excerpted from America's Working Women, *ed. Rosalyn Baxandall, Linda Gordon and Susan Reverby. (New York, 1976), 120–25.*

1887

. . . Upon the strength of my observation and experience I would ask of officers and members of this Order that more consideration be given, and more thorough educational measures be adopted on behalf of the working-women of our land, the majority of whom are entirely ignorant of the economic and industrial question which is to them of such vital importance; and they must ever remain so while the selfishness of their brothers in toil is carried to such an extent as I find it to be among those who have sworn to demand equal pay for equal work. Thus far in the history of our Order that part of our platform has been but a mockery of the principles intended.

1888

My understanding of the duties implied in my office was that I was to do everything in my power that would in my judgement have a tendency to educate and elevate the workingwomen of America and ameliorate their condition. Therefore, when I spoke to a public audience of American citizens, exposing existing evils and showing how, through the demands of Knighthood, they could be remedied, I felt that I was fulfilling the duties of my office. . . . When I found an opportunity of laying before other organizations of women the cause of their less fortunate sisters and mold a favorable sentiment, I felt I was doing that which is an actual necessity, as woman is often unconsciously woman's oppressor. . . .

It has been intimated that the Woman's Department was started on sentiment. Well, if so, it has turned out to be one of the most thoroughly practical departments in the Order. Without egotism I can safely say it has done as much effective work in cheering, encouraging, educating and instructing the women of this Order in the short year of its existence as was done by the organization in the whole time of women's connection with it previous to its establishment.

As you will all doubtless remember, I instituted a Beneficial Department for women, of our Order by way of encouragement and that they might have some tangible proof of the benefits of our organization. Owing to the lack of business methods and selfishness of others, and a general apathy with which comfortably-situated women are afflicted, it did not become the universal success I had hoped. . . .

1889

My work has not been confined solely to women and children, but to all of earth's toilers, as I am of the opinion that the time when we could separate the interests of the toiling masses on sex lines is past. If it were possible, I wish that it were not necessary for women to learn any trade but that of domestic duties, as I believe it was intended that man should be the bread-winner. But as that is impossible under present conditions, I believe women should have every opportunity to become proficient in whatever vocation they choose or find themselves best fitted for.

A few words about the Woman's Department. When I took a position at its head I fondly hoped to weld together in organization such a number of women as would be a power for good in the present, and a monument to their honor in the relief it would establish for the women of the future. I was too sanguine, and I am forced to acknowledge that to fulfill my best hopes is a matter of impossibility; and I believe now we should, instead of supporting a Woman's Department, put more women in the field as Lecturers to tell women why they should organize as a part of the industrial hive, rather than because they are women. There can be no separation or distinction of wage-workers on account of sex, and separate departments for their interests is a direct contradiction of this, and also of that part of our declaration which says "we know no sex in the laws of Knighthood." Therefore, I recommend the abolition of the Woman's Department, believing, as I now do, that women should be Knights of Labor without distinction, and should have all the benefits that can be given to men—no more, no less—thereby making it incumbent upon all to work more earnestly for the general good, rather than for sex, Assembly or trade.

Questions

1. *What three or four words used by Powderly do you feel best reveal the social values underlying his view of unionism?*
2. *What key words and phrases used by Gompers best delineate his perspective on unionism that is different from Powderly's viewpoint?*
3. *In what ways does the IWW rhetoric differ from and/or compliment the rhetoric of Gompers and Powderly?*
4. *Despite their limitations, which approach do you think offered the most promising avenue for advancement for female workers—Gompers's, Powderly's, or the IWW's perspective on women?*

FURTHER READING

For a fuller treatment of the lives and ideas of Terence V. Powderly, Samuel Gompers, and William D. "Big Bill" Haywood, see the respective essays by Richard Oestreicher, John H. M. Laslett, and Joseph R. Conlin in Labor Leaders in America, *ed. Melvyn Dubofsky and Warren Van Tine (Urbana, Illinois, 1987). Two still viable treatments of the differences between the Knights of Labor and the American Federation of Labor can be found in Norman J. Ware,* The Labor Movement in the United States, 1860–1895 *(New York, 1964); and Gerald N. Grob,* Workers and Utopia: A Study of Ideological Conflict in the American Labor Movement, 1865–1900 *(Chicago, 1961). The best history of the IWW is Melvyn Dubofsky's* We Shall Be All: A History of the Industrial Workers of the World *(Chicago, 1969). For a wonderful collection of IWW songs, poems, pictures, and essays, see* Rebel Voices: An I.W.W. Anthology, *ed. Joyce L. Kornbluh (Ann Arbor, Michigan, 1964).*

The Grueling Battle
for Woman Suffrage

Susan M. Hartmann

INTRODUCTION

Women voiced their first formal demand for the ballot at the Seneca Falls convention in 1848. It took seventy-two years to win ratification of the Nineteenth Amendment to the Constitution granting women throughout the United States the right to vote in 1920. Not all women had to wait that long. By 1890 women in sixteen states had partial suffrage, that is, they could vote in school board or other local elections. Wyoming became the first state to grant women full suffrage in 1890, followed by Colorado, Utah, and Idaho in the next six years. These victories invigorated anti-suffrage forces, and thereafter the suffrage movement endured one defeat after another. Using a state-by-state approach, between 1896 and 1909 women attempted dozens of times to get legislatures to authorize popular referenda on suffrage. They obtained only six referenda, and lost every one. But after 1910, when the state of Washington enfranchised women, the momentum shifted to the suffrage forces.

Suffragists were overwhelmingly native born, white, and middle class, and they sometimes used nativist and racist arguments to advance their cause. The National American Woman Suffrage Association (NAWSA) distanced itself from black women eager to work for the ballot, but by 1910 some activists had begun to strengthen the crusade by mobilizing across class and ethnic lines. With an expanded constituency, suffragists continued to struggle state by state, but they increasingly focused on the national level and an amendment to the federal Constitution.

The effort gained momentum when a new group split off from NAWSA. First called the Congressional Union and then the National Woman's Party (NWP), it energized the movement with *its more militant, radical tactics. NWP women picketed the White House, and once the United States entered World War I, they taunted President Woodrow Wilson with the contradiction between fighting a war for democracy abroad while failing to practice it at home. When they resisted police orders to disperse, NWP militants were sent to jail where they went on hunger strikes and officials forced nutrients down their throats. NAWSA members criticized and disavowed the NWP activists, but the militants gained publicity for the cause and helped the NAWSA by making it appear more moderate, the lesser evil. The decades of persistent organizing by mainstream suffragists, the NWP's militant actions, and the wartime environment, which highlighted women's contributions to the public sphere and exposed the nation's failure to live up to its ideal of representative government, all combined to secure congressional passage of the Nineteenth Amendment in 1919 and its ratification in 1920.*

Three years later, two suffrage leaders looked back on the struggle with awe: "How much of time and patience, how much work, energy and aspiration, how much faith, how much hope, how much despair went into it." To the women involved, "its success became a monumental thing."

WHY DID IT TAKE SO LONG FOR WOMEN TO WIN THE VOTE?

In recounting the history of the woman suffrage campaign, NAWSA President Carrie Chapman Catt noted that "America's history, her principles, her traditions stood forth to . . . suggest that she would normally be the first country in the world to give the vote to women." But twenty-six nations enfranchised women before the United States did. "Why the delay?" Catt queried. "It is a question that was the despair of two generations of American women."

Historians have examined a number of forces arrayed against votes for women, including southern politicians, northern political machines, and various business interests, most notably the liquor industry. Although men alone had the power to enfranchise women, scholars have also investigated the role of women who joined the countermovement and became its most visible participants and spokespersons. Their national organization, the National Association Opposed to Woman Suffrage, claimed 350,000 members by 1916 and included twenty-five state groups. The relative importance of each of these forces in resisting the suffrage movement continues to be a subject of debate among scholars.

Who Opposed Woman's Suffrage?

In her analysis of the resistance to woman suffrage, historian Eleanor Flexner downplays the role of women themselves and emphasizes the liquor industry, other business interests, and southern politicians. The following is taken from her book, Century of Struggle: The Woman's Rights Movement in the United States *(New York, 1974), 294–305.*

⸢Some of the opposition to the enfranchisement of women was obviously based on the prejudices of individuals. But the more closely one looks, the clearer it becomes that suffragists faced far more than mere conservative opinion; no distaste for women in new social roles, no feeling about the sanctity of motherhood or the sacredness of the home could account for the animus that expressed itself in highly organized and articulate form against women as voters, becoming increasingly intemperate as woman suffrage spread slowly from one state to another.⸥

Where did the multitude of anti-suffrage organizations, male and female, that cropped up across the country come from? Who supplied the organizers and the witnesses at legislative and Congressional hearings, so often masculine in gender? Who paid the bills for the stream of newspaper articles and advertisements, the hoardings and handbills? Who bought the referendum votes that were stolen from the suffragists? . . . Who paid for the immigrant and saloon vote in city after city, state after state, in suffrage elections from the Dakotas to New Jersey? . . .

Inevitably the main source of opposition varied from one part of the country to the other. In the South the source of sentiment lay in fear of the Negro vote—in fear of strengthening any attempts to overthrow the system of Jim Crow restrictions (including the poll tax) which, in defiance of the Fourteenth and Fifteenth amendments, disfranchised the colored population. In the Middle West much of the opposition stemmed from the brewing interests; in the East from industrial and business sources.

The original "anti" leaders were women of irreproachable social position, like the wives of General Sherman and Admiral Dahlgren, who as early as 1872 headed one thousand signers to a petition to the United States Senate against granting woman suffrage. In 1882, in opposition to the campaign for the municipal vote for women in Massachusetts, two women "remonstrants" appeared at a legislative hearing on the bill, but preserved their modesty by presenting a written statement instead of verbal testimony against the proposed bill. . . .

In 1895 to combat the drive to put woman suffrage into the revised New York state constitution (an attempt which failed), anti-suffragists, men and women, organized in New York, and the Massachusetts group re-formed itself into the Massachusetts Association Opposed to the Further Extension of Suffrage to Women; it continued the most active and vocal, although similar organizations eventually appeared in some twenty states. In 1911 a National Association Opposed to Woman Suffrage was formed in New York, headed by Mrs. Arthur M. Dodge.

Almost without exception the women in these organizations were ladies of means and social position. The main burden of their argument was that woman suffrage placed an additional and unbearable burden on women, whose place was in the home; the fact that this argument came largely from women whose housework was done by an adequate force of servants and that they presumed to speak for women less fortunately placed, never seemed to disturb the "antis," who also argued that they did not need political suffrage since their menfolk represented them and cared for their interests.

No one in the suffrage camp credited the "antis" with great effectiveness. Their arguments seemed too puerile and roused more than one woman who eventually became a suffrage leader to thought and action. While the antis' appearance at hearings and in print, through a flood of pamphlets and letters to the newspapers, did furnish legislators with the excuse that a body of respectable women did not want the vote, their real role in the opinion of the women working with Mrs. Catt was to serve as a front for more potent forces working against woman suffrage, principally the liquor interests. Mrs. Catt declared categorically that "a trail led from the women's organizations into the liquor camp and it was traveled by the men the women antis employed. . . .["]

The anonymity in which the brewers preferred to carry on their opposition to woman suffrage was punctured in 1918 by a Senate Judiciary Committee investigating charges of propaganda carried on by them during the war in both Bolshevik and German interests. The complaints which had for years flooded suffrage headquarters after every referendum received unexpected authoritative documentation when the subpoenaing of the files of Percy Andreae, who masterminded much of the brewers' publicity, turned up such letters as one marked "confidential" to a Milwaukee brewing concern in 1914:

> In regard to the matter of woman suffrage, we are trying
> to keep from having any connection with it whatever. We

These suffragists picketing the White House in 1917 carry a banner exposing the contradiction between President Woodrow Wilson's wartime rhetoric about democracy and his refusal to support democracy at home by supporting woman suffrage. Their banner quotes his war message, "We shall fight for the things which we have always carried near our hearts, for Democracy, for the right of those who submit to authority to have a voice in their government." (Courtesy of The Library of Congress.)

are, however, in a position to establish channels of communication with the leaders of the anti-suffrage movement for our friends in any state where suffrage is an issue. I am under the impression that a new anti-suffrage association has been organized in Illinois and is a retail liquor dealers affair. I consider it most dangerous to have the retailers identified or active in any way in this fight, as it will be used against us everywhere.

A brewers' strategy conference on October 13, 1913, whose minutes unaccountably survived (since it was the practice of the brewers' organizations to keep neither minutes nor financial records), revealed their role in more than one woman suffrage referendum defeat. An organizer for the brewers declared that in Nebraska, woman suffrage was defeated in 1911 at tremendous expense. His report for Wisconsin stated: "We have had the usual bills, like every other state—county option (liquor selling), women's suffrage in about six different forms and we have had everything else, which were all defeated; and I say that can be done only by organization and by active work of the brewers being on the job all the time and not leaving it to somebody else." . . .

The means employed by the liquor groups to achieve their goal went beyond buying editorial support for their "educational campaigns" or open editorial opposition, or allocating quotas to saloon keepers and bartenders of the number of customers for whose appearance and "no" vote at the polls they would be held accountable. Their influence reached openly into the halls of legislation. The Lieutenant-Governor of Wisconsin, as one instance alone, told Mrs. Ben Hooper, one of Mrs. Catt's most active co-workers, that he had seen the Milwaukee lawyer who "lobbied" for the brewers "sit in the gallery of the Senate and tell his men with his hands how to vote." As late as 1918, with Prohibition staring them in the face, lobbyists for the brewers were still lobbying against the woman suffrage amendment in Washington.

It is more difficult to pinpoint some of the other elements in the opposition to woman suffrage. Easiest to identify, after the liquor groups, were the political machines, whose weight was invariably thrown against votes for women until Tammany Hall gave up in 1917. Machine men were plainly uncertain of their ability to control an addition to the electorate which seemed to them relatively unsusceptible to bribery, more militant, and bent on disturbing reforms ranging from better sewage control to the abolition of child labor and, worst of all, "cleaning up" politics. The arguments many suffragists used in their own behalf, such as the inherent interest of women in such improvements as better schools or protective legislation for women workers, sounded in the ears of the machine bosses like the trumpet of doom. . . .

Most difficult of all to link with the opposition to woman suffrage were the business interests. The proceedings of the annual conventions of the National Association of Manufacturers and the U. S. Chamber of Commerce, or the pages of the *Wall Street Journal*, do not contain a word of protest against granting women the vote. There was no nation-wide mobilization of Big Business against woman suffrage. Yet some business groups fought suffrage tenaciously and bitterly, albeit with the greatest circumspection. One suffrage organizer after another reported the presence and activity of railroad, oil, and general manufacturing lobbies, whenever suffrage was up for legislative action or referendum.

In March 1916 Mrs. Catt was in Iowa, with a state referendum scheduled for June and what looked like a good chance of victory. Yet already a cloud no bigger than one man's hand was visible:

> That man Maling is in Iowa doing dirty work. I had a talk with him myself, and . . . I have called on one and all to institute an investigation as to who or what is backing this man. He is saying that it is the business interests of Colorado. I half believe it. I am a bit fearful that the banks, mine owners and other big business are really sending along an official warning to the men of the other states to beware of this terrible menace of woman suffrage, but, if it is so, it is better to smoke our enemy out and know where he is.

There were other instances. In the course of a Congressional investigation into the affairs of Swift & Company, the meat packers were shown to have made secret contributions to the "antis"— secret because the company recognized that eventually woman suffrage was likely to "sweep the country." An appeal to Nebraska voters to vote against the woman suffrage referendum in that state in 1914 carried the signatures of nine railroad and municipal transit executives, seven bankers, and other assorted businessmen, leavened by those of two Episcopalian ministers. . . .

In Massachusetts, where the "antis" were so entrenched that defeat of the state referendum in 1915 left suffrage workers hopeless of progress by the state method, the *Woman's Journal* looked

Five thousand suffragists marched in the first suffrage parade in 1913 in Washington, D.C. The parade was scheduled to coincide with the inauguration of President Woodrow Wilson. (Courtesy of Brown Brothers, Sterling, PA.)

into the election expense reports which the law required be filed with the Secretary of State. Reports from three anti-suffrage organizations showed the majority of their contributions coming from individuals, four fifths of them from men. An amount of $31,695 was reported from 135 men, an average of $235 apiece. The outraged *Journal* asked, "What sort of man can afford to sign a check for $235 with which to fight the enfranchisement of women?" and answered its own question: "the powerful directors of the moneyed section of Boston."

It is not too difficult to see why such corporate interests as railroads, oil companies, and other manufacturers were opposed to giving women the vote. The Federal Income Tax, which had been authorized by the Sixteenth Amendment to the constitution in 1913, had been bitterly opposed as "communistic"; so had popular election of United States Senators, provided by the Seventeenth Amendment in the same year. Other elements of the "New Freedom," such as the institution of the Federal Reserve banking system, the Tariff Commission and the Federal Trade Commission, along with new anti-trust legislation and a widespread movement for the initiative and referendum, all appeared as cumulative threats to vested interests. In such circumstances, the addition of a large body of new voters, control of which appeared uncertain and many of whose leaders were vocal in the cause of further reform, presented a fresh menace. What might not such an infusion into the body politic do to the enormous advantages concealed in grants to railroads, franchises of various kinds, and rate schedules? . . .

There was also a strong feeling, particularly in some of the industries that would be most closely affected, that women would use the vote to improve the conditions of working women. The National Council of Women Voters, which had been organized in 1911 as an abortive attempt to gather together the voting strength of the enfranchised women in the West, had stated as its threefold purpose: extension of equal suffrage to other states; changing conditions in the suffrage states to improve conditions for women, children and the home; and "to claim justice for women in the political and economic world." The legislative record of some states which had enjoyed woman suffrage for a number of years could be used to substantiate such a view; so could innumerable speeches and articles by women like Florence Kelley, Margaret Dreier Robins, Leonora O'Reilly, and others, as well as publications issued by the National [Council of Women Voters] itself.

The men from northern states who led the fight against the suffrage amendment on the floor of the United States Senate were spokesmen for business interests, and the fact was spread out in their voting record on a score of measures. Senator Wadsworth of New York who did not alter by one jot his opposition to suffrage after his state gave its women the vote in 1917 also voted against the income tax, the direct primary, the taxation of war profits, and an investigation of Wall Street. Senator Weeks, leader of the Republican machine in Massachusetts, voted against the direct election of senators, the income tax, taxation of war profits, and the establishment of the Federal Trade Commission. . . . The reputation of Brandegee of Connecticut was such that even the impersonal Dictionary of American Biography noted that "his influence was largely negative, if not reactionary in effect"; he opposed the direct election of Senators, extension of parcel post, the Federal Reserve system, and the income tax.

These men alone would not have been able to delay the suffrage amendment as long as they did without the support of the large majority of southern Democrats. For decades the question of woman suffrage had carried, for politicians and the dominant interests in the South, some of the same explosive impact of desegregation today [1974], as a threat to established social, economic, and political patterns. . . .

This keynote sounded through most of the speeches in the Senate against the amendment in the closing battle, as in the words of Senator Smith of South Carolina, who was assailing the few southerners who supported woman suffrage by constitutional amendment:

> I warn every man here today that when the test comes, as it will come, when the clamor for Negro rights shall have come, that you Senators from the South voting for it have started it here this day. . . . If it was a crime to enfranchise the male half of this race, why is it not a crime to enfranchise the other half? . . . [A]nd when the time comes, as it will, when you meet the results of this act, you cannot charge that it was a crime to pass the 15th amendment. . . . By thus adding the word "sex" to the 15th amendment you have just amended it to liberate them all, when it was perfectly competent for the legislatures of the

several states to so frame their laws as to preserve our civilization without entangling legislation involving women of the black race.

Nor were the Southerners alone in voicing this point of view. Senators Wadsworth of New York and Reed of Missouri took the states' rights position to the point where they declared they would vote against a federal amendment *forbidding* woman suffrage! And Borah of Idaho, who always based his opposition on the states' rights issue, declared that he had no wish to add to the already heavy burden borne by the South. . . .

Borah was not the most striking example of the strange coalition which, despite everyday partisan alignments, faced the suffrage amendment down to the final vote. With regard to the tacit filibuster which prevented a vote on the amendment a whole year before the end, the *Woman Citizen,* in the person of Alice Stone Blackwell, commented acidly:

> It was clear that Senator Lodge (Rep.) of Massachusetts was the leader and general floor manager for the opposition, but the loving camaraderie between the "wilful few" Republicans and the "wilful few" Democrats who in normal relations do not waste time in each other's company, was an amazing sight to the galleries. Mr. Lodge of Massachusetts and Mr. Ellison Smith of South Carolina, Mr. Brandegee of Connecticut, Mr. Martin of Virginia, Mr. Wadsworth of New York, Mr. Underwood of Alabama, as divided as the Kaiser and the King of England in most matters, were as united as twin brothers in defending the nation against the "awful disaster to the nation should women be enfranchised by the Federal Amendment." . . . [B]ut it cannot record the pictures of Republicans and Democrats with arms around each other's necks, with Democrats slapping Republicans on the back in token of a common jubilation that they had scored a mighty victory in preventing the Senate from taking a vote!

"The unholy alliance," Mrs. Catt christened this combination after she and Mrs. Park, watching from the gallery, had once seen Lodge of Massachusetts and Martin of Virginia standing arm-in-arm at the back of the chamber, comparing notes. It did not in the end prevent women from getting the vote, but it caused far more delay and difficulty than one would ever imagine from reading the usual phrase in the history books, announcing that American women were enfranchised after World War I.

Ladies Against Women

Suffragists tended to dismiss their female opponents as members of an economic elite who feared losing their privileges and/or as dupes of the liquor interests. In the following account, however, historian Carl Degler argues that women played the crucial role in blocking the suffrage campaign and suggests reasons why some women would oppose their own emancipation. The account is taken from Carl N. Degler, At Odds: Women and the Family in America from the Revolution to the Present *(New York, 1980), 349–58, 360–61.*

[T]he active opposition of thousands of women was one of the most striking aspects of the struggle for the vote . . . Historians who favor woman suffrage have either ignored the anti-suffragists or dismissed them as women who were merely expressing the opposition of their husbands. But the size, persistence, and activities, not to mention the character of the leadership of the anti-suffrage groups, beginning in the 1890s, belie the argument that the opposition was male-directed. . . .

The reason why women, alone of all social groups, organized against their own political emancipation is that many women perceived in the suffrage a threat to the family, a threat so severe that the vote did not seem worth the possible cost. Although the anti-suffrage case comprised almost an infinite number of arguments and justifications—as the pro-suffrage case did, too—behind all the arguments and justifications loomed the fear that bestowing the ballot upon women would force an alteration in the traditional family. The argument runs all through the anti-suffrage literature from the 1880s right down to 1920.

Underlying the anti-suffrage arguments was the fundamental assumption that the natures of women and men were different. As an anti-suffrage document submitted to the Illinois legislature in 1897 phrased it, the pivotal question is that "of sex. We believe that men are ordained to govern in all forceful and material matters, *because they are men,* physically and intellectually strong, virile, aggressive; while women, by the same decree of God and nature, are equally fitted to bear rule in a higher and more spiritual realm, where the strong frame and the weighty brain count for less, but the finer fibre of the woman's body and the spiritual uplift of her affection and her soul are the indications of a power not less than that of a man, and even more necessary to the progress and elevation of the race." This was, of course, a biological justification of the old principle of the separate spheres. And though it denied the identity of the sexes, it asserted their equality, with perhaps a slight edge to women.

Some anti-suffragists were even more precise in equating the intellectual abilities of men and women, while asserting their basic difference in character. "You cannot dodge the fact women have work in the world that men cannot do, and it is equally true that men have work that women cannot do," contended Ann Watkins in 1912. "Neither man nor woman is superior or inferior to the other; the two are just different, positive and negative, two great manifestations of a still greater force." . . .

What differentiated the Antis from the Suffs was not their conceptions of the differences between men and women, but the Antis' denial of *individual* differences in women. The Antis thought and acted much as racists—they assumed that all people in a given biological category—in this case women—were alike and so much so that social policy—the suffrage—should be based on that assumption. "The Anti-Suffragists grant the equality of sexes," wrote a well-known Anti in 1909. "Men are no better than women and science assures us that they are no more intelligent. But the Anti insists that the *difference* between the sexes shall not be ignored." The work of the two sexes, wrote another anti-suffragist, was "not to be measured by the same standard of values." It was their differences that made "any home a symmetrical thing. . . . We do those things for which we are best fitted by physical and mental powers." The response of the Antis to the suffragists' contention that sex had nothing to do with work, she continued, was that "sex happens to be the pivot upon which the whole *question turns.* It has fixed our place in the home and in the world, and no matter how far astray we go mentally from our right appreciation of this truth, sex will inexorably drive us back to wifehood and motherhood until the world ends." It was the feminists' and suffragists' counter-assertion that some women could perform the work of men that fully exposed the quasi-racist, antiindividualist assumptions of the Antis. "That woman could develop better under masculine conditions of life," contended Margaret Robinson in 1916, "is a totally unsupported theory. Woman cannot become man—she can only become a poor imitation. She develops best along the lines of her aptitudes and instincts." . . .

Alice George thought the suffrage must disrupt the family because of its emphasis upon women's individuality. Should the vote be granted, she wrote, "the whole sweep of relations of the sexes must be revised, if the woman's vote is to mean anything more than two people doing what one does now." For if women simply duplicated the votes of men there would be no purpose in giving them the suffrage. Yet if women used the vote as individuals with interests different from those of their husbands, then we "reinforce those who clamor for individual rights" and "strike at the family as the self-governing unit upon which the state is built." . . . To Helen Johnson, the fundamental threat of the suffrage was that it brought "the possibility of civil war . . . to the door of every family."

If the suffragists worried about the lack of interest the mass of women showed in achieving the suffrage, the anti-suffragists made capital out of it. The more perceptive of them recognized the women's apathy or hostility toward the suffrage stemmed from the threat it posed to the family. Caroline Corbin, one of the leading anti-suffragists in Illinois, made the point in the form of a question as early as 1887. If women become politically and economically independent, she inquired, "what then becomes of marriage and the home? Is there any escape from the conviction that the industrial and political independence of women would be the wreck of our present domestic institutions? May it not be possible," she asked, "that an intuitive sense that woman suffrage is incompatible with the present relations of men and women in the home, has something to do with the fact that . . . an overwhelming majority of women do not desire the ballot?" She might have added that the refusal of most suffragists and feminists to acknowledge the conflict between the family and women's emancipation was in itself a sure sign that there was a threat. . . .

In the end, then, the conflict between the Suffs and the Antis was over whether women ought to be treated as individuals or as subordinates who served the family. . . . The Antis attacked Elizabeth Cady Stanton's *Woman's Bible* because it frankly emphasized women's thinking of themselves rather than of others—that is, acting as self-interested individuals. "What sort of a 'next generation' would evolve," asked the *Anti-Suffragist* in 1909, "if all women considered their 'first duty' to be themselves, and overlooked the fact that their strongest power and highest possibility is that of unselfish—and often unnoticed—service." This is also why many anti-suffragist women were among the leaders in the opposition to easier divorce laws, for they saw in divorce not only a sign of family instability but a heightened sense of self among women, which they could only deplore. Helen K. Johnson, the author of a major anti-suffrage book, for example, was also a leader in the opposition to any easing of the divorce laws. The Antis also asserted that divorce was easier in those states where woman suffrage prevailed. . . .

If a perceived threat to the family explains why women were reluctant to support the suffrage, we are still left with the question of how it was that the suffrage finally was accepted in 1920. Two kinds of reasons suggest themselves.

First of all, there was the powerful and well-organized campaign mounted by the suffragists, especially after 1910. Just about then a decision was made by the suffrage leadership to abandon the fifty-year-long campaign to win the suffrage state by state and to concentrate upon amending the federal Constitution. After all, as late as 1910 no more than four states, all of them small and western, had enacted full suffrage for women. Once the decision was made to fight for a federal amendment, the suffrage leaders moved to win over Congress and the President, much more concentrated targets than some forty state legislatures. Notable in this regard was the intense and often violent campaign of the radical wing of the suffragists in 1913–14, led by the indefatigable Alice Paul. Emulating the passive-resistance tactics of the contemporary English women's movement, suffragists picketed the White House, chained themselves to fences, and, when taken to jail, went on hunger strikes. There they resisted the brutality of forced feeding and, when freed, went back to jail immediately and eagerly. Meanwhile membership in the more conventional organizations swelled, and the propaganda and political pressure mounted. Although in 1915 referenda on woman suffrage were defeated in four eastern states, the proponents came close to winning. They captured 46 per cent of the total in Pennsylvania, 42 per cent in New York and New Jersey, and 35 per cent in Massachusetts. President Wilson himself supported suffrage when he voted that year in New Jersey. Membership in the National American Woman Suffrage Association reached almost two million members, with a gross income of three-quarters of a million dollars a year. In short, by 1915 the suffrage had been raised to a national political issue, causing the Progressive and Republican parties officially to endorse the suffrage in time for the election of 1916. . . .

The second reason why resistance to the suffrage was finally overcome has to do with a decline in the fear that the suffrage threatened the family. During the first decade or so of the 20th century it became increasingly clear that, whatever the suffrage might portend in theory, in fact it was not a threat to the family. By 1910 woman suffrage had been tried in four states for over a decade; yet there nothing much had changed, one way or another. . . .

The most important reason of all why many women could forget about their apprehension that the suffrage threatened the family was that the justifications for the suffrage shifted ground in the early 20th century. The original and most common argument on behalf of woman suffrage in the 19th century had been that which has been sketched in previous pages—namely, that votes for women symbolized their individuality, their sense of self-interest, their need to be able to speak politically as individuals. Feminists and suffragists like Elizabeth Cady Stanton pushed that argument hard, contending that no man could speak for a woman, any more than a white person could speak for a black. Suffrage was justified on the grounds that women were individual human beings, who must express their own preferences individually.

By the opening years of the 20th century, however, the original suffragist leaders had passed from the scene, and the old appeal to individual rights as the basis for the suffrage for women was gradually abandoned. The principal reason it was dropped was that it was not working. . . . At the same time, the advancement of women in education, business, professions, and in a great variety of social and reform organizations by the early 20th century suggested a more practical argument in support of the suffrage. The new justification was that women had a special contribution to make to society, something that men could not provide. This special contribution, so the argument went, came from their character as women—as wives and mothers, as homemakers. Jane Addams, for example, pointed out early in the 20th century that the problems of modern cities were those that women had long been familiar with: child labor, unsanitary housing, adulterated food, and so forth. "May we not say," she asked, "that city housekeeping has failed partly because women, the traditional housekeepers,

WOMEN
bring all
VOTERS
into the world
~
Let Women Vote

This poster presents a typical suffrage argument—that women should have the right to vote because of their role as mothers. (Courtesy of the North Carolina Museum of History.)

have not been consulted as to its multiform activities?" And in 1914 Alice Stone Blackwell urged woman suffrage on the ground that it would have a salutary effect on foreign policy because women were different from men. "Let us do our utmost to hasten the day when the wishes of the mothers shall have their due weight in public affairs, knowing that by so doing we hasten the day when wars shall be no more." In short, politics and voting were but an extension of the home, so they needed the special character of women to improve them. Suffrage now became a way of extending women's special sphere to society, rather than being a way of providing political expression for women's self-interest as individuals. Those suffragists who advanced such a defense of the suffrage were, in effect, arguing that women's character as a sex should be represented, but not a woman's interest as an individual. This new justification for the suffrage was thus very close to the Antis' assertion that women as a group were basically different from men. In the process, of course, that assertion played down, if it did not deny outright, a woman's individuality. It fitted in well, however, with the idea that woman's place in the family was as helper and nurturer of others, and thus supported, rather than threatened, the traditional relation between husband and wife in the family. . . .

⌐ . . . [T]he suffrage fight has been treated as a conservative reform, which is certainly the way it was defended in the last stages of the campaign. In fact, though, the suffrage was the political side of a drive for woman's individuality that was re-shaping the traditional family. The suffrage may have been only a first step in the achievement of women's equality, rather than the last one that the suffragists contended. Yet it was certainly an integral and necessary part of that long revolution concerning woman's place through which American society is still passing.⌐

Questions

---

1. *Why would liquor interests devote funds to blocking woman suffrage instead of focusing their resources on preventing prohibition? Does Flexner's evidence convince you that other corporate interests worked against suffrage? According to Flexner, why did they do so? Why did the strongest opposition to woman suffrage come from the South?*

2. *To what extent can we say that women's opposition to suffrage represented a rational calculation of their self-interest?*

3. *Should the woman suffrage movement be characterized as conservative or radical? How great a change do you think its achievement brought to American society?*

4. *Do you find any parallels between the opponents of woman suffrage and the groups that oppose feminist goals today?*

ARGUMENTS AND ACTIONS

As befitted their views of women's appropriate roles, anti-suffrage women conducted their campaigns more quietly than their opponents. They testified before state legislatures and Congress, gave public speeches, and wrote profusely, as did the men on their side. Suffragists used words just as vigorously, but the elusiveness of their goal drove them to bolder, more innovative, and more extensive efforts. The following documents illustrate the arguments used by anti-suffragists and the strategies and tactics employed by suffragists.

The Threat to the Home

From 1911 to 1916, Mrs. Arthur M. Dodge, a Vassar-educated, wealthy widow and mother of six sons, led the National Association Opposed to Woman Suffrage. Dodge devoted her public life to the anti-suffrage cause and to the day nursery movement, whose goals were to provide care for children of employed mothers and inculcate American middle-class values into the children of immigrants. In this selection, Dodge's views on suffrage are quoted in Edward Marshall, "Our Suffrage Movement is Flirtation on a Big Scale," New York Times, May 25, 1913, Sec. V.

"Never has there been a propaganda so destructive of great values as that which women now are preaching, marching, dancing, dressing. While suffrage must inevitably lead to the destruction of the old home idea, it offers for it not the slightest substitute.

"Even the word 'home' is becoming a rare joke among the suffragists. From their platforms they continually ridicule us—the anti-suffragists—because we talk of it.

"That is a sad state of things isn't it? Home has been the woman's business and her love and life for centuries. It is the foundation of society, the basis of all morals. Without the home we should become unmoral and without morals society, in turn, must perish.

"No man ever made a home. It has been ever women's work. If she refuses to accomplish it, then it must remain undone; if it remains undone, what can ensue but something close related to a social reign of terror? . . .

"When women cease to strive to learn the art of home-making then will the world indeed go wrong. And all this agitation of the present day trends certainly in that direction.

"The tendencies toward feminism and toward socialism both find in home the chief object of attack, although only the Socialists are brave enough to make acknowledgment of this. One, not less than the other, means its loss.

"The old-time woman made herself the idol of the world not through stump speeches or mad 'hikes,' (leaving her little ones to hired nurses' care,) but through her sacrifices. Each of the great moral teachers has assured us and has proved by his own life that in sacrifice must lie the greatest of achievements. . . .

"To offset the suspicion in the public mind that suffrage means destruction to the home, the leaders of the movement are now bending every effort to prove otherwise. Watch the newspapers and periodicals of recent days and those of days immediately to come and you will find a flood of pictures showing suffrage leaders with their progressive cheeks pressed tight against the velvet faces of their babies. They doubtless have decided that this variation of the plan of their publicity is necessary as a means of proving to the public that a suffragist can be a mother.

"And in thinking of this matter men must not fail to take count of the link between the suffragists and Socialists. I have already spoken of it. It cannot too often be brought to the public mind. As suffrage grows in strength so socialism grows in strength, and vice versa. California, Oregon, Kansas—all these States were carried for the suffrage cause by Socialistic votes. . . .

Don't Know What They Are Doing.

"I don't want to seem discourteous toward my sisters in the suffrage movement. I believe the greater portion of them are not really aware of what they do. I am certain the majority of them do not desire to bring about destruction of the home, with all that must imply—of loose or no domestic life; I believe many of them to be good mothers, and that among their younger workers may be many girls who are not infected and who will not become infected with a horror of the highest function given to woman by her God, that of motherhood. . . .

"I am no advocate of retrogression among women. I believe in education, culture, full development. In these days woman, to do the best which in her lies for her own home, must get much for it from outside. My point is that she must get these outside things for the benefit of her home and not neglect her home so that she may go adventuring for them for her own benefit, amusement, and dissipation.

"I am not certain that in suffrage influences may not be found the causes which are making good homes fewer, families smaller, marriages later. Suffrage and the voluntary or forced entrance of woman into industrial life is the greatest threat against the home. In a nation's homes lies its strength. It would be a world-tragedy if woman, in her blind and mistaken efforts to uplift herself, should bring ruin on the Nation and with it destroy herself.

"And what does the vote amount to? Women do not need it to accomplish really good things. . . .

"A woman can do anything if she does not vote; she is likely to do little if she does. Only through constructive methods has any nation ever thrived. We women must be wives and mothers, and as wives and mothers, through increasingly good education, must build our children's character.

"We need more, not less, of the mother-daughter and mother-son influence. We must continue to build citizens through individual efforts: machinery can never do it.

"These things being true, is it not obvious that anything which takes woman from her home is dangerous? May I call attention to the fact that immigration of undesirable Europeans is coincident with our own decreasing birth-rate?

"Is not that inevitable? Our country will be stocked with human beings of one kind of another. Would it not be better business if our women ceased their thinking and their prating, their hiking and hurrahing about votes and took some thought of this condition?

"If they keep their eyes upon their homes and those within them, the ballot box will take care of itself; if they keep their eyes upon the ballot box, the homes will not."

147

The Threat to American Institutions

Many opponents of suffrage portrayed it as a radical threat to American values and institutions. Helen Kendrick Johnson, a prolific anti-suffrage writer, makes this case in a letter to the New York Times, *March 12, 1911.*

Woman suffrage, like Socialism, has been the enemy of sound government and of true republican progress since the days of the ancient republics, when Sparta, the commune, brought up its women like men, and progressive Athens builded homes. Socialism has given the Old World every particle of constitutional woman suffrage that exists there. There is no such woman suffrage in the Republics of Switzerland and France.

As to our own country, woman suffrage was introduced into it by Mormonism, when Utah was still a Territory. Populism and a ridiculous incident gave it to Wyoming; Populism and the free silver madness were its sponsors in Colorado, and to Mormonism it owes its entrance in Idaho. Its late success in Washington was a Socialistic triumph, which, according to a decision of the Court of Appeals in a case brought in Texas, is likely to be pronounced unconstitutional. In the past twelve years suffrage bills in various States have been defeated, on an average, oftener than once a month. The movement was originally the child of Communism, and that the mother has come to claim her child is evident from the present merging of suffrage and Socialism in our city. One Saturday evening recently I heard the Socialist pleaders for woman suffrage denounce the home, marriage, religion, and the Republic. If in these rests our hope of progress, then woman suffrage is an obstacle that will continue to be swept aside by sound legislation. There is evidence that many American women are beginning to realize that they must either rush into the destructive tide or renounce the delusion that has been fostered with a zeal that blinded their womanly vision. This is the hour when patriotic, progressive citizens must devote thought and energy to maintaining American institutions.

HELEN KENDRICK JOHNSON

Essential Differences between the Sexes

Female anti-suffragists offered abundant reasons why they did not want the ballot. But that did not stop men from claiming to speak for women, as did Lyman Abbott, a retired Congregational minister and editor of Outlook, *an influential journal espousing progressive Christianity. Abbott focuses on two popular arguments against woman suffrage in this selection from his article, "Why Women Do Not Wish the Suffrage,"* Atlantic Monthly 92 *(September 1903): 289–93.*

Certainly few men or women will doubt that at the present time an overwhelming majority of women are either reluctant to accept the ballot or indifferent to it. Why this indifference, this reluctance? This is the question which in this article I seek to answer. Briefly, I believe it is because woman feels, if she does not clearly see, that the question of woman suffrage is more than merely political; that it concerns the nature and structure of society,—the home, the church, the industrial organism, the state, the social fabric. And to a change which involves a revolution in all of these she interposes an inflexible though generally a silent opposition. . . .

The first and most patent fact in the family is the difference in the sexes. Out of this difference the family is created: in this difference the family finds its sweet and sacred bond. This difference is not merely physical and incidental. It is also psychical and essential. It inheres in the temperament; it is inbred in the very fibre of the soul; it differentiates the functions; it determines the relation between man and woman; it fixes their mutual service and their mutual obligations. . . .

This difference in the sexes is the first and fundamental fact in the family; it is therefore the first and fundamental fact in society, which is but a large family. . . . And the fundamental fact, without which there could be no family, is the temperamental, inherent, and therefore functional difference between the sexes.

Because their functions are different, all talk of equality or non-equality is but idle words, without a meaning. Only things which have the same nature and fulfill the same function can be said to be superior to or equal with one another. . . . Man is not an inferior woman. Woman is not an inferior man. They are different in nature, in temperament, in function. We cannot destroy this difference if we would; we would not if we could. In preserving it lies the joy of the family; the peace, prosperity, and well-being of society. If man attempts woman's function, he will prove himself but an inferior woman. If woman attempts man's function, she will prove herself but an inferior man. Some masculine women there are; some feminine men there are. These are the monstrosities of Nature. . . .

[It] is not woman's function to fight against human foes who threaten the home. She is not called to be a soldier. She is not to be welcomed with the volunteers nor coerced into military service by the draft. It is in vain to recite the story of Joan of Arc; it is in vain to narrate the efforts of the Amazons. The instinct of humanity revolts against the employment of woman as a soldier on the battlefield. No civilized man would wish to lay this duty upon her; no civilized woman would wish to assume it. . . . For like reason society exempts woman from police functions. She is not called to be sheriff or constable or night watchman. . . .

. . . The question, "Shall woman vote?" is really, in the last analysis, the question, "Ought woman to assume the responsibility for protecting person and property which has in the past been assumed by man as his duty alone?" It is because women see . . . that the first and fundamental function of government is the protection of person and property, and because women do not think that they ought to assume this duty any more than they ought to assume that police and militia service which is involved in every act of legislature, that they do not wish to have the ballot thrust upon them.

Let us not here make any mistake. Nothing is law which has not *authority* behind it; and there is no real authority where there is not *power* to compel obedience. It is this power to compel which distinguishes law from advice. Behind every law stands the sheriff, and behind the sheriff the militia, and behind the militia the whole military power of the Federal government. No legislature ever ought to enact a statute unless it is ready to pledge all the power of government—local, state, and Federal—to its enforcement, if the statute is disregarded. A ballot is not a mere expression of opinion; it is an act of the will; and behind this act of the will must be power to compel obedience. Women do not wish authority to compel the obedience of their husbands, sons, and brothers to their will. . . .

. . . She is glad to counsel: she is loath to command. She does not wish to arm herself, and, as police or soldier, enforce her will on the community. Nor does she wish to register her will, and leave her son, her brother, or her husband to enforce it. If she can persuade them by womanly influence she will; but just in the measure in which she is womanly, she is unwilling to say to her son, to her brother, or to her husband, "I have decreed this; you must see that my decree is enforced on the reluctant or the resisting."

Suffrage Strategies in Ohio

Proponents of political change always have a harder time than those who want merely to preserve the status quo. This account of suffrage efforts in Ohio indicates the enormous amount of effort women expended, the succession of defeats they endured, their changing strategies, and their perceptions of their opponents. It is written by Mrs. Harriet Taylor Upton, president of the Ohio Woman Suffrage Association for the years 1899–1908 and 1911–1920, for The History of Woman Suffrage, *ed. Ida Husted Harper (New York, 1922), 6:508–17.*

The history of woman suffrage in Ohio is a long one, for the second woman's rights convention ever held took place at Salem, in April, 1850, and the work never entirely ceased. . . . Other States did more spectacular work and had larger organizations but none finished its tasks with a stronger spirit of loyalty and love for the work and the workers.

The State Woman Suffrage Association was organized in 1885 and held annual conventions for the next thirty-five years. . . .

From the first gathering of Ohio suffragists in 1850 until . . . 1920, few years passed when some suffrage measure was not asked for and few Legislatures went out of existence without having considered some legislation referring to women. In 1894 a law gave them the right to vote for members of the boards of education. In 1904 and 1905, the Legislature was asked to submit to the voters an amendment to the State constitution giving full suffrage to women but the resolution was not reported out of the committees. In 1908 it was reported but no vote was taken. In 1910 it was defeated on the floor. This was the experience for years.

Periodically attempts had been made to revise the State constitution of 1851 without success but the Legislature of 1910 provided for submitting to the voters the question of calling a convention, which was carried in the fall of that year. . . .

Interests, vicious and commercial, fought the suffrage amendment from every possible angle but on March 7 the convention adopted it by a vote of 76 to 34. If accepted by the voters it would eliminate the words "white male" from Section I, Article V, of the present constitution. The enemies secured the submission of a separate amendment eliminating the word "white." This was done to alienate the negro vote from the suffrage amendment and the negroes were told that it was a shame they should be "tied to the women's apron strings." . . .

. . . The constitution was ready on May 31 and the special election was set for Sept. 3, 1912. Three months of vigorous campaign for the amendment followed. The German-American Alliance and the Personal Liberty League, two associations representing the brewers' interests, fought it in the field as they had done in the convention. It was estimated that the suffragists spent $40,000 and it was learned that the liquor forces first appropriated $500,000 and later added $120,000 to defeat the suffrage amendment. The chief work of the suffragists was done in the cities, although women spoke at picnics, county fairs, family reunions, circuses, beaches, institutes, labor meetings, at country stores, school houses and cross roads. More than fifty workers came into Ohio from all directions to assist, the larger number from the eastern States. They received no financial recompense and gave splendid service. In August an impressive suffrage parade of 5,000 took place in Columbus.

The president of the German-American Alliance at a meeting in Youngstown boasted openly that it defeated the amendment. It advertised everywhere, by posters and in street cars, and had no voluntary workers. It was evident that huge sums were being spent. The amendment was lost by a majority of 87,455—ayes, 249,420; noes, 336,875. Only 24 out of 88 counties were carried and but one Congressional district, the Eighteenth.

There was never any state-wide anti-suffrage association of women but only small groups in Cleveland, Cincinnati, Dayton and Columbus. Most of them were rich, well situated, not familiar with organized reform work and not knowing the viciousness of their associates. The real foe was the associated liquor men, calling themselves at first the Personal Liberty League, later the Home Rule Association, appearing under different names in different campaigns and they had in their employ a few women who were connected with the Anti-Suffrage Association. The amendment was lost in 1912 because of the activity of the liquor interests and the indifference of the so-called good people. . . .

The amendment eliminating the word "white," left over from ante bellum days, also was defeated and the new constitution retained a clause which had been nullified by the 15th Amendment to the National Constitution forty years before! The initiative and referendum amendment was carried. The State Suffrage Association, therefore, early in 1913, decided to circulate a petition initiating a woman suffrage amendment to the constitution, as there was no hope that the Legislature would submit one. It required the signatures of ten per cent. of the voters at the last election, in this instance 130,000 names. . . .

Who but women fighting for their freedom could ever have had the courage to keep on? They had no money to pay circulators and all was volunteer work. Over 2,000 women circulated these petitions. To have more than 130,000 men write their names and addresses on a petition and the circulator see them do it and swear that she did was no light task but it was accomplished. On July 30 petitions bearing 131,271 names were filed with the Secretary of State. A petition was secured in every county, although the law requires them from a majority only, and each was presented by a worker from that county. The sight of scores of men and women with arms laden with petitions marching up to the State House to deposit them brought tears to the eyes of some of the onlookers.

The campaign opened in Toledo, April 14, 15, was hectic. Everything possible was done to bring the amendment to the attention of the voters. Cleveland suffragists put on a beautiful pageant, A Dream of Freedom. A pilgrimage was made to the Friends' Meeting House in Salem where the suffrage convention of 1850 was held and the resolutions of those pioneers were re-adopted by a large, enthusiastic audience. Women followed party speakers, taking their audiences before and after the political meeting. State conventions of all sorts were appealed to and many gave endorsement, those of the Republicans and the Democrats refusing. Groups of workers would visit a county, separate and canvass all the towns and then keep up their courage by returning to the county seat at night and comparing notes. Street meetings and noon meetings for working people were held. Everything which had been tried out in any campaign was done.

From the beginning of 1913 to the election in November, 1914, there was constant work done for the amendment. The total number of votes cast on it was 853,685; against, 518,295; for 335,390; lost by 182,905 votes. There were gains in every county but only 14 were carried, where there had been 24 in 1912.

That the liquor interests and the anti-suffragists worked together was clearly established. The Saturday preceding the election the president of the State Suffrage association saw in her own city of Warren a man distributing literature from door to door and accompanied by a witness she followed him and picked up several packages in different parts of the city. They contained two leaflets, one giving information on how to vote on the Home Rule or "wet" amendment, the other giving instructions how to vote against the suffrage amendment. The latter had a facsimile ballot marked against it and was signed by five women. . . .

After the defeats of 1912 and 1914 the suffragists abandoned the idea of carrying an amendment. The revised constitution provided for "home rule" for cities, which allowed them to adopt their own charters instead of going to the Legislature. Suffragists believed that these charters could provide for woman suffrage in municipal affairs. In 1916 East Cleveland decided to frame a charter and they saw a chance to make a test. This campaign was the work of the Woman Suffrage Party of Greater Cleveland. On June 6 a city charter was submitted to the voters and adopted including woman suffrage. . . .

In the fall of 1917 the women of Lakewood, a city adjoining Cleveland on the west, gave municipal suffrage to its women by charter after a vigorous campaign. Columbus undertook to put this in its charter and a bitter campaign took place. It was the house to house canvass and the courageous work of the Columbus women and State suffrage officers which brought the victory when it was voted on at the election in August, 1917. Sandusky was not successful.

A partial poll of the Legislature on the subject of Presidential suffrage for women in 1915 had shown that it would be futile to attempt it but after endorsements of woman suffrage by the national party conventions in 1916 it was determined to try. [The bill passed and the governor signed it on February 21, 1917.] . . .

Very soon the opponents opened headquarters in Columbus and circulated petitions to have the Presidential suffrage bill referred to the voters for repeal. The story of these petitions is a disgraceful one. Four-fifths of the signatures were gathered in saloons, the petitions kept on the back and front bars. Hundreds of names were certified to by men who declared they saw them signed, an impossibility unless they stood by the bar eighteen hours each day for some weeks and watched every signature. Some petitions, according to the dates they bore, were circulated by the same men in different counties on the same day. Some of them had whole pages of signatures written in the same hand and some had names only, no addresses. The suffragists copied some of these petitions after they were filed in Columbus and although the time was short brought suit to prove them fraudulent in six counties. . . .

The law made no provision to meet the expenses of petition suits and the suffragists had to bear the cost, no small undertaking. The election boards which were dominated by politicians who had been notorious for their opposition to suffrage, interposed every possible obstacle to the attempt of the suffragists to uncover fraud. In some counties it was impossible to bring cases. Women were absorbed in war work and thousands of them bitterly resented the fact that at such a time their right to vote should be questioned. The referendum was submitted with the proposal so worded on the ballot that it was extremely difficult to know whether to vote yes or no.

At the election in November, 1917, the majority voted in favor of taking away from women the Presidential suffrage. The vote for retaining it was 422,262; against 568,382; the law repealed by a majority of 146,120. . . .

Ohio suffragists now turned their attention entirely towards national work. It was apparent that while the liquor interests continued their fight, women with a few thousand dollars, working for principle, could never overcome men with hundreds of thousands of dollars working for their own political and financial interests. Intensive organized congressional work was carried on henceforth for the Federal Suffrage Amendment.

Suffrage Tactics in New York

New York suffragists waged a massive referendum campaign in 1915 for an amendment to the state constitution. This account of the effort in New York City reveals the detailed planning, imaginative tactics, and huge amounts of sheer legwork that went into the campaign. Written by Mrs. Oreola Williams Haskell, head of the Press Bureau of the New York City Woman Suffrage Party, the narrative is taken from The History of Woman Suffrage, *ed. Ida Husted Harper (New York, 1922), 6:460–64.*

The Woman Suffrage Party of Greater New York was launched . . . at Carnegie Hall, October 29, 1909, modelled after that of the two dominant political parties. Its first convention with 804 delegates and 200 alternates constituted the largest delegate suffrage body ever assembled in New York State. The new party announced that it would have a leader for each of the 63 assembly districts of the city and a captain for each of the 2,127 election districts, these and their assistant officers to be supervised by a borough chairman and other officers in each borough, the entire force to be directed by a city chairman assisted by city officers and a board of directors. Mrs. Catt, with whom the idea of the Party originated, and her co-workers believed that by reaching into every election district to influence its voters, they would bring suffrage close to the people and eventually influence parties and legislators through public opinion.

The population of Greater New York was 4,700,000 and the new party had a task of colossal proportions. It had to appeal to native Americans of all classes and conditions and to thousands of foreign born. It sent its forces to local political conventions; held mass meetings; issued thousands of leaflets in many languages; conducted street meetings, parades, plays, lectures, suffrage schools; gave entertainments and teas; sent appeals to churches and all kinds of organizations and to individual leaders; brought pressure on legislators through their constituents and obtained

Suffragists demonstrate in New York City in 1912; their banner refers to the fact that women in some western states, including Colorado, Utah, and Washington, had already won the right to vote. (Courtesy of Corbis-Bettmann.)

wide publicity in newspapers and magazines. It succeeded in all its efforts and increased its membership from 20,000 in 1910 to over 500,000 in 1917. . . .

The City Party began the intensive work of the campaign in January, 1915. . . . It was decided to canvass all of the 661,164 registered voters and hundreds of women spent long hours toiling up and down tenement stairs, going from shop to shop, visiting innumerable factories, calling at hundreds of city and suburban homes, covering the rural districts, the big department stores and the immense office buildings with their thousands of occupants. It was estimated that 60 per cent of the enrolled voters received these personal appeals. The membership of the party was increased by 60,535 women secured as members by canvassers. . . .

The spectacular activities of the campaign caught and held public attention. Various classes of men were complimented by giving them "suffrage days." The appeal to the firemen took the form of an automobile demonstration, open air speaking along the line of march of their annual parade and a ten dollar gold piece given to one of their number who made a daring rescue of a yellow-sashed dummy—a suffrage lady. A circular letter was sent to 800 firemen requesting their help for all suffragists. "Barbers' Day" produced ten columns of copy in leading New York dailies. Letters were sent in advance to 400 barbers informing them that on a certain day the suffragists would call upon them. The visits were made in autos decorated with barbers' poles and laden with maps and posters to hang up in the shops and then open air meetings were held out in front. Street cleaners on the day of the "White Wings" parade were given souvenirs of tiny brooms and suffrage leaflets and addressed from automobiles. . . .

Forty-five banks and trust companies were treated to a "raid" made by suffrage depositors, who gave out literature and held open meetings afterward. Brokers were reached through two days in Wall Street where the suffragists entered in triumphal style, flags flying, bugles playing. . . . [H]undreds of colored balloons were sent up to typify "the suffragists' hopes ascending." Workers in the subway excavations were visited with Irish banners and shamrock fliers; Turkish, Armenian, French, German and Italian restaurants were canvassed as were the laborers on the docks, in vessels and in public markets.

A conspicuous occasion was the Night of the Interurban Council Fires, when on high bluffs in the different boroughs huge bonfires were lighted, fireworks and balloons sent up, while music, speeches and transparencies emphasized the fact that woman's evolution from the campfire of the savage into a new era was commemorated. Twenty-eight parades were a feature of the open air demonstrations. There were besides numbers of torch-light rallies; street dances on the lower East Side; Irish, Syrian, Italian and Polish block parties; outdoor concerts, among them a big one in Madison Square, where a full orchestra played, opera singers sang and eminent orators spoke; open air religious services with the moral and religious aspects of suffrage discussed; a fête held in beautiful Dyckman Glen; flying squadrons of speakers whirling in autos from the Battery to the Bronx; an "interstate meet" on the streets where suffragists of Massachusetts, New Jersey and New York participated. . . . [T]he suffragists ended their campaign valiantly with sixty speakers talking continuously in Columbus Circle for twenty-six hours.

On the night of November 2, election day, officers, leaders, workers, members of the Party and many prominent men and women gathered at City headquarters in East 34th Street to receive the returns, Mrs. Catt and Miss Hay at either end of a long table. At first optimism prevailed as the early returns seemed to indicate victory but as adverse reports came in by the hundreds all hopes were destroyed. . . . [T]hough many workers wept openly, the gathering took on the character of an embattled host ready for the next conflict. After midnight many of the women joined a group from the State headquarters and in a public square held an outdoor rally which they called the beginning of the new campaign.

The vote was as follows: . . . Total opposed, 320,853; in favor, 238,098; adverse majority, 82,755.

Two days after the election the City Party united with the National Association in a mass meeting at Cooper Union, where speeches were made and $100,000 pledged for a new campaign fund. The spirit of the members was shown in the words of a leader who wrote: "We know that we have gained over half a million voters in the State, that we have many new workers, have learned valuable lessons and with the knowledge obtained and undiminished courage we are again in the field of action."

Questions

---

1. *How did anti-suffragists argue that suffrage would be bad for the nation? How did they argue that it would be bad for women?*
2. *What were the most compelling of anti-suffragist arguments?*
3. *To what extent do you think anti-suffragists' concerns about woman suffrage actually proved true once women had the ballot?*
4. *What different routes to suffrage did women attempt? What strategies or tactics might have proved more effective?*
5. *From what you have learned about other reform movements in American history, how was the woman suffrage movement similar to or different from them?*

FURTHER READING

Eleanor Flexner, Century of Struggle: The Woman's Rights Movement in the United States *(New York, 1974), remains the best overall history of the suffrage movement. Aileen S. Kraditor*, The Ideas of the Woman Suffrage Movement, 1890–1920 *(New York, 1965), provides a good analysis of the arguments on both sides. Rosalyn Terborg-Penn's article, "Discontented Black Feminists," in* Decades of Discontent, *ed. Lois Scharf and Joan M. Jensen (Boston, 1987), explores the suffrage experiences of African American women. For the broader context of American feminism before and after suffrage, see Nancy F. Cott*, The Grounding of Modern Feminism *(New Haven, 1987). For more on the militant suffragists, see Christine A. Lunardini*, From Equal Suffrage to Equal Rights: Alice Paul and the National Woman's Party *(New York, 1986).*

The First
Sexual Revolution

Leila J. Rupp

INTRODUCTION

In the decades before and after 1900, profound changes in American society constituted what historians have called a "sexual revolution." By this they mean a transformation of sexual behavior and attitudes, in particular an increase in sexual contact outside of both marriage and prostitution among some groups in society and a new openness about sexuality, especially women's sexuality. As more white working and middle-class women moved out of the home and into the factories, offices, department stores, and college classrooms of a rapidly industrializing society, the nineteenth-century separation of male and female spheres began to erode. As the economy shifted from the stage of heavy industrialization to the production of consumer goods, the societal emphasis on thrift gave way to the glorification of spending and pleasure. In the newly respectable world of commercialized entertainment—consisting of dance halls, amusement parks, and the movies—young men and women socialized freely with strangers, setting the stage for what commentators came to call the "revolution in manners and morals."

Urban areas served as the crucible for change. Here the massive wave of immigration from southern and eastern Europe and the northward trek of African Americans introduced different sexual attitudes and practices to the white native-born population. In addition, an influx of young, white, rural men and women contributed to the growth of urban working-class subcultures where changes in social and sexual behavior flourished. In traditional rural communities, young people socialized on the front porch or at church, under the watchful eyes of family or community, but in the cities "women adrift"—young women living apart from their families—mingled with strange men in public places. The automobile, too, for those who could afford one, provided privacy that facilitated greater intimacy. The phenomenon of dating, including various kinds of sexual activity, came to replace the more serious "courting" signified by the pairing off of a couple.

As social barriers between men and women crumbled, the nineteenth-century notion of women as "passionless" in contrast to men as inherently lustful came under attack. Women, too, were recognized as sexual beings, a perception underscored by their adoption of shorter skirts, bobbed hair, and makeup. Although a large gap remained between the sexual experience of men and women, both faced new societal demands for "sex appeal." Couples increasingly came to expect sexual satisfaction and fun in marriage. Sexuality separated from the demands of reproduction necessitated access to birth control, a battle originally fought by "emancipated" and radical women in the first decades of the century.

In accordance with the breakdown of social barriers between women and men, sexologists and psychologists emphasized the naturalness of heterosexuality, thereby stigmatizing the same-sex "romantic friendships" that had been widely accepted in the nineteenth century. The usage of the terms "heterosexual" and "homosexual" in the U.S. date from the turn of the century, when the idea that sexual behavior defined categories of people first developed. Commentators began to notice subcultures of what they termed "inverts"—a description that associated "reversed" gender characteristics with same-sex sexual behavior—in American cities. The sexual revolution both sexualized relationships that had previously seemed non-sexual and categorized people by the sexual acts in which they engaged.

At the heart of all these transformations, then, lay a sexualizing of society. People talked more openly about sexuality, ironically spurred by the social hygiene movement that sought to fight the spread of venereal disease by controlling sexual behavior. People engaged more openly in sexual activity outside the confines of marriage and beyond the world of prostitution. Changes that began in the working-class urban subcultures attracted the attention of a bohemian vanguard in such places as Greenwich Village and Harlem, who then spread the word through their novels, paintings, and music. The "flapper" style of the 1910s and 1920s represented the acceptance by young middle-class women, particularly on college campuses, of styles of behavior pioneered by their working-class sisters. American society would never be the same again.

DATING AND PETTING

Historians often tend to assume that changes in behavior percolate down from the upper or middle classes. The sexual revolution of the early twentieth century first came to light in investigations of middle-class youth. But social historians investigating the working-class subcultures of cities such as New York and Chicago have discovered changes in sexual mores even before those that swept the middle class in the 1920s. Young single women and men, living in boarding houses or furnished rooms, pioneered many of the changes in sexual attitudes and behavior previously associated with college youth.

Paula Fass details the changing sexual norms among native-born, white, middle-class college students in the 1920s, a group that left readily accessible sources by which we can chart new attitudes and behavior. Certainly they played an important role in the transformation of modern American sexuality. But they were not as pioneering as we once thought, as Kathy Peiss's work makes clear. Her interpretation of working-class life in turn-of-the-century cities is based on a careful reading of the reports of middle-class observers—reformers, social workers, and journalists—who often reacted with alarm to what they saw as violations of decent morality. Peiss "reads against the grain" in order to try to understand, through the filter of middle-class minds, how working-class men and women viewed their own sexuality. Both Fass and Peiss are interested in the development of peer subcultures that challenged, to a lesser and greater extent, traditional understandings of morality.

Sexuality on Campus in the 1920s

Paula S. Fass, in a commentary on sexuality among white college youth, argues that young people "appeared suddenly, dramatically, even menacingly on the social scene" in the 1920s. By that she means that the stage of youth became increasingly significant for young people themselves and for the setting of trends in society as a whole. Excerpted from Paula S. Fass, The Damned and the Beautiful: American Youth in the 1920's *(New York, 1977), 260–68, 271–72.*

Students of modern sexual behavior have quite correctly described the twenties as a turning point, a critical juncture between the strict double standard of the age of Victoria and the permissive sexuality of the age of Freud. Too often, however, the sexual revolution of the twenties has been described exclusively in terms of scattered data suggesting an increase in premarital sexual intercourse on the part of women. One is tempted to picture investigators hunting for that special morning between 1919 and 1929 when 51% of the young unmarried women in America awoke to find that they were no longer virgins. Instead, of course, investigators are forced to deduce revolutionary changes from small, though important, increases in what remained a minority pattern of behavior. This kind of thinking, not unlike the Victorian concept of all or nothing, overlooks the fact that changes in sexual habits, as in most other areas of social relations, are evolutionary and take place through a gradual accretion of behavioral and value changes. These changes must be located not in sudden reversals of traditional beliefs and habits but in adaptations to new circumstances and in a reorientation to new social groups that set the standards and establish the patterns which most individuals imitate.

By concentrating so exclusively on the incidents of premarital coitus, analysts have overlooked the most fruitful area for understanding the changes in sexual patterns among the majority of the middle-class population. For it is to the behavior and attitudes of young men and women in the twenties, who had to deal with emerging sexual impulses and had the least vested interest in maintaining older norms, that one must look for the readjustments that underlay the process of change. From this perspective the post-war decade was indeed critical for the evolution of modern sexual patterns. The young, reared in a moral standard in which all sex was taboo, redefined that standard according to their own needs and laid the basis for a change in the standard itself. The college campus, especially, provided a fertile social environment for the new mores concerning the relationships between men and women. On the coeducational campuses of the 1920's (matrimonial bureaus, they were sometimes called), sex was a perpetual peer concern.

College youth of the 1920's redefined the relationship between men and women. In good part this resulted from a simple rediscovery—love is erotic. The remainder drew on an old assumption—that the goal of relations between men and women was marriage. Together the new insight and the old tradition resulted in a significant restructuring of premarital forms of sexual behavior as relationships were charged by a new sexual dynamism and a vigorous experimentalism. Sex for middle-class youths of the 1920's had become a significant premarital experience, but it continued to be distinctly marriage-oriented and confined by stringent etiquettes and sharply etched definitions. In the process of defining their future roles in the new society and within the context of already potent changes, the young helped to create the sexual manners of the twentieth century.

The norms established by college youths had a dual purpose. They provided room for the exploration of immediate sexual interests, and they facilitated mate selection for future marriage. The result was a sexual revolution: not, however, as often implied, a revolution erupting in a sudden and drastic increase in sexual intercourse among the unmarried young, but a revolution growing out of new patterns of sexual play. The young evolved a code of sexual behavior that was, in effect, a middle ground between the no-sex-at-all taboo officially prescribed by the adult world and inculcated by their families, and their own burgeoning sexual interests and marital aspirations. To this dual purpose, youths elaborated two basic rituals of sexual interaction—dating and petting. These behavior patterns accompanied and emphasized several important value changes: more tolerance for non-norma-

In the dance halls; painting by Thomas Hart Benton, "City Activities with Dance Hall." (Courtesy of The Equitable Life Assurance Soceity of the United States.)

tive sexual behavior, the recognition and approval of female sexuality, and a positive evaluation of emotional response and expression in relations between men and women. This nexus of behavior and value was the heart of the sexual revolution of the 1920's.

Dating was something definitely new in the ritual of sexual interaction. It was unlike the informal get-togethers that characterized youth socializing in the village or small town of the nineteenth century, for at such events there was no pairing early in an acquaintance. It was also unlike courting, which implied a commitment between two people. Dating permitted a paired relationship without implying a commitment to marriage and encouraged experimental relations with numerous partners. Dating emerged in response to a modern environment in which people met casually and irregularly, and in response to new kinds of recreations like movies, dance halls, and restaurants, where pairing was the most convenient form of boy-girl relation. . . . The lack of commitment permitted close and intimate associations and explorations of personality, and isolation and privacy laid the ground for sexual experimentation, both as a means for testing future compatibility and as an outlet for present sexual energies.

With the isolation of relations, the young were forced to rely on their own judgment in determining the degree and limits of permissible eroticism. It was this latitude for self-determination that produced the haunting fear of sexual promiscuity in the jeremiads of the twenties. The fear was unfounded. The young were thrown back on their own resources, but they were not free, either from the influence of childhood training or, more immediately, from the controls and sanctions of their peers. Basing their actions on an unyielding taboo against sexual intercourse and an elaborate network of peer norms and standards, they proceeded to open up the possibilities of sexual play without overstepping the bounds of family prohibition and peer propriety. . . .

"Petting" described a broad range of potentially erotic physical contacts, from a casual kiss to more intimate caresses and physical fondling. Even such limited eroticism would have automatically defined a woman as loose and disreputable in the nineteenth century. To the Victorians, who divided good women from bad, revered ideal purity, and were suspicious of female sexuality, all forms of eroticism on the part of women could be equated with total submission. Even in the twenties, it was not unknown for reformers to introduce legislation that would prohibit petting and define it along with fornication as illegal as well as immoral. But the young drew distinct boundaries between what was acceptable erotic behavior and what was not. Petting was the means to be safe and yet not sorry, and around this form of sexual activity they elaborated a code of permissible eroticism. As a result, while there remained two kinds of women among college students in the twenties, the difference was not between sexual women and non-sexual women but between sexual women who lived by the rules and those who did not. A Trinity College editor put it well when he asserted, "There are only two kinds of co-eds, those who have been kissed and those who are sorry they haven't been kissed." And he later added just the right note about the group norms that carefully tailored female behavior: "Although a girl will not always let you kiss her when you ask her, she usually appreciates your asking her, often so much that she has to tell her friends." . . . [T]he youth of the twenties were incorporating dating and petting into a wholly new ritual of graded relationships. A casual first date might thus entail a good-night kiss, but greater intimacies and a certain amount of erotic play were permitted and expected of engaged couples. . . . The young first sanctioned eroticism and then imposed degrees and standards of acceptability.

College youths were fully aware of, and highly sensitive to, the criticism that petting evoked from their elders. But the editors of college papers were quick to deny any widespread evil in the behavior or intentions of the young. They did not, however, deny the existence of petting or its importance in the social relations between the sexes. What they denied was the adult evaluation of such behavior as promiscuous or immoral, as in fact it was by an earlier standard. Peer norms, which deviated from adult attitudes, were now legitimate criteria for evaluating conduct. By the standards of the young, petting was not immoral. It was inappropriate when abused and when the rigid boundaries the young imposed on their own behavior were overstepped. In decrying the inordinate amount of attention that youth's morals were receiving from the public, the *Daily Illini,* for example, illustrated how out of touch older people were with the life of the young by referring to a recent questionnaire where the term "spooning" had been used. A sure way of antagonizing youth, the *Illini* noted, was to be so removed from the realities of their lives as to use an expression as archaic and wholly unreal as "spooning."

In view of the strength of peer-group influence, youth were unlikely to bypass the restrictions and staged ritual associated with sexual behavior. But neither was petting restricted to only a small minority of wildly experimental youths, for petting had become a convention and a necessary demonstration of conformity. One investigation of coed behavior found that 92% of all women admitted petting at one time or another. . . . One observed the restrictions on petting in order to remain respectable to peers, but given the occasion and the desire, one could and did pet because it was commonly accepted behavior. There was undoubtedly also considerable pressure to pet at least a little in order to remain in good standing in the eyes of peers and to assure that future dates would be forthcoming. One result of this peer compulsion was that experimental erotic exploration was often a group phenomenon. The petting party was probably the major contribution of the twenties to group sex, and it was in such groups that the first hesitant initiations into erotic play were often made. . . .

The rating system by which social connections were made and by which eligibility was established and maintained worked within a tight system of gossip, reference, bull-session discussions, and careful conformity to standards. A correspondent to the *Daily Illini* . . . asked pointedly, "At what fraternity house will you not find sooner or later just such a discussion of 'Girls Who Pet'?" If a woman could be criticized for the way she wore her hair, for excessive reliance on the paint box, or for overly suggestive dancing, and when it was generally known whether she was "a first-night petter," how much more would her reputation be affected by an imputation of officially and unofficially proscribed behavior? One study of undergraduate life noted, "Men are very dependent on one another's estimate of a girl. Some fraternities blacklist a girl for being obviously 'a speed,' too giddily dressed, or lacking sex attraction." There was a very clear differentiation between positive sex appeal and offensive behavior. For the majority, "a petting party is the right thing to do," but a really "fast woman" was disreputable. Sexual irregularity on the part of coeds, as one investigator of campus ethics discovered, was universally condemned by men and women as the worst of all possible offenses on the campus. Significantly, women still condemned such irregularities more consistently than men, and since it was women who usually regulated sexual behavior, there was still a tight lid on intercourse with campus women. Despite an easing of the double standard and an erosion of distinctions between virtuous women and sexual women, students still clung to a double standard in their own behavior and described illicit sexual behavior as far worse for women than for men. . . .

Dating and petting were, moreover, distinctly marriage-oriented in the twenties. Since mating was one of the chief aims of both rituals, immediate sexual satisfactions had to be carefully weighed in view of long-term goals. And while virginity in a bride was no longer an absolute prerequisite for most men, it was still considered desirable. For men, female chastity appears to have taken a back seat to considerations of compatibility, but there was still some ambiguity on this point, and the devaluation of virginity in the bride was probably related to a growing acceptance of intercourse among engaged couples rather than to a tolerance of casual promiscuity. Women too continued to display considerable anxiety about the consequences of lost virginity. These multiple ambivalences reinforced the sense of acceptable limitations on sexual indulgence. . . .

The controlled ritual of petting had opened up the possibilities of intimacy and response in the relationship between young men and women. At the same time, it also restricted complete spontaneity and laid the basis for the emotionally inhibiting cat-and-mouse game of staged seductions and "scoring" that continued to govern sexual relations among the young throughout the first half of the twentieth century. It was a first and necessary step toward modern patterns of sexual behavior, for the youths of the twenties redefined sexuality in erotic and emotional terms. But in ritualizing a process of personal and cultural experimentation, the youth of the twenties had also placed bonds on individual expression and behavior quite as real and determinate as those which ruled in the heyday of Victorian morals.

"Charity Girls" and City Pleasures

Beginning in the last decades of the nineteenth century, urban working-class youths created their own peer subculture that in many ways foreshadowed what would happen on campuses in the 1920s. Excerpted from Kathy Peiss, "'Charity Girls' and City Pleasures: Historical Notes on Working-Class Sexuality, 1880–1920" in Powers of Desire: The Politics of Sexuality, *ed. Ann Snitow, Christine Stansell, and Sharon Thompson (New York, 1983), 75–78, 81–84.*

My discussion focuses on one set of young, white working women in New York City in the years 1880 to 1920. Most of these women were single wage earners who toiled in the city's factories, shops, and department stores, while devoting their evenings to the lively entertainment of the streets, public dance halls, and other popular amusements. Born or educated in the United States, many adopted a cultural style meant to distance themselves from their immigrant roots and familial traditions. Such women dressed in the latest finery, negotiated city life with ease, and sought intrigue and adventure with male companions. For this group of working women, sexuality became a central dimension of their emergent culture, a dimension that is revealed in their daily life of work and leisure.

These New York working women frequented amusements in which familiarity and intermingling among strangers, not decorum, defined normal public behavior between the sexes. At movies and cheap theaters, crowds mingled during intermissions, shared picnic lunches, and commented volubly on performances. Strangers at Coney Island's amusement parks often involved each other in practical jokes and humorous escapades, while dance halls permitted close interaction between unfamiliar men and women. At one respectable Turnverein ball, for example, a vice investigator described closely the chaotic activity in the barroom between dances:

> Most of the younger couples were hugging and kissing, there was a general mingling of men and women at the different tables, almost everyone seemed to know one another and spoke to each other across the tables and joined couples at different tables, they were all singing and carrying on, they kept running around the room and acted like a mob of lunatics let lo[o]se.

As this observer suggests, an important aspect of social familiarity was the ease of sexual expression in language and behavior. Dances were advertised, for example, through the distribution of "pluggers," small printed cards announcing the particulars of the ball, along with snatches of popular songs or verse; the lyrics and pictures, noted one offended reformer, were often "so suggestive that they are absolutely indecent." . . .

Other forms of recreation frequented by working-class youth incorporated a free and easy sexuality into their attractions. Many social clubs and amusement societies permitted flirting, touching, and kissing games at their meetings. One East Side youth reported that "they have kissing all through pleasure time, and use slang language, while in some they don't behave nice between [sic] young ladies." Music halls and cheap vaudeville regularly worked sexual themes and suggestive humor into comedy routines and songs. At a Yiddish music hall popular with both men and women, one reformer found that "the songs are suggestive of everything but what is proper, the choruses are full of double

Luna Park—Coney Island Amusement Park, site of the working-class urban heterosocial subculture. (Courtesy of Culver Pictures, Inc.)

meanings, and the jokes have broad and unmistakable hints of things indecent." Similarly, Coney Island's Steeplechase amusement park, favored by working-class excursionists, carefully marketed sexual titillation and romance in attractions that threw patrons into each other, sent skirts flying, and evoked instant intimacy among strangers. . . .

The heterosocial orientation of these amusements made popularity a goal to be pursued through dancing ability, willingness to drink, and eye-catching finery. Women who would not drink at balls and social entertainments were often ostracized by men, while cocktails and ingenious mixtures replaced the five-cent beer and helped to make drinking an acceptable female activity. Many women used clothing as a means of drawing attention to themselves, wearing high-heeled shoes, fancy dresses, costume jewelry, elaborate pompadours, and cosmetics. As one working woman sharply explained, "If you want to get any notion took of you, you gotta have some style about you." The clothing that such women wore no longer served as an emblem of respectability. "The way women dress today they all look like prostitutes,"

The dance craze. (Courtesy of The Library of Congress.)

reported one rueful waiter to a dance hall investigator, "and the waiter can some times get in bad by going over and trying to put some one next to them, they may be respectable women and would jump on the waiter."

Underlying the relaxed sexual style and heterosocial interaction was the custom of "treating." Men often treated their female companions to drinks and refreshments, theater tickets, and other incidentals. Women might pay a dance hall's entrance fee or carfare out to an amusement park, but they relied on men's treats to see them through the evening's entertainment. Such treats were highly prized by young working women; as Belle Israels remarked, the announcement that "he treated" was "the acme of achievement in retailing experiences with the other sex."

Treating was not a one-way proposition, however, but entailed an exchange relationship. Financially unable to reciprocate in kind, women offered sexual favors of varying degrees, ranging from flirtatious companionship to sexual intercourse, in exchange for men's treats. "Pleasures don't cost girls so much as they do young men," asserted one saleswoman. "If they are agreeable they are invited out a good deal, and they are not allowed to pay anything." Reformer Lillian Betts concurred, observing that the working woman held herself responsible for failing to wangle men's invitations and believed that "it is not only her misfortune, but her fault; she should be more attractive." Gaining men's treats placed a high premium on allure and personality, and sometimes involved aggressive and frank "overtures to men whom they desire to attract," often with implicit sexual proposals. One investigator, commenting on women's dependency on men in their leisure time, aptly observed that "those who are unattractive, and those who have puritanic notions, fare but ill in the matter of enjoyments. On the other hand those who do become popular have to compromise with the best conventional usage." . . .

The extent of the sexual culture . . . is particularly difficult to establish, since the evidence is too meager to permit conclusions about specific groups of working women, their beliefs about sexuality, and their behavior. Scattered evidence does suggest a range of possible responses, the parameters within which most women would choose to act and define their behavior as socially acceptable. Within this range, there existed a subculture of working women who fully bought into the system of treating and sexual exchange, by trading sexual favors of varying degrees for gifts, treats, and a good time. These women were known in underworld slang as "charity girls," a term that differentiated them from prostitutes because they did not accept money in their sexual encounters with men. As vice reformer George Kneeland found, they "offer themselves to strangers, not for money, but for presents, attention, and pleasure, and most important, a yielding to sex desire." Only a thin line divided these women and "occasional prostitutes," women who slipped in and out of prostitution when unemployed or in need of extra income. Such behavior did not result in the stigma of the "fallen woman." Many working women apparently acted like Dottie: "When she needed a pair of shoes she had found it easy to 'earn' them in the way that other girls did." Dottie, the investigator reported, was now known as a respectable married woman. . . .

The charity girl's activities form only one response in a wide spectrum of social and sexual behavior. Many young women defined themselves sharply against the freer sexuality of their pleasure-seeking sisters, associating "respectability" firmly with premarital chastity and circumspect behavior. One working woman carefully explained her adherence to propriety: "I never go out in the evenings except to my relatives because if I did, I should lose my reputation and that is all I have left." Similarly, shop girls guarded against sexual advances from co-workers and male customers by spurning the temptations of popular amusements. "I keep myself to myself," said one saleswoman. "I don't make friends in the stores very easily because you can't be sure what any one is like." Settlement workers also noted that women who freely attended "dubious resorts" or bore illegitimate children were often stigmatized by neighbors and workmates. Lillian

Betts, for example, cites the case of working women who refused to labor until their employer dismissed a co-worker who had born a baby out of wedlock. To Betts, however, their adherence to the standard of virginity seemed instrumental, and not a reflection of moral absolutism: "The hardness with which even the suggestion of looseness is treated in any group of working girls is simply an expression of self-preservation."

Other observers noted an ambivalence in the attitudes of young working women toward sexual relations. Social workers reported that the critical stance toward premarital pregnancy was "not always unmixed with a certain degree of admiration for the success with the other sex which the difficulty implies." According to this study, many women increasingly found premarital intercourse acceptable in particular situations: "'A girl can have many friends,' explained one of them, 'but when she gets a "steady," there's only one way to have him and to keep him; I mean to keep him long.'" Such women shared with charity girls the assumption that respectability was not predicated solely on chastity.

Perhaps few women were charity girls or occasional prostitutes, but many more must have been conscious of the need to negotiate sexual encounters in the workplace or in their leisure time. Women would have had to weigh their desire for social participation against traditional sanctions regarding sexual behavior, and charity girls offered to some a model for resolving this conflict. This process is exemplified in Clara Laughlin's report of an attractive but "proper" working woman who could not understand why men friends dropped her after a few dates. Finally she receives the worldly advice of a co-worker that social participation involves an exchange relationship: "Don't yeh know there ain't no feller goin' t'spend coin on yeh fer nothin'?" . . .

For . . . young working women, respectability was not defined by the strict measurement of chastity employed by many middle-class observers and reformers. Instead, they adopted a more instrumental and flexible approach to sexual behavior. Premarital sex *could* be labeled respectable in particular social contexts. Thus charity girls distinguished their sexual activity from prostitution, a less acceptable practice, because they did not receive money from men. Other women, who might view charity girls as promiscuous, were untroubled by premarital intimacy with a steady boyfriend.

This fluid definition of sexual respectability was embedded within the social relation of class and gender, as experienced by women in their daily round of work, leisure, and family life. Women's wage labor and the demands of the working-class household offered daughters few resources for entertainment. At the same time, new commercial amusements offered a tempting world of pleasure and companionship beyond parental control. Within this context, some young women sought to exchange sexual goods for access to that world and its seeming independence, choosing not to defer sexual relations until marriage. Their notions of legitimate premarital behavior contrast markedly with the dominant middle-class view, which placed female sexuality within a dichotomous and rigid framework. Whether a hazard at work, fun and adventure at night, or an opportunity to be exploited, sexual expression and intimacy comprised an integral part of these working women's lives.

Questions

1. *How similar and how different were the definitions of acceptable sexual behavior shaped by the college culture in the 1920s and the working-class subculture in the period from 1890-1920?*
2. *What class differences in attitudes toward sexuality do you see in comparing working-class and middle-class Americans, including both middle-class college students and middle-class observers of the working-class subculture?*
3. *How "revolutionary" was the first sexual revolution?*
4. *In what ways might the changes described by Paula Fass and Kathy Peiss have set the stage for contemporary relations between the sexes?*

PERSPECTIVES ON SEXUALITY IN THE EARLY TWENTIETH-CENTURY UNITED STATES

Dating and petting among white, urban, working-class youth and college students represent an important sign of the first sexual revolution, but there were other manifestations of this important transformation in American society. Commentators from the 1910s on noticed the greater openness in discussions of sexuality, often linking them to public discourse about prostitution, venereal disease, and birth control. Perhaps nothing shocked the arbiters of traditional morality so much as young women—the "flappers" who revealed their boyish bodies, used cosmetics, and claimed the right to smoke and drink with men—who talked of "white slavery"—a term that implicitly contrasted involuntary prostitution to the enslavement of Africans and African Americans—without batting an eye. So, too, public discussion of birth control, pioneered by anarchist Emma Goldman and socialist Margaret Sanger, threatened the traditional order by validating sexuality apart from reproduction.

The changes associated with the sexual revolution also affected diverse groups of Americans. Alongside the cafes and dance halls catering to the heterosexual crowd, establishments for men (and to a far lesser extent women) attracted to members of the same sex grew up in urban areas. That the freer expression of sexuality—both heterosexual and same-sex—affected not just young white people is clear from the art, music, and social life that flowered during the Harlem Renaissance of the 1920s. Following the massive migration of African Americans from the rural South to the urban North, the vibrant mixed-class neighborhood of Harlem fostered both artistic and sexual experimentation. Novels, plays, poetry, and especially the blues celebrated sexuality and even fostered the recognition and grudging toleration of same-sex relationships. The fol-

lowing documents illustrate a range of perspectives on the widespread changes that comprised the sexual revolution.

"Sex O'Clock" in America

"Sex O'Clock in America," a much-cited article published in 1913, heralds the new openness about sexuality and discusses the views of a number of commentators who disagreed about what was going on and whether or not the new developments should be viewed as dangerous. This article appeared in Current Opinion, *55, no. 2 (August 1913): 113–14.*

A WAVE of sex hysteria and sex discussion seems to have invaded this country. Our former reticence on matters of sex is giving way to a frankness that would even startle Paris. Prostitution, as *Life* remarks, is the chief topic of polite conversation. It has struck "sex o'clock" in America, to use [journalist] William Marion Reedy's memorable phrase. The White Slave appears in the headlines of our newspapers. . . . [Journalist] Witter Bynner in *The Forum* exploits the White Slave in blank verse. *Leslie's Weekly* points out her lesson in short stories. *The Smart Set* makes her the subject of a novelette. In the theater, "Damaged Goods," a play of which the action springs from venereal disease, marks an epoch of new freedom in sex discussion. . . . Vice reports leap into print. Vice commissions meet and gravely attempt to rebuild in a fortnight the social structure of the world. Is this overemphasis of sex a symptom of a new moral awakening or is it a sign that the morbidity of the Old World is overtaking the New? Does it indicate a permanent change in our temper or is it merely the concomitant of the movement for the liberation of woman from the shackles of convention that will disappear when society has readjusted itself to the New Woman and the New Man? Has it struck sex o'clock permanently or will time soon point to another hour?

One writer in the St. Louis *Mirror*, James F. Clark, asserts that we must grant to-day to woman the same promiscuity that society tacitly grants to the male. This statement has aroused a storm of discussion and protest. Mr. Reedy himself, tho a radical, strongly dissents from the attitude of his aggressive contributor. . . .

"The laxity in sex matters in this and other countries cannot be said to be due to the broadening of women's views. The women who have entered upon the life of civic and social enlargement are not those who 'go astray.' The sexually loose women are not the so-called advanced women. They are the parasite women, the indulged women, the women who do not think. And I want to say that I don't believe in the theory that the woman has the same passions as a man. I, too, have been to Cyprus, and the woman of passion, from Sappho to Catherine of Russia, is a fake or a physio-psychological freak. Woman's passion is mostly a pretence. The idea that women in any great number would resort to promiscuity is absurd. The removal of the fear of consequences won't count for much with an intelligent womanhood. Not intelligence, but ignorance recruits the ranks of the social evil."

The brilliant Saint Louis editor has little use for the anti-vice crusades financed by Standard Oil money. There are, he says, and he speaks with the authority of a man of wide experience, plenty of women of evil life in all large cities. But these are not "White Slaves." The inmates of houses may be in debt to mistresses, but they are not held prisoners and cannot be. "But as young Rockefeller is putting up the money for the White Slave hunt, of course," Mr. Reedy goes on to say, somewhat cynically, "'White Slaves' have to be produced." Vice and crime, he insists, are the symptoms of poverty, which itself is a symptom of the disease known as privilege. We should strike at the root, not at the branches.

The vice crusade business in Chicago, New York, San Francisco, everywhere, thinks Reedy, is being overdone. There is too much sensationalism in its campaigns. There is too much censorship of songs and dances. . . .

"No one is particularly in favor of vice. But most thinking people are in favor of liberty and there cannot prevail much liberty when the raiding plan of reform is so generally adopted. I have an idea that people have a right to go to hell in their own way. And that a good way to drive them to hell is to begin to coerce and drive them towards other people's ideals of righteousness. Raids are going to produce more harm than good. If society is going to hell by way of the tango and the turkey trot and the cabaret show, who started it in that direction? Why, 'the best people.' It is 'the best people' that have exalted vaudeville and girl shows above the genuine drama. It is the best people who have made the cabaret show and demanded that it be ever more and more highly spiced. When the habits and customs of the best people broaden down to the common people, lo, there is a wild cry for reform. And it is all done now in the name of the working girl. Balderdash! The working girl is a working girl, not a bawd at large. The working girl doesn't keep the hot joints in the big town running. That is done mostly by folks who think themselves in the know and in the swim. The prevalent looseness in society is not to be checked by sensational raids or slumming expeditions by legislative committees of investigation. We must begin farther back than the patrol-wagon."

Reedy places the blame for the sex hysteria upon the hedonistic materialistic philosophy that pervades American life. The poor, he says, learn their worst vices from the rich. Everybody lives for a good time in the upper world, and the infection spreads downward. "Is there," he asks, "anything of the spiritual left in education in America, broadly speaking? There is not."

"Education is now directed to the end of enabling a man to get money. Our youths study what they think will enable them to get there quickest. No classics. No arts and no metaphysics. No religion. And science—well, science is fallen into the hands of those who pursue it not to *know*, but to *get*. Education is not to draw a man out of himself, but to draw material things to himself. No one is concerned with eternal things. All that interests us is the immediate gratification. And some few of us have the idea that, because we think we are better than other people, we have a right to say what they shall sing or dance and whom they shall marry and whether they shall marry at all. We want to make people good by science." . . .

Dr. Cecile L. Greil, a Socialist writer, welcomes the fact that society is drawing its head out of the sand of prudery where it had hidden it, ostrich-like. But she, too, fears the hysteria of sex discussion. She especially warns the members of her own sex. The pendulum with women swings more rapidly to extreme degrees, she asserts. This may be because of her highly sensitized nervous organism, which fastens with almost hysterical tenacity to anything which produces an emotional appeal. And surely nothing that has come to her for study or reflection in all the ages has been as important to her, and through her to posterity, as is this freedom of sex knowledge, which guards the citadel of society and makes for a better, finer race of citizens. "But one danger lurks in her midst. Sex freedom is frequently hysterically interpreted into meaning sex license. And the science which shall give her the right to freer, happier motherhood entails all the responsibilities that freedom in any other sense does." The modern social system, the writer continues in *The Call*, is a terrific endurance test against the forces within ourselves and the forces that attack us without. Vanity and love and sport she admits, quoting a Judge of one of the Night Courts, make more prostitutes than economic pressure and exploitation.

"Youth is extravagant to prodigality with itself. It is drunk with its own intoxicating perfume. It looks down into the glass of life as did Narcissus into the brook, and like Narcissus falls in love with its own beauty. And we surround that young, passionate, bursting blossom with every temptation to break down its resistant power, lure it into sentient, pulsating desire and eroticism by lurid literature, moving pictures, tango dances, suggestive songs, cabarets, noise, music, light, life, rhythm, everywhere, until the senses are throbbing with leashed-in physical passion—everything done to lure, but nothing to instruct. So one day the leash snaps, and another boy or girl is outside the pale. We do much for the developing of the intellect and for the use of our hands so that we may send our young people out into the big battle that lies beyond the home, but for the battle against the physical forces, the law of the magnetic attraction of the sexes, at the dangerous period of puberty and adolescence, we do nothing. Education is the only thing that can save, rational libertarian education on the subjects pertaining to the laws of personal and social hygiene."

Society is apt to regard the fourteen-year-old adolescent as a little dreamy school-girl, ties pretty ribbons in her hair, and keeps her dresses well confined to knee length, forgetting that all the externals of the child mask the seething turbulent ocean underneath. In the child dwells a fully awakened woman. Nature goes through a vicarious process of sex awakening with all its stupendous morbid psychology and complexes. The position of the boy at puberty, contends Dr. Greil, is still worse. He has not even the hereditary instincts of inhibition that his little sister has.

"Society smiles on his acts, calls them 'sport,' sowing his wild oats, etc. He becomes a moral coward and sneak, conscious only of strong animal impulses that he need not curb, and these drive him early to secret vice, to the brothel, to dissipation and roguery. And the crop he reaps from the wild oats he sows fill our streets with prostitutes, fill our foundling asylums with nameless babies and give him a heritage of venereal disease to wreck his future usefulness and hand down as a sad legacy to his posterity. He fears no moral code! His mother and sisters live in a rarified atmosphere of imaginary purity that cuts him off from intimacy, and the understanding which his mother could impart to him if she were his friend instead of a transcendental ideal far up on a pedestal out of his reach. His father, perhaps the only human being who could save him at the crucial period, is his bitterest foe or at best a total stranger to him, shielding himself after exhausting all the phases of sex liberty for himself in an armor of virtue and respectability, which simply antagonizes the boy and widens the breach between himself and society.

"He becomes an alien in his own home, an outcast free to mingle with the world of vicious freedom that welcomes him with open arms, makes him the tool of lost souls and stains him with a smear of filth that ruins him utterly before he is old enough to learn that his much-prized sex freedom is a bondage that makes him pay exorbitant prices in loss of strength, ideals and health. Truly, life does teach as thoroly [thoroughly] as any academy, but how it makes us pay!"

The necessity of sex education is generally recognized. Yet there are also evidences of reaction. Thus the Chicago Board of Education rescinded the order issued by Mrs. Ella Flagg Young, in whose hands rests the school system of Chicago, providing for lectures on sex hygiene in the schools. *The Ecclesiastical Review,* a Roman Catholic publication, maintains that whatever warning and instruction may be necessary should be left in the hands of the priest. Nevertheless, the editor, tho grudgingly, prints a list of books on eugenics for the use of Roman Catholic teachers and priests to aid them in following intelligently the trend of public opinion. Another Roman Catholic publication, *America,* asks for the suppression of vice reports and of vice commissions, except for restricted particular investigations. The publication attacks Doctor Eliot's championship of the Society of Sanitary and Moral Prophylaxis. Eliot has no right, in the opinion of *America,* to declare that before the advent of the Society and its head, Dr. Morton, the policy of the world was "absolute silence" with regard to sex hygiene. "There is," we are told, "a world of difference between absolute silence and the wise and prudent discretion which bids father and mother and teacher refrain from handling the topic in public and without discriminating sense, whilst it at the same time inspires them to say at the fitting time the right word which shall safeguard their children, and to say it with a circumspection not likely to destroy the sense of shame, which is the best natural protection of the innocence of these little ones."

Radicals and conservatives, Free-thinkers and Catholics, all seem to believe in solving the sex problem by education, but as to the method that is to be followed there are abysmal differences of opinion.

The Flapper

This unsigned article written in 1915 by the renowned journalist and social critic H.L. Mencken caricatures the young upper- or middle-class woman who had embraced the flapper style and could discuss prostitution or venereal disease without blushing. Taken from H.L. Mencken, "The Flapper," in The Smart Set 45, no. 2 (February 1915): 1–2.

THE American language, curiously enough, has no name for her. In German she is *der Backfisch*, in French she is *l'Ingénue*, in English she is the Flapper. But in American, as I say, she is nameless, for Chicken will never, never do. Her mother, at her age, was a Young Miss; her grandmother was a Young Female. But she herself is no Young Miss, no Young Female. Oh, dear, no! . . .

Observe, then, this nameless one, this American Flapper. Her skirts have just reached her very trim and pretty ankles; her hair, newly coiled upon her skull,

Flapper fashions. (Courtesy of UPI/Corbis-Bettmann.)

has just exposed the ravishing whiteness of her neck. A charming creature! Graceful, vivacious, healthy, appetizing. It is a delight to see her bite into a chocolate with her pearly teeth. There is music in her laugh. There is poetry in her drive at tennis. She is an enchantment through the plate glass of a limousine. Youth is hers, and hope, and romance, and—

Well, well, let us be exact: let us not say innocence. This Flapper, to tell the truth, is far, far, far from a simpleton. An Ingénue to the Gaul, she is actually as devoid of ingenuousness as a newspaper reporter, a bartender or a midwife. The age she lives in is one of knowledge. She herself is educated. She is privy to dark secrets. The world bears to her no aspect of mystery. She has been taught how to take care of herself.

For example, she has a clear and detailed understanding of all the tricks of white slave traders, and knows how to circumvent them. She is on the lookout for them in matinée lobbies and railroad stations—benevolent-looking old women who pretend to be ill, plausible young men who begin business with "Beg pardon," bogus country girls who cry because their mythical brothers have failed to meet them. She has a keen eye for hypodermic needles, chloroform masks, closed carriages. She has seen all these sinister machines of the devil in operation on the screen. . . . She has followed the war upon them in the newspapers.

Life, indeed, is almost empty of surprises, mysteries, horrors to this Flapper of 1915. She knows the exact percentage of lunatics among the children of drunkards. . . . She knows exactly what the Wassermann reaction [a blood test for venereal disease] is, and has made up her mind that she will never marry a man who can't show an unmistakable negative. . . . She is opposed to the double standard of morality, and favors a law prohibiting it.

This Flapper has forgotten how to simper; she seldom blushes; it is impossible to shock her. She saw "Damaged Goods" without batting an eye, and went away wondering what the row over it was all about. The police of her city having prohibited "Mrs. Warren's Profession," [a novel about prostitution] she read it one rainy Sunday afternoon, and found it a mass of platitudes. . . . She slaved at French in her finishing school in order to read Anatole France. . . . She plans to read Havelock Ellis during the coming summer. . . .

As I have said, a charming young creature. There is something trim and trig and confident about her. She is easy in her manners.

She bears herself with dignity in all societies. She is graceful, rosy, healthy, appetizing. It is a delight to see her sink her pearly teeth into a chocolate, a macaroon, even a potato. There is music in her laugh. She is youth, she is hope, she is romance—she is wisdom!

Emma Goldman Lectures on Sex

Harry Kemp, a Bohemian writer known as the "Don Juan of Greenwich Village," relates part of the story of his life on the road as a tramp. Kemp, using the name "Johnnie," describes a lecture by the anarchist advocate of emancipation, Emma Goldman, here called "Emma Silverman." Goldman lectured widely on sex, birth control, and the emancipation of women. She was deported after the First World War for her radical views. Excerpted from Harry Kemp, Tramping on Life: An Autobiographical Narrative *(New York, 1922), 285–88. (Note: Kemp uses a modified form of ellipses in the text.)*

Emma Silverman, the great anarchist leader, came to Laurel, with her manager, Jack Leitman. I went to the Bellman House, the town's swellest hotel, to see her. I had never met her but had long admired her for her activities and bravery. . . .

Her first lecture was on Sex. The hall was jammed to the doors by a curiosity-moved crowd.

She began by assuming that she was not talking to idiots and cretins, but to men and women of mature minds—so she could speak as she

Emma Goldman, anarchist, birth control advocate, and apostle of sexual freedom. (Courtesy of UPI/Corbis-Bettmann.)

thought in a forthright manner. She inveighed against the double standard. When someone in the auditorium asked what she meant by the single standard she replied, she meant sexual expression and experience for man and woman on an equal footing . . the normal living of life without which no human being could be really decent—and that regardless of marriage and the conventions!

"The situation as it is, is odious . . all men, with but few exceptions, have sexual life before marriage, but they insist that their wives come to them in that state of absurd ignorance of their own bodily functions and consequent lack of exercise of them, which they denominate 'purity.' . . I doubt if there is a solitary man in this audience—a married man—who has not had premarital intercourse with women."

All the while I kept my eye on Professor Wilton, who sat near me, in the row ahead . . he was flushing furiously in angry, puritanic dissent . . and I knew him well enough to foresee a forthcoming outburst of protest.

"Yes, I think I can safely say that there is not one married man here who can honestly claim that he came to his wife with that same physical 'purity' which he required of her."

Wilton leaped to his feet in a fury . . the good, simple soul. He was so indignant that the few white hairs on his head worked up sizzling with his emotion. . .

"*Here's one!*" he shouted, forgetting in his earnest anger the assembled audience, most of whom knew him.

There followed such an uproar of merriment as I have never seen the like before nor since. The students, of course, howled with indescribable joy . . Emma Silverman choked with laughter. Jack Leitman rolled over the side table on which he had set the books to sell as the crowd passed out——

After the deafening cries, cat-calls and uproars, Emma grew serious.

"I don't know who you are," she cried to Professor Wilton, "but I'll take chances in telling you that you're a liar!"

Again Wilton was on his feet in angry protest.

"Shame on you, woman! have you no shame!" he shouted.

Excerpt from *Tramping on Life: An Autobiographical Narrative* by Harry Kemp, published by Boni and Liveright Publishers, New York, 1922. Copyright © 1922 by Boni and Liveright, Inc.

This sally brought the house down utterly. The boys hooted and cat-called and stamped again. . .

Emma Silverman laughed till the tears streamed down her face. . .

"I have something on my conscience," remarked Miss Silverman to me, "Johnnie, do you really think that old professor was speaking the truth?"

"I'm sure of it, Miss Silverman."

"Why, then, I'm heartily sorry . . and it was rough of me . . and will you tell the professor for me that I sincerely apologise for having hurt his feelings . . tell him I have so many jackasses attending my lectures all over the country, who rise and say foolish and insincere things, just to stand in well with the communities they live in—that sometimes it angers me, their hypocrisy— and then I blaze forth pretty strong and lay them flat!"

Same-Sex Subcultures

An excerpt from British sexologist Havelock Ellis's Sexual Inversion, *the second volume of a multi-volume work called* Studies in the Psychology of Sex, *describes the existence of same-sex sexual subcultures in U.S. cities. Most observers of such subcultures, like the middle-class reformers who described the heterosexual urban working-class world, expressed the kind of disapproval evident in Ellis's account. The term "invert," introduced by medical commentators at the turn of the century, reflected the assumption that men attracted to men were feminine and women attracted to women were masculine—their gender was "inverted." Taken from Havelock Ellis,* Studies in the Psychology of Sex, *vol. 2,* Sexual Inversion, *3d ed. (Philadelphia, 1933), 351–52, 299–300.*

As regards the prevalence of homosexuality in the United States, I may quote from a well-informed American correspondent:—

"The great prevalence of sexual inversion in American cities is shown by the wide knowledge of its existence. Ninety-nine normal men out of a hundred have been accosted on the streets by inverts, or have among their acquaintances men whom they know to be sexually inverted. Everyone has seen inverts and knows what they are. The public attitude toward them is generally a negative one—indifference, amusement, contempt.

"The world of sexual inverts is, indeed, a large one in any American city, and it is a community distinctly organized—words, customs, traditions of its own; and every city has its numerous meeting-places: certain churches where inverts congregate; certain cafés well known for the inverted character of their patrons; certain streets where, at night, every fifth man is an invert. The inverts have their own 'clubs,' with nightly meetings. These 'clubs' are, really, dance-halls, attached to *saloons*, and presided over by the proprietor of the saloon, himself almost invariably an invert, as are all the waiters and musicians. The frequenters of these places are male sexual inverts (usually ranging from 17 to 30 years of age); sightseers find no difficulty in gaining entrance; truly, they are welcomed for the drinks they buy for the company—and other reasons. Singing and dancing turns by certain favorite performers are the features of these gatherings, with much gossip and drinking at the small tables ranged along the four walls of the room. The habitués of these places are, generally, inverts of the most pronounced type, *i.e.*, the completely feminine in voice and manners, with the characteristic hip motion in their walk; though I have never seen any approach to feminine dress there, doubtless the desire for it is not wanting and only police regulations relegate it to other occasions and places. You will rightly infer that the police know of these places and endure their existence for a consideration; it is not unusual for the inquiring stranger to be directed there by a policeman." . . .

. . . [I]t is notable that of recent years there has been a fashion for a red tie to be adopted by inverts as their badge. This is especially marked among the "fairies" (as a *fellator* is there termed) in New York. "It is red," writes an American correspondent, himself inverted, "that has become almost a synonym for sexual inversion, not only in the minds of inverts themselves, but in the popular mind. To wear a red necktie on the street is to invite remarks from newsboys and others—remarks that have the practices of inverts for their theme. A friend told me once that when a group of street-boys caught sight of the red necktie he was wearing they sucked their fingers in imitation of *fellatio*. Male prostitutes who walk the streets of Philadelphia and New York almost invariably wear red neckties. It is the badge of all their tribe. The rooms of many of my inverted friends have red as the prevailing color in decorations. Among my classmates, at the medical school, few ever had the courage to wear a red tie; those who did never repeated the experiment."

"Prove It On Me Blues"

The blues played an important role as a cultural medium for the expression of sexuality, especially within African American culture. The lesbian lyrics of "Prove It On Me Blues," by bisexual blues singer Ma Rainey, is an example of the unconventional sexuality associated with the Harlem Renaissance. Written by Ma Rainey in 1928, the lyrics of this song are reprinted from Sandra R. Lieb, Mother of the Blues: A Study of Ma Rainey *(Amherst, 1981), 124.*

"Prove It On Me Blues"

Went out last night, had a great big fight,
Everything seemed to go on wrong;
I looked up, to my surprise,
The gal I was with was gone.

Where she went, I don't know,
I mean to follow everywhere she goes;
Folks said I'm crooked, I didn't know where she took it,
I want the whole world to know:

They say I do it, ain't nobody caught me,
Sure got to prove it on me;
Went out last night with a crowd of my friends,
They must've been women, 'cause I don't like no men.

It's true I wear a collar and a tie,
Make the wind blow all the while;
They say I do it, ain't nobody caught me,
They sure got to prove it on me.

Say I do it, ain't nobody caught me,
Sure got to prove it on me;
I went out last night with a crowd of my friends,
They must've been women, 'cause I don't like no men.

Wear my clothes just like a fan,
Talk to the gals just like any old man;
'Cause they say I do it, ain't nobody caught me,
Sure got to prove it on me.

Questions

---

1. *What different perceptions of and attitudes about the sexualiza-tion of American society can you identify in these documents?*
2. *What different changes in sexual life can you identify from these documents?*
3. *Do you think the changes were greater for women or for men?*
4. *What evidence can you identify in these documents supporting the idea that urban life facilitated changes in sexual behavior?*

FURTHER READING

Intimate Matters: A History of Sexuality in America, *by John D'Emilio and Estelle B. Freedman (New York, 1988), provides a comprehensive overview of changes in sexual attitudes and behavior throughout the history of the U.S.* Kathy Peiss, Cheap Amusements: Working Women and Leisure in Turn-of-the-Century New York *(Philadelphia, 1986), and Joanne J.* Meyerowitz, Women Adrift: Independent Wage Earners in Chicago, 1880–1930 *(Chicago, 1988) discuss the lives of women in the urban working-class subcultures. Kevin White,* The First Sexual Revolution: The Emergence of Male Heterosexuality in Modern America *(New York, 1993), analyzes the impact of the sexual revolution on men.* Gay New York: Gender, Urban Culture, and the Making of the Gay Male World, 1890–1940, *by George Chauncey (New York, 1994), tells the story of changes in the male same-sex subculture of New York.*

United States Entry into World War II

Peter L. Hahn,
Michael J. Hogan, and Amy L. S. Staples

INTRODUCTION

World War II began in September 1939 when Nazi Germany invaded Poland and subsequently traded declarations of war with Great Britain and France. The European war ran parallel to a major Asian conflict that had started years earlier with a Japanese attack on China and continued with Japanese expansion into Southeast Asia. U.S. officials had opposed Japanese aggression but had done little to stop it. Nor did they rush to intervene in the European conflict. Many Americans believed that their country had been dragged into World War I by bankers and businessmen who had invested heavily in the Allied cause and by misleading British propaganda about German behavior. They were sadly disillusioned about the results of that conflict. It had failed to "make the world safe for democracy," as President Woodrow Wilson had predicted it would, and there was no reason to believe that involvement in a second world war would reach such an ideal objective. Other Americans believed that World War II, like World War I and earlier European conflicts, lacked real importance to the United States. They affirmed the principles of the Monroe Doctrine, which established America's realm of interest as the Western Hemisphere, and George Washington's Farewell Address, which warned of the dangers of entangling alliances with European powers. American isolationism was manifested in a series of neutrality laws, passed by Congress in the 1930s, designed to regulate public and private actions in order to avert involvement in the brewing European conflict.

Although he had earlier accepted the neutrality laws, President Franklin D. Roosevelt came to believe that German and Japanese aggression posed serious threats to America's national security and political and economic way of life. This conviction became stronger in 1940-41 after Germany conquered most of continental Europe and Japan continued its expansion into Southeast Asia. The president slowly chipped away at the neutrality laws and isolationist sentiment in the United States. He acted to aid the Allied powers of Britain and France, even though some of his actions violated international law and risked involving the United States in war. Despite Roosevelt's actions, however, only Japan's devastating attack on Pearl Harbor on 7 December 1941 would overcome isolationism in the United States and trigger American entry into World War II.

HISTORIANS DEBATE
FDR's LEADERSHIP

The debate over American entry into World War II, and Roosevelt's leadership, continued long after the attack on Pearl Harbor. Historians divided sharply on these issues. One group, often identified with isolationist sentiment, accused the president of deceiving the American people about the nature of his efforts to aid the Allies and the risks that his efforts entailed. They considered Roosevelt's decisions to supply Britain with American destroyers and the Allies with lend-lease aid as unduly provocative and risky. Some of these historians argued that Roosevelt was so determined to enter the war that he took an unnecessarily tough stand against Japanese expansion, and thereby provoked the Japanese attack on Pearl Harbor.

Other historians have disputed these conclusions. More internationalist in their views, they have argued that Roosevelt moved reluctantly from a policy of neutrality, to a policy of aiding the Allies without entering the war, to a policy of military intervention. This transformation stemmed from the president's sincere conviction that a German-Japanese victory would imperil American security and interests. These internationalist historians acknowledge that Roosevelt was less than honest in explaining his policies to the American people, but they also point out that he had to maneuver within a domestic political context in which popular isolationism limited his options.

The Isolationist Argument

Historian Charles Callan Tansill became one of the most outspoken critics of American entry into World War II. According to Tansill's "back door" thesis, the president deceitfully orchestrated a series of moves to bring a reluctant nation into war. By supplying destroyers to Britain, establishing the lend-lease program, and maneuvering Japan into attacking Pearl Harbor, Tansill argues, Roosevelt created circumstances in which U.S. entry became unavoidable. The following selection is from Charles Callan Tansill, Back Door to War: The Roosevelt Foreign Policy, 1933–1941 *(Chicago, 1952), 558, 595–96, 598-99, 602–3, 605–6, 609, 612–15, 645–46, 649–52.*

IMMEDIATELY after the outbreak of World War II, President Roosevelt made a radio address in which he reminded the American people that they should master "at the outset a simple but unalterable fact in modern foreign relations. When peace has been broken anywhere, peace of all countries everywhere is in danger." . . . [Roosevelt] then glibly gave the following assurance: "Let no man or woman thoughtlessly or falsely talk of America sending its armies to European fields. At this moment there is being prepared a proclamation of American neutrality." . . . America would remain "a neutral nation." But he closed his address with a curtain line that had an ominous implication: *"As long as it remains within my power to prevent,* there will be no blackout of peace in the United States." . . .

The fall of France [in May 1940] imparted a sense of urgency to the Administration's program for aiding Britain by the sale or lease of war matériel. The President's qualms about constitutional limitations slowly disappeared under the drumfire of repeated requests from [British Prime Minister Winston] Churchill. Moreover, he [Roosevelt] brought into his Cabinet certain new members who were not averse to a prowar inclination. This was particularly true of the new Secretary of War, Henry L. Stimson, who was a notorious war hawk. It is apparent that after June 1940 the

Administration embarked upon a phony bipartisan policy that pointed directly to American intervention in the European conflict. . . .

. . . On June 24 he [Churchill] wrote to [British Ambassador to Washington] Mackenzie King and once more emphasized the danger that if England fell there was the possibility that Hitler would get the British fleet. . . . He also complained that Britain had "really not had any help worth speaking of from the United States so far." After more than a month of silence he wrote again to the President . . . to inform him that the need for destroyers had "become most urgent." The whole fate of the war

A construction worker reads the San Francisco Chronicle *on 8 December 1941. (Courtesy of The Library of Congress.)*

might rest upon the speed with which these destroyers were delivered. . . .

There was no doubt in Churchill's mind that any transfer of American destroyers to Britain would be a "decidedly unneutral act by the United States." It would justify a declaration of war by Hitler. Such action would be eminently agreeable to Churchill who would ardently welcome American help in the struggle against the dictatorships. . . .

[Attorney General Robert] Jackson blandly pushed aside the pertinent provisions of the Treaty of Washington (May 8, 1871) and Article 8 of the Hague Convention XIII of 1907 which required that a neutral government take measures to prevent the departure from its jurisdiction of any vessel intended to engage in belligerent operations, if the vessel was specially adapted within the neutral's jurisdiction to warlike use. The one precedent that Mr. Jackson adduced to support his contention concerning the transfer of destroyers was a most dubious one. Indeed, the opinion of the Attorney General was distinctly "phony" and was based upon the familiar dictum: "What's the Constitution between friends." The way was now prepared for the destroyer deal. . . .

From the viewpoint of international law the destroyer deal was definitely illegal. As Professor Herbert Briggs correctly remarks: "The supplying of these vessels by the United States Government to a belligerent is a violation of our neutral status, a violation of our national law, and a violation of international law." . . . The whole matter was correctly described by the *St. Louis Post-Dispatch* in a pertinent headline: "Dictator Roosevelt Commits an Act of War." . . .

It was entirely fitting that lend-lease legislation should have a prelude of promises by the President that American boys would not be sent abroad to die along far-flung frontiers. It had been evident to the President in the summer of 1940 that American involvement in World War II might be just around the corner of the next year. . . . When the election currents in the fall of 1940 appeared to be making a turn towards [Republican nominee] Wendell Willkie, the President made some new pledges . . . : "While I am talking to you mothers and fathers, I give you one more assurance. I have said this before, but I shall say it again and again and again: Your boys are not going to be sent into any foreign wars." . . .

. . . Under the impact of appeals from Churchill in England the entire structure of American neutrality was finally demolished by the legislative bomb of lend-lease. . . .

Although Admiral [Harold R.] Stark expressed on January 13 [1941] the opinion that "we are heading straight for this war," the lend-lease program was sold to the American people as a form of peace insurance. On March 11, 1941, the lend-lease bill was signed by the President, and it was not long before a forecast of Senator [Robert] Taft was proved correct: "I do not see how we can long conduct such a war [undeclared war] without actually being in the shooting end of the war." . . .

. . . [I]n January 1941 a series of secret [American-British-Canadian military] staff conversations began in Washington. Two months later (March 27, 1941), the ABC-I Staff Agreement was consummated which envisaged a "full-fledged war co-operation when and if Axis aggression forced the United States into the war."

One of the sections of this agreement was aimed at creating an incident that would "force the United States into the war." It contained the following explosive phraseology: "Owing to the threat to the sea communications of the United Kingdom, the principal task of the United States naval forces in the Atlantic will be the protection of shipping of the Associated Powers." In order to carry out this task the Royal Navy hastened to give the United States Navy the "benefit of its experience, and of the new devices and methods for fighting submarines that had already been evolved." The responsibility "now assumed by the United States Navy meant the organization of a force for escort-of-convoy." . . .

. . . [A series of] naval incident[s] involving German-American relations . . . [included] the sinking of the American merchant ship (May 21, 1941) *Robin Moor*, New York to Cape Town, by a German submarine. There was no visit or search but the crew and passengers were allowed to take to open lifeboats. As the sinking occurred outside the blockade zone it is evident that the submarine commander disregarded orders concerning American ships. [German] Admiral [Eric] Raeder immediately issued orders to prevent further incidents of this nature, and Hitler, after confirming these instructions, remarked that he wished to "avoid any incident with the U.S.A." On June 20 the President sent a message to Congress in which he bitterly criticized Germany as an international outlaw. He followed this message with another move in the direction of war. On July 7 he ordered American occupation of Iceland. Two days later Secretary [of War Frank] Knox gave a statement to the press which implied that the American patrol force in the North Atlantic had the right to use its guns when the occasion arose.

This occasion arose on September 4, 1941, when the destroyer *Greer*, bound for Iceland, was informed by a British plane that a submerged U-boat lay athwart her course some ten miles ahead. The *Greer* at once laid a course for the reported submarine, and after having made sound contact with it, kept it on her bow for more than three hours. During this period a British plane dropped four depth charges in the vicinity of the submarine without effect. Finally, the submarine commander grew tired of this game of hide-and-seek and launched a torpedo which the *Greer* was able to dodge. When the *Greer* counterattacked with depth charges, the submarine launched another torpedo which was avoided. When sound contact with the submarine could not be re-established, the *Greer* resumed course for Iceland.

On September 11 the President gave a broadcast which presented a distorted version of the *Greer* incident. He conveniently forgot to tell that the initiative had been taken by the *Greer*. . . . [T]his serious incident . . . clearly showed the aggressive character of American naval patrolling. . . .

This *de facto* war in the Atlantic soon produced another incident. On October 16 five American destroyers rushed from Reykjavik, Iceland, to the help of a convoy that was being attacked by submarines. On the following day, while in the midst of the fighting, the destroyer *Kearny* was struck by a torpedo. . . . It had deliberately moved into the center of a pitched battle between German submarines and British and Canadian warships and had taken the consequences. It was not long before President Roosevelt gave to the American people a twisted account of the incident. . . . [Roosevelt] asserted that he had "wished to avoid shooting." America had "been attacked. The U.S.S. *Kearny* is not just a Navy ship. She belongs to every man, woman, and child in this Nation. . . . Hitler's torpedo was directed at every American." . . . The American Navy had been given orders to "shoot on sight." The Nazi "rattlesnakes of the sea" would have to be destroyed.

This declaration of war was confirmed by the *Reuben James* incident. On October 31, while the *Reuben James* was escorting a convoy to Iceland, some German submarines were encountered. . . . The American destroyer was struck by a torpedo and rapidly sank. Only 45, out of a crew of about 160, were saved. . . .

. . . [I]t was obvious that America was really in the war. But the American people did not realize that momentous fact, nor did they know that they were pledged "to spare no effort and no sacrifice in bringing to pass the final defeat of Hitlerism." . . . The war hawks of 1941 were never tired of sneering at the majority of Americans as benighted isolationists who had tried to build a Chinese wall around the United States and thus cut it off from all foreign contacts. They knew their sneers were patent lies. America had never been isolated from the social, economic, religious, and cultural forces that shaped the modern world. Thanks to its geographical position it had escaped the recurring tides of conflict that had crumbled the walls of ancient civilizations and washed away the heritage men had earned through dauntless courage and high endeavor. Americans had been isolationists only against war and its evident evils, and their country had grown prosperous beyond the dreams of the founding fathers. But in 1915, President Wilson began to nurse the thought of sharing America's ideals and wealth with the rest of the world, and two years later he led us into a foreign war that he hoped would make the world safe for democracy. But this theme song turned sour in American ears when it led to the great parade of 1917 which ended for many men in the vast cemeteries in France. It gained new popularity after 1933, and with Roosevelt as maestro, the old macabre accents began to haunt every home. In 1941 his orchestra of death was anxiously waiting for the signal to begin the new symphony. He had hoped for a German motif but Hitler had refused to assist with a few opening martial notes. Perhaps some Japanese states- man would prove more accommodating! At any rate, after the *Reuben James* incident had fallen flat he turned his eyes towards the Orient and sought new inspiration from the inscrutable East. He found it at Pearl Harbor when Japanese planes sounded the first awesome notes in a chorus of war that is still vibrating throughout the world. . . .

In the second week in November 1941 tension began to mount in Tokyo. On November 10 the Japanese Foreign Minister ex-

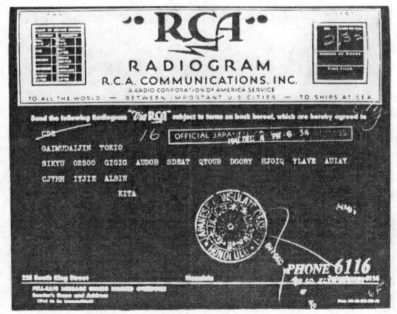

A radiogram from the Japanese government carries an encoded message, 1941. (Courtesy of RCA Communications, Inc.)

pressed to [U.S. Ambassador Joseph] Grew the opinion that the . . . Japanese Government had "repeatedly made proposals calculated to approach the American point of view, but the American Government . . . had taken no step toward meeting the Japanese position." On this same day (November 10), [Japanese] Ambassador Nomura presented to President Roosevelt a further explanation of his Government's proposals. In the meantime the Japanese Foreign Office instructed Nomura that November 25 was the deadline. All negotiations would have to be concluded by that date. . . . Under pressure from the Foreign Office, Nomura was extremely anxious to secure an early answer to the Japanese proposals of November 7 and 10. . . .

Secretary [of State Cordell] Hull knew of this deadline through intercepted Japanese instructions to Nomura, so on November 15 he handed to Nomura a long oral statement setting forth the bases of an agreement. He knew they would not be acceptable to Japan. Complete control over "its economic, financial and monetary affairs" should be restored to China, and Japan should abandon any thought of preserving in China, or anywhere else in the Pacific area, a "preferential position."

The abrupt tone of this note was a challenge that could easily lead to a break in diplomatic relations. Japan had long feared that such a break was inevitable, but in a final attempt to stave off such an emergency it had been decided to send to Washington another diplomat who would assist Nomura in the delicate negotiations that were hanging by a very slender thread. The new appointee, Saburo Kurusu, had served as consul in Chicago and New York. . . . His happy marriage to an American girl gave him a personal interest in maintaining friendly relations between Japan and the United States. . . .

On the afternoon of November 26 he [Hull] abandoned all thought of a truce with Japan and put into final shape a ten-point proposal. Both he and the President knew this program would be rejected by Japan. There was no thought of compromise or conciliation: "The Government of Japan will withdraw all military, naval, air and police forces from China and from Indochina." When Kurusu read the ten-point proposal of Secretary Hull he immediately inquired if this was the American answer to the Japanese request for a *modus vivendi* or truce. Was not the American Government interested in a truce? Hull merely replied that "we have explored that" but had arrived at no real decision. Kurusu could only reply that the Secretary's attitude "could be inter-preted as tantamount to meaning the end." It was obvious that the next step was war.

On the morning of December 4, the Navy radio receiving station at Cheltenham, Maryland, intercepted a Japanese overseas news broadcast from Station JAP in Tokyo, in which there was inserted a false weather report, "east wind rain." On November 19 the Japanese government had instructed its ambassador in Wash-ington that such a weather forecast would indicate imminence of war with the United States. After intercepting this Japanese in-struction the radio receiving stations of the American armed forces were on the alert for the "east wind rain" message. As soon as it was translated, Lieutenant Commander [Alvin D.] Kramer handed it to Commander [Laurence F.] Safford with the exclama-tion: "This is *it*." Safford got in touch immediately with Rear Admiral [Leigh] Noyes who telephoned the substance of the inter-cepted message "to the naval aide to the President." . . .

The unaccountable failure of high naval officers to convey a warning to Honolulu about the imminence of war was given additional highlights on the evening of December 6 when the Japanese reply to the American note of November 26 was sent secretly to Ambassador Nomura. It was intercepted by Navy receiving stations and decoded. When the President read this message to Nomura he at once exclaimed: "This means war!" . . .

It would ordinarily be assumed that the President, after read-ing this intercepted Japanese message, would hurriedly call a conference of the more important Army and Navy officers to concert plans to meet the anticipated attack. The testimony of General [of the Army George C.] Marshall and Admiral Stark would indicate that the Chief Executive took the ominous news so calmly that he made no effort to consult with them. Did he delib-erately seek the Pearl Harbor attack in order to get America into the war? What is the real answer to this riddle of Presidential composure in the face of a threatened attack upon some American outpost in the faraway Pacific? This problem grows more compli-cated as we watch the approach of zero hour. At 9:00 A.M. on December 7, Lieutenant Commander Kramer delivered to Admi-ral Stark the final installment of the Japanese instruction to Nomura. Its meaning was now so obvious that Stark cried out in great alarm: "My God! This means war. I must get word to Kimmel at once." [Admiral Husband Kimmel, Command-in-

Chief, U.S. Pacific Fleet at Pearl Harbor] But he made no effort to contact Honolulu. Instead he tried to get in touch with General Marshall, who, for some strange reason, suddenly decided to go on a long horseback ride. It was a history-making ride. . . . In the early hours of World [War] II, General Marshall took a ride that helped prevent an alert from reaching Pearl Harbor in time to save an American fleet from serious disaster and an American garrison from a bombing that cost more than two thousand lives. Was there an important purpose behind this ride? . . .

It was 11:25 A.M. when General Marshall returned to his office. If he carefully read the reports on the threatened Japanese attack (on Pearl Harbor) he still had plenty of time to contact Honolulu by means of the scrambler telephone on his desk, or by the Navy radio or the FBI radio. For some reason best known to himself he chose to send the alert to Honolulu by RCA [telegraph] and did not even take the precaution to have it stamped, "priority." As the Army Pearl Harbor Board significantly remarked: "We find no justification for a failure to send this message by multiple secret means either through the Navy radio or the FBI radio or the scrambler telephone or all three." Was the General under Presidential orders to break military regulations with regard to the transmission of important military information? Did he think that the President's political objectives outweighed considerations of national safety? Was the preservation of the British Empire worth the blood, sweat, and tears not only of the men who would die in the agony of Pearl Harbor but also of the long roll of heroes who perished in the epic encounters in the Pacific, in the Mediterranean area, and in the famous offensive that rolled at high tide across the war-torn fields of France? New cemeteries all over the world would confirm to stricken American parents the melancholy fact that the paths of military glory lead but to the grave.

The Internationalist Argument

Historian Robert A. Divine rejects the isolationist argument advanced by Charles Callan Tansill and others. Divine argues instead that Roosevelt was motivated initially by a sincere desire to keep the U.S. out of the war. As international events seemed to impinge on American security, however, Roosevelt moved incrementally toward belligerency. Divine is critical of Roosevelt's pre-Pearl Harbor policy, but for very different reasons than those cited by Tansill. Selected from Robert A. Divine, Roosevelt and World War II *(Baltimore, 1969), 38–40, 43–47.*

After his triumphant election to a third term, Roosevelt relaxed on a Caribbean cruise. But after only a week, a navy seaplane arrived with an urgent dispatch from Winston Churchill. The Prime Minister gave a lengthy and bleak description of the situation in Europe and then informed the President that England was rapidly running out of money for continued purchases of American goods. "The moment approaches when we shall no longer be able to pay cash for shipping and other supplies," Churchill wrote, concluding with the confident assertion that Roosevelt would find "ways and means" to continue the flow of munitions and goods across the Atlantic.

When the President returned to Washington in mid-December [1940], he called in the press, and in his breeziest and most informal manner began to outline the British dilemma and his solution to it. His advisers were working on several plans, he said, but the one that interested him most was simply to lend or lease to England the supplies she needed, in the belief that "the best defense of Great Britain is the best defense of the United States." Saying that he wanted to get rid of the dollar sign, Roosevelt compared his scheme to the idea of lending a garden hose to a neighbor whose house was on fire. When the fire is out, the neighbor either returns the hose or, if it is damaged, replaces it with a new one. So it would be, Roosevelt concluded, with the munitions the United States would provide Britain in the war against Nazi Germany.

In a fireside chat to the American people a few days later, Roosevelt justified this lend-lease concept on grounds of national security. Asserting that Hitler aimed not just at victory in Europe but at world domination, Roosevelt repeated his belief that the United States was in grave peril. If England fell, he declared, "all of us in the Americas would be living at the point of a gun." He admitted that the transfer of arms and munitions to Britain risked American involvement in the conflict, but he argued that "there is far less chance of the United States getting into war if we do all we can now to support the nations defending themselves against attack by the Axis than if we acquiesce in their defeat, submit tamely to an Axis victory and wait our turn to be the object of attack in another war later on." He declared that he had no intention of sending American troops to Europe; his sole purpose was to "keep war away from our country and our people." Then, in a famous phrase, he called upon the United States to become "the great arsenal of democracy."

Congress deliberated over the lend-lease bill for the next two months, and a strong consensus soon emerged in favor of the measure. Leading Republicans, including Wendell Willkie, endorsed the bill, and most opponents objected only to the leasing provision, suggesting instead an outright loan to Britain. The House acted quickly, approving lend-lease by nearly 100 votes in February [1941]; the Senate took longer but finally gave its approval by a margin of almost two to one in early March. After the President signed the legislation into law, Congress granted an initial appropriation of seven billion dollars to guarantee the continued flow of vital war supplies to Great Britain.

Roosevelt had thus taken another giant step forward, and this time without any hesitation. His election victory made him bolder than usual, and Churchill's candid plea had convinced him that speed was essential. The granting of lend-lease aid was very nearly an act of war, for it gave Britain unrestricted access to America's enormous industrial resources. But the President felt with great sincerity that this policy would lead not to American involvement but to a British victory that alone could keep the nation out of war. . . .

In the six months preceding Pearl Harbor, Franklin Roosevelt moved slowly but steadily toward war with Germany. On July 7, he announced that he had sent 4,000 American marines to Iceland to prevent that strategic island from falling into German hands. Secretary of War Stimson, though pleased with this action, expressed disappointment over the President's insistence on describing it solely as a measure of hemispheric self-defense. Iceland was the key to defending the supply route across the Atlantic, and

Stimson believed that the President should have frankly told Congress that the United States was occupying the island to insure the delivery of goods to Britain.

Once American forces landed in Iceland, Roosevelt authorized the Navy to convoy American ships supplying the marines on the island. In addition, he at first approved a naval operations plan which permitted British ships to join these convoys and thus receive an American escort halfway across the Atlantic, but in late July he reversed himself, ordering the Navy to restrict its convoys to American and Icelandic vessels. In August, at the famous Atlantic Conference with Churchill, Roosevelt once again committed himself to the principle of convoying British ships halfway across the Atlantic, but he failed to give the necessary order to the Navy after his return to Washington.

Roosevelt's hesitancy and indecision finally ended in early September when a German submarine fired a torpedo at the American destroyer *Greer*. Though subsequent reports revealed that the *Greer* had been following the U-boat for more than three hours and had been broadcasting its position to nearby British naval units, Roosevelt interpreted this incident as a clear-cut case of German aggression. . . .

In biting phrases, Roosevelt lashed out against Hitler and Nazi Germany. . . . The attack on the *Greer* was an act of piracy, Roosevelt declared; German submarines had become the "rattlesnakes of the Atlantic." Then, implying but never openly saying that American ships would shoot German submarines on sight, Roosevelt declared that henceforth the United States Navy would escort "all merchant ships—not only American ships but ships of any flag—engaged in commerce in our defensive waters."

Contemporary observers and many historians labeled this the "shoot-on-sight" speech. . . . "The undeclared war" speech would be a better label, for its real importance was that Roosevelt had finally made a firm decision on the convoy issue on which he had been hedging ever since the passage of lend-lease by Congress. Branding the Germans as "pirates" and their U-boats as "rattlesnakes" distracted the American people from the fact that the President was now putting into practice the policy of convoying British ships halfway across the ocean, and thereby assuming a significant share of the responsibility for the Battle of the Atlantic. . . . In the long run, the President's decision meant war with Germany. . . . Only Hitler's reluctance to engage in war with the United States while he was still absorbed in the assault on Russia prevented an immediate outbreak of hostilities.

With the convoy issue now resolved, Roosevelt moved to revise the Neutrality Act. In mid-October he asked the House to permit the arming of American merchant ships with deck guns, and then later in the month he urged the Senate to remove the "carry" provision of the law so that American merchantmen could take supplies all the way across the Atlantic to British ports. When a German submarine torpedoed the [American] destroyer *Kearney* near Iceland, Roosevelt seized on the incident to speed up action in Congress.

"America has been attacked," the President declared in a speech on October 27. "The U.S.S. *Kearney* is not just a Navy ship. She belongs to every man, woman, and child in this Nation." . . .

Two weeks later, by quite slim majorities, Congress removed nearly all restrictions on American commerce from the Neutrality Act. For the first time since the war began in 1939, American merchant vessels could carry supplies all the way across the Atlantic to British ports. The significance of this action was obscured by the Japanese attack on Pearl Harbor which triggered American entry into the war in December and gave rise to the subsequent charge that Roosevelt led the nation into the conflict via the back door. Revision of the Neutrality Act was bound to lead to war with Germany within a matter of months. Hitler . . . could not have permitted American ships to carry a major portion of lend-lease supplies to Britain without giving up the Battle of the Atlantic. With the German offensive halting before Leningrad and Moscow in December, Hitler would have been compelled to order his submarine commanders to torpedo American ships as the only effective way to hold Britain in check. And once Germany began sinking American ships regularly, Roosevelt would have had to ask Congress for a declaration of war.

The crucial question, of course, is why Roosevelt chose such an oblique policy which left the decision for peace or war in the hands of Hitler. His apologists . . . insist that he had no choice. The isolationists were so powerful that the President could not lay the issue squarely before Congress and ask for a declaration of war. If he had, . . . he would have "invited a prolonged, bitter, and divisive debate" and thereby have risked a defeat which would have discredited the administration and turned the nation back to isolationism. . . .

. . . Roosevelt was the prisoner of his own policies. He had told the nation time and time again that it was not necessary for the United States to enter the war. He had propounded the doctrine that America could achieve Hitler's downfall simply by giving all-out aid to England. He had repeatedly denied that his measures would lead the nation to war. In essence, he had foreclosed to himself the possibility of going directly to the people and bluntly stating that the United States must enter the war as the only way to guarantee the nation's security. All he could do was edge the country closer and closer, leaving the ultimate decision to Germany and Japan.

We will never know at what point Roosevelt decided in his own mind that it was essential that the United States enter the war.

A Composite View

In the late 1970s and early 1980s historians agreed with the isolationists that Roosevelt often manipulated public opinion in order to lead the country into World War II, but they also accepted the internationalists' position in denying Roosevelt's foreknowledge of the attack on Pearl Harbor. Historian Robert Dallek argues that Roosevelt's leadership showed a masterful balance. Roosevelt was able to assemble a Congressional majority that provided the Allies with the goods they desperately required to continue the war while simultaneously preserving his ability to lead a unified nation into World War II. The president understood that domestic politics limited his options in foreign policy, and these limits, more than some sinister conspiracy, help to explain the direction of Roosevelt's policy. Excerpted from Robert Dallek, Franklin D. Roosevelt and American Foreign Policy, 1932–1945 *(New York, 1979), 530–32.*

[Roosevelt's] acceptance of the Neutrality laws of the thirties was less an act of conviction than of realistic calculation about what he could achieve at home and abroad. Since winning congressional approval for domestic programs essential to national economic and political stability ruled out bold initiatives in foreign affairs, Roosevelt acquiesced in the widespread preference for a passive foreign policy. Instead, he aimed to meet worldwide attacks on democracy by preserving it in the United States. . . .

Yet Roosevelt's contribution to the survival of international democracy came not through symbolic gestures in the thirties [changes to the Neutrality laws] but through substantive actions during World War II. His appreciation that effective action abroad required a reliable consensus at home and his use of dramatic events overseas to win national backing from a divided country for a series of pro-Allied steps were among the great presidential achievements of this century. In the years 1939-41 Roosevelt had to balance the country's desire to stay out of war against its contradictory impulse to assure the defeat of Nazi power. Roosevelt's solution was not to intensify the conflict by choosing one goal over the other but rather to weave the two together: the surest road to peace, he repeatedly urged the nation to believe throughout this difficult period, was material aid to the Allies. And even when he concluded that the country would eventually have to join the fighting, as I believe he did in the spring of 1941, he refused to force an unpalatable choice upon the nation by announcing for war.

Roosevelt's dissembling created an unfortunate precedent for arbitrary action in foreign affairs which subsequent Presidents have been quick to use. This consequence, however, needs to be evaluated alongside two other considerations: first, that Roosevelt's indirection forestalled a head-on clash with the Congress and majority opinion which would have weakened his ability to lead before and after Pearl Harbor; and, second, that for all his willingness to deceive the public in the interest of persuading it to go to war, he never lost sight of the fact that a national commitment to fight required events beyond his control to arrange. Indeed, what seems most striking in this period was not Roosevelt's arbitrariness in pushing the country toward war but rather his caution and restraint. . . . [H]e refused to ask for a declaration of war until a genuine provocation from abroad made the nation ready to fight.

Did Roosevelt, then, maneuver or, at the very least, permit the country to become involved in a war with Japan as a backdoor to the European fighting? "Had FDR been determined to avoid war with the Japanese if at all possible," George Kennan [a State Department official] has argued, "he would have conducted American policy quite differently . . . than he actually did. He would not, for example, have made an issue over Japanese policy in China, where the Japanese were preparing, anyway, to undertake a partial withdrawal . . . and where this sort of American pressure was not really essential.

Surrounded by congressional leaders, President Roosevelt signs the Declaration of War against Japan at his White House desk on December 8, 1941. (Courtesy of AP/ Wide World Photos.)

He would not have tried to starve the Japanese navy of oil. And he would have settled down to some hard and realistic dealings with the Japanese." This picture of Roosevelt's options leaves out the domestic context in which he had to operate. The struggle against fascism in American minds was indelibly linked with China's fight against Japan. Though mindful of the advantage of concentrating American power against Berlin, Roosevelt also appreciated that opposition to Japan was an essential part of the moral imperative Americans saw for fighting. To have acquiesced in Japan's domination of China and allowed oil and other vital supplies to fuel Japan's war machine would have provoked an outcry in the United States against cynical power politics and weakened the national resolve to confront fascist power outside of the Western Hemisphere. In short, to gain a national consensus for fighting fascism overseas, Roosevelt could not discriminate between Germany and Japan; both had to be opposed at the same time.

None of this is meant to suggest that Roosevelt foresaw and accepted the surprise attack at Pearl Harbor as a necessary means of bringing a unified nation into the war. Seeing the Fleet in Hawaii as a deterrent rather than a target, lulled by the belief that the Japanese lacked the capability to strike at Pearl Harbor and by the information . . . indicating that an attack might come at any one of a number of points, Roosevelt, like the rest of the nation, failed to anticipate the Pearl Harbor attack. Later contentions to the contrary had less to do with the actuality of Roosevelt's actions than with isolationist efforts to justify the idea that the country had never in fact been vulnerable to attack.

Questions

1. *Was President Roosevelt justified in implementing lend-lease, Atlantic convoys, and other policies that broke international law governing the activities of neutral nations in time of war? Was he justified in distorting facts in his reports to the American people about naval incidents in the Atlantic? Why or why not?*

2. *If the Japanese had not attacked Pearl Harbor and thereby united American public opinion, do you think that the United States would have entered World War II? Why or why not?*

3. *In light of both foreign and domestic political circumstances, was Roosevelt's leadership in the period preceding Pearl Harbor wise or faulty?*

THE CONTEMPORARY DEBATE ABOUT AMERICAN ENTRY INTO WORLD WAR II

The period preceding the attack on Pearl Harbor witnessed a vigorous debate between Americans who wished to remain isolated from the war and those who wished to enter the conflict. Historian Charles A. Beard and groups such as the America First Committee clearly articulated the isolationist position. On the other hand, President Franklin D. Roosevelt delivered a series of public addresses that progressively called for involvement in the war. His campaign culminated in an address to Congress on 8 December 1941 that asked for a declaration of war against Japan.

Beard Favors Neutrality

The prominent historian Charles A. Beard outspokenly opposed American intervention in any foreign conflict. He tried to influence public opinion through publications and testimony to Congress. The selection below, written by Beard in anticipation of the outbreak of war, clearly expresses the isolationists' view of history and current events. Abridged from Charles A. Beard, Giddy Minds and Foreign Quarrels: An Estimate of American Foreign Policy *(New York, 1939), 8, 12, 27–29, 45–47, 49–51, 53–59, 61–62, 64–65, 86–87.*

Since the foundation of the American Republic there has been an endless procession of foreign quarrels with which giddy minds could have been busied.... [T]he Government of the United States kept aloof from the aggressions, wars, and quarrels of Europe....

. . . [During the Great Depression] the American people had enough jitters at home to keep their giddy minds away from foreign affairs, and in a quest for relief they swept into office Franklin D. Roosevelt, who promised to get them out of the slough of economic despond. . . . The state of jitters in domestic economy has not been cured by the New Deal, despite the best of intentions. And Great Britain, after playing Germany off against France and treating Russia with studied contempt, has once more got . . . "the grizzly German terror" on her doorstep, and needs American help again. . . .

The return to constant jitters over European affairs came after the election of 1936. In the campaign of that year President Roosevelt gave no hint that he intended to take a strong hand in European quarrels. The Democratic platform, made in his own office, declared positively: "We shall continue to observe a true neutrality in the disputes of others; to be prepared resolutely to resist aggression against ourselves; to work for peace and to take the profits out of war; to guard against being drawn, by political commitments, international banking, or private trading, into any war which may develop anywhere." This looked like a pledge to keep out of foreign conflicts and wars. The pledge President Roosevelt confirmed in his Chautauqua address of August 14, 1936: "We can keep out of war if those who watch and decide have a sufficiently detailed understanding of international affairs to make certain that the small decisions of each day do not lead toward war and if, at the same time, they possess the courage to say 'no' to those who selfishly or unwisely would let us go to war." If words meant anything in 1936, those words confirmed an evident desire to avoid meddling with the incessant quarrels of Europe and Asia. . . .

. . . But on October 5, 1937, President Roosevelt went to Chicago and called, in effect, for collective action by all the "democracies" against Germany, Italy, and Japan. He declared that if a holocaust came the United States could not avoid it and appealed to "the peace loving nations" to put a quarantine on aggressors. The significance of this address was grasped immediately. Advocates of collective security and collaboration with Brit-

---

Excerpts from *Giddy Minds and Foreign Quarrels: An Estimate of American Foreign Policy* by Charles A. Beard, published by The Macmillan Company, 1939. Copyright © 1939 by Charles A. Beard.

A newspaper reports the Japanese attack on Pearl Harbor. (Courtesy of The Library of Congress.)

ain and France hailed it as a sharp change of front on the part of the President. But the counter blast of criticism from all parts of the country was startling and for a few weeks President Roosevelt lapsed into silence. Nevertheless he had evidently made up his mind that he was going to take a big hand in European and Asiatic affairs anyway and that the country would have to bend to his will or break.

Additional proof of his resolve soon came. On January 28, 1938, President Roosevelt . . . demanded an enormous increase in naval outlays, with special emphasis on battleships, and called for a mobilization bill which had no meaning unless he wanted a huge army that could be used in Europe. . . .

. . . President Roosevelt renewed his battle in 1939. His message to Congress in January . . . asserted that the United States is directly menaced by "storms from abroad." These storms, the President said, challenge "three institutions indispensable to Americans. The first is religion. It is the source of the other two— democracy and international good faith." Evidently he was clearing a way to make the next war a real holy war. This clarion call President Roosevelt followed by another demand for an increase in armaments on a scale more vast. . . .

. . . In the summer of 1939 they [President Roosevelt and Secretary of State Hull] opened a public campaign to break down the provision of the Neutrality Act which imposed an embargo on munitions in case of a foreign war. . . . [T]hey were . . . resolved if possible to erase every line of the Neutrality Act that stood in the way of their running the foreign affairs of the United States on the basis of constant participation in the quarrels of Europe and Asia, with war as their *ultima ratio.*

Now President Roosevelt's foreign policy is clear as daylight. He proposes to collaborate actively with Great Britain and France in their everlasting wrangle with Germany, Italy, and Japan. He wants to wring from Congress the power to throw the whole weight of the United States on the side of Great Britain and France in negotiations, and in war if they manage to bungle the game. That using measures short of war would, it is highly probable, lead the United States into full war must be evident to all who take thought about such tactics.

From the point of view of the interest of the United States as a continental nation in this hemisphere, the Roosevelt policy is, in my opinion, quixotic and dangerous. . . . [I]t is not based upon a realistic comprehension of the long-time history of Europe and Asia and of the limited power which the United States has over the underlying economies and interests of those two continents. It assumes that the United States can in fact bring those continents into a kind of stable equilibrium, assure them the materials of a peaceful economic life, and close their history in a grand conference of the powers. . . . It assumes that somebody in the White House or State Department can calculate the consequences likely to come out of the explosive forces which are hidden in the civilizations of those immense areas. . . .

. . . [I]t seems to me, it would be wiser to suggest that those countries of Europe which are immediately menaced by Germany and Italy put aside their jealousies, quarrels, and enmities, and join in a combination of their own to effect control over the aggressors. If countries whose very existence seems at stake will not unite for self-protection, how can the United States hope to effect a union among them? . . .

On what then should the foreign policy of the United States be based? . . . It is the doctrine formulated by George Washington, supplemented by James Monroe, and followed by the Government of the United States until near the end of the nineteenth century, when the frenzy for foreign adventurism burst upon the country. This doctrine is simple. Europe has a set of "primary interests" which have little or no relation to us, and is constantly vexed by "ambition, rivalship, interest, humor, or caprice." The United States is a continental power separated from Europe by a wide ocean which, despite all changes in warfare, is still a powerful asset of defense. In the ordinary or regular vicissitudes of European politics the United States should not become implicated by any permanent ties. . . .

Those Americans who refuse to plunge blindly into the maelstrom of European and Asiatic politics are not defeatist or neurotic. They are giving evidence of sanity, not cowardice; of adult thinking as distinguished from infantilism. Experience has educated them and made them all the more determined to concentrate their energies on the making of a civilization within the circle of their continental domain. They do not propose to withdraw from the world, but they propose to deal with the world as it is and not as romantic propagandists picture it. They propose to deal with it in American terms, that is, in terms of national interest and security on this continent. Like their ancestors who made a revolution, built the Republic, and made it stick, they intend to preserve and defend the Republic, and under its shelter carry forward the work of employing their talents and resources in enriching American life. They know that this task will call for all the enlightened statesmanship, the constructive energy, and imaginative intelligence that the nation can command. America is not to be Rome or Britain. It is to be America.

Roosevelt's Fireside Chat after the Invasion of Poland, 3 September 1939

Roosevelt realized that public opinion strongly opposed U.S. intervention in World War II. In his first fireside chat, a nationwide radio broadcast, after the invasion of Poland, therefore, he declared American neutrality and expressed his determination to isolate the United States from the hostilities. But at the same time he clearly leaned toward the Allied powers of Britain and France and began to prepare the American people for future actions to support these nations. Excerpted from The Public Papers and Addresses of Franklin D. Roosevelt, 1939, War—and Neutrality, *comp. Samuel I. Rosenman (New York, 1941), 460–64.*

My fellow Americans and my friends:

. . . Until four-thirty this morning I had hoped against hope that some miracle would prevent a devastating war in Europe and bring to an end the invasion of Poland by Germany.

For four long years a succession of actual wars and constant crises have shaken the entire world and have threatened in each case to bring on the gigantic conflict which is today unhappily a fact. . . .

You must master at the outset a simple but unalterable fact in modern foreign relations between nations. When peace has been broken anywhere, the peace of all countries everywhere is in danger.

It is easy for you and for me to shrug our shoulders and to say that conflicts taking place thousands of miles from the continental United States, and, indeed, thousands of miles from the whole American Hemisphere, do not seriously affect the Americas—and that all the United States has to do is to ignore them and go about its own business. Passionately though we may desire detachment, we are forced to realize that every word that comes through the air, every ship that sails the sea, every battle that is fought, does affect the American future.

Let no man or woman thoughtlessly or falsely talk of America sending its armies to European fields. At this moment there is being prepared a proclamation of American neutrality. . . .

. . . And I trust that in the days to come our neutrality can be made a true neutrality. . . .

. . . Most of us in the United States believe in spiritual values. Most of us, regardless of what church we belong to, believe in the spirit of the New Testament—a great teaching which opposes itself to the use of force, of armed force, of marching armies and falling bombs. The overwhelming masses of our people seek peace—peace at home, and the kind of peace in other lands which will not jeopardize our peace at home.

We have certain ideas and certain ideals of national safety, and we must act to preserve that safety today, and to preserve the safety of our children in future years.

That safety is and will be bound up with the safety of the Western Hemisphere and of the seas adjacent thereto. We seek to keep war from our own firesides by keeping war from coming to the Americas. . . .

This nation will remain a neutral nation, but I cannot ask that every American remain neutral in thought as well. Even a neutral has a right to take account of facts. Even a neutral cannot be asked to close his mind or his conscience.

I have said not once, but many times, that I have seen war and that I hate war. I say that again and again.

I hope the United States will keep out of this war. I believe that it will. And I give you assurance and reassurance that every effort of your Government will be directed toward that end.

As long as it remains within my power to prevent, there will be no black-out of peace in the United States.

Roosevelt's "Arsenal of Democracy" Address, 29 December 1940

With France occupied by the Nazis and Britain anticipating a German invasion, Roosevelt in late 1940 urged the nation toward greater participation in the war. In a fireside chat broadcast on 29 December 1940, he defined Great Britain's continued ability to fight Germany as vital to America's national security. Despite continuing protests by isolationists, this speech ultimately inspired the passage of lend-lease legislation, which enabled Roosevelt "to sell, transfer title to, exchange, lease, lend, or otherwise dispose of war matériel to any country whose defense the President deems vital to the defense of the United States." Selected from The Public Papers and Addresses of Franklin D. Roosevelt, 1940, War—and Aid to Democracies, *comp. Samuel I. Rosenman (New York, 1941), 633–36, 638–41, 643–44.*

My friends:

THIS is not a fireside chat on war. It is a talk on national security; because the nub of the whole purpose of your President is to keep you now, and your children later, and your grandchildren much later, out of a last-ditch war for the preservation of

American independence and all the things that American independence means to you and to me and to ours. . . .

Never before since Jamestown and Plymouth Rock has our American civilization been in such danger as now.

For, on September 27, 1940, by an agreement signed in Berlin, three powerful nations, two in Europe and one in Asia, joined themselves together in the threat that if the United States of America interfered with or blocked the expansion program of these three nations—a program aimed at world control—they would unite in ultimate action against the United States.

The Nazi masters of Germany have made it clear that they intend not only to dominate all life and thought in their own country, but also to enslave the whole of Europe, and then to use the resources of Europe to dominate the rest of the world. . . .

In view of the nature of this undeniable threat, it can be asserted, properly and categorically, that the United States has no right or reason to encourage talk of peace, until the day shall come when there is a clear intention on the part of the aggressor nations to abandon all thought of dominating or conquering the world.

At this moment, the forces of the states that are leagued against all peoples who live in freedom, are being held away from our shores. The Germans and the Italians are being blocked on the other side of the Atlantic by the British, and by the Greeks, and by thousands of soldiers and sailors who were able to escape from subjugated countries. In Asia, the Japanese are being engaged by the Chinese nation in another great defense. . . .

Does anyone seriously believe that we need to fear attack anywhere in the Americas while a free Britain remains our most powerful naval neighbor in the Atlantic? Does anyone seriously believe, on the other hand, that we could rest easy if the Axis powers were our neighbors there?

If Great Britain goes down, the Axis powers will control the continents of Europe, Asia, Africa, Australasia, and the high seas—and they will be in a position to bring enormous military and naval resources against this hemisphere. It is no exaggeration to say that all of us, in all the Americas, would be living at the

---

point of a gun—a gun loaded with explosive bullets, economic as well as military.

We should enter upon a new and terrible era in which the whole world, our hemisphere included, would be run by threats of brute force. To survive in such a world, we would have to convert ourselves permanently into a militaristic power on the basis of war economy.

Some of us like to believe that even if Great Britain falls, we are still safe, because of the broad expanse of the Atlantic and of the Pacific.

But the width of those oceans is not what it was in the days of clipper ships. . . . Even today we have planes that could fly from the British Isles to New England and back again without refueling. And remember that the range of the modern bomber is ever being increased. . . .

The experience of the past two years has proven beyond doubt that no nation can appease the Nazis. No man can tame a tiger into a kitten by stroking it. There can be no appeasement with ruthlessness. There can be no reasoning with an incendiary bomb. We know now that a nation can have peace with the Nazis only at the price of total surrender.

Even the people of Italy have been forced to become accomplices of the Nazis; but at this moment they do not know how soon they will be embraced to death by their allies.

The American appeasers ignore the warning to be found in the fate of Austria, Czechoslovakia, Poland, Norway, Belgium, the Netherlands, Denmark, and France. . . .

With all their [the Nazis] vaunted efficiency, with all their parade of pious purpose in this war, there are still in their background the concentration camp and the servants of God in chains.

The history of recent years proves that shootings and chains and concentration camps are not simply the transient tools but the very altars of modern dictatorships. They may talk of a "new order" in the world, but what they have in mind is only a revival of the oldest and worst tyranny. In that there is no liberty, no religion, no hope.

The proposed "new order" is . . . not a Government based upon the consent of the governed. It is not a union of ordinary, self-respecting men and women to protect themselves and their freedom and their dignity from oppression. It is an unholy alliance of power and pelf to dominate and enslave the human race.

The British people and their allies today are conducting an active war against this unholy alliance. Our own future security is greatly dependent on the outcome of that fight. Our ability to "keep out of war" is going to be affected by that outcome.

Thinking in terms of today and tomorrow, I make the direct statement to the American people that there is far less chance of the United States getting into war, if we do all we can now to support the nations defending themselves against attack by the Axis than if we acquiesce in their defeat, submit tamely to an Axis victory, and wait our turn to be the object of attack in another war later on.

If we are to be completely honest with ourselves, we must admit that there is risk in any course we may take. But I deeply believe that the great majority of our people agree that the course that I advocate involves the least risk now and the greatest hope for world peace in the future.

The people of Europe who are defending themselves do not ask us to do their fighting. They ask us for the implements of war, the planes, the tanks, the guns, the freighters which will enable them to fight for their liberty and for our security. Emphatically we must get these weapons to them in sufficient volume and quickly enough, so that we and our children will be saved the agony and suffering of war which others have had to endure. . . .

Our national policy is not directed toward war. Its sole purpose is to keep war away from our country and our people.

Democracy's fight against world conquest is being greatly aided, and must be more greatly aided, by the rearmament of the United States and by sending every ounce and every ton of munitions and supplies that we can possibly spare to help the defenders who are in the front lines. It is no more unneutral for us to do that than it is for Sweden, Russia and other nations near Germany, to send steel and ore and oil and other war materials into Germany every day in the week. . . .

We must be the great arsenal of democracy. For us this is an emergency as serious as war itself. We must apply ourselves to our task with the same resolution, the same sense of urgency, the same spirit of patriotism and sacrifice as we would show were we at war.

We have furnished the British great material support and we will furnish far more in the future. . . .

We have no excuse for defeatism. We have every good reason for hope—hope for peace, hope for the defense of our civilization and for the building of a better civilization in the future.

I have the profound conviction that the American people are now determined to put forth a mightier effort than they have ever yet made to increase our production of all the implements of defense, to meet the threat to our democratic faith.

As President of the United States I call for that national effort. I call for it in the name of this nation which we love and honor and which we are privileged and proud to serve. I call upon our people with absolute confidence that our common cause will greatly succeed.

Roosevelt Justifies "Shoot on Sight," 11 September 1941

In 1941, German submarines attacked American merchant ships that were transporting war matériel to the British Empire and the U.S.S. Greer, a destroyer that had provided the British navy with detailed information on German U-boat locations. In an address on 11 September 1941, Roosevelt publicized these incidents in order to enrage the public against Germany and thereby build support for American involvement in the war. In this speech, Roosevelt committed the United States Navy to escort convoys of merchant ships of all nations halfway across the Atlantic Ocean and to "shoot on sight" any German submarines. Taken from The Public Papers and Addresses of Franklin D. Roosevelt, 1941, The Call to Battle Stations, *comp. Samuel I. Rosenman (New York, 1950), 384–91.*

THE Navy Department of the United States has reported to me that on the morning of September fourth the United States destroyer *Greer*, proceeding in full daylight toward Iceland, had

---

Reprinted from *The Public Papers and Addresses of Franklin D. Roosevelt, 1941: The Call to Battle Stations,* compiled by Samuel I. Rosenman, published by Harper & Brothers Publishers, 1950. Copyright © 1950 by Samuel I. Rosenman.

reached a point southeast of Greenland. She was carrying American mail to Iceland. She was flying the American flag. Her identity as an American ship was unmistakable.

She was then and there attacked by . . . a German submarine. The submarine deliberately fired a torpedo at the *Greer*, followed later by another torpedo attack. In spite of what Hitler's propaganda bureau has invented, and in spite of what any American obstructionist organization may prefer to believe, I tell you the blunt fact that the German submarine fired first upon this American destroyer without warning, and with deliberate design to sink her.

Our destroyer, at the time, was in waters which the Government of the United States had declared to be waters of self-defense— surrounding outposts of American protection in the Atlantic.

In the North of the Atlantic, outposts have been established by us in Iceland, in Greenland, in Labrador and in Newfoundland. Through these waters there pass many ships of many flags. They bear food and other supplies to civilians; and they bear matériel of war, for which the people of the United States are spending billions of dollars, and which, by Congressional action, they have declared to be essential for the defense of our own land.

The United States destroyer, when attacked, was proceeding on a legitimate mission. . . .

This was piracy—piracy legally and morally. It was not the first nor the last act of piracy which the Nazi Government has committed against the American flag in this war. For attack has followed attack.

A few months ago an American flag merchant ship, the *Robin Moor*, was sunk by a Nazi submarine in the middle of the South Atlantic, under circumstances violating long-established international law and violating every principle of humanity. The passengers and the crew were forced into open boats hundreds of miles from land, in direct violation of international agreements signed by nearly all Nations including the Government of Germany. No apology, no allegation of mistake, no offer of reparations has come from the Nazi Government.

In July, 1941, an American battleship in North American waters was followed by a submarine which for a long time sought to maneuver itself into a position of attack. The periscope of the submarine was clearly seen. No British or American submarines were within hundreds of miles of this spot at the time, so the nationality of the submarine is clear.

Five days ago a United States Navy ship on patrol picked up three survivors of an American-owned ship operating under the flag of our sister Republic of Panama—the *S.S. Sessa*. On August seventeenth, she had been first torpedoed without warning, and then shelled, near Greenland, while carrying civilian supplies to Iceland. It is feared that the other members of her crew have been drowned. In view of the established presence of German submarines in this vicinity, there can be no reasonable doubt as to the identity of the flag of the attacker.

Five days ago, another United States merchant ship, the *Steel Seafarer*, was sunk by a German aircraft in the Red Sea two hundred and twenty miles south of Suez. She was bound for an Egyptian port. . . .

It would be unworthy of a great Nation to exaggerate an isolated incident, or to become inflamed by some one act of violence. But it would be inexcusable folly to minimize such incidents in the face of evidence which makes it clear that the incident is not isolated, but is part of a general plan. . . .

. . . It is the Nazi design to abolish the freedom of the seas, and to acquire absolute control and domination of these seas for themselves.

For with control of the seas in their own hands, the way can obviously become clear for their next step—domination of the United States—domination of the Western Hemisphere by force of arms. . . .

To be ultimately successful in world mastery, Hitler knows that he must get control of the seas. He must first destroy the bridge of ships which we are building across the Atlantic and over which we shall continue to roll the implements of war to help destroy him, to destroy all his works in the end. He must wipe out our patrol on sea and in the air if he is to do it. He must silence the British Navy. . . .

Generation after generation, America has battled for the general policy of the freedom of the seas. And that policy is a very simple one—but a basic, a fundamental one. It means that no Nation has the right to make the broad oceans of the world at great distances from the actual theater of land war unsafe for the commerce of others.

That has been our policy, proved time and time again, in all our history. . . .

And I am sure that even now the Nazis are waiting to see whether the United States will by silence give them the green light to go ahead on this path of destruction. . . .

We have sought no shooting war with Hitler. We do not seek it now. But neither do we want peace so much, that we are willing to pay for it by permitting him to attack our naval and merchant ships while they are on legitimate business. . . .

But when you see a rattlesnake poised to strike, you do not wait until he has struck before you crush him.

These Nazi submarines and raiders are the rattlesnakes of the Atlantic. They are a menace to the free pathways of the high seas. They are a challenge to our sovereignty. They hammer at our most precious rights when they attack ships of the American flag—symbols of our independence, our freedom, our very life. . . .

The time for active defense is now. . . .

. . . Their very presence in any waters which America deems vital to its defense constitutes an attack.

In the waters which we deem necessary for our defense, American naval vessels and American planes will no longer wait until Axis submarines lurking under the water, or Axis raiders on the surface of the sea, strike their deadly blow—first.

Upon our naval and air patrol—now operating in large number over a vast expanse of the Atlantic Ocean—falls the duty of maintaining the American policy of freedom of the seas—now. That means, very simply, very clearly, that our patrolling vessels and planes will protect all merchant ships—not only American ships but ships of any flag—engaged in commerce in our defensive waters. They will protect them from submarines; they will protect them from surface raiders.

This situation is not new. The second President of the United States, John Adams, ordered the United States Navy to clean out European privateers and European ships of war which were infesting the Caribbean and South American waters, destroying American commerce.

The third President of the United States, Thomas Jefferson, ordered the United States Navy to end the attacks being made upon American and other ships by the corsairs of the Nations of North Africa.

My obligation as President is historic; it is clear. It is inescapable.

It is no act of war on our part when we decide to protect the seas that are vital to American defense. The aggression is not ours. Ours is solely defense.

But let this warning be clear. From now on, if German or Italian vessels of war enter the waters, the protection of which is necessary for American defense, they do so at their own peril.

The orders which I have given as Commander in Chief of the United States Army and Navy are to carry out that policy—at once.

America First Committee Charges Roosevelt with Fighting a One-Man War

Roosevelt's addresses convinced many Americans to endorse an interventionist policy toward the war in Europe. But diehard isolationists vigorously resisted what they perceived as an inexorable slide toward war by seeking to rally the public against the president. The isolationist America First Committee, in a treatise published on 13 September 1941, disputed Roosevelt's account of the American-German naval incidents and demanded that Congress check his war-making authority. Excerpted from the America First Committee's newsletter Did You Know 22 *(September 13, 1941): 1–5.*

In his speech on September 11, 1941, President Roosevelt informed the nation that, without consultation with, or approval by, the Congress of the United States, he had ordered our naval and air patrols to clear all German and Italian warships from any waters considered vital to American defense, and had, in effect, ordered our armed forces to "shoot on sight." . . . His asserted justification for this sudden move, admittedly involving danger of involvement in a "shooting war," arose out of the sinking of three merchant ships and attacks on two American warships. . . .

Reprinted from *Did You Know*, #22, prepared by America First Committee Research Bureau, September 13, 1941.

. . . [The] important criticisms of the President's speech are these: 1) shooting war is not justified; 2) it circumvents the spirit of the Neutrality Act and the Lease-Lend law; 3) the doctrine which the President calls "freedom of the seas" is really "freedom to aid one country at war without interference from that country's enemies"; 4) it takes the war-making power away from Congress.

Examination of the circumstances under which occurred the attacks upon American ships cited by the President, demonstrates clearly that they fail utterly to justify participation in a "shooting war." The three merchant ships were the Robin Moor, the Steel Seafarer and the Sessa. The Robin Moor was sunk in the South Atlantic while carrying contraband to British South Africa, a country at war. . . .

The Steel Seafarer was sunk without loss of life in the Red Sea, some 12,000 miles from the United States, while carrying war supplies for Britain, a country at war. . . .

The Sessa was not even sailing under the American flag when sunk. . . . [The ship] had been transferred to the flag of Panama in order that she might be used to carry supplies into war zones in clear violation of the intent of the Neutrality Act. . . .

The attacks upon the destroyer Greer . . . were of course unjustified. But those attacks arose because of the one-man policy pursued by the President of occupying Iceland (nearer to the heart of the European war zone . . . [than] to the United States) and of keeping American troops there along with the British. . . . That is a policy whose implementation requires the use of American naval vessels for patrol purposes in order to keep the surrounding waters clear. It is inevitable that they will come into conflict with Nazi warships which are seeking British ships in those waters, part of the Nazi-declared war zone. . . . Certainly these five attacks, resulting in no loss of American lives on any ship operating under the American flag, do not justify American participation in a "shooting" war. . . .

Nor can the President's "shoot on sight" order be justified, as he claims, as necessary to protect "freedom of the seas." It must be recalled that American armed protection is to be given, not only to American ships, but also to the ships of any flag, and that the waters in which that protection is to be given extend . . . to any waters the President chooses to declare vital to our "defense." This would enable our fleet to give what amounts to "convoy protection" to British ships or the ships of any other allied nation, as well as American ships, carrying war supplies for Britain or Russia or China. It would enable American patrols even to convoy British ships right into English ports. . . .

. . . But there is a remedy, a means of checking the drive towards an all-out shooting war. Congress still has the constitutional power to assert its control over the war power. . . . Congress can still assert its control over the pursestrings. . . . Congress can still investigate and bring to the public view the orders given our patrols and their implications. . . . Assertion by the American people of their will to remain out of war, and of their intention to retain our constitutional form of government, can compel the repudiation of Presidential war moves. It is late, but not yet too late.

Roosevelt's War Message, 8 December 1941

Isolationists who opposed Roosevelt's policy toward the war were overwhelmed by a surge of emotional public opinion favoring immediate entry into World War II, a surge triggered by the surprise Japanese attack on U.S. forces at Pearl Harbor and other locations in the Pacific Ocean on 7 December 1941. The next day, Roosevelt asked Congress to declare war on Japan, and Congress complied within an hour by votes of 82-0 in the Senate and 388-1 in the House. Days later the United States also traded declarations of war against Germany and Italy. Pearl Harbor thus ended the debate that had raged between isolationists and interventionists since the 1930s. Roosevelt's war address is taken from The Public Papers and Addresses of Franklin D. Roosevelt, 1941, The Call to Battle Stations, *comp. Samuel I. Rosenman (New York, 1950), 514–15.*

Mr. Vice President, and Mr. Speaker, and Members of the Senate and House of Representatives:

YESTERDAY, December 7, 1941—a date which will live in infamy—the United States of America was suddenly and deliberately attacked by naval and air forces of the Empire of Japan.

The United States was at peace with that Nation and, at the solicitation of Japan, was still in conversation with its Government and its Emperor looking toward the maintenance of peace in the Pacific. Indeed, one hour after Japanese air squadrons had commenced bombing in the American Island of Oahu, the Japanese Ambassador to the United States and his colleague delivered to our Secretary of State a formal reply to a recent American message. And while this reply stated that it seemed useless to continue the existing diplomatic negotiations, it contained no threat or hint of war or of armed attack.

It will be recorded that the distance of Hawaii from Japan makes it obvious that the attack was deliberately planned many days or even weeks ago. During the intervening time the Japanese Government has deliberately sought to deceive the United States by false statements and expressions of hope for continued peace.

The attack yesterday on the Hawaiian Islands has caused severe damage to American naval and military forces. I regret to tell you that very many American lives have been lost. In addition American ships have been reported torpedoed on the high seas between San Francisco and Honolulu.

Yesterday the Japanese Government also launched an attack against Malaya.

Last night Japanese forces attacked Hong Kong.

Last night Japanese forces attacked Guam.

Last night Japanese forces attacked the Philippine Islands.

Last night the Japanese attacked Wake Island.

And this morning the Japanese attacked Midway Island.

Japan has, therefore, undertaken a surprise offensive extending throughout the Pacific area. The facts of yesterday and today speak for themselves. The people of the United States have already formed their opinions and well understand the implications to the very life and safety of our Nation.

As Commander in Chief of the Army and Navy I have directed that all measures be taken for our defense.

But always will our whole Nation remember the character of the onslaught against us.

No matter how long it may take us to overcome this premeditated invasion, the American people in their righteous might will win through to absolute victory.

I believe that I interpret the will of the Congress and of the people when I assert that we will not only defend ourselves to the uttermost but will make it very certain that this form of treachery shall never again endanger us.

Hostilities exist. There is no blinking at the fact that our people, our territory, and our interests are in grave danger.

With confidence in our armed forces—with the unbounding determination of our people—we will gain the inevitable triumph—so help us God.

I ask that the Congress declare that since the unprovoked and dastardly attack by Japan on Sunday, December 7, 1941, a state of war has existed between the United States and the Japanese Empire.

Questions

1. *Do you think that Roosevelt was correct in believing that Nazi Germany posed a threat to the national security of the United States? Why or why not?*

2. *How do you explain the different views of the isolationists and the president about events and their significance to American security?*

3. *What dimension of the isolationists' arguments seem most convincing? What were President Roosevelt's most effective arguments for greater American involvement in the war?*

FURTHER READING

The isolationists' impact on American diplomacy during World War II is discussed in In Danger Undaunted: The Anti-Interventionist Movement of 1940–1941 as Revealed in the Papers of the America First Committee, *ed. Justus D. Doenecke (Stanford, 1990); Wayne S. Cole,* Roosevelt and the Isolationists, 1932–45 *(Lincoln, Nebraska, 1983); and Manfred Jonas,* Isolationism in America, 1935–1941 *(Ithaca, 1966). Charles A. Beard made a strong isolationist argument about Roosevelt's World War II diplomacy in* President Roosevelt and the Coming of the War, 1941: A Study in Appearances and Realities *(New Haven, 1948). Frederick W. Marks III developed a related argument in* Wind Over Sand: The Diplomacy of Franklin Roosevelt *(Athens, Georgia, 1988). For internationalist viewpoints see Herbert Feis,* The Road to Pearl Harbor: The Coming of the War Between the United States and Japan *(Princeton, 1950), and Roberta Wohlstetter,* Pearl Harbor: Warning and Decision *(Stanford, 1962). Historians who have produced more nuanced accounts include Akira Iriye,* Power and Culture: The Japanese-American War, 1941–1945 *(Cambridge, Massachusetts, 1981); and Waldo Heinrichs,* Threshold of War: Franklin D. Roosevelt and American Entry into World War II *(New York, 1988). An abridged version of Pearl Harbor investigations is Roland H. Worth, Jr.,* Pearl Harbor: Selected Testimonies, Fully Indexed, from the Congressional Hearings (1945–1946) and Prior Investigations of the Events Leading Up to the Attack *(Jefferson, North Carolina, 1993).*

The Expulsion
and Relocation of
Japanese Americans in
World War II

Michael Les Benedict

INTRODUCTION

*On 7 December 1941, following years of growing tension be-
tween Japan and the United States, Japan launched a surprise
bombing of Pearl Harbor, the home port of the United States
Pacific fleet. Japan's allies, Germany and Italy, quickly joined it
in declaring war on the United States, bringing the Americans
fully into World War II.*

*Claiming that Japanese and Japanese Americans on the
Pacific coast were sympathetic to Japan and preparing to aid
Japanese air raids and even invasion, many people there called
for their expulsion from the coast. Within two months the
government of the United States ordered all persons of Japanese
ancestry—both aliens and "non-aliens" (that is, citizens)—to
leave a large swath of territory along the Pacific coast. This
included both Japanese immigrants (called Issei or "first generation") and their children (Nisei or "second generation"). The
small number previously identified as pro-Japan by U.S. intelligence agencies were interned at special locations. Over 100,000
others who had nowhere to go and no means of support outside
of their homes in California, western Oregon, and western
Washington were expelled from the region and taken to "relocation" camps in a process military authorities called "controlled
evacuation." While German Americans had been subject to
harassment during World War I, and both German and Italian
aliens were interned during World War II, the scope of the
forced Japanese evacuation was unprecedented. Moreover, unlike German and Italian immigrants, who could acquire American citizenship after five years' residence, Japanese immigrants*

had been barred from acquiring American citizenship by laws that limited naturalization to white immigrants and those of African descent.

After the war, more and more Americans came to doubt the practical and legal justification for wrenching Japanese and Japanese Americans from their homes and sending them to the relocation camps. Many of the relocated Japanese were outraged; after the war some returned to Japan rather than continue to live in the United States. The vast majority who remained did little to protest their treatment after the war, but by the 1970s many Japanese Americans demanded apologies and restitution. After a long struggle, Congress passed the Civil Liberties Act of 1988, acknowledging the injustice of the "controlled evacuation" and making reparations. The readings that follow describe the evacuation and relocation program, the reaction of the people subjected to it, life in the camps, and the demand for redress.

THE JAPANESE RELOCATION: EVENTS AND ATTITUDES

Most historians have condemned the expulsion and relocation of the Japanese and Japanese Americans during World War II, attributing the decision to domestic racism, fear of the "Yellow Peril" in foreign affairs, and the hysteria surrounding the sneak attack on Pearl Harbor. But some of those who supported the evacuation policy and a few modern analysts still defend the decision. The following readings provide a more detailed account of events and their effect on the forced evacuee. The readings demonstrate the continuing disagreement over whether the policy was justified.

A Daughter of an Evacuee Describes the History of the Expulsion and Relocation

In this essay, Donna K. Nagata, whose grandparents and parents were relocated, gives an overview of the history of the evacuation. Abridged from Donna K. Nagata, Legacy of Injustice: Exploring the Cross-Generational Impact of the Japanese American Internment *(New York, 1993), 1–15.*

The Decision to Evacuate

Japanese Americans recognize February 19 as the official Day of Remembrance for the Internment. On that date in 1942, President Franklin D. Roosevelt signed Executive Order 9066, ten weeks after the Japanese attacked Pearl Harbor. The order provided the secretary of war and his designated officers with the authority to exclude all persons, both citizens and aliens, from designated areas in order to provide security against sabotage or espionage. The army took charge of implementing Executive Order 9066 by removing all Japanese Americans from the West Coast of the United States, placing them first into temporary "assembly centers" and later into concentration camps located in desolate areas of the country. No formal charges were brought against the Japanese Americans, and there was no opportunity for an individual review of their loyalty.

The stated rationale for Executive Order 9066 concerned national security; removal of Japanese Americans from the West Coast was necessary to provide safeguards against espionage or sabotage. The order was signed at a time when the military activities of Japan generated increased concern in the United States. The Japanese struck the Malay Peninsula, Hong Kong, Wake and Midway islands, and the Philippines on the same day they attacked Pearl Harbor. By the time Executive Order 9066 was signed, they had successfully taken Guam, Wake Island, most of the Philippines, and Hong Kong. Rumors that the Pearl Harbor attack had been aided by ethnic Japanese in Hawaii ran rampant in newspapers and on radio, fueled by a December 12, 1941, press report from Secretary of the Navy Frank Knox. Although Knox falsely stated that Japanese spies operated in Hawaii prior to the Pearl Harbor attack, his press statements "carried considerable weight and gave credence to the view that ethnic Japanese on the mainland were a palpable threat and danger." In an atmosphere of paranoia and general panic, Japanese American fishing boats were accused of signaling Japanese submarines with their lights, and Japanese American farmers were suspected of planting their fields in rows pointing to nearby airports.

The fears for American security were not founded on fact. Intelligence reports, including those from the Federal Bureau of Investigation (FBI) and Naval Intelligence, concluded that mass

---

Excerpts from "Historical Background" reprinted from *Legacy of Injustice: Exploring the Cross-Generational Impact of the Japanese American Internment* by Donna K. Nagata, published by Plenum Publishing Corporation, 1993. Copyright © 1993 by Plenum Press, a division of Plenum Publishing Corporation.

incarceration was *not* a military necessity. Indeed, many of the fears were founded in racial prejudice evident both in the public and within the military itself. The views of Lieutenant General John L. DeWitt, who recommended the exclusion of Japanese from the West Coast, illustrate the extremity of this prejudice. DeWitt was in charge of West Coast security under Secretary of War Henry L. Stimson. Encouraged by both Major General Allen W. Gullion, the provost marshal for the army, and Colonel Karl R. Bendetsen, chief of Gullion's Aliens Division, he pressured the Department of Justice to adopt stricter enemy alien controls and informed Secretary of War Stimson that there were "indications that ethnic Japanese were organized and ready for concerted action within the United States." DeWitt saw the evacuation as a military necessity because he saw no distinction between the Japanese and Japanese Americans. Ethnic heritage alone determined one's loyalty. Transcripts of a conference between DeWitt and newspaper reporters on April 14, 1943, recorded him stating bluntly to reporters that "a Jap is a Jap" and on February 14, 1942, five days before the signing of Executive Order 9066, he stated to Secretary Stimson:

> In the war in which we are now engaged racial affinities are not severed by migration. The Japanese race is an enemy race and while many second and third generation Japanese born on United States soil, possessed of the United States citizenship, have become "Americanized," the racial strains are undiluted. That Japan is allied with Germany and Italy in this struggle is no ground for assuming that any Japanese, barred from assimilation by convention as he is, though born and raised in the United States, will not turn against this nation when the final test of loyalty comes. It follows that along the Pacific Coast over 112,000 potential enemies, of Japanese extraction, are at large today.

In an incredible "catch-22," DeWitt also noted that "the very fact that no sabotage has taken place to date is a disturbing and confirming indication that such action will be taken."

Research suggests that U.S. intelligence had monitored Japanese immigrants and their activities *before* the war, and as early as August 1941, Army Intelligence inquired about the possibility of arresting and detaining those civilians who were American citizens. Prior to Pearl Harbor there were also government officials who considered the use of Japanese in America as "barter" and "reprisal" reserves in case the United States needed to trade "prisoners of war" or wanted to ensure the humane treatment of American soldiers who were held as prisoners.

Individuals did oppose DeWitt's recommendations, but such opposition was neither unified nor focused. Both the Justice Department and J. Edgar Hoover of the FBI proposed that restrained actions would be preferable to a mass evacuation. Secretary of War Stimson, Assistant Secretary of War John J. McCloy, and Attorney General Francis Biddle also disagreed with DeWitt's plans but did not protest them vigorously. However, stronger political forces pressed for mass internment along with DeWitt.

That the motivations behind the internment could not be justified simply on the basis of military necessity was evident when contrasting the sequence of events in Hawaii with those on the mainland. The military interned only 1% of the Japanese population in Hawaii, which was significantly closer to Japan, compared with more than 90% of the Japanese Americans on the mainland. Several factors contributed to the differential treatment of the Hawaiian Japanese. Japanese Americans composed a significant portion, more than one-third, of Hawaii's population, and the territory's population was more pluralistic and ethnically tolerant than the mainland. Anti-Asian sentiment, although present, did not occur at the levels evident along the West Coast. Because they were so numerous, an internment of all Japanese Americans would severely hamper day-to-day functioning on the islands. In addition, General Delos Emmons of the War Department, the commanding general of Hawaii, urged a restrained response to the presence of ethnic Japanese, recommended that the size of the areas prohibited to Japanese Americans be reduced, and objected to the exclusion of persons not actually or potentially dangerous. The difference in treatment between the Hawaiian and mainland Japanese Americans is striking. . . .

The racism underlying the internment did not emerge suddenly, for although Executive Order 9066 may serve as an official "beginning" to the internment, decades of anti-Asian prejudice prior to World War II set the context for its inception. As [historian Roger] Daniels notes, the Japanese were initially welcomed in the mid-1800s in Hawaii as a source of cheap labor on sugar plantations. The Chinese, who had been brought earlier to Hawaii as a source of inexpensive labor, came to be seen as problematic when their numbers increased. By the 1800s, Japanese labor groups were recruited in large numbers from Hawaii to come to the mainland and work in agriculture.

As the numbers of Japanese increased on the mainland, so did the levels of prejudice and hostility around them. The media portrayed the Japanese as a "yellow peril," and by 1908, the Gentleman's Agreement (an executive agreement between the United States and Japan) restricted immigration from Japan. The Gentleman's Agreement prevented the immigration of Japanese men but did allow for a significant number of Japanese women to immigrate as picture brides and begin families in this country. However, in 1924 the Immigration Act effectively stopped all Japanese immigration until 1965. These immigration restrictions had important long-term consequences in defining the demographics of the Japanese American community, isolating Japanese couples in the United States and creating a population with "unique age distributions" and distinct age peaks for each generation. For example, by 1940 the Issei (first-generation Japanese immigrant) men were generally between the ages of 50 and 64, whereas the Issei women tended to be approximately 10 years younger. Most of their U.S.-born children (the Nisei) were born between 1918 and 1922.

Pre-World War II discrimination against the Japanese was also evident in other forms of anti-Japanese legislation. Antimiscegenation laws prohibited Japanese Americans from intermarrying with whites. In addition, Japanese were considered "aliens ineligible for citizenship," and the 1913 Alien Land Law in California (where the vast majority of mainland Japanese lived) barred such aliens from purchasing land and owning property. In fact, Japanese immigrants could not become citizens until 1952.

Economic competition fueled anti-Japanese sentiment along the West Coast prior to the war. More than 50% of all Japanese men along the West Coast made their living through agriculture, forestry, and fishing. In 1940, Japanese American farms in California, Washington, and Oregon numbered over 6,000 and comprised a total of 250,000 acres. Most were small family businesses that specialized in "a labor-intensive, high-yield agricultural technique as opposed to the resource-intensive, low-yield agriculture characteristic of American farming." Altogether, these farms were valued at $72.6 million, and the productivity of the Japanese

Soldiers guarding Japanese and Japanese-Americans at Santa Anita Park, where evictees were gathered for relocation to desert camps. (Courtesy of The National Archives.)

American farmers benefitted the West Coast. Nonetheless, their success threatened many white American groups. Fears that the Japanese farmers were driving whites out of business heightened negative feelings, as did the erroneous perception that the Japanese population was exploding and creating a "yellow peril." Records show that, in reality, the Japanese farmers in California were not displacing existing farmers.

Years of the anti-Japanese sentiment prior to World War II set the emotional and economic stage for the removal of Japanese Americans. Then came the shock of Pearl Harbor, which crystallized these views into a panic. Not surprisingly, the majority of citizens favored harsh treatment of Japanese Americans. In March 1942, the National Opinion Research Center found that a vast majority of the public supported internment. Ninety-three percent of those questioned approved of the relocation of Japanese aliens, and 60% favored the evacuation of U.S. citizens as well. Two-thirds thought that once the Japanese Americans were incarcerated, they should not be allowed to move freely within the camps, but rather they ought to be kept "under strict guard like prisoners of war." Additional polls revealed that more than half of those sampled wanted to send all Japanese Americans to Japan after the war.

Those who had typically advocated for civil rights also remained silent or endorsed the internment orders. A majority of members of the Northern California Civil Liberties Union actually *favored* the evacuation orders in the spring of 1942. Japanese Americans clearly were excluded from the moral community of most other Americans at that time. Moral exclusion occurs when "individuals or groups are perceived as *outside the boundary in which moral values, rules, and considerations of fairness apply.* Those who are morally excluded are perceived as nonentities, expendable, or undeserving; consequently, harming them appears acceptable, appropriate, or just." Japanese Americans, viewed as treacherous, racially inferior, and unassimilable, were easily excluded. On the other hand, German and Italian Americans, who were racially similar to the dominant group, much more numerous, and politically powerful, did not suffer the extreme pressures toward mass incarceration; they remained within the boundaries of inclusion.

The Evacuation Process

Pearl Harbor affected Japanese Americans immediately. On the night of December 7, 1941, the FBI arrested approximately 1,500 Issei aliens who were considered to be potentially disloyal. Virtually all the leaders of Japanese American communities were removed, often with no explanation or indication of their fate. The void in leadership within the communities left Japanese Americans with few options. . . . [T]here was no political group in the larger community to support a resistance of the internment orders. As a result, the vast majority of Japanese Americans "played a passive role—waiting to see what their government would do with them."

Initially, General DeWitt attempted to implement a plan of "voluntary" resettlement. According to the plan, Japanese Americans would be restricted from military zones of the West Coast . . . [see map] but free to move outside of those zones. Data from the U.S. army indicated that approximately 5,000 individuals chose this option and "voluntarily" migrated east between March and October of 1942, in addition to an uncounted number who fled the

West Coast between December 7, 1941, and March 1942. The plan, however, was destined to fail. It was impossible for Issei and Nisei to sell their businesses and homes quickly. Many had no funds with which to move because their monies had been frozen by the government. They feared the hostility of an unknown destination. Japanese Americans could easily be recognized wherever they went, and interior states such as Idaho and Wyoming were no more welcoming than West Coast states. Recognizing the inad-

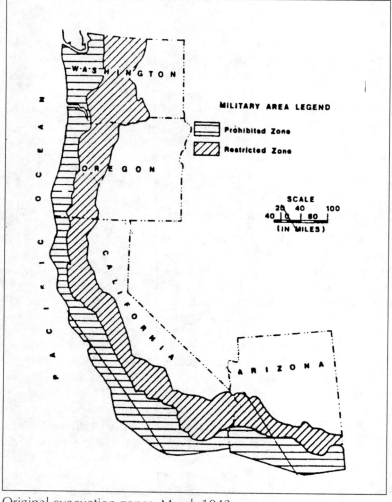

Original evacuation zones, March 1942.

equacy of the voluntary relocation program, the government took control over the evacuation process and implemented a plan for compulsory removal of Japanese Americans.

Because it was impossible to evacuate and relocate such a large group of people at the same time, the Japanese Americans first had to be transported to temporary "assembly centers." Later, when the more permanent camps were built, the internees would be moved again. The evacuation to assembly centers was carried out under military supervision of the army between March and August of 1942. Although there were Japanese Americans who were aware of the potential for some kind of evacuation, the army typically withheld details about the impending move, leaving little time or information for preparations. Many were given but a few days' notice that they would be leaving their homes. They took what they could carry. The economic losses stemming from the enforced evacuation were tremendous. Real estate, cars, appliances, farm equipment, crops ready for harvest, and personal possessions were sold for a fraction of their worth or simply left behind in haste. The fact that the military would not inform the Japanese Americans of their destination made the decision of what to bring more difficult. Families did not know whether to pack for cold or warm climates.

Throughout the evacuation families wore impersonal numbered tags. Travel by train or bus to the assembly centers was stressful and dehumanizing. Some trains had inadequate food supplies. Window shades blocked out the scenery, and passengers could not tell their whereabouts. As armed guards patrolled the trains, gossip arose that the military planned to take the Japanese Americans to an isolated area and shoot them.

After traveling hours without clear information about their destination or what fate lay in store for them, the internees arrived at the assembly centers. Sixteen of the hastily converted assembly centers were located in California, and an additional three were in Washington, Oregon, and Arizona. Many were located at race tracks and fairgrounds, where the Japanese Americans lived in horse stalls and animal quarters. Although whitewashed, they still smelled of manure. A family of eight was squeezed into a 20- by 24-foot space, four persons into an 8- by 20-foot space. Married couples often shared one large space, living in sections partitioned by a hanging sheet. Inadequate food, sanitation, and medical facilities proved equally problematic. Military police with ma-

Evicted Japanese and Japanese-Americans forced to leave the small town of Byron, California, May 2, 1942. (Courtesy of The National Archives.)

chine guns guarded the perimeter of the centers, while internal police instituted curfews, roll calls, and searches within the camps.

Although most internees lived with their families at the assembly center, others arrived without their complete family. Often, the father or husband had been taken by the FBI prior to the evacuation, but in other circumstances families were separated from loved ones who were institutionalized or incapacitated. Non-Japanese spouses of interracial couples also faced internment if they wanted to remain with their husband or wife.

Although assembly centers were labeled "temporary," the Japanese Americans remained in the centers for an average of 3 months. Then, at the end of May 1942, the process of uprooting began again. This time the long, tiresome train rides ended at the more permanent concentration camps. These 10 camps . . . were located in barren areas outside the exclusion area.

Many Japanese Americans hoped that the concentration

camps (euphemistically called "relocation centers") would provide better living conditions than the assembly centers. Unfortunately, the conditions were not significantly better. Barbed wire
and armed guards persisted, as did the harsh living conditions.
No camp housed less than 7,000 internees, and the largest held
over 18,000. Barrack-style housing was constructed specifically
for the purpose of containing the Japanese Americans. Each
"block" consisted of 12 to 14 barracks, a communal mess hall,
toilet and bath facilities, a laundry, and a recreation hall. A bar-
rack measured approximately 20 by 100 feet and was divided into
four to six rooms. At Topaz, a camp that was typical of the others,
rooms ranged in size from 20 feet by 8 feet, to 20 feet by 24 feet.
Each room contained one family. Sparse furnishings included a
cot, a coal-burning stove with no coal, and a light bulb hanging
from the ceiling. There was no running water. Internees braved
extreme temperatures throughout the year. In the deserts, where
many of the camps were located, winter temperatures could reach
as low as 35 below zero and summers could be as high as 115
degrees. Dust storms arose frequently.

The War Relocation Authority (WRA), a newly formed civilian agency, was responsible for the camps. It planned to act as a
facilitator of the resettlement rather than a warden for prisoners
and proposed a policy that would entitle the Japanese Americans
to the same treatment as other American citizens. As noted in the
CWRIC [Commission on Wartime Relocation and Internment of
Civilians] final report, however, the actual experience of the Japanese Americans fell far short of this initial goal. The institutional
mess-hall meals were minimally adequate. Dairy items were in
continual shortage, and some centers had no meat for several days
each week. Facilities for the sick, elderly, and mothers with infants
were particularly poor. The WRA did prepare special meals for
those with health problems, but the elderly and sick who needed
the special meals might have to walk a mile three times a day to
get them because the meals were prepared in a building separate
from the mess halls. The shortage of medical care, evident in the
assembly centers, also continued. At one point, the camp in
Jerome, Arkansas, had only seven doctors to provide care to
10,000 people. Epidemics of dysentery, typhoid, and tuberculosis
were reported in several camps.

The Japanese Americans had meager opportunities for work
while interned and performed a variety of jobs: Many worked in

agriculture or food preparation, while others constructed camouflage nets or operated sawmills. According to the 1982 [CWRIC] . . ., the WRA encouraged their participation because they hoped that outsiders would view such work as a sign of Japanese American loyalty. However, a strict limit on earnings was set. Camp internees could earn no more than $19.00 a month, regardless of whether they worked as nurses or field workers. In contrast, a white WRA librarian might earn $167.00 a month in camp.

Some 30,000 Japanese American children attended public school at the time of the internment. Although inadequate numbers of textbooks, equipment, and trained teachers severely limited what could be accomplished, both the Issei and older Nisei remained committed to providing an education for the young internees. Within weeks, the Japanese American residents themselves set up kindergarten and English classes, even in the temporary assembly centers. However, once the internees were transferred to the more permanent concentration camps, the WRA made little effort to retain the educational initiatives from the assembly centers and instead instituted inadequate and paternalistic educational policies. . . . Approximately 600 Caucasian American teachers, 50 certified Japanese American teachers, and 400 Japanese American assistant teachers eventually taught in the camps.

The WRA's system of governance gave it veto power over all legislative activities. It also barred the Issei from holding elected office and created conflicts between the Issei and Nisei generations by placing greater official authority in the hands of the children and disenfranchising their parents. Such a structure directly opposed Japanese cultural values of filial piety and deference to one's elders.

Other government policies produced friction among internees. In early 1943, all Japanese Americans over age 16 in the camps were required to answer loyalty questions. These questions were to serve two purposes. First, they would be used to help camp authorities process internees requesting work furloughs and resettlement outside the camps. Second, because the government had decided to open enlistment into the armed forces to Japanese Americans in 1944, a system was needed by which "loyal" and "disloyal" Japanese could be distinguished. To accomplish this latter task, army officers and WRA staff distributed questionnaires to all draft-age males that contained two critical questions about loyalty. Question 27 asked, "Are you willing to serve in the armed forces of the United States on combat duty, wherever ordered?" Question 28 asked, "Will you swear unqualified allegiance to the United States of America and faithfully defend the United States from any or all attack by foreign or domestic forces, and forswear any form of allegiance or obedience to the Japanese emperor, or any other government, power or organization?" The answers to the required questions were then used in registering Nisei men for the draft. The Issei and women internees were required to answer loyalty questions as well, although Question 27 was rephrased to ask whether they were willing to serve in the WACS or Army Nurse Corps.

The loyalty questionnaire raised significant and painful conflicts for Issei and Nisei alike and again demonstrated the government's blatant insensitivity to the circumstances of the Japanese Americans. The Issei struggled over Question 28. To answer "yes" would require them to renounce their Japanese nationality. Yet, because they were legally prevented from becoming American citizens, this would leave them without a country of citizenship at all! On the other hand, an answer of "no" would be seen as disloyal and could lead to being transferred to another camp and separated from one's children who were citizens of the United States. The loyalty oath essentially asked the Issei to "voluntarily assume stateless status," a request that was "a clear violation of the Geneva convention."

Loyalty questions concerned the Nisei as well. Some wondered if Question 28 were a trick question, since forswearing allegiance to the emperor might also be construed as admitting that allegiance had once existed. Question 27 asked them to fight for the country that had so unjustly imprisoned them. Tensions and debates over how to respond to the loyalty questions arose between family members and friends. In the end, the majority of internees (87%) answered the question with an unqualified "yes." Qualified answers and unanswered questions were interpreted as "no's." The approximately 8,000 who answered "no" to both Question 27 and 28 were considered "disloyals" and eventually shipped to a special high-security camp at Tule Lake. There the so-called "no-no's" joined individuals who wished to expatriate or repatriate to Japan.

By January 1944, following the loyalty questionnaire, the government reinstituted the draft for Japanese Americans. According to the selective service, approximately 23,000 Nisei served during World War II. About half came from the continental United States, and among these were 2,800 Nisei inductees from the camps. Some of the young Nisei males willingly joined the armed forces. The all-Japanese American 100th Battalion and the 442nd Regimental Combat Team, composed of volunteers from Hawaii and the camps, became famous for their bravery and loyalty. Other Nisei contributed to the war effort through their service in the intelligence or by acting as interrogators of Japanese war prisoners in combat. Ironically, the Japanese heritage that made them targets for suspected disloyalty had become an asset.

Dissension and Resistance

The outstanding service record of Japanese Americans who served in the military might lead one to believe that all internees supported the recruitment effort. Other statistics, however, indicate that there were Nisei who did not accept military service as a positive alternative. Twenty-two percent of the total Nisei males eligible for the draft refused to answer "yes" to both of the loyalty questions. In addition, the army eventually recruited only 1,208 volunteers from the camps. The proportion of volunteers from the noninterned Hawaiian Japanese was significantly higher. Daniels also points out that many Japanese American soldiers who fought in Europe were farmers. White farmers of draft age would have received deferments as "essential agricultural workers," but no such occupational deferments were available to Japanese Americans. And while the 442nd Regiment and 100th Battalion were exemplary combat units, Company K, another all-Nisei unit, was plagued by low morale and insubordination. Not all Nisei welcomed the draft as a sign of reinstated rights. For them, the loyalty questionnaire and the draft represented additional insults to their citizenship and rights. At the Heart Mountain camp, some 85 men were indicted and convicted for draft resistance.

Draft resistance represented only one example of the Japanese American disillusionment. Renunciation of citizenship represented yet another. By January 1945, over 5,000 Nisei had renounced their American citizenship. Some regretted their decision several months later when an end to the war appeared near and the Justice Department announced that Nisei renunciants would be deported to Japan while their Issei parents would be relocated in the United States. Eventually, after negotiating considerable legal and bureaucratic complexities, all who wished to invalidate their renunciations were able to do so. Other Japanese Americans filed for repatriation (in the case of aliens) or expatriation (in the case of citizens) to Japan.

In the assembly and relocation centers, applications to go to Japan had been one of the few nonviolent ways to protest degrading treatment. During three years of rising humiliation, 20,000 people chose this means to express their pain, outrage and alienation, in one of the saddest testaments to the injustice of exclusion and detection. . . . The cold statistics fail . . . to convey the scars of mind and soul that many carried with them from the camps.

As was the case with the renunciants, most repatriation and expatriation applicants eventually remained in the United States. It is nonetheless sobering that 4,724 Japanese Americans actually left the camps for Japan.

Resettlement

Beginning in 1943, Nisei who answered "yes" to the loyalty oath but did not enlist in the service began receiving clearance to leave the camps for areas outside the restricted zones of the West Coast. Resettlement was a slow process. Those who left the camps were given one-way transportation costs and $25 to begin a new life. Young Nisei between the ages of 15 and 35 relocated in cities such as Chicago, Denver, and New York and took whatever form of work they could find. Many became domestics or performed other forms of manual labor. Between 2,300 and 2,700 ended up working at Seabrook Farms in New Jersey. These individuals were influenced by farm recruiters who went to the camps to solicit resettlers by feedback from trial groups sent from the camps and letters from those already resettled in Seabrook.

Although resettlement had been a goal of the WRA from early on in the internment, there were many reasons why the Japanese Americans were reluctant to leave the camps. In addition to experiencing the physical and emotional stress of imprisonment, many were fearful to leave the camps and distrustful of resettlement offers. This was especially true of the older Issei. Government records showed that by January 1945, only one of six Issei had left the camps, and it was not until June 1946 that all camps (with the exception of Tule Lake, where hearings on detainees were held) closed. . . .

. . . Greater than two-thirds of those who left the camps eventually returned to their previous region of residence. Both those who resettled in cities away from the West Coast and those who returned to their home towns faced many adjustments. [Historian Tetsuden] Kashima, in fact, refers to the resettlement years between 1945 and 1955 as a crisis period for Japanese Americans, a time when they were forced to readjust to a normal life after the camps, find jobs and a place to live, and confront an often hostile environment. Most found their original neighborhoods greatly changed. Areas that had once been the "Japantowns" and centers of Japanese American community life had, over the war years, become occupied by other ethnic minority groups. In addition, anti-Japanese sentiments remained high, and 31 major attacks on California relocatees were reported between January and June of 1945.

We have seen that by spring of 1943, following the loyalty review of internees, there was evidence that the incarceration of the Japanese Americans was not a military necessity. Yet, many Japanese Americans remained in the camps through 1945. Why was this so? The following quote taken from the CWRIC report provides the sobering answer to this question:

> . . . the President was unwilling to act to end the exclusion until the first Cabinet meeting following the Presidential election of November, 1944. The inescapable conclusion from this . . . pattern is that the delay was motivated by political considerations. By the participants' own accounts, there is no rational explanation for maintaining the exclusion of loyal ethnic Japanese from the West Coast for eighteen months after May, 1943—except political pressure and fear.

From the beginnings of the decision to evacuate, to the closing of the camps, the Japanese Americans were the victims of racial, economic, and political injustices. By the end of the internment, with their community dispersed across the country, their lives would never be the same.

A Defense of the Relocation Policy

In the following selection, Dwight D. Murphey, a lawyer who has written on social and political philosophy, defends the relocation policy, arguing that it was justified and that conditions in the camps were good. From Dwight D. Murphey, The Dispossession of the American Indian—And Other Key Issues in American History *(Washington, D.C., 1995), 31-35, 39-41.*

On February 19, 1942, President Franklin D. Roosevelt signed Executive Order 9066. This authorized the establishment of military areas from which people of all kinds could be excluded. Lt. General John L. DeWitt was appointed the military commander to carry out the Executive Order. In March, Gen. DeWitt declared large parts of the Pacific Coast states military areas in which no one of Japanese descent would be allowed to remain. The exclusion order affected Japanese-Americans living on the West Coast by forcing them to move inland. Its only effect upon those who already lived inland was to bar them from going to the quarantined areas on the West Coast. . . .

A short-lived plan originally was to assist the Japanese-Americans in a process by which they would move inland "on their own recognizance" as individuals and families. [Karl R.] Bendetsen [who directed the evacuation for the government] says that "funds were provided for them [and] we informed them . . . where there were safe motels in which they could stay overnight." This was ended almost immediately, by late March, however . . . the need for a more organized system became apparent when most of the Japanese-Americans were not able to make arrangements to relocate quickly even with some help. A second reason was that the governors of western states (reflecting public opinion in their states) objected strongly to thousands of people of Japanese origin moving into their states without oversight. . . .

Excerpt from "The Relocation of the Japanese-Americans During World War II" in *The Dispossession of the American Indian — And Other Key Issues in American History* by Dwight D. Murphey, published by Scott-Townsend Publishers, copyright © 1995, Council for Social and Economic Studies, Inc. Reprinted by permission of the author.

Relocated Japanese-Americans play baseball at the Lone Pine Relocation Camp, with other residents looking on. (Courtesy of The Library of Congress.)

This led to the "assembly center phase," during which the evacuees were moved to improvised centers such as race tracks and fairgrounds along the West Coast pending the construction of ten "relocation centers" in eastern California, Arizona, Utah, Idaho, Wyoming, Colorado, and as far east as Arkansas. . . .

Hastily improvised and purely temporary quarters for thousands of people who have been uprooted from their homes on short notice could not have been pleasant. There is no incongruity, however, between this and the fact, also true, that the government worked with the evacuees to take extraordinary measures to make the centers as comfortable as possible. In the short time they existed, some centers opened libraries; movies were shown regularly; there were Scout troops, arts and crafts classes, musical groups, and leagues for basketball and baseball. Three hundred and fifty people signed up for a calisthenics class at Stockton. All had playgrounds for children, and one even had a pitch-and-putt golf course. The centers were run almost entirely by the Japanese-Americans themselves.

As the ten relocation centers became ready, the evacuees were moved to them from the assembly centers. These were under the jurisdiction of the War Relocation Authority. . . . It is worth noting that no families were ever separated during the process.

As with the assembly centers, the critics find fault with much about the relocation centers. For example, the health care has been the subject of continuing dispute. Dillon Myer [director of the War Relocation Authority (WRA), which supervised the camps], however, says that "the professional care was excellent [and] was free."

There were messhalls for meals, and a large number of community enterprises, which included stores, theaters, hairdressers, community theaters, and newspapers. There was ping-pong, judo, boxing, badminton, and sumo wrestling. Again, there were basketball and baseball leagues (along with some touch football). The Santa Fe center had "gardens, two softball diamonds, two tennis courts, a miniature nine-hole golf course, a fenced forty-acre hiking area, . . . classes in calligraphy, Chinese and Japanese poetry. . . ." The Massachusetts Quakers sponsored art competitions. Libraries featured Japanese-language sections. There were chapters of the American Red Cross, YMCA, YWCA, Boy Scouts, and Girl Scouts. State Shinto, with its emperor-worship, was barred, but otherwise the evacuees worshiped as they pleased. The government paid a salary equal to an American soldier's pay ($21 per month) to those who worked in the centers.

Each of the camps (except Tule Lake . . .) had fully accredited schools through the high school level. There were nursery schools, kindergarten, the teaching of instrumental music, school choruses, achievement testing, high school newspapers and annuals, dances, active Parent-Teacher Associations, student councils and class officers. . . .

Much of the credit for the livability of the centers goes to the Japanese-Americans themselves, whose energy and intelligence immediately made the best of the situation. This was accomplished in an active relationship with the WRA.

Subject to a veto that the WRA could exercise, each relocation center was governed internally (as had been the assembly centers) by the Japanese-Americans themselves, who elected representatives from each block.

Even before the relocation centers became filled, college-age students began to leave to attend American universities. By the beginning of the fall semester in 1942, approximately 250 students had left for school, attending 143 colleges and universities. By the time the war was over, 4,300 college-age students were attending more than 300 universities around the country (though not on the West Coast). Scholarships were granted based on financial ability. Foundations and churches funded a "National Japanese American Student Relocation Council" to help with college attendance.

The centers were intended, as their name suggests, to be places in which the evacuees could stay while they were being relocated around the country. Myer says "never was there any policy of confinement for the duration." . . . That is why the camps were called "relocation centers" rather than "internment camps."

Many of the evacuees, however, remained in the centers for the duration of the war. Critics attribute this to a lack of alternatives, as though the evacuees were trapped, but Bendetsen credits the fact that life was acceptable within the centers. "Many elected to stay in the relocation centers while being gainfully employed in nearby pursuits in the general economy . . . The climate of hostility which presented intractable problems in the very early phases had long since subsided." . . .

The critics of the evacuation often argue that there was no demonstrated military necessity for it. The Report of the Commission on Wartime Relocation speaks of "the clamor" by California officials for protective action, and says that "these opinions were not informed by any knowledge of actual military risks." The extensive critical literature mocks the perception of danger, suggesting that it was a figment of hysterical imaginations.

But this is nonsense. The danger was apparent to anyone who considered the situation. Earl Warren, as attorney general of California, testified before a select committee of Congress (the "Tolan Committee") on February 21, 1942, and submitted letters from a number of local officials. Some pointed to the vulnerability of the water supply and of the large-scale irrigation systems: "It would be absolutely humanly impossible," one of them wrote, "for the small force now available in the sheriff's office to make even a pretense of guarding this tremendous farm territory and the irrigation system." Another pointed out that "a systematic campaign of incendiarism would cause terrific disaster" during the California dry season from May until October. . . .

In addition to the civilian population, there was much that was important militarily and economically along the West Coast; it was clearly exposed; and there were few means to defend it. This was enough in itself to create a critical emergency, to be met as humanely but as effectively as possible. It should not be necessary for the American government to have known specifically of plans for espionage and sabotage.

Just the same, there *was* definitive evidence of Japan's intent to exploit (and actual exploitation of) the situation. On December 4, 1941, the Office of Naval Intelligence reported a Japanese "intelligence machine geared for war, in operation, and utilizing west coast Japanese." On January 21, 1942, a bulletin from Army Intelligence "stated flat out that the Japanese government's espionage net containing Japanese aliens, first and second generation Japanese and other nationals is now thoroughly organized and working underground," according to the testimony of David D. Lowman, a retired career intelligence officer who has written extensively on declassified intelligence from World War II. . . .

Amazingly, the Commission ignored the most important source of information about espionage, which is the dispatches sent by the Japanese government to its own officials before and during the war. U. S. Navy codebreakers had broken the Japanese diplomatic code in 1938, and the decoded messages were distributed, on a basis "higher than Top Secret," to a small handful of the very highest American officials under the codename "MAGIC." Lowman testified in 1984 that "included among the diplomatic communications were hundreds of reports dealing with espionage activities in the United States and its possessions." . . .

Several officials within the Roosevelt administration opposed the evacuation of the Japanese-Americans from the West Coast, but Lowman makes a telling point: that the President, the Secretary of War, the Army Chief of Staff, the Director of Military Intelligence, the Secretary of the Navy, the Chief of Naval Operations, the Director of Naval Intelligence, and the Chiefs of Army and Navy Plans—all of whom received MAGIC—*favored* evacuation. It was those who did not have knowledge of the Japanese dispatches who found it possible, somewhat incongruously in light of the self-evident factors I have mentioned, to doubt the military necessity.

Questions

1. *What role did racism play in encouraging the government to order the forced relocation of Japanese and Japanese Americans from the Pacific coast? Do you think that military necessity alone can explain the decision? Do you think that government officials' perception of military necessity alone can explain the decision?*

2. *Does Dwight Murphey's justification of the expulsion and relocation policy help you to understand the feelings of those who supported it in 1941?*

3. *How persuasive do you find Murphey's defense of the government's policy? Did the fears and evidence of Japanese disloyalty that Murphey describes justify mass relocation? Explain.*

4. *Defenders of the evacuation of Japanese Americans from the Pacific coast describe their transfer to the relocation camps as "voluntary." Nagata, like many who have described the events, refers to the relocation as "internment," suggesting the transfer was involuntary. How voluntary does it appear to have been? If you are unsure, keep this question in mind as you read the original documents that follow.*

5. *Defenders of the evacuation and relocation policy point out that Japanese and Japanese Americans were treated much better than enemy aliens in Germany and Japan. How does this affect your evaluation of the expulsion and relocation policy?*

THE JAPANESE RELOCATION: DOCUMENTS AND FIRST-HAND ACCOUNTS

After their release from the relocation camps, few of the residents were willing to describe their experiences. For some the memory was too painful. Many adult Japanese considered their time in the camps to be a mark of shame, to be hidden. Moreover, many Japanese and Japanese Americans had been taught not to express anger openly. But over time, Japanese Americans—especially the younger generation—began to describe their experiences and express their outrage. The following documents and first-hand accounts describe their experiences and the actions of the United States government.

Executive Order 9066

After several months of debate within his administration, on 19 February 1942, President Franklin D. Roosevelt signed an executive order authorizing the military to relocate the Japanese and Japanese Americans living on the West coast. Did the president allege any actual evidence of sabotage or disloyalty? Excerpted from U.S. House of Representatives, Report of the Select Committee Investigating National Defense Migration *(hereafter cited as* Tolan Committee*),* House Report No. 2124, *77th Cong., 2d sess. (1942), 314.*

WHEREAS the successful prosecution of the war requires every possible protection against espionage and against sabotage to national defense material, national defense premises, and national defense utilities. . . .

Now, THEREFORE, by virtue of the authority vested in me as President of the United States, and Commander in Chief of the Army and Navy, I hereby authorize and direct the Secretary of War, and the Military Commanders who he may from time to time designate, whenever he or any designated Commander deems such action necessary or desirable, to prescribe military areas in such places and of such extent as he or the appropriate Military Commander may determine, from which any or all persons may be excluded, and with respect to which, the right of any person to enter, remain in, or leave shall be subject to whatever restrictions the Secretary of War or the appropriate Military Commander may impose in his discretion. The Secretary of War is hereby authorized to provide for residents of any such area who are excluded therefrom, such transportation, food, shelter, and other accommodations as may be necessary, in the judgment of the Secretary of War or the said Military Commander, and until other arrangements are made, to accomplish the purpose of this order.

An Evacuation Order

The following was the first of the evacuation orders that forced over 100,000 Japanese Americans from their homes on the West coast and led to their relocation to camps in the interior. Abridged from Tolan Committee, House Report No. 2124, *332–33.*

CIVILIAN EXCLUSION ORDER NO. 1
HEADQUARTERS, WESTERN DEFENSE COMMAND AND FOURTH ARMY, *Presidio of San Francisco, California, March 24, 1942.*

1.   Pursuant to the provisions of Public Proclamations Nos. 1 and 2, this headquarters, dated March 2, 1942, and March 16, 1942, respectively, it is hereby ordered that all persons of Japanese ancestry, including aliens and nonaliens, be excluded from that portion of Military Area No. 1 described as "Bainbridge Island," in the State of Washington,

on or before 12 o'clock noon, P. W. T., of the 30th day of March 1942.

2. Such exclusion will be accomplished in the following manner:

(a) Such persons may, with permission, on or prior to March 29, 1942, proceed to any approved place of their choosing beyond the limits of Military Area No. 1 and the prohibited zones established by said proclamations or hereafter similarly established, subject only to such regulations as to travel and change of residence as are now or may hereafter be prescribed by this headquarters and by the United States Attorney General. Persons affected hereby will not be permitted to take up residence or remain within the region designated as Military Area No. 1 or the prohibited zones heretofore or hereafter established. Persons affected hereby are required on leaving or entering Bainbridge Island to register and obtain a permit at the Civil Control Office to be established on said Island at or near the ferryboat landing.

(b) On March 30, 1942, all such persons who have not removed themselves from Bainbridge Island in accordance with Paragraph 1 hereof shall, in accordance with instructions of the Commanding General, Northwestern Sector, report to the Civil Control Office referred to above on Bainbridge Island for evacuation in such manner and to such place or places as shall then be prescribed.

(c) A responsible member of each family affected by this order and each individual living alone so affected will report to the Civil Control Office described above between 8 a. m. and 5 p. m. Wednesday, March 25, 1942.

3. Any person affected by this order who fails to comply with any of its provisions or who is found on Bainbridge Island after 12 o'clock noon, P. W. T., of March 30, 1942, will be subject to the criminal penalties provided by Public Law No. 503, 77th Congress, approved March 21, 1942, entitled "An Act to Provide a Penalty for Violation of Restrictions or Orders with Respect to Persons Entering, Remaining in, Leaving, or Committing Any Act in Military Areas or

Zone", and alien Japanese will be subject to immediate apprehension and internment.

J. L. DE WITT,
Lieutenant General,
U.S. Army, Commanding

The Uchida Family is Evacuated

Like many other community leaders, Yoshiko Uchida's father, Dwight Takashi Uchida, the manager of a leading department store serving the Japanese community in Berkeley, California, was arrested and interned immediately after the bombing of Pearl Harbor. His family, including his daughter Yoshiko, a student at the University of California, remained in Berkeley until ordered to evacuate on 21 April 1942. From Yoshiko Uchida, Desert Exile: The Uprooting of a Japanese American Family *(Seattle, 1982), 58–60, 62.*

Each day we watched the papers for the evacuation orders covering the Berkeley area. On April 21, the headlines read: "Japs Given Evacuation Orders Here." I felt numb as I read the front page story. "Moving swiftly, without any advance notice, the Western Defense Command today ordered Berkeley's estimated 1,319 Japanese, aliens and citizens alike, evacuated to the Tanforan Assembly Center by noon, May 1." (This gave us exactly ten days' notice.) "Evacuees will report at the Civil Control Station being set up in Pilgrim Hall of the First Congregational Church . . . between the hours of 8:00 A.M. and 5:00 P.M. next Saturday and Sunday."

This was Exclusion Order Number Nineteen, which was to uproot us from our homes and send us into the Tanforan Assembly Center in San Bruno, a hastily converted racetrack.

All Japanese were required to register before the departure date, and my sister, as head of the family, went to register for us.

Excerpts from "Evacuation" reprinted from *Desert Exile: The Uprooting of a Japanese American Family* by Yoshiko Uchida, published by the University of Washington Press, 1982. Copyright © 1982 by Yoshiko Uchida.

She came home with baggage and name tags that were to bear our family number and be attached to all our belongings. From that day on we became Family Number 13453.

Although we had been preparing for the evacuation orders, still when they were actually issued, it was a sickening shock.

"Ten days! We have only ten days to get ready!" my sister said frantically. Each day she rushed about, not only taking care of our business affairs, but, as our only driver, searching for old crates and cartons for packing, and taking my mother on various errands as well.

Mama still couldn't seem to believe that we would have to leave. "How can we clear out in ten days a house we've lived in for fifteen years?" she asked sadly.

But my sister and I had no answers for her.

Mama had always been a saver, and she had a tremendous accumulation of possessions. Her frugal upbringing had caused her to save string, wrapping paper, bags, jars, boxes, even bits of silk thread left over from sewing, which were tied end to end and rolled up into a silk ball. Tucked away in the corners of her desk and bureau drawers were such things as small stuffed animals, wooden toys, *kokeshi* dolls, marbles, and even a half-finished pair of socks she was knitting for a teddy bear's paw. Many of these were "found objects" that the child in her couldn't bear to discard, but they often proved useful in providing diversion for some fidgety visiting child. These were the simple things to dispose of.

More difficult were the boxes that contained old letters from her family and friends, our old report cards from the first grade on, dozens of albums of family photographs, notebooks and sketch pads full of our childish drawings, valentines and Christmas cards we had made for our parents, innumerable guest books filled with the signatures and friendly words of those who had once been entertained. These were the things my mother couldn't bear to throw away. Because we didn't own our house, we could leave nothing behind. We had to clear the house completely, and everything in it had either to be packed for storage or thrown out.

We surveyed with desperation the vast array of dishes, lacquerware, silverware, pots and pans, books, paintings, porcelain and pottery, furniture, linens, rugs, records, curtains, garden tools, cleaning equipment, and clothing that filled our house. We put up a sign in our window reading, "Living room sofa and chair for sale." We sold things we should have kept and packed away foolish trifles we should have discarded. We sold our refrigerator, our dining room set, two sofas, an easy chair, and a brand new vacuum cleaner with attachments. Without a sensible scheme in our heads, and lacking the practical judgment of my father, the three of us packed frantically and sold recklessly. Although the young people of our church did what they could to help us, we felt desperate as the deadline approached. Our only thought was to get the house emptied in time, for we knew the Army would not wait.

Organizations such as the First Congregational Church of Berkeley were extremely helpful in anticipating the needs of the panic-stricken Japanese and provided immediate, practical assistance. Families of the church offered storage space to those who needed it, and we took several pieces of furniture to be stored in the basement of one such home. Another non-Japanese friend offered to take our books and stored more than eight large cartons for us. In typical Japanese fashion, my mother took gifts to express her gratitude to each person who helped us. . . .

By now I had to leave the university, as did all the other Nisei students. We had stayed as long as we could to get credit for the spring semester, which was crucial for those of us who were seniors. My professors gave me a final grade on the basis of my midterm grades and the university granted all Nisei indefinite leaves of absence.

During the last few weeks on campus, my friends and I became sentimental and took pictures of each other at favorite campus sites. The war had jolted us into a crisis whose impact was too enormous for us to fully comprehend, and we needed these small remembrances of happier times to take with us as we went our separate ways to various government camps throughout California.

A Description of a Camp

Minoru Yasui, a California-born lawyer and U.S. Army reserve officer, refused to report for relocation. He was taken from his home in Oregon, interned with 3,000 other Japanese Americans in Portland for five months, and then transported to the Minidoka camp in Idaho. Abridged

The belongings of relocated Japanese and Japanese-Americans, piled behind the barbed-wire fence at the Salinas Relocation Center. (Courtesy of The Library of Congress.)

from John Tateishi, And Justice for All: An Oral History of the Japanese American Detention Camps *(New York, 1984), 76–77.*

We arrived late afternoon, at some isolated siding in the desert area, north of Twin Falls, although we did not know where we were. No houses were in sight, no trees or anything green— only scrubby sagebrush and an occasional low catcus, and mostly dry, baked earth. There was a slight rise to the north, and one could not see to the horizon.

Baggage was unloaded and piled up next to the road, and Army trucks were rolling in, kicking up huge clouds of dust. People came off the train, were lined up and loaded into the trucks, and went off into the distance. The seats were hard planks, and after riding all day on the train, most were sore and tired.

We had left the dark, dank confines of a livestock barn hoping to breathe the fresh, open air. But because the virgin desert had been bulldozed and disturbed by men and machinery, instead of

Excerpts reprinted from *And Justice for All: An Oral History of the Japanese American Detention Camps* by John Tateishi, published by Random House, 1984. Copyright © 1984 by John Tateishi.

fresh air, we got to breathe dust. I remember groups of women getting off the train, looking bewildered. After the lush greenness of the Willamette Valley, to see the sterile, dusty desert which was to be our home "for the duration," many sat on the baggage in the middle of nowhere and wept. . . .

We saw again the barbed-wire fences, the watchtowers, guard houses, the MP detachments, the administration housing, warehouse areas, and block after block of black, tar-paper barracks, about 120 feet long and about 20 feet wide. I remember that at least the mess halls and kitchens were completed, and that evening we had hot meals, perhaps spam and canned vegetables. The barracks were supplied with army cots with metal springs, and we got padding-filled ticks and a couple of army blankets. There was a potbellied stove, and each block had a coal depot. One bare bulb hung from the center of the room. There were real composition-board ceilings but the walls were unfinished with open two-by-four studs. The floor was wood, and single layered, so one could see the earth below, through the cracks. The smaller units for childless couples were on the end of the building, with two windows on each side, or a total of four windows. There was only one entrance to each unit. No chairs or tables were furnished; however, later the evacuees scrounged scrap lumber and built chairs, tables, bunk beds, dressers, and other things. But only those who were handy with tools could do this. The internee wives with small children were not always able to furnish their rooms comfortably. There was, however, a great deal of sharing and exchange going on.

The Loyalty Questionnaire

In February 1943 the government began to register the people it had relocated to camps. To facilitate the release of those considered loyal and to encourage loyal Japanese Americans to enlist in the armed forces, the government prepared a questionnaire to accompany registration. Question 27 asked Nisei men if they were willing to serve in the armed forces in combat wherever ordered. Question 28 amounted to a loyalty oath— asking respondents to reaffirm allegiance to the United States and renounce allegiance to Japan. In the camps, Japanese Americans divided bitterly about how to respond. In the end about 5,000 refused to take the oath of allegiance and refused to express a willingness to fight for the United States against "any or all" of its enemies, including Japan. Extremists among the refusers worked to foment resistance to American authorities among camp residents, resorting at times to violence and intimidation. The following describes how Frank Chuman, a California-born law student in the Manzanar camp in the California desert, anguished over what to do. Taken from John Tateishi, And Justice for All: An Oral History of the Japanese American Detention Camps, 230–32.

I didn't get the full brunt of the anti-Japanese hostility which was a hell of a good thing, because when I went to Manzanar there was a delayed reaction for me. What the hell am I doing in camp? I thought. While I was very busy working in the hospital, I said to myself, Why should the United States Government doubt our loyalty to the United States? We haven't done anything to justify this kind of treatment. Certainly not myself and certainly none of the others that I know of. And yet here I am in a camp of ten thousand people—men, women, and children. So I began to think to myself, because I had studied law—constitutional law and constitutional rights and due process and equal protection and all the rest of it—Jesus Christ, we've been deprived of our constitutional rights. There's been no accusations against me, and yet I'm suspect and I'm arbitrarily told to go into a camp. It's completely in violation of my rights. . . . And I really got angry and very, very upset at the United States Government for doing this kind of thing to not only me, but all Japanese Americans. I really got upset.

The Army recruiting team came into Manzanar around the early part of 1943. We had a big meeting in this mess hall of all persons eligible for military duty with two white soldiers and a person of Japanese ancestry, and this guy was trying to persuade us all to volunteer for the Army, and I'm not too sure whether I got up and spoke back to him or whether I said it in my own mind, but I said, "Why should we fight for the United States Government as soldiers, when the United States Government distrusts us? Why do they now want us to serve when they consider us to be disloyal? Why do they want us to serve when they have taken us out of our homes and schools and businesses, and now they want us to become loyal to the United States? It doesn't make sense, and so far as I'm concerned I'm not going to do anything to go into the

United States Army until the United States Government does something to remedy this unjust situation." I cannot remember whether I stood up and said it or whether I felt it.

In any event, that's the way it was. In the latter part of 1943, this questionnaire came out sponsored by the WRA, and in that questionnaire it had something like "request for relocation" as well as the questionnaire. It was in two parts. And there were these questions 27 and 28, "Are you willing to foreswear any allegiance to any foreign potentate and say that you are loyal to the United States?" and, "Are you willing to bear arms for the United States?" The first answer that I gave to both questions was no. I was so goddamned mad at that questionnaire. It was insulting, impugning without any evidence, just from the top down that there was something that made us Japanese Americans suspect in loyalty, allegiance, that we wouldn't fight for the government and saying now you're going to fight. They don't have to push it down my throat—are you willing to bear arms to defend the United States? That's so goddamned obvious that I would do that that it just really made me angry. . . .

I did not remain a no-no, because all of a sudden I thought to myself, after I had said that, I regretted it, because it wasn't my true feelings. There was no way that I could hate the United States Government, but I was goddamned angry at them for doing things like that about us.

The Supreme Court Upholds Japanese Relocation: *Korematsu* v. *U.S.* (1944)

Several Japanese Americans resisted the government exclusion orders in order to challenge their constitutionality in the courts. In 1943 the Supreme Court sustained a curfew applying to all people of Japanese ancestry along the Pacific Coast. A year later, to the dismay of civil libertarians, it upheld Executive Order 9066 and the relocation program instituted under its authority. Abridged from Korematsu v. U.S., 323 US 214, (1944), 216, 218–20, 233–34, 240, 242.

Opinion of the Court

It should be noted, to begin with, that all legal restrictions which curtail the civil rights of a single racial group are immediately suspect. That is not to say that all such restrictions are unconstitutional. It is to say that courts must subject them to the most rigid scrutiny. Pressing public necessity may sometimes justify the existence of such restrictions; racial antagonism never can. . . .

. . . [E]xclusion of those of Japanese origin was deemed necessary because of the presence of an unascertained number of disloyal members of the group, most of whom we have no doubt were loyal to this country. It was because we could not reject the finding of the military authorities that it was impossible to bring about an immediate segregation of the disloyal from the loyal that we sustained the validity of the curfew order as applying to the whole group. In the instant case, temporary exclusion of the entire group was rested by the military on the same ground. The judgment that exclusion of the whole group was for the same reason a military imperative answers the contention that the exclusion was in the nature of group punishment based on antagonism to those of Japanese origin. . . .

We uphold the exclusion order as of the time it was made and when the petitioner violated it. . . . In doing so, we are not unmindful of the hardships imposed by it upon a large group of American citizens. . . . Citizenship has its responsibilities as well as its privileges, and in time of war the burden is always heavier. Compulsory exclusion of large groups of citizens from their homes, except under circumstances of direst emergency and peril, is inconsistent with our basic governmental institutions. But when under conditions of modern warfare our shores are threatened by hostile forces, the power to protect must be commensurate with the threatened danger. . . .

Mr. Justice Murphy, dissenting.
This exclusion of "all persons of Japanese ancestry, both alien and non-alien," from the Pacific Coast area on a plea of military necessity in the absence of martial law ought not to be approved. Such exclusion goes over "the very brink of constitutional power" and falls into the ugly abyss of racism. . . .

. . . [I]t is essential that there be definite limits to military discretion, especially where martial law has not been declared.

Individuals must not be left impoverished of their constitutional rights on a plea of military necessity that has neither substance nor support. . . .

. . . No one denies, of course, that there were some disloyal persons of Japanese descent on the Pacific Coast who did all in their power to aid their ancestral land. Similar disloyal activities have been engaged in by many persons of German, Italian and even more pioneer stock in our country. But to infer that examples of individual disloyalty prove group disloyalty and justify discriminatory action against the entire group is to deny that under our system of law individual guilt is the sole basis for deprivation of rights. . . . To give constitutional sanction to that inference in this case, however well intentioned may have been the military command on the Pacific Coast is to adopt one of the cruelest of the rationales used by our enemies to destroy the dignity of the individual and to encourage and open the door to discriminatory actions against other minority groups in the passions of tomorrow. . . .

. . . All residents of this nation are kin in some way by blood or culture to a foreign land. Yet they are primarily and necessarily a part of the new and distinct civilization of the United States. They must accordingly be treated at all times as the heirs of the American experiment and as entitled to all the rights and freedoms guaranteed by the Constitution.

The Government Reinvestigates

In response to agitation by Japanese Americans in the 1970s and renewed public interest in the events surrounding Japanese exclusion and relocation, Congress established a commission to investigate the subject. After taking testimony from those who organized and administered the program, those subjected to it, and historians of it, the Commission concluded that the exclusion and relocation had been unjustified and unjustifiable. It recommended a formal apology and restitution. Excerpted from Personal Justice Denied: Report of the Commission on Wartime Relocation and Internment of Civilians *(Washington, D.C., 1982), 2–3, 18.*

This policy of exclusion, removal and detention was executed against 120,000 people without individual review, and exclusion was continued virtually without regard for their demonstrated loyalty to the United States. Congress was fully aware of and supported the policy of removal and detention; it sanctioned the exclusion by enacting a statue which made criminal the violation of orders issued pursuant to Executive Order 9066. The United States Supreme Court held the exclusion constitutionally permissible in the context of war, but struck down the incarceration of admittedly loyal American citizens on the ground that it was not based on statutory authority.

All this was done despite the fact that not a single documented act of espionage, sabotage or fifth column activity was committed by an American citizen of Japanese ancestry or by a resident Japanese alien on the West Coast.

No mass exclusion or detention, in any part of the country, was ordered against American citizens of German or Italian descent. Official actions against enemy aliens of other nationalities were much more individualized and selective than those imposed on the ethnic Japanese.

The exclusion, removal and detention inflicted tremendous human cost. There was the obvious cost of homes and businesses sold or abandoned under circumstances of great distress, as well as injury to careers and professional advancement. But, most important, there was the loss of liberty and the personal stigma of suspected disloyalty for thousands of people who knew themselves to be devoted to their country's cause and to its ideals but whose repeated protestations of loyalty were discounted—only to be demonstrated beyond any doubt by the record of Nisei solders, who returned from the battlefields of Europe as the most decorated and distinguished combat unit of World War II, and by the thousands of other Nisei who served against the enemy in the Pacific, mostly in military intelligence. The wounds of the exclusion and detention have healed in some respects, but the scars of that experience remain, painfully real in the minds of those who lived through the suffering and deprivation of the camps.

The personal injustice of excluding, removing and detaining loyal American citizens is manifest. Such events are extraordinary and unique in American history. For every citizen and for American public life, they pose haunting questions about our country and its past. . . .

The promulgation of Executive Order 9066 was not justified by military necessity, and the decisions which followed from it—detention, ending detention and ending exclusion—were not driven by analysis of military conditions. The broad historical causes which shaped these decisions were race prejudice, war hysteria and a failure of political leadership. Widespread ignorance of Japanese Americans contributed to a policy conceived in haste and executed in an atmosphere of fear and anger at Japan. A grave injustice was done to American citizens and resident aliens of Japanese ancestry who, without individual review or any probative evidence against them, were excluded, removed and detained by the United States during World War II.

The Civil Liberties Act of 1988

In response to the report of the Commission on Wartime Relocation and Internment of Civilians, on 10 August 1988, Congress passed the Civil Liberties Act of 1988. The act requested the president to issue pardons to those convicted of violating the curfew, exclusion, and relocation orders; authorized restitution in the amount of $20,000 to every person expelled, interned, or relocated; and set up a fund to finance educational programs to inform the public about the expulsion and relocation "so as to prevent the recurrence of any similar event." Taken from U.S. Statutes at Large, *vol. 102, 1988 (1990), 903–4.*

SEC. 2. STATEMENT OF THE CONGRESS.

(a) WITH REGARD TO INDIVIDUALS OF JAPANESE ANCESTRY.—The Congress recognizes that, as described by the Commission on Wartime Relocation and Internment of Civilians, a grave injustice was done to both citizens and permanent resident aliens of Japanese ancestry by the evacuation, relocation, and internment of civilians during World War II. As the Commission documents, these actions were carried out without adequate security reasons and without any acts of espionage or sabotage documented by the Commission, and were motivated largely by racial prejudice, wartime hysteria, and a failure of political leadership. The excluded individuals of Japanese ancestry suffered enormous damages, both material and intangible, and there were incalculable losses in education and job training, all of which resulted in significant human suffering for which appropriate compensation has not been made. For these fundamental violations of the basic civil liberties and constitutional rights of these individuals of Japanese ancestry, the Congress apologizes on behalf of the Nation.

Questions

1. *Many non-Japanese tried to help their Japanese and Japanese American neighbors as they were forced to leave the Pacific Coast. Should they have done more? What more could they have done?*

2. *Should the Nisei have resisted the relocation program more forcefully? What might have inhibited such resistance?*

3. *Why did some of the Japanese and Japanese Americans in the relocation camps refuse to reaffirm their allegiance to the United States and refuse to agree to fight in the armed forces when presented with Questions 27 and 28 of the registration questionnaire in 1943? How would you have answered the questions?*

4. *On what basis did the Supreme Court sustain the constitutionality of Japanese expulsion and relocation in* Korematsu v. U.S.? *On what basis did Justice Murphy disagree? Do you think an occurrence similar to Japanese relocation could take place in a future time of war? Do you think the Supreme Court might intervene?*

5. *Do you think it was appropriate for Congress to apologize formally for the actions taken during World War II? Do you think the formal apology and the Civil Liberties Act might deter similar actions by government in the future? Explain.*

FURTHER READING

Page Smith, Democracy on Trial: The Japanese American Evacuation and Relocation in World War Two *(New York, 1995) is a balanced chronicle of the events leading up to the relocation of the Japanese and their experiences afterwards. Smith argues that perceived military necessity, rather than racism, motivated the government's decision. Roger Daniels takes the opposite view in* Concentration Camps USA: Japanese Americans and World War II *(New York, 1971). In* Justice at War *(New York, 1983), Peter H. Irons also argues that political considerations and the racism of the Pacific coast military leaders overcame the resistance to relocation on the part of some officials of the Roosevelt administration. John Tateishi compiled the remembrances of camp inmates in* And Justice for All: An Oral History of the Japanese American Detention Camps *(New York, 1984).* Righting a Wrong: Japanese Americans and the Passage of the Civil Liberties Act of 1988 *(Stanford, California, 1993), by Leslie T. Hatamiya, tells how crusaders secured compensation and the official apology of the United States government for its treatment of Japanese American citizens during World War II. Lillian Baker trenchantly defends the expulsion and relocation policy in* American and Japanese Relocation in World War II: Fact, Fiction & Fallacy *(Medford, Oregon, 1990).*

The Feminine Mystique and the Organization Man

Leila J. Rupp

INTRODUCTION

Following on the heels of a global war, the decade of the 1950s has gone down in history as a period of prosperity, conformity, domesticity, and suburbanization, perhaps indelibly imprinted on the American imagination as the world of the popular television program "Leave It to Beaver." This was the era of the Cold War, fought beyond the country's borders and flaring up into hot war in Korea; this was the era of McCarthyism, the homefront war against Communist subversion. Threatened from without and within, retreating from the disruptions of war, Americans, according to the standard picture, clung to home and family as a safe haven in a heartless world. Men, taking advantage of the educational benefits of the G.I. Bill, flocked to college and into corporate jobs, giving rise to the image of the "Organization Man," the loyal and conformist white-collar employee. On weekends they barbecued and took up "do-it yourself" projects in their suburban ranch houses. Women stayed home in the expanding suburbs, raising a larger number of children, drinking coffee with their neighbors, and acting out the societal ideal of familial "togetherness." For the outsized Baby Boom generation, born between the end of the Second World War and the early 1960s, and even for the generations that have followed, the 1950s have come to represent normality and tradition, even though the decade's family roles were in fact more aberrant than typical in the context of American history.

But there is another side to the 1950s, one that historians are just beginning to explore. The dream-come-true of life in the suburbs was in reach of only a portion of the population, and a variety of developments spoke to the quite different experience of diverse groups. Most obviously, the decade witnessed the resurgence of the Civil Rights movement, despite the McCarthyite threat to any kind of collective protest against the social order. African American men and women organized their communities and launched massive protests against segregation and discrimination, and white progressives began to join the battle. The first legal victories—most notably the 1954 Brown v. Board of Education *Supreme Court decision declaring segregated schools unconstitutional—came to fruition in the 1950s. In the West, Mexican American working-class women and men also took up civic activism on the local level, setting the stage for the national Chicano/a movement of the 1970s. Within the beleaguered union movement, in the peace movement, in the remnants of the women's movement, in the vilified Communist Party, individuals fought for social change despite the proclaimed contentment of the era.*

Belying the image of domesticity, the 1950s also witnessed the growth of the female labor force, including married middle-class women who swelled the ranks of women workers and quietly countered the assumption that all women were housewives. More directly, unwed mothers, participants in the growing lesbian and gay subcultures, and the cultural radicals known as the "Beats" rebelled against the conformity embodied in the idea of the organization man and the "feminine mystique," the ideal of complete fulfillment for women through marriage, motherhood, and domesticity.

On the basis of recent historical work, the old image of contentment and domesticity, a decidedly white and middle-class image that did not even apply to that limited group in American society, has been forever fractured. Diverse groups—from Chinese immigrants in urban areas to African American professional women to gay male government employees—experienced the fifties in profoundly different ways. Like other decades, the 1950s can be seen as more complex than we previously imagined.

This new recognition that a great deal was going on beneath the surface calm makes the explosive decade of the 1960s more comprehensible. Why, we might have asked, if these were "Happy

Days," did they end in an upsurge of social movement activism—among African Americans, women, students, lesbians and gay men, Mexican Americans—that shook the very base of American society? We can see now that the tensions and contradictions of the 1950s nurtured the roots of such social protest movements.

THE HAPPY HOUSEWIFE AND THE MAN IN THE GRAY FLANNEL SUIT

The following excerpts are from two classic and emormously influential works on the 1950s: Betty Friedan's The Feminine Mystique, *published in 1963, and William H. Whyte, Jr.'s* The Organization Man, *which appeared in 1956. These books present the analyses of women's and men's lives that are only now under revision by historians.*

Betty Friedan's bestseller is often credited with launching the contemporary wave of the women's movement by calling attention to what she calls "the problem that has no name," that is, the pervasive discontent of white, middle-class, suburban housewives, the most privileged women in American society. She attributes women's dissatisfaction to the limitations of traditional femininity attached to the housewife role and blames the writers and editors of mass circulation women's magazines, as well as educators, psychologists, and other social scientists, for perpetuating what she calls the feminine mystique. In the excerpt reproduced here, Friedan connects the portrayal of women in women's magazines to the demands of the capitalist system, targeting advertisers and motivational researchers as the men responsible for the portrayal of the "Happy Housewife Heroine."

William H. Whyte, Jr., a sociologist, bestowed the term "the Organization Man" on the conformist male ideal of the 1950s. Whyte explores the ideology associated with the concentration of economic power in large corporations and of political power in civil service bureaucracies, lamenting the decline of competitive capitalism and rugged individualism associated with the Protestant Ethic. In its place he finds a new "Social Ethic" of conformity, collectivization, and "team work."

In the second excerpt reproduced here, Whyte discusses the impact of the new ethic on college seniors in the 1950s, on the brink of donning their gray flannel suits and joining the world of the organization.

"The Sexual Sell"

Betty Friedan played a leading role in the resurgence of the women's movement in the mid-1960s, serving as the first president of the National Organization for Women, founded in 1966. This excerpt comes from her The Feminine Mystique *(New York, 1963), 197–201, 203-4, 217–18.*

There are certain facts of life so obvious and mundane that one never talks about them. . . . Why is it never said that the really crucial function, the really important role that women serve as housewives is *to buy more things for the house.* In all the talk of femininity and woman's role, one forgets that the real business of America is business. But the perpetuation of housewifery, the growth of the feminine mystique, makes sense (and dollars) when one realizes that women are the chief customers of American business. Somehow, somewhere, someone must have figured out that women will buy more things if they are kept in the underused, nameless-yearning, energy-to-get-rid-of state of being housewives. . . .

It is easy to see why it [the perpetuation of traditional femininity] happened. I learned *how* it happened when I went to see a man who is paid approximately a million dollars a year for his professional services in manipulating the emotions of American women to serve the needs of business. This particular man got in on the ground floor of the hidden-persuasion business in 1945, and kept going. The headquarters of his institute for motivational manipulation is a baronial mansion in upper Westchester. The walls of a ballroom two-stories high are filled with steel shelves holding a thousand-odd studies for business and industry, 300,000 individual "depth interviews," mostly with American housewives.

He let me see what I wanted, said I could use anything that was not confidential to a specific company. Nothing there for anyone to hide, to feel guilty about—only, in page after page of those depth studies, a shrewd cheerful awareness of the empty, purposeless, uncreative, even sexually joyless lives that most

American housewives lead. In his own unabashed terms, this most helpful of hidden persuaders showed me the function served by keeping American women housewives—the reservoir that their lack of identity, lack of purpose, creates, to be manipulated into dollars at the point of purchase.

Properly manipulated ("if you are not afraid of that word," he said), American housewives can be given the sense of identity, purpose, creativity, the self-realization, even the sexual joy they lack—by the buying of things. I suddenly realized the significance of the boast that women wield seventy-five per cent of the purchasing power in America. I suddenly saw American women as *victims* of that ghastly gift, that power at the point of purchase. The insights he shared with me so liberally revealed many things. . . .

The dilemma of business was spelled out in a survey made in 1945 for the publisher of a leading women's magazine on the attitudes of women toward electrical appliances. The message was considered of interest to all the companies that, with the war about to end, were going to have to make consumer sales take the place of war contracts. It was a study of "the psychology of housekeeping"; "a woman's attitude toward housekeeping appliances cannot be separated from her attitude toward homemaking in general," it warned.

On the basis of a national sample of 4,500 wives (middle-class, high-school or college-educated), American women were divided into three categories: "The True Housewife Type," "The Career Woman," and "The Balanced Homemaker." While 51 per cent of the women then fitted "The True Housewife Type" ("From the psychological point of view, housekeeping is this woman's dominating interest. She takes the utmost pride and satisfaction in maintaining a comfortable and well-run home for her family. Consciously or subconsciously, she feels that she is indispensable and that no one else can take over her job. She has little, if any, desire for a position outside the home, and if she has one it is through force or circumstances or necessity"), it was apparent that this group was diminishing, and probably would continue to do so as new fields, interests, education were now open to women.

The largest market for appliances, however, was this "True Housewife"—though she had a certain "reluctance" to accept new devices that had to be recognized and overcome. ("She may even fear that they [appliances] will render unnecessary the old-fashioned way of doing things that has always suited her.") After

A typical white suburban family gathered around the television set—the ideal image of contentment and domesticity in the 1950s.

all, housework was the justification for her whole existence. ("I don't think there is any way to make housework easier for myself," one True Housewife said, "because I don't believe that a machine can take the place of hard work.")

The second type—The Career Woman or Would-Be Career Woman—was a minority, but an extremely "unhealthy" one from the sellers' standpoint; advertisers were warned that it would be to their advantage not to let this group get any larger. For such women, though not necessarily job-holders, "do not believe that a woman's place is primarily in the home." ("Many in this group have never actually worked, but their attitude is: 'I think house-keeping is a horrible waste of time. If my youngsters were old enough and I were free to leave the house, I would use my time to better advantage. If my family's meals and laundry could be taken care of, I would be delighted to go out and get a job.' ") The point to bear in mind regarding career women, the study said, is that, while they buy modern appliances, they are not the ideal type of customer. *They are too critical.*

The third type—"The Balanced Homemaker"—is "from the market standpoint, the ideal type." She has some outside interests, or has held a job before turning exclusively to homemaking; she "readily accepts" the help mechanical appliances can give— but "does not expect them to do the impossible" because she needs to use her own executive ability "in managing a well-run household."

The moral of the study was explicit: "Since the Balanced Homemaker represents the market with the greatest future potential, it would be to the advantage of the applicance manufacturer to make more and more women aware of the desirabilty of belonging to this group. Educate them through advertising that it is possible to have outside interests and become alert to wider intellectual influences (without becoming a Career Woman). The art of good homemaking should be the goal of every normal woman." . . .

By the mid-fifties, the surveys reported with pleasure that the Career Woman ("the woman who clamored for equality—almost for identity in every sphere of life, the woman who reacted to 'domestic slavery' with indignation and vehemence") was gone, replaced by the "less worldly, less sophisticated" woman whose activity in PTA gives her "broad contacts with the world outside her home," but who "finds in housework a medium of expression for her femininity and individuality." She's not like the old-fashioned self-sacrificing housewife; she considers herself the equal of man. But she still feels "lazy, neglectful, haunted by guilt feelings" because she doesn't have enough work to do. The advertiser must manipulate her need for a "feeling of creativeness" into the buying of his product.

> After an initial resistance, she now tends to accept instant coffee, frozen foods, precooked foods, and labor-saving items as part of her routine. But she needs a justification and she finds it in the thought that "by using frozen foods I'm freeing myself to accomplish other important tasks as a modern mother and wife."
>
> Creativeness is the modern woman's dialectical answer to the problem of her changed position in the household. Thesis: I'm a housewife. Antithesis: I hate drudgery. Synthesis: I'm creative!
>
> This means essentially that even though the housewife may buy canned food, for instance, and thus save

time and effort, she doesn't let it go at that. She has a great need for "doctoring up" the can and thus prove her personal participation and her concern with giving satisfaction to her family.

The feeling of creativeness also serves another purpose: it is an outlet for the liberated talents, the better taste, the freer imagination, the greater initiative of the modern woman. It permits her to use at home *all the faculties that she would display in an outside career.*

The yearning for creative opportunities and moments is a major aspect of buying motivations. . . .

One day, having immersed myself in the varied insights these reports have been giving American advertisers for the last fifteen years, I was invited to have lunch with the man who runs this motivational research operation. He had been so helpful in showing me the commercial forces behind the feminine mystique, perhaps I could be helpful to him. Naively I asked why, since he found it so difficult to give women a true feeling of creativeness and achievement in housework, and tried to assuage their guilt and disillusion and frustrations by getting them to buy more "things"—why didn't he encourage them to buy things for all they were worth, so they would have time to get out of the home and pursue truly creative goals in the outside world.

"But we have helped her rediscover the home as the expression of her creativeness," he said. "We help her think of the modern home as the artist's studio, the scientist's laboratory. Besides," he shrugged, "most of the manufacturers we deal with are producing things which have to do with homemaking."

"In a free enterprise economy," he went on, "we have to develop the need for new products. And to do that we have to liberate women to desire these new products. We help them rediscover that homemaking is more creative than to compete with men. This can be manipulated. We sell them what they ought to want, speed up the unconscious, move it along. The big problem is to liberate the woman not to be afraid of what is going to happen to her, if she doesn't have to spend so much time cooking, cleaning."

"That's what I mean," I said. "Why doesn't the pie-mix ad tell the woman she could use the time saved to be an astronomer?"

"It wouldn't be too difficult," he replied. "A few images—the astronomer gets her man, the astronomer as the heroine, make it glamorous for a woman to be an astronomer . . . but no," he shrugged again. "The client would be too frightened. He wants to sell pie mix. The woman has to want to stay in the kitchen. The manufacturer wants to intrigue her back into the kitchen—and we show him how to do it the right way. If he tells her that all she can be is a wife and mother, she will spit in his face. But we show him how to tell her that it's creative to be in the kitchen. We liberate her need to be creative in the kitchen. If we tell her to be an astronomer, she might go too far from the kitchen. Besides," he added, "if you wanted to have a campaign to liberate women to be astronomers, you'd have to find somebody like the National Education Association to pay for it."

"A Generation of Bureaucrats"

This excerpt comes from William H. Whyte, Jr.'s The Organization Man *(New York, 1956), 63–68, 70–71.*

When I was a college senior in 1939, we used to sing a plaintive song about going out into the "cold, cold world." It wasn't really so very cold then, but we did enjoy meditating on the fraughtness of it all. It was a big break we were facing, we told ourselves, and those of us who were going to try our luck in the commercial world could be patronizing toward those who were going on to graduate work or academic life. We were taking the leap.

Seniors still sing the song, but somehow the old note of portent is gone. There is no leap left to take. The union between the world of organization and the college has been so cemented that today's seniors can see a continuity between the college and the life thereafter that we never did. Come graduation, they do not go outside to a hostile world; they transfer.

For the senior who is headed for the corporation it is almost as if it were part of one master scheme. The locale shifts; the training continues, for at the same time that the colleges have been changing their curriculum to suit the corporation, the corporation has responded by setting up its own campuses and classrooms. By now the two have been so well molded that it's difficult to tell where one leaves off and the other begins.

The descent, every spring, of the corporations' recruiters has now become a built-in feature of campus life. If the college is large and its placement director efficient, the processing operation is visibly impressive. I have never been able to erase from my mind the memory of an ordinary day at Purdue's placement center. It is probably the largest and most effective placement operation in the country, yet, much as in a well-run group clinic, there seemed hardly any activity. In the main room some students were quietly studying company literature arranged on the tables for them; others were checking the interview timetables to find what recruiter they would see and to which cubicle he was assigned; at the central filing desk college employees were sorting the hundreds of names of men who had registered for placement. Except for a murmur from the row of cubicles there was little to indicate that scores of young men were, every hour on the half hour, making the decisions that would determine their whole future life.

Someone from a less organized era might conclude that the standardization of this machinery—and the standardized future it portends—would repel students. It does not. For the median senior this is the optimum future; it meshes so closely with his own aspirations that it is almost as if the corporation was planned in response to an attitude poll.

Because they are the largest single group, the corporation-bound seniors are the most visible manifestation of their generation's values. But in essentials their contemporaries headed for other occupations respond to the same urges. The lawyers, the doctors, the scientists—their occupations are also subject to the same centralization, the same trend to group work and to bureaucratization. And so are the young men who will enter them. Whatever their many differences, in one great respect they are all of a piece: more than any generation in memory, theirs will be a generation of bureaucrats.

They are, above all, conservative. Their inclination to accept the status quo does not necessarily mean that in the historic sweep of ideas they are conservative—in the more classical sense of conservatism, it could be argued that the seniors will be, in effect if not by design, agents of revolution. But this is a matter we must leave to later historians. For the immediate present, at any rate, what ideological ferment college men exhibit is not in the direction of basic change.

This shows most clearly in their attitude toward politics. It used to be axiomatic that young men moved to the left end of the spectrum in revolt against their fathers and then, as the years went on, moved slowly to the right. A lot of people still believe this is true, and many businessmen fear that twenty years of the New Deal hopelessly corrupted our youth into radicalism. After the election of 1952 businessmen became somewhat more cheerful, but many are still apprehensive, and whenever a poll indicates that students don't realize that business makes only about 6 per cent profit, there is a flurry of demands for some new crusade to rescue our youth from socialistic tendencies.

If the seniors do any moving, however, it will be from dead center. Liberal groups have almost disappeared from the campus, and what few remain are anemic. There has been no noticeable activity at the other end of the spectrum either. When William Buckley, Jr., produced *God and Man at Yale,* some people thought this signaled the emergence of a strong right-wing movement among the young men. The militancy, however, has not proved particularly contagious; when the McCarthy issue roused and divided their elders, undergraduates seemed somewhat bored with it all.

Their conservatism is passive. No cause seizes them, and nothing so exuberant or willfully iconoclastic as the Veterans of Future Wars has reappeared. There are Democrats and Republicans, and at election time there is the usual flurry of rallies, but in comparison with the agitation of the thirties no one seems to care too much one way or the other. There has been personal unrest— the suspense over the prospect of military service assures this— but it rarely gets resolved into a thought-out protest. Come spring and students may start whacking each other over the head or roughing up the townees and thereby cause a rush of concern over the wild younger generation. But there is no real revolution in them, and the next day they likely as not will be found with their feet firmly on the ground in the recruiters' cubicles.

Some observers attribute the disinterest to fear. I heard one instructor tell his colleagues that in his politics classes he warned students to keep their noses clean. "I tell them," he said, "that they'd better realize that what they say might be held against them, especially when we get to the part about Marx and Engels. Someday in the future they might find their comments bounced back at them in an investigation."

The advice, as his colleagues retorted, was outrageously unnecessary. The last thing students can be accused of now is dangerous discussion; they are not interested in the kind of big questions that stimulate heresy and whatever the subject—the corporation, government, religion—students grow restive if the talk tarries on the philosophical. Most are interested in the philosophical only to the extent of finding out what the accepted view is in order that they may accept it and get on to the practical matters. This spares the bystander from the lofty bulling and the elaborate pose of unorthodoxy that my contemporaries often used to affect, but it does make for a rather stringent utilitarianism. . . .

In judging a college generation, one usually bases his judgment on how much it varies from one's own, and presumably superior, class, and I must confess that I find myself tempted to do so. Yet I do not think my generation has any license to damn the acquiescence of seniors as a weakening of intellectual fiber. It is easy for us to forget that if earlier generations were less content with society, there was a great deal less to be contented about. In the intervening years the economy has changed enormously, and even in retrospect the senior can hardly be expected to share former discontents. Society is not out of joint for him, and if he acquiesces it is not out of fear that he does so. He does not want to rebel against the status quo because he really likes it—and his elders, it might be added, are not suggesting anything bold and new to rebel *for*.

Perhaps contemporaryism would be a better word than conservatism to describe their posture. The present, more than the past, is their model; while they share the characteristic American faith in the future also, they see it as more of same. As they paraphrase what they are now reading about America, they argue that at last we have got it. The big questions are all settled; we know the direction, and while many minor details remain to be cleared up, we can be pretty sure of enjoying a wonderful upward rise. . . .

The urge to be a technician, a collaborator, shows most markedly in the kind of jobs seniors prefer. They want to work for somebody else. Paradoxically, the old dream of independence through a business of one's own is held almost exclusively by factory workers—the one group, as a number of sociologists have reported, least able to fulfill it. Even at the bull-session level college seniors do not affect it, and when recruiting time comes around they make the preference clear. Consistently, placement officers find that of the men who intend to go into business—roughly one half of the class—less than 5 per cent express any desire to be an entrepreneur. About 15 to 20 per cent plan to go into their fathers' business. Of the rest, most have one simple goal: the big corporation. . . .

In turning their back on the Protestant Ethic they are consistent; if they do not cherish venture, neither do they cherish what in our lore was its historic reward. They are without avarice. . . .

. . . One recruiter went through three hundred interviews without one senior's mentioning salary, and the experience is not unusual. Indeed, sometimes seniors react as if a large income and security were antithetical. . . .

In popular fiction . . . heroes aren't any less materialistic than they used to be, but they are decidedly more sanctimonious about it. So with seniors. While they talk little about money, they talk a great deal about the good life. This life is, first of all, calm and ordered. Many a senior confesses that he's thought of a career in teaching, but as he talks it appears that it is not so much that he likes teaching itself as the sort of life he associates with it—there is a touch of elms and quiet streets in the picture. For the good life is equable; it is a nice place out in the suburbs, a wife and three children, one, maybe two cars (you know, a little knock-about for the wife to run down to the station in), and a summer place up at the lake or out on the Cape, and, later, a good college education for the children. It is not, seniors explain, the money that counts.

Questions

1. *In what ways are Friedan's and Whyte's analyses linked to the stage of economic development of the U.S. in the 1950s?*
2. *What assumptions about human agency—about people's ability to determine their own destiny—underlie these analyses?*
3. *How might a broader vision of the diversity of American society challenge these interpretations?*
4. *How have images of and ideals for women and men changed since the 1950s?*

RETHINKING THE FEMININE MYSTIQUE AND THE ORGANIZATION MAN

The following essays challenge the notion that American popular culture in the 1950s set forth a monolithic vision of the Happy Housewife married to the conformist Organization Man. Joanne Meyerowitz goes beyond the argument that the "feminine mystique" did not correspond to the reality of most women. She takes issue directly with the widely accepted notion, expounded by Betty Friedan in her classic work, The Feminine Mystique, *that the popular ideology made no place for women in the labor force or politics. Systematically sampling the mass-circulation monthlies published in the period from 1946 to 1958, ranging from "highbrow" to "middlebrow" to African American to women's magazines, she presents the middle-class popular discourse on women as more varied than we have traditionally assumed. The enormous popularity of Friedan's 1963 analysis, which emphasized the pervasive discontent of women subjected to the feminine mystique, can be understood, Meyerowitz argues, as a response to the articulation of themes already present in the popular culture.*

The second essay in this section reinterprets the image of the Organization Man. Barbara Ehrenreich sees the 1950s as the beginning of a "male revolt" against the breadwinner ethic—against the expectation that adult men would marry, buy a home, and support their wives. Despite the emphasis on maturity and adult responsibility in such famous novels as The Man in the Gray Flannel Suit *and* Marjorie Morningstar, *Ehrenreich finds evidence in the popular culture for an alternative ideal of the male rebel. Sociologist David Riesman, author of* The Lonely Crowd *(1950), distinguished the old-fashioned "inner-directed" person from the new conformist "outer-directed" one. Like other social scientists and novelists, he associated conformity with the*

*emasculation of men and thus championed revolt against the expecta-
tions of the male role. In his criticism of the organization man, sociologist
William Whyte also qualifies as part of the male revolt.*

Beyond the Feminine Mystique:
A Reassessment of
Postwar Mass Culture, 1946–1958

---

*This essay is taken from Joanne Meyerowitz, "Beyond the Feminine
Mystique: A Reassessment of Postwar Mass Culture, 1946–1958,"*
Journal of American History *79, (March 1993): 1465–74.*

The postwar popular discourse on women . . . did not simply
exhort women to stay at home. Its complexity is . . . seen in the
articles that addressed questions of gender directly. The topics of
those articles ranged from women in India to premenstrual tension, but most fell into four broad categories: women's paid work,
women's political activism, marriage and domesticity, and glamour and sexuality. Most of these articles did not pose profound
challenges to the variegated oppression of women. But they do
differ significantly from most historical descriptions of a postwar
domestic ideology. The articles in this sample reveal ambivalence
and contradictions in postwar mass culture, which included a
celebration of nondomestic as well as domestic pursuits and a
tension between individual achievement and domestic ideals.

On the issue of paid employment, there was rough consensus.
Despite concerns for the postwar economy, journalists in this
sample consistently defended wage work for women. Articles
insisted that women, including married women, worked for
wages because they needed money. One early article, published in
1946, spelled this out in its opening lines: "Most American working women need their jobs. That's the stark and simple reason
why hiring and firing policies arbitrarily based on sex discrimina-

---

tion don't make sense." By the 1950s, arguments for wage work often included the personal "satisfaction" jobs offered as well as the economic benefits. These articles generally advocated part-time as well as full-time work, and they often stressed the opportunities available to older women. According to one such article, "a part-time job can bring a feeling of full-time usefulness and satisfaction." . . .

Beneath the consensus, though, a quiet debate exposed the tensions between the ideals of nondomestic achievement and of domestic duty. Echoing earlier debates of the 1920s, some authors advised women to subordinate careers to home and motherhood while others invited women to pursue public success. The question of careers was rarely discussed at any length, and the relative silence itself underscores how postwar popular magazines often avoided contended issues. But throwaway lines in various articles sometimes landed on one side of the debate or the other. In a single article in *Ebony*, for example, one unmarried career woman warned readers, "Don't sacrifice marriage for career," while another stated, "I like my life just as it is." Another article, "Profile of Success," published in the *Ladies' Home Journal* in 1946, captured the ambivalence in postwar discourse. The bulk of the article celebrated the achievements of career women, "the cream of the working-woman population," and analyzed the ingredients of their success. But toward the end of the article two paragraphs questioned whether a married career woman had time enough for her husband and children. The article concluded more positively: "In moments of weakness the woman at the top eyes with envy the occasional leisure of the housewife . . . the joys of total family life. The moment passes. . . . She knows what she wants, after all—and she wants what she has." . . .

The postwar popular magazines were more unequivocally positive on increased participation of women in politics. The *Ladies' Home Journal*, not known for its feminist sympathies, led the way with numerous articles that supported women as political and community leaders. In 1947, lawyer and longtime activist Margaret Hickey, former president of the National Federation of Business and Professional Women's Clubs, launched the *Journal's* monthly "Public Affairs Department," which encouraged women's participation in mainstream politics and reform. In one article, Hickey stated bluntly, "Make politics your business. Voting, office holding, raising your voice for new and better laws are just as important to your home and your family as the evening meal or spring house cleaning." Like earlier Progressive reformers, Hickey sometimes justified nondomestic political action by its benefits to home and family, but her overall message was clear: women should participate outside the home, and not just by voting. . . .

Historians sometimes contend that the Cold War mentality encouraged domesticity, that it envisioned family life and especially mothers as buffers against the alleged Communist threat. But Cold War rhetoric had other possible meanings for women. In the *Ladies' Home Journal,* authors often used the Cold War to promote women's political participation. One such approach contrasted "free society" of the United States with Soviet oppression, including oppression of women. [Dorothy] Thompson condemned the Soviet Union not only because women there worked as "beasts of burden" in menial jobs but also because they held no positions of political leadership. Other articles stressed that Soviet citizens, male and female, did not participate in a democratic process. American women could prove the strength of democracy by avoiding "citizen apathy," by "giving the world a lively demonstration of how a free society can serve its citizens," by making "free government work well as an example for the undecided and unsatisfied millions elsewhere in the world." Sen. Margaret Chase Smith made the case most strongly: "The way to reverse this socialistic, dictatorial trend and put more *home* in the Government is for you women, the traditional homemakers, to become more active in your Government." In this line of argument, the Cold War made women's political participation an international obligation.

In general, then, popular magazines incorporated women's public participation as part of a positive image of the modern American woman in the postwar world. In an article on women in the Soviet Union, John Steinbeck defended the American woman: "[The Russians] had an idea that in America we have only overdressed, neurotic, kept women. . . . It had not occurred to them that we have farms and factories, and offices, too, and that our women also help to run our country."

The popular literature generally gave facile support to women in a variety of activities. A celebratory photo essay in *Coronet* magazine in 1948, titled "The American Woman," presented a graphic depiction of the dominant view. The photographs ran from childhood to old age with laudatory comments at every stage of the life cycle. The photos of adulthood began with six pictures of women at work, including a young salesclerk, an elderly worker in light industry, and a middle-aged judge on her bench. A caption claimed, "The challenge of a career is irresistible." The essay proceeded with five pictures of brides and mothers. The captions here waxed more sentimental: "Proudest of all American women are those who know the joys of motherhood . . . For in motherhood alone are all [their] girlhood dreams fulfilled." The section on adulthood continued with two more photos of middle-aged women involved in community activism. The captions said, "her desire to be useful beyond the home keep[s] her active and vital . . . [in] the building of democracy in religious, political, and charitable movements." Such stories do not imply that postwar popular magazines condemned or disparaged domesticity. To the contrary, marriage and motherhood stood strategically at the literal and emotional center, yet wage work and political activism also won resolute praise.

Despite the support for marriage and motherhood, the role of the housewife and mother was problematic in the postwar popular discourse. On the one hand, all of the magazines assumed that women wanted to marry, that women found being wives and mothers rewarding, and that women would and should be the primary parents and housekeepers. In the midst of the baby boom, some articles glorified the housewife, sometimes in conscious attempts to bolster her self-esteem. On the other hand, throughout the postwar era, numerous articles portrayed domesticity itself as exhausting and isolating, and frustrated mothers as overdoting and smothering. Such articles hardly glorified domesticity. They provided their postwar readers with ample references to housewife's discontent. . . .

In the postwar magazines, marriage also presented problems. Although journalists expected most women to marry, they portrayed the search for a husband as a potentially troubling task. An article in *Ebony* stated, "Most women would rather be married than single but there are many who would rather remain single than be tied to the wrong man." The magazines gave readers contrasting advice on how to find a good husband. One article told women, "Don't fear being aggressive!," while another considered "aggressive traits" as "handicaps . . . in attracting a husband." Within marriage as well, journalists seemed to anticipate constant problems, including immaturity, incompatibility, and infidelity. They saw divorce as a difficult last resort and often advised both husbands and wives to communicate and adjust. . . .

. . . [T]he postwar popular literature generally did not offer any serious challenge to marriage or to the sexual division of labor in the home. . . .

The postwar magazines seemed least willing to entertain alternatives in the area of sexuality. As Friedan argued, popular magazines emphasized glamour and allure, at least for young women, and as [historian] Elaine Tyler May has elaborated, they tried to domesticate sexual intercourse by containing it within marriage. Magazines presented carefully framed articles with explicit directives about appropriate behavior. Young women were to make themselves attractive to men, and married women were to engage in mutually pleasing sexual intercourse with their mates. Articles presented "normal" sex through voyeuristic discussion of sexual problems, such as pregnancy before marriage and frigidity after. Other forms of sexual expression were rarely broached, although one article in *Ebony* did condemn "lesbians and nymphomaniacs" in the Women's Army Corps.

While all of the magazines endorsed a manicured version of heterosexual appeal, the African-American magazines displayed it most heartily. This may have reflected African-American vernacular traditions, such as the blues, that rejected white middle-class injunctions against public sexual expression. But it also reflected an editorial decision to construct glamour and beauty as political issues in the fight against racism. Articles admired black women's sex appeal in a self-conscious defiance of racist white standards of beauty. In this context what some feminists today might read as sexual "objectification" presented itself as racial advancement, according black womanhood equal treatment with white. Thus, *Ebony*, which in most respects resembled a white family magazine like *Life*, also included some of the mildly risqué cheesecake seen in white men's magazines like *Esquire*. One editorial explained: "Because we live in a society in which standards of physical beauty are most often circumscribed by a static concept of whiteness of skin and blondness of hair, there is an aching need for someone to shout from the housetops that black women are beautiful." . . .

Still, despite the magazines' endorsement of feminine beauty and heterosexual allure, Friedan's polemical claim that "American women have been successfully reduced to sex creatures" seems unabashedly hyperbolic. Try as they might, popular magazines could not entirely dictate the responses of readers. In most cases, we have little way of knowing how readers responded to magazine articles, but in the case of sex appeal we have explicit letters of dissent. In the African-American magazines, some readers, women and men both, objected to the photos of semiclad women. One woman complained that the "so-called beauties" were "really a disgrace to all women." And another protested "those girl covers and the . . . so-called realism (just a cover up name for cheapness, coarseness, lewdness, profanity and irreverence)."

In *Ladies' Home Journal,* too, readers responded with rare indignation to one article on sex appeal. In the offending article, "How to Be Loved," movie star Marlene Dietrich lectured housewives on enhancing their allure. Dietrich linked appeal to unadorned self-subordination. "To be completely a woman," she wrote, "you need a master." She advised women to plan their clothes, their conversation, and their meals to please their husbands. After washing their dishes, "like Phoenix out of the ashes," women should emerge "utterly desirable." And they should not grumble. "Some women," Dietrich proclaimed, "could do with a bit of spanking to answer their complaining." The article evoked what the *Journal*'s editors called an "intense" response. Sarcastic letter writers objected to Dietrich's call for servile pampering of men and "utterly desirable" behavior. As one writer stated, "How *could* you hand the American woman such an article?" The letter writers portrayed themselves as down-home and unglamorous housewives, "all straight-haired and plain," who could not and would not emulate Dietrich's version of sexual allure. One woman wrote: "I resemble Eleanor Roosevelt more than I do La Dietrich, so that alters the visual effect." Another writer proclaimed: "Pish, tosh and hooey! Could be that Marlene could emerge from a stack of dirty dishes . . . and still be glamorous and desirable, but the housewife and mother I know gets dishpan hands and another twinge in the old back. . . . Marlene should talk about something she understands." For these women, marriage was a working partnership. Their husbands, they claimed, helped with the housework, accepted their scolding, and respected their "whims and fatigue." "Out here where I live," one woman wrote, "reasonably intelligent [married couples] . . . learn to live and work together." These readers used their domestic identities as hardworking housewives, not to berate women of public achievement, but to reject a competing image of women as subservient sexual bait.

A handful of letters, written by only a few readers, scarcely begins to suggest the range of responses that women probably had when reading the magazines. The frequent articles on work, politics, domesticity, and sexuality may have encouraged some women to take pride in, long for, or emulate magazine versions of public participation, home life, or glamour. At the same time, the flood of competing images—of housewives, workers, politicians, and sex bombs—may have inundated women who could not possibly identify with or remake themselves in all of the proffered models.

The response to one article suggests that readers may have chosen among alternative versions of womanhood, appropriating the images that rang true or appealed to them and rejecting the others. In this set of letters, some housewives accepted the "plight of the young mother" as a true description of their experience. They appreciated an article that validated their sense of domestic discontent. For these women, the article was a "morale lifter." "I have no words to tell what it means," one woman wrote, "to have all the facets of housewifery (that seemed to have sprung from my own deficiencies) held up as situations of national import." Other women rejected the article as a "very unfair picture." They resented an article that depicted them as overworked victims who could not cope with their housework. "Oh, for pity's sake," one woman asked, "What old plight am I in that no one has told me about? . . . I have four children . . . and I don't put in a forty-hour week. . . . I think it's a great life." In short, both readers and articles were varied enough and ambivalent enough to enable more than one possible reading.

Playboy Joins the Battle of the Sexes

In the excerpt reproduced here, Ehrenreich focuses on the male revolt as embodied in the Playboy ideal. Men's rejection of responsibility and domesticity—whether as playboys or Beats—culminated, Ehrenreich argues, in the transformation of expectations for men in the 1970s and 1980s. Men, rather than women, she argues, were the first to rebel against their traditional roles, and thus the male revolt, rather than feminism, brought about the antifeminist backlash of the 1980s.

This excerpt comes from Barbara Ehrenreich, The Hearts of Men: American Dreams and the Flight from Commitment *(Garden City, New York, 1983), 42–51.*

The first issue of *Playboy* hit the stands in December 1953. The first centerfold—the famous nude calendar shot of Marilyn Monroe—is already legendary. Less memorable, but no less prophetic of things to come, was the first feature article in the issue. It was a no-holds-barred attack on "the whole concept of alimony," and secondarily, on money-hungry women in general, entitled "Miss Gold-Digger of 1953." From the beginning, *Playboy* loved women—large-breasted, long-legged young women, anyway—and hated wives.

The "Miss Gold-Digger" article made its author a millionaire—not because Hugh Hefner paid him so much but because Hefner could not, at first, afford to pay him at all, at least not in cash. The writer, Burt Zollo (he signed the article "Bob Norman"; even Hefner didn't risk putting his own name in the first issue), had to accept stock in the new magazine in lieu of a fee. The first print run of 70,000 nearly sold out and the magazine passed the one-million mark in 1956, making Hefner and his initial associates millionaires before the end of the decade.

But *Playboy* was more than a publishing phenomenon, it was like the party organ of a diffuse and swelling movement. Writer Myron Brenton called it the "Bible of the beleaguered male." . . . The magazine encouraged the sense of membership in a fraternity of male rebels. After its first reader survey, *Playboy* reported on the marital status of its constituency in the following words: "Approximately half of PLAYBOY'S readers (46.8%) are free men and the other half are free in spirit only."

In the ongoing battle of the sexes, the *Playboy* office in Chicago quickly became the male side's headquarters for wartime propaganda. Unlike the general-audience magazines that dominated fifties' newsstands—*Life, Time,* the *Saturday Evening Post, Look,* etc.—*Playboy* didn't worry about pleasing women readers. The first editorial, penned by Hefner himself, warned:

> We want to make clear from the very start, we aren't a "family magazine." If you're somebody's sister, wife or mother-in-law and picked us up by mistake, please pass us along to the man in your life and get back to your *Ladies' Home Companion.*

When a Memphis woman wrote in to the second issue protesting the "Miss Gold-Digger" article, she was quickly put in her place. The article, she wrote, was "the most biased piece of tripe I've ever read," and she went on to deliver the classic anti-male rejoinder:

> Most men are out for just one thing. If they can't get it any other way, sometimes they consent to marry the girl. Then they think they can brush her off in a few months and move on to new pickings. They *ought* to pay, and pay, and pay.

The editors' printed response was, "Ah, shaddup!"

Hefner laid out the new male strategic initiative in the first issue. Recall that in their losing battle against "female domination," men had been driven from their living rooms, dens and even their basement tool shops. Escape seemed to lie only in the great outdoors—the golf course, the fishing hole or the fantasy world of Westerns. Now Hefner announced his intention to reclaim *the indoors for men.* "Most of today's 'magazines for men' spend all their time out-of-doors—thrashing through thorny thickets or splashing about in fast flowing streams," he observed in the magazine's first editorial. "But we don't mind telling you in advance—we plan [on] spending most of our time inside. We like our apartment." For therein awaited a new kind of good life for men:

> We enjoy mixing up cocktails and an *hors d'oeuvre* or two, putting a little mood music on the phonograph and inviting in a female acquaintance for a quiet discussion on Picasso, Nietzsche, jazz, sex.

Women would be welcome after men had reconquered the indoors, but only as guests—maybe overnight guests—but not as wives.

In 1953, the notion that the good life consisted of an apartment with mood music rather than a ranch house with barbecue pit was almost subversive. Looking back, Hefner later characterized himself as a pioneer rebel against the gray miasma of conformity that gripped other men. At the time the magazine began, he wrote in 1963, Americans had become "increasingly concerned with security, the safe and the sure, the certain and the known . . . it was unwise to voice an unpopular opinion . . . for it could cost a man his job and his good name." Hefner himself was not a political dissident in any conventional sense; the major intellectual influence in his early life was the Kinsey Report [world renowned study on human sexuality], and he risked his own good name only for the right to publish bare white bosoms. What upset him was the "conformity, togetherness, anonymity and slow death" men were supposed to endure when the good life, the life which he himself came to represent, was so close at hand. . . .

If Hefner was a rebel, it was only because he took the new fun morality seriously. As a guide to life, the new imperative to enjoy was in contradiction with the prescribed discipline of "conformity" and *Playboy*'s daring lay in facing the contradiction head-on. Conformity, or "maturity," as it was more affirmatively labeled by the psychologists, required unstinting effort: developmental "tasks" had to be performed, marriages had to be "worked on," individual whims had to be subordinated to the emotional and financial needs of the family. This was true for both sexes, of course. No one pretended that the adult sex roles—wife/mother and male breadwinner—were "fun." They were presented in popular culture as achievements, proofs of the informed acquiescence praised as "maturity" or, more rarely, lamented as "slow death." Women would not get public license to have fun on a mass scale for more than a decade, when Helen Gurley Brown took over *Cosmopolitan* and began promoting a tamer, feminine version of sexual and material consumption. But *Playboy* shed the burdensome aspects of the adult male role at a time when businessmen were still refining the "fun morality" for mass consumption, and the gray flannel rebels were still fumbling for responsible alternatives like Riesman's "autonomy." Even the magazine's name defied the convention of hard-won maturity— *Playboy*.

Playboy's attack on the conventional male role did not, however, extend to the requirement of earning a living. There were

two parts to adult masculinity: One was maintaining a monoga-
mous marriage. The other was working at a socially acceptable
job; and *Playboy* had nothing against work. The early issues barely
recognized the white-collar blues so fashionable in popular sociology. Instead, there were articles on accoutrements for the rising
executive, suggesting that work, too, could be a site of pleasurable
consumption. Writing in his "*Playboy* Philosophy" series in 1963,
Hefner even credited the magazine with inspiring men to work
harder than they might: " . . . *Playboy* exists, in part, as a motivation for men to expend greater effort in their work, develop their
capabilities further and climb higher on the ladder of success."
This kind of motivation, he went on, "is obviously desirable in our
competitive, free enterprise system," apparently unaware that the
average reader was more likely to be a white-collar "organization
man" or blue-collar employee rather than a free entrepreneur like
himself. Men should throw themselves into their work with
"questing impatience and rebel derring-do." They should overcome their vague, ingrained populism and recognize wealth as an
achievement and a means to personal pleasure. Only in one respect did Hefner's philosophy depart from the conventional, Dale
Carnegie-style credos of males success: *Playboy* believed that men
should make money; it did not suggest that they share it.

Playboy charged into the battle of the sexes with a dollar sign
on its banner. The issue was money: Men made it; women wanted
it. In *Playboy*'s favorite cartoon situation an elderly roué [a rake]
was being taken for a ride by a buxom bubblebrain, and the joke
was on him. The message, squeezed between luscious full-color
photos and punctuated with female nipples, was simple: You can
buy sex on a fee-for-service basis, so don't get caught up in a long-
term contract. [Comedian] Phil Silvers quipped in the January
1957 issue:

> A tip to my fellow men who might be on the brink of
> disaster: when the little doll says she'll live on your in-
> come, she means it all right. But just be sure to get another
> one for yourself. . . .

To stay free a man had to stay single. . . . Hefner's friend Burt Zollo
wrote in one of the early issues:

> Take a good look at the sorry, regimented husbands
> trudging down every woman-dominated street in this

woman-dominated land. Check what they're doing when you're out on the town with a different dish every night . . . Don't bother asking their advice. Almost to a man, they'll tell you marriage is the greatest. *Naturally.* Do you expect them to admit they made the biggest mistake of their lives?

This was strong stuff for the mid-fifties. The suburban migration was in full swing and *Look* had just coined the new noun "togetherness" to bless the isolated, exurban family. Yet here was *Playboy* exhorting its readers to resist marriage and "enjoy the pleasures the female has to offer without becoming emotionally involved"—or, of course, financially involved. Women wrote in with the predictable attacks on immaturity: "It is . . . the weak-minded little idiot boys, not yet grown up, who are afraid of getting 'hooked.'" But the men loved it. One alliterative genius wrote in to thank *Playboy* for exposing those "cunning cuties" with their "suave schemes" for landing a man. And, of course, it was *Playboy*, with its images of cozy concupiscence and extra-marital consumerism, that triumphed while *True* was still "thrashing through the thorny thickets" in the great, womanless outdoors.

One of the most eloquent manifestos of the early male rebellion was a *Playboy* article entitled, "Love, Death and the Hubby Image," published in 1963. It led off with a mock want ad:

TIRED OF THE RAT RACE?
FED UP WITH JOB ROUTINE?

Well, then . . . how would you like to make $8,000, $20,000—*as much as $50,000 and More*—working at Home in Your Spare Time? No selling! No commuting! No time clocks to punch!

BE YOUR OWN BOSS!!!

Yes, an Assured Lifetime Income can be yours *now*, in an easy, low-pressure, part-time job that will permit you to spend most of each and every day as *you please!*—relaxing, watching TV, playing cards, socializing with friends! . . .

"Incredible though it may seem," the article began, "the above offer is completely legitimate. More than 40,000,000 Americans are already so employed . . ." They were, of course, wives. . . .

Playboy had much more to offer the "enslaved" sex than rhetoric: It also proposed an alternative way of life that became ever more concrete and vivid as the years went on. At first there were only the Playmates in the centerfold to suggest what awaited the liberated male, but a wealth of other consumer items soon followed. Throughout the late fifties, the magazine fattened on advertisements for imported liquor, stereo sets, men's colognes, luxury cars and fine clothes. Manufacturers were beginning to address themselves to the adult male as a consumer in his own right, and they were able to do so, in part, because magazines like *Playboy* (a category which came to include imitators like *Penthouse*, *Gent* and *Chic*) allowed them to effectively "target" the potential sybarites among the great mass of men. New products for men, like toiletries and sports clothes, appeared in the fifties, and familiar products, like liquor, were presented in *Playboy* as accessories to private male pleasures. The new male-centered ensemble of commodities presented in *Playboy* meant that a man could display his status or simply flaunt his earnings without possessing either a house or a wife—and this was, in its own small way, a revolutionary possibility.

Domesticated men had their own commodity ensemble, centered on home appliances and hobby hardware, and for a long time there had seemed to be no alternative. A man expressed his status through the size of his car, the location of his house, and the social and sartorial graces of his wife. The wife and home might be a financial drag on a man, but it was the paraphernalia of family life that established his position in the occupational hierarchy. *Playboy*'s visionary contribution—visionary because it would still be years before a significant mass of men availed themselves of it—was to give the means of status to the single man: not the power lawn mower, but the hi-fi set in mahogany console; not the sedate, four-door Buick, but the racy little Triumph; not the well-groomed wife, but the classy companion who could be rented (for the price of drinks and dinner) one night at a time.

So through its articles, its graphics and its advertisements *Playboy* presented, by the beginning of the sixties, something approaching a coherent program for the male rebellion: a critique of marriage, a strategy for liberation (reclaiming the indoors as a realm for masculine pleasure) and a utopian vision (defined by its unique commodity ensemble). It may not have been a revolutionary program, but it was most certainly a disruptive one. If even a fraction of *Playboy* readers had acted on it in the late fifties, the "breakdown of the family" would have occurred a full fifteen years before it was eventually announced. Hundreds of thousands of women would have been left without breadwinners or stranded in court fighting for alimony settlements. Yet, for all its potential disruptiveness, *Playboy* was immune to the standard charges leveled against male deviants. You couldn't call it anticapitalist or un-American, because it was all about making money and spending it. Hefner even told his readers in 1963 that the *Playboy* spirit of acquisitiveness could help "put the United States back in the position of unquestioned world leadership." You *could* call it "immature," but it had already called itself that, because maturity was about mortgages and life insurance and *Playboy* was about fun. Finally, it was impervious to the ultimate sanction against male rebellion—the charge of homosexuality. The playboy didn't avoid marriage because he was a little bit "queer," but, on the contrary, because he was so ebulliently, evenly compulsively heterosexual.

Later in the sixties critics would come up with what seemed to be the ultimately sophisticated charge against *Playboy*: It wasn't really "sexy." There was nothing erotic, *Time* wrote, about the pink-cheeked young Playmates whose every pore and perspiration drop had been air-brushed out of existence. . . . But the critics misunderstood *Playboy*'s historical role. *Playboy* was not the voice of the sexual revolution, which began, at least overtly, in the sixties, but of the male rebellion, which had begun in the fifties. The real message was not eroticism, but escape-literal escape, from the bondage of breadwinning. For that, the breasts and bottoms were necessary not just to sell the magazine, but to protect it. When, in the first issue, Hefner talked about staying in his apartment, listening to music and discussing Picasso, there was the Marilyn Monroe centerfold to let you know there was nothing queer about these urbane and indoor pleasures. And when the articles railed against the responsibilities of marriage, there were the nude torsos to reassure you that the alternative was still within the bounds of heterosexuality. Sex—or Hefner's Pepsi-clean version of it—was there to legitimize what was truly subversive about *Playboy*. In every issue, every month, there was a Playmate to prove that a playboy didn't have to be a husband to be a man.

Questions

1. *What elements of traditional female and male roles do these authors find in the popular culture of the 1950s?*
2. *In what ways do their findings challenge the housewife and breadwinner ideals?*
3. *What factors determine the images portrayed in popular magazines?*
4. *What kinds of male and female ideals can be found in contemporary popular culture?*

FURTHER READING

Eugenia Kaledin's Mothers and More: American Women in the 1950s *(Boston, 1984) details the public accomplishments of women that belie their victimization in the 1950s. Elaine Tyler May's* Homeward Bound: American Families in the Cold War Era *(New York, 1988) analyzes middle-class family life in the 1950s, using personal testimonies to detail the dissatisfaction that the domestic ideal denied and attempted to contain. Wini Breines's* Young, White, and Miserable: Growing Up Female in the Fifties *(Boston, 1992) explores the dissatisfaction and rebellion of young white women in the decade. Joanne Meyerowitz's anthology,* Not June Cleaver: Women and Gender in Postwar America, 1945–1960 *(Philadelphia, 1994) brings together the recent work that challenges the traditional image of women's roles in the 1950s.*

Nonviolence and the Civil Rights Movement

Penny A. Russell

INTRODUCTION

Some histories of the civil rights movement begin in 1954 with the **Brown v. Board of Education** *decision that struck down separate but equal in public education. Other writers insist that the movement began in August 1955 with the decision of an all-white Mississippi jury to set free the two white men who brutally tortured and murdered fourteen-year-old Chicago native Emmett Till for allegedly whistling at a white woman. Many scholars begin their analysis with Rosa Parks, Martin Luther King, Jr., and the Montgomery Bus Boycott that started in December 1955. Recently, a few scholars have searched for the origins of the movement in the decades before the 1950s.*

Historians also disagree on how to characterize the ideology, politics, strategies, and tactics of the movement. A few have insisted that the commonly used term "the civil rights movement" is inadequate because this social movement was concerned with more than securing citizenship rights for Blacks. Some people saw the movement as a search for community, others spoke of it as a religious crusade, and still others believed it was a battle for the soul of America. To understand how and why African-American activism and politics came to be one of the dominant forces in American life from the mid-1950s to the mid-1960s, you must understand the origins and the foundation of the civil rights movement.

African Americans attempted to mobilize mass movements before the 1950s. The first call for a march on Washington came in May 1941, twenty-two years before Martin Luther King, Jr., told the nation about his dream of equality for all people. In May 1941,

A. *Philip Randolph urged African Americans to demonstrate in Washington for an end to discrimination in defense industries and in the military. The march was canceled only after President Franklin D. Roosevelt issued Executive Order 8802, which outlawed discrimination in employment in defense industries that held government contracts and created a Fair Employment Practices Committee (FEPC) to investigate companies that violated the order.*

The mass movement that Randolph had wanted to create became a reality fourteen years later. On 1 December 1955, Rosa Parks left her seamstress job in a tailor shop, boarded a city bus for home, and was arrested for refusing to give up her seat to a white passenger, a violation of Alabama's segregation laws. In response, the Women's Political Council, a black women's organization that had been petitioning Montgomery's mayor about discrimination and segregation on the city buses, called for a boycott of the buses on 5 December when Parks's case went to trial. E. D. Nixon and other black men in Montgomery met to discuss the situation and they endorsed the idea of a boycott and called for a mass meeting on the night of 5 December as well.

The city buses were virtually empty of black riders on the morning of the boycott. That same afternoon, Nixon and other male leaders created the Montgomery Improvement Association and elected a young minister, Martin Luther King, Jr., as head of the organization. African Americans in Montgomery walked for a year, enduring intimidation, loss of employment, violence, and bombings until the U.S. Supreme Court declared Montgomery's bus segregation laws unconstitutional.

African-American college students became the leaders and innovators during the next phase of the movement. On 1 February 1960, Franklin McCain, David Richmond, Joseph McNeil, and Izell Blair, Jr., four black college students attending North Carolina Agricultural and Technical College in Greensboro, asked to be served at a Woolworth's lunch counter and refused to leave their seats when they were denied service. Their actions sparked sit-ins by black college students, who were sometimes joined by a few white students, all across the South. In mid-April 1960 local student sit-in leaders met at Shaw University in Raleigh, North Carolina, and, with the assistance of Ella Baker of the Southern Christian Leadership Conference (SCLC), created the Student Nonviolent Coordinating Committee (SNCC) to organize their struggles against segregation.

SNCC's first efforts to register African-American voters were in McComb, Mississippi, under the direction of Robert Moses, a Harlem school teacher who had attended graduate school at Harvard and who had worked with Ella Baker in the past. Despite intimidation, humiliation, violence, and arrests, SNCC members worked with local activists to establish voting rights projects in other communities in Mississippi where they supported the efforts of African Americans to register to vote. SNCC workers were often arrested for their actions and chose to serve their sentences instead of accepting bail. This was a dangerous choice, for African Americans were routinely beaten and mistreated in southern jails.

In April 1963, Martin Luther King, Jr., was arrested in Birmingham, Alabama. While he was incarcerated, in response to a letter from white clergymen, he composed the most famous statement on the philosophy of nonviolent direct action. They had accused King and the SCLC of promoting violence and argued that civil rights activists were outsiders who should not have come to the city. In his letter from jail, King explained the use of nonviolence and assured the clergymen that they would join African Americans in their protests if they knew how the police had tortured Blacks both in the streets and the jails of Birmingham.

Most African-American organizations involved in the struggle for social and political change from the mid-1950s to the mid-1960s adopted the philosophy of nonviolence and the tactics of nonviolent direct action. The definition of nonviolence and how it should be used differed from individual to individual and from group to group, but most civil rights activists agreed on the goals of their movement. They wanted to destroy segregation and transform the nation. They embraced the spirit of urgency that Martin Luther King, Jr., spoke about at the August 1963 March on Washington: "Now is the time to make real the promises of democracy; now is the time to rise from the dark and desolate valley of segregation to the sunlit path of racial justice; now is the time to lift our nation from the quicksands of racial justice to the solid rock of brotherhood; now is the time to make justice a reality for all God's children."

WAS IT MORE THAN
A CIVIL RIGHTS MOVEMENT?

In his search for the beginning of the civil rights movement, Adam Fairclough discovers a history of struggle against segregation dating back to the 1930s and reveals a long-forgotten period highlighted by the radicalism of the National Association for the Advancement of Colored People (NAACP). Arguing that civil rights activists constructed a radical, new kind of politics, Clayborne Carson shows the relationship between their politics and traditional sources of struggles against discrimination and segregation. He also argues for a new interpretation of the civil rights movement that questions established ideas about Martin Luther King, Jr., SNCC, and the ideological foundation of their strategies for social change. Both Fairclough and Carson are interested in the roots of this social movement and are dissatisfied with traditional analysis of this period.

When Did the Civil Rights Movement Begin?

Emphasizing "the courage and determination with which ordinary blacks challenged the status quo," Adam Fairclough finds activists in Louisiana using tactics in their struggle against segregation years before they would become common strategies used throughout the South in the early 1960s.

Excerpted from Adam Fairclough, "The Civil Rights Movement in Louisiana, 1939-54," in The Making of Martin Luther King and the Civil Rights Movement, *ed. Brian Ward and Tony Badger (Washington Square, New York, 1996), 15-19, 21-22, 26.*

In 1950, in the sweltering heat of a June evening, blacks gathered in a small church in the tiny hamlet of Lebeau, Louisiana, to hear a distinguished guest speaker talk to them about democracy. Alvin Jones held degrees from Columbia University and the University of Pennsylvania; a former schoolteacher, and until recently executive secretary of the New Orleans Urban League, he worked for the Louisiana Progressive Voters League, an off-shoot of the NAACP. A broad-shouldered, distinguished-looking black man in his late forties, Jones reminded the audience that St. Landry Parish, where the tiny hamlet of Lebeau stood, did not have a single black voter. He insisted that now was the time to remedy this situation. The following morning he accompanied five people to the parish court house in Opelousas, which housed the office of the registrar of voters. When they entered the room several policemen assaulted and chased them away. 'I was slugged with the butt of a gun and pounded with a pair of brass knuckles', Jones recounted. 'They left a hole in my head.' Dazed and bloody, he received first aid from a black doctor and then returned to New Orleans. Within eighteen months he was dead.

Although St. Landry Parish lay in the heart of the Acadian triangle, a Catholic area of south Louisiana often regarded as less racially oppressive than the northern, Protestant, half of the state, many blacks regarded it as one of Louisiana's worst. A few months earlier an alleged rapist, Edward Honeycutt, had escaped a lynching party only by diving into the Atchafalaya river. An NAACP lawyer who saw him after his recapture found the surliness of Honeycutt's jailers unnerving: 'I have never in my life experienced a more hostile situation.' Honeycutt's confession had been so obviously beaten out of him that the state supreme court ordered a retrial. (Convicted a second time, Honeycutt went to the electric chair.) A local Catholic priest told black civil rights lawyer A. P. Turead that whites in St. Landry Parish were 'immovably opposed' to black voting.

The beating of Alvin Jones, however, gave the NAACP an opportunity that it eagerly seized: here was a dramatic illustration

---

Abridged from "The Civil Rights Movement in Louisiana, 1939–1954" by Adam Fairclough as it appeared in *The Making of Martin Luther King and the Civil Rights Movement*, edited by Dr. Brian Ward and Dr. Tony Badger. Published by New York University Press, 1996. Reprinted by permission of the publisher.

of southern brutality that could advance the cause of black suffrage by goading the federal government into action. Under pressure from the Association, the Attorney General ordered the FBI to conduct a full investigation. But in a pattern that was becoming wearily familiar to civil rights activists, the 'G-men' drew a blank. The registrar of voters admitted that he *did* remember some kind of commotion in his office, but 'he was busy registering voters at the time and did not notice any of the details of the commotion.' Nothing fazed, blacks in St. Landry Parish pressed on with their quest for the ballot. Forming a local branch of the NAACP, they found three men willing to file suit in federal court against the registrar of voters. A few days after the litigation began, a deputy sheriff shot and killed one of the plaintiffs. The other two plaintiffs fled to the comparative safety of Baton Rouge.

White politicians in St. Landry, however, recognized that if the NAACP backed suit went to trial, the registrar of voters would probably lose. In 1950, in the first ruling of its kind in Louisiana, federal district judge J. Skelly Wright had ordered the registrar of Washington Parish to enrol black applicants; two years later judge Gaston Porterie slapped a similar injunction on the registrar of Bossier Parish, in the northern part of the state. Black determination and NAACP pressure paid off: in 1953, for the first time since the wholesale disfranchisement of the black population in 1898-1904, blacks started to vote in St. Landry Parish. Indeed, black registration soared. It soon exceeded 80 per cent and composed two-fifths of the total electorate. Blacks helped to elect a new sheriff, a new mayor, and a new city council.

To any student of the civil rights movement this is a familiar tale; it could have happened in any one of hundreds of counties throughout the length and breadth of the South. Yet, because this particular story unfolded between 1950 and 1954—before *Brown* v. *Board of Education*, before the Montgomery bus boycott, before the civil rights movement 'began'—the name of Alvin Jones is absent from the list of martyrs that is inscribed on the Civil Rights Memorial in Montgomery. Nor will Jones's name be encountered in any of the standard histories of the civil rights movement.

When *did* the civil rights movement begin? Precisely when the term 'civil rights movement' became common currency is unclear. Historians commonly use it to describe the wave of black protest that swept the South between 1955 and 1965. Those were the years when black southerners, even in the most oppressive areas of the

327

Deep South, challenged white supremacy head-on. They developed an insurgency so insistent, so broadly based and so morally appealing that they overcame every obstacle that white racists threw at them—legal repression, economic coercion, physical brutality, and murder. The civil rights movement achieved a decisive breakthrough in the long struggle for racial equality. It tore up the fabric of segregation and transformed the South's political landscape. The words 'civil rights movement' carry such specific connotations of time, place and character that they immediately conjure up powerful images: images of sit-ins and freedom rides, of mass meetings and demonstrations; above all, images of Martin Luther King Jr, on his heroic journey from Montgomery to Memphis.

Yet, in many parts of the South an organized struggle against white supremacy developed much earlier, and had already made giant strides by the time of the Montgomery bus boycott. In a few short years, for example, St. Landry Parish had undergone a dramatic transformation. So had hundreds of other southern counties.

The breakthroughs came earlier and faster in Louisiana than elsewhere in the South. . . . .

These gains did not simply flow from federal court decisions: they also reflected the courage and determination with which ordinary blacks challenged the status quo. Moreover, many acts of opposition utilized direct action tactics. . . .

Baton Rouge, the state capital, witnessed the most striking example of direct action. There, in June 1953, blacks boycotted city buses to protest against segregation laws that compelled them to stand over empty seats that had been reserved for whites. An ad hoc organization, the United Defense League, coordinated the boycott, and a young Baptist minister, Theodore J. Jemison, led it. . . . During the week-long protest, hardly any blacks rode the city buses. 'Operation Free Lift', a car pool made up of about a hundred private vehicles, ferried people to and from work.

The Baton Rouge bus boycott did not gain much national attention; it was too short-lived. Nor did it achieve any great victory: blacks soon accepted a compromise that embodied a more equitable form of segregation. They then made the tactical error of challenging segregation in the state rather than the federal courts, losing the case. Even so, the fact that the boycott happened at all, and that it took place in the heart of the Deep South, was immensely significant. An entire black community had been speedily and effectively mobilized in a protest against segregation. Such examples of pre-1955 direct action are not, perhaps, all that surprising. Historical epochs do not come in neatly-wrapped chronological parcels; there is always overlapping and fuzziness around the edges. . . .

. . . Nevertheless, the central assertion of this paper is that the 'Montgomery-to-Selma' account of the civil rights movement, which focuses almost exclusively on the period 1955 to 1965, needs to be extended and revised. As Gerald Horne has argued, this narrative has become a historical myth. It is a myth not in the sense of being untrue, but in the sense of providing a simplified version of history that is readily comprehensible, morally edifying and politically acceptable. 'The traditional myth', writes Horne, 'is centred on Martin Luther King, Jr, with Rosa Parks and the Student Non-Violent Coordinating Committee playing pivotal and supporting roles. All of a sudden, in the mid-1950s—during a period, we are told, for some reason otherwise somnolent—Negroes, led by Dr. King and assisted by brilliant attorneys . . . started marching and getting their rights.' This is a caricature, of course, but we can recognize various elaborations of that myth in many, if not most, histories of the civil rights movement. . . .

Here is another advantage of a longer perspective: by examining specific black communities over time the remarkable depth and duration of black protest becomes evident. As historians redirect their gaze from the top leadership of the civil rights movement to the grass roots activists, and away from the few famous confrontations toward the many unheralded struggles, we can see how the work of SNCC, CORE [Congress of Racial Equality] and SCLC in the 1960s depended upon the efforts of 'local people' . . . who had been organizing and struggling for many years. And we can recognize that the civil rights movement began to take shape in the 1930s and 1940s. . . .

The example of Louisiana suggests that one can find, if one only looks, a long and continuous history of black organization and protest in many cities, towns and counties. For many local activists the struggle for civil rights was not merely a year-by-year affair but often a decade-by-decade one. And for many who joined the NAACP it was a lifetime commitment. . . .

The NAACP supplied, in most cases, the core element of continuity in local black activism. Yet, historians have until quite recently both neglected and underestimated that organization. In most histories of the civil rights movement it receives short shrift, virtually disappearing from sight after *Brown* v. *Board of Education* save for an occasional comment disparaging its effectiveness. . . .

Assessments of the NAACP's effectiveness circa 1960, however, must take into account the segregationist counter-attack known as Massive Resistance. In 1956 ultra-segregationists across the South unleashed a campaign to smash the NAACP. This onslaught almost succeeded. . . .

Hence the generation of 1960 encountered the NAACP in an enfeebled state. Moreover, they usually knew little of the history of the civil rights struggle in particular local communities and made little effort to find out. What happened in 1956, let alone 1946, was ancient history. Historians, however, should not be so present-minded. . . . Southern whites tried to destroy the NAACP not because the organization was ineffective, but because its combination of courtroom action, political pressure and popular mobilization was proving all *too* effective. It would be a great irony if Massive Resistance achieved a posthumous triumph by erasing the NAACP's golden age from the history books. . . .

The relationship between the pre-Montgomery and post-Montgomery phases of the civil rights struggle is a complex one. But an awareness of discontinuities, and an appreciation for the distinctive qualities of the Montgomery-to-Selma years, does not lessen the argument for treating the two periods as inextricably linked. Instead of viewing 1940 to 1955 as a mere prelude to something much bigger, we should see it as the first act of a two-act drama.

. . . . In 1940, lynching was still an ever-present threat; by 1955 it had become such a rarity that each incident evoked national condemnation and international opprobrium. In 1940 southern whites were still implacably opposed to black voting; by 1955 the areas of hard-core white resistance were increasingly isolated. I am not arguing, of course, that the voter registration and direct action campaigns of the 1960s were a mere mopping-up operation. I am simply asserting that the registration of one and a quarter million black voters between 1944 and 1956 represent an achievement of equal magnitude and significance.

As King was the first to acknowledge, his leadership was created by, and responded to, the aspirations and activism of ordinary people. By the same token, ordinary people became stronger and more courageous when they found a leader such as King. The Montgomery bus boycott and the emergence of King were critically important in intensifying black protest. But they also represented a further stage in a struggle that went back ten, fifteen, twenty years. And these earlier years were just as critical; they should not be lightly passed over. At stake is more than the remembrance of civil rights martyrs like . . . Alvin Jones; more than the apportioning of credit to this or that organization. At stake is our understanding of what shaped and propelled the most important social movement of twentieth-century America.

Rethinking African-American Politics and Activism

Clayborne Carson argues that King's awareness "of the potential power of non-violent tactics when used by militant, disciplined practitioners in close association with mass movements" marked an important change in black political thought and activism.

Taken from Clayborne Carson, "Rethinking African-American Political Thought in the Post-Revolutionary Era," in The Making of Martin Luther King and the Civil Rights Movement, *ed. Brian Ward and Tony Badger (Washington Square, New York, 1996), 117-22.*

Although the ideas that emerged from the African-American activism of the 1950s and early 1960s are often seen as precursors to the black power and New Left radicalism of the late 1960s, they can best be understood as the outgrowth of efforts by King, by youthful organizers of the SNCC, and other civil rights activists to create radical alternatives to both traditional black nationalism and Marxism. Once Rosa Parks's defiance of southern segregation thrust King into a leadership role, he and other activists began

Abridged from "Rethinking African-American Political Thought in the Post Revolutionary Era" by Clayborne Carson as it appeared in *The Making of Martin Luther King and the Civil Rights Movement*, edited by Dr. Brian Ward and Dr. Tony Badger. Published by New York University Press, 1996. Reprinted by permission of the publisher.

formulating a strategy of social change that departed from mainstream liberalism and from the two main ideological traditions of militant African-American struggle—that is, black nationalism and Marxism. ⌋

King's alternative radicalism was constructed, first of all, on the foundation of social gospel Christianity, especially the African-American variant of this tradition to which his father and grandfather had contributed. Reviving this tradition of prophetic dissent, King publicly criticized Cold War liberalism and capitalist materialism while also rejecting communism. Acknowledging in *Stride Toward Freedom: The Montgomery Story* that the works of Karl Marx had reinforced his long-held concern 'about the gulf between superfluous wealth and abject poverty', King charged that capitalist materialism was 'always in danger of inspiring men to be more concerned about making a living than making a life.' His version of social gospel Christianity also incorporated socialist ideas as well as anti-colonial sentiments spurred by the African independence movements.

In short, King made an important contribution to what later became known as liberation theology, which has enabled activists around the world to redefine widely held spiritual beliefs that are often used as supports for the status quo. . . . ⌈King understood that Christianity could serve either as a basis for African-American accommodation or for resistance. As a privileged insider within the largest African-American denomination, he fought an uphill struggle to transform the black church into an institutional foundation for racial struggles.

King also continued the efforts of Howard Thurman, James Farmer, Benjamin Mays, James Lawson and others to combine social gospel Christianity with Gandhian ideas of non-violent struggle. . . . Under the guidance of more experienced Gandhians, such as Bayard Rustin, Glenn Smiley and Lawson, King came to recognize that Gandhian non-violence represented more than simply a tactical option for oppressed people. He became increasingly aware of the potential power of non-violent tactics when used by militant, disciplined practitioners in close association with mass movements. Moreover, he discerned the importance of the ethos of non-violence as a cohesive force within the black struggle and as a spiritual foundation for what Gandhians called the Beloved Community.

At the beginning of the 1960s, the activists associated with SNCC were more willing than King to explore the radical implications of social gospel Christianity and Gandhism. At the time of SNCC's founding, however, many young black activists were drawn more to Lawson than to King. Having tutored Nashville student activists in Gandhian principles, Lawson encouraged SNCC activists to transform the lunch-counter sit-ins into a 'nonviolent revolution' to destroy 'segregation slavery, serfdom, paternalism', and 'industrialization which preserves cheap labour and racial discrimination.' Although some SNCC activists later abandoned Lawson's idealism in favour of instrumental rather than philosophical rationales for non-violence, those in the group continued to see themselves as involved in a freedom struggle rather than simply in an effort to achieve civil rights reforms. Several of the graduates of Lawson's Nashville workshop—especially Diane Nash, James Bevel and John Lewis—were more tactically audacious than was King, who often backed away from confrontations that lacked federal legal sanction or were likely to result in violence.

Moreover, SNCC workers quickly moved from conventional liberalism toward their own distinctive radicalism, which was more secular and innovative than King's Christian Gandhianism. SNCC field secretaries, especially those working with Bob Moses in Mississippi, resisted ideological conformity and derived their evolving worldview from their experiences as community organizers in the Deep South. SNCC developed a distinctive style of community organizing that self-consciously avoided the creation of new dependent relationships to replace the traditional racial dependencies of southern blacks. SNCC organizers were inspired by the example of Ella Baker, a woman who abhorred the elitism she had encountered as a field secretary of the NAACP and as the executive director of King's hierarchically organized SCLC. Rejecting King's charismatic leadership style, Baker encouraged the development of 'group-centered leaders' rather than leader-centered groups. SNCC's notion of organizing emphasized the development of grassroots leaders. SNCC organizers often stated, and some of them actually believed, that their job was to work themselves out of a job and that organizers should never seek leadership positions for themselves.

SNCC's radicalism was greatly influenced by the example of activists of earlier generations. Although SNCC workers generally avoided Marxian sectarianism, they borrowed tactics and rhetoric from the dedicated Communist Party organizers who had played significant roles in southern black movements of the pre-1960 era. SNCC also borrowed from Miles Horton and Septima Clark at the Highlander Folk School in Tennessee and from the Students for a Democratic Society, although SDS was more influenced by SNCC than vice versa. Finally, during the period after 1963, SNCC borrowed ideas from Malcolm X and the black nationalist tradition, most notably concepts of consciousness-raising and institution-building.

During the first half of the 1960s, King and the college-student organizers in SNCC were, in their different ways, responsible for mobilizations of large masses of black people willing to confront white authority on a scale unequalled during the last half of the decade. These militant mobilizations compelled a reluctant federal government to enact civil rights legislation, and they established a foundation for a fundamental restructuring of African-American participation in the electoral politics of the United States.

Nevertheless, by the mid 1960s, many SNCC activists, recognizing the need to move beyond civil rights reform to address issues of poverty and political powerlessness, adopted the black power slogan. Initially, the slogan represented an extension of SNCC's organizing efforts in the deep South, but after it became popularized by Stokely Carmichael the slogan came to symbolize a sharp break with SNCC's past. Rather than continuing to develop the radicalism of the early 1960s, many black power advocates abandoned the radical perspectives that grew out of the civil rights movement in favour of racial separatist ideologies. Veterans of SNCC's earlier organizing efforts, such as Carmichael, were embittered by their experiences and abandoned interracialism and non-violence as guiding principles. As the black power proponents pursued the mirage of a successful black nationalist revolution, they also abandoned many of the valuable insights that SNCC had acquired during its years of growth.

The key individual in this transformation of African-American political thought was Malcolm X. Malcolm's ideological contribution to the black power era would consist largely of his bitter critique of the non-violent civil rights movement; yet ironically, at the time of his assassination in February 1965, he was seeking to forge ties with King and SNCC organizers. While a member of

Elijah Muhammad's Nation of Islam, Malcolm had supported his group's policy of non-engagement, which prevented members from joining in any protest activity. Even as he fiercely attacked King's strategy of non-violent resistance, however, Malcolm increasingly recognized that the Nation [of Islam] offered no real alternative to black people facing vicious white racists in the South. Unlike many of his posthumous followers, Malcolm realized that the militant racial rhetoric of his years in the Nation of Islam obscured the group's accommodationism. Indeed, he knew that the Nation of Islam was not above making deals with white people when it served the leaders' interests. Malcolm later admitted that in 1961, even while he criticized civil rights activists for working with white liberals, his own organization sent him to Atlanta to negotiate a mutual non-interference agreement with the Ku Klux Klan. . . .

After his break with the Nation of Islam, Malcolm publicly acknowledged the radical potential of what he called the grassroots forces of the civil rights movement. Rather than attempting to supplant the radical ideas that were emerging from the grassroots, Malcolm saw the need for a convergence of those ideas and his own version of revolutionary nationalism. . . . In March 1964, after leaving the Nation of Islam and establishing his own Organization of Afro-American Unity (OAAU), he immediately began reaching out to civil rights leaders he had once harshly criticized. . . .

Soon afterwards, in his 'Ballot or the Bullet' speech delivered in April 1964, Malcolm sought to erase the ideological boundaries that had previously separated him from the civil rights organizations: 'The political philosophy of black nationalism is being taught in the Christian church . . . in the NAACP . . . in CORE meetings . . . in SNCC . . . It's being taught everywhere'. Malcolm broadened his own political perspective as a result of his tour of several African nations, including Nigeria and Ghana, following the *Hajj* to Mecca. . . .

Returning to the United States, Malcolm established increasingly close links with the southern black struggle. In December 1964 he invited Fannie Lou Hamer and the SNCC Freedom Singers to be guests of honour at an OAAU meeting in Harlem. He also hosted a delegation of 37 teenage activists from the McComb Mississippi movement. On 1 February 1965, he sent a telegram to the head of the American Nazi Party, warning, 'I am no longer held in check from fighting white supremacists by Elijah Muhammad's separatist Black Muslim movement, and if your present racist agitation of our people there in Alabama causes physical harm to Reverend King or any other Black Americans . . . you and your KKK friends will be met with maximum physical retaliation. . . .' Malcolm also sought to make amends for his previous harsh personal criticisms of Martin Luther King Jr. A few weeks before his assassination, while in Selma, Alabama, to lend support to the ongoing voting rights struggle, he met Coretta Scott King and made clear that he did not want to make her husband's job more difficult, explaining that, if whites knew that Malcolm was the alternative, 'it might be easier for them to accept Martin's proposals.'

Despite Malcolm's effort to achieve an alliance of black nationalism and the civil rights movement, black power militancy after Malcolm's death was often characterized by hostility toward any black leader who advocated non-violent tactics and racial integration. Malcolm's call for liberation 'by any means necessary' became a rationale for the abandonment of militant Gandhian tactics, despite the fact that Malcolm himself came to realize the necessity of non-violent tactics as part of any sustained mass struggle. Serious ideological conflicts within the African-American political community undermined the unity Malcolm was attempting to achieve. This disunity culminated in violent clashes between militant blacks, such as the one that took place in January 1969, at UCLA, when members of Maulana Karenga's US group shot and killed two Black Panthers in the campus dining-hall. By the end of the 1960s, the rhetorical violence of many self proclaimed black revolutionaries had been transformed into self-destructive violence that ravaged the fabric of black communities. Initially the Panthers advised blacks to 'pick up the gun', but the drug dealers of the 1970s were far better armed and more ruthless than were the black revolutionaries of the 1960s. . . .

Ultimately, the black power movement of the last half of the 1960s promised more than the civil rights movement but delivered less. Black Power militants talked of power yet exercised only transitory power within black communities and none outside those communities. They proclaimed that they acted on behalf of African Americans whose needs had been ignored by the civil rights leaders, but black power militancy did not prevent a rapid deterioration in the economic status of the black masses during more than two decades since the late 1960s. Black power militants talked of revolution but the veterans of the black power movement have generally found ways of accommodating to the existing white-dominated social order. After Malcolm's assassination in 1965, the black power movement adopted many of his ideas, but the lasting contributions of the black power period were more significant in the intellectual and cultural rather than the political arena. Black power militancy survives not as insurgencies but as unthreatening expressions of Afrocentrism.

While failing to produce greater power for black people, black power militancy actually led to a decline in the ability of African-Americans to affect the course of American politics. The emergence of Stokley [Stokely] Carmichael and H. Rap Brown as nationally known black advocates of black power prompted more effective repression once J. Edgar Hoover's FBI recognized that the black struggle could be crippled through the elimination of a few leaders. Moreover, the rhetorical violence and racism of some black militants spurred the increasing popularity among whites of 'law and order' politics. Brown, in fact, helped to create the conditions that made it possible for Spiro Agnew to transform himself from a minor Maryland politician to Vice-President within little more than a year. In the larger context of American politics, the black power controversy encouraged a conservative political trend which has led to a Republican ascendancy in national electoral politics.

Questions

---

1. *What are the reasons that Adam Fairclough gave for reconsidering the beginning of the civil rights movement? Would Clayborne Carson agree with him?*

2. *Is it possible to combine Fairclough's and Carson's analyses to create a new narrative of the civil rights movement or are their ideas too dissimilar?*

3. *How does Carson's view of Martin Luther King, Jr., differ from popular views of King that are presented during the King holiday?*

4. *What are the major differences between the philosophical approaches of Martin Luther King, Jr., and Malcolm X?*

THE STRATEGIES OF NONVIOLENCE AND THE DANGERS OF ACTIVISM

These documents offer different views of nonviolence, activism, and resistance by African Americans. Some of these people, such as Rosa Parks, Malcolm X, and King, are familiar while others, such as Ella Baker, James Forman, or A. Philip Randolph, are not. These selections are a small example of the creativity and innovation that activists employed in their efforts to transform the United States into a nation where all citizens could enjoy justice, equality, and freedom.

A. Philip Randolph Calls for a March on Washington, 1941

A. Philip Randolph was the head of the Brotherhood of Sleeping Car Porters, a predominantly African-American labor union, an early civil rights activist, and publisher of The Black Worker, *a labor magazine. In this excerpt from his May 1941 call for a march on Washington, Randolph wanted "mass action that is orderly and lawful, but aggressive and militant, for justice, equality and freedom."*

Taken from "To March On Washington for Jobs and Equal Participation in National Defense," The Black Worker, *May 1941, p. 4.*

Greetings:

We call upon you to fight for jobs in National Defense.

We call upon you to struggle for the integration of Negroes in the armed forces, such as the Air Corps, Navy, Army and Marine Corps of the Nation.

We call upon you to demonstrate for the abolition of Jim-Crowism in all Government departments and defense employment.

This is an hour of crisis. It is a crisis of democracy. It is a crisis of minority groups. It is a crisis of Negro Americans.

What is this crisis?

To American Negroes, it is the denial of jobs in Government defense projects. It is racial discrimination in Government departments. It is widespread Jim-Crowism in the armed forces of the nation. . . .

What shall we do? . . .

With faith and confidence of the Negro people in their own power for self-liberation, Negroes can break down the barriers of discrimination against employment in National Defense. . . .

Most important and vital to all, Negroes, by the mobilization and coordination of their mass power, can cause PRESIDENT ROOSEVELT TO ISSUE AN EXECUTIVE ORDER ABOLISHING DISCRIMINATIONS IN ALL GOVERNMENT DEPARTMENTS, ARMY, NAVY, AIR CORPS AND NATIONAL DEFENSE JOBS. . . .

In this period of power politics, nothing counts but pressure, more pressure, and still more pressure, through the tactic and strategy of broad, organized, aggressive mass action behind the vital and important issues of the Negro. To this end, we propose that ten thousand Negroes MARCH ON WASHINGTON FOR JOBS IN NATIONAL DEFENSE AND EQUAL INTEGRATION IN THE FIGHTING FORCES OF THE UNITED STATES.

An "all-out" thundering march on Washington, ending in a monster and huge demonstration at Lincoln's Monument will shake up white America.

It will shake up official Washington.

It will give encouragement to our white friends to fight all the harder by our side, with us, for our righteous cause.

It will gain respect for the Negro people.

It will create a new sense of self-respect among Negroes. . . .

We summon you to mass action that is orderly and lawful, but aggressive and militant, for justice, equality and freedom.

From "To March on Washington for Jobs and Equal Participation in National Defense" by A. Philip Randolph as it appeared in *The Black Worker*, p. 4, May 1941.

Rosa L. Parks is Arrested in Montgomery, Alabama on 1 December 1955

In a 1977 interview Rosa Parks remembers that she told the city bus driver to "go on and have me arrested" for not giving up her seat to a white man who boarded the bus after her. In this selection, she discusses the events that ignited a community-wide protest.

Taken from Howell Raines, My Soul Is Rested: Movement Days in the Deep South Remembered *(New York, 1977)*, 40-42.

As I got up on the bus and walked to the seat I saw there was only one vacancy that was just back of where it was considered the white section. So this was the seat I that I took, next to the aisle, and a man was sitting next to me. . . . The third stop is when all the front seats were taken, and this one man was standing and when the driver looked around and saw he was standing, he asked the four of us, the man in the seat with me and the two women across the aisle, to let him have those front seats.

At his first request, didn't any of us move. Then he spoke again and said, "You'd better make it light on yourselves and let me have those seats." At this point, of course, the passenger who would have taken the seat hadn't said anything. In fact, he never did speak to my knowledge. When the three people, the man who was in the seat with me and the two women, stood up and moved into the aisle, I remained where I was. When the driver saw that I was still sitting there, he asked if I was going to stand up. I told him no, I wasn't. He said, "Well, if you don't stand up, I'm going to have you arrested." I told him to go on and have me arrested.

He got off the bus and came back shortly. A few minutes later, two policemen got on the bus, and they approached me and asked if the driver had asked me to stand up, and I said yes, and they wanted to know why I didn't. I told them I didn't think I should have to stand up. After I had paid my fare and occupied a seat, I didn't think I should have to give it up. They placed me under arrest then and had me to get in the police car, and I was taken to jail and booked on suspicion, I believe. The questions were asked, the usual questions they ask a prisoner or somebody that's under arrest. They had to determine whether or not the driver wanted to press charges or swear out a warrant, which he did. Then they took me to jail and I was placed in a cell. In a little while I was taken from the cell, and my picture was made and fingerprints taken. I went back to the cell then, and a few minutes later I was called back again, and when this happened I found out that Mr. E.D. Nixon and Attorney and Mrs. Clifford Durr had come to make bond for me.

In the meantime before this, of course . . . I was given permission to make a telephone call after my picture was taken and fingerprints taken. I called my home and spoke to my mother on the telephone and told her what had happened, that I was in jail. She was quite upset and asked me had the police beaten me. I told her, no, I hadn't been physically injured, but I was being held in jail, and I wanted my husband to come and get me out. . . . He didn't have a car at that time, so he had to get someone to bring him down. At the time when he got down, Mr. Nixon and the Durrs had just made bond for me, so we all met at the jail and we went home.

Student Nonviolent Coordinating Committee Statement of Purpose

The Reverend James Lawson was a divinity student who was expelled from Vanderbilt University after sit-ins in the spring of 1960. Later that year he would be influential in the founding of the Student Nonviolent Coordinating Committee. In May 1960, he drafted the statement of purpose for the new organization that appeared in the first issue of the newspaper the students created, The Student Voice 1 *(June 1960): 1.*

Statement of Purpose

"Carrying out the mandate of the Raleigh Conference to write a statement of purpose for the movement, the Temporary Student Nonviolent Coordinating Committee submits for careful consideration the following draft. We urge all local state or regional groups to examine it closely. Each member of our movement must work diligently to understand the depths of nonviolence.

We affirm the philosophical or religious ideal of nonviolence as the foundation of our purpose, the pre-supposition of our faith, and the manner of our action. Nonviolence as it grows from Judaic-Christian tradition seeks a social order of justice permeated by love. Integration of human endeavor represents the crucial first step towards such a society.

Through nonviolence, courage displaces fear; love transforms hate. Acceptance dissipates prejudice; hope ends despair. Peace dominates war; faith reconciles doubt. Mutual regards cancel enmity. Justice for all overthrows injustice. The redemptive community supercedes [supersedes] systems of gross social immorality.

Love is the central motif of nonviolence. Love is the force by which God binds man to himself and man to man. Such love goes to the extreme; it remains loving and forgiving even in the midst of hostility. It matches the capacity of evil to inflict suffering with an even more enduring capacity to absorb evil, all the while persisting in love.

By appealing to conscience and standing on the moral nature of human existence, nonviolence nurtures the atmosphere in which reconciliation and justice become actual possibilities."

Prepared by-Rev. J.M. Lawson, Jr. Saturday, May 14, 1960

Bigger Than A Hamburger

Ella Baker, executive director of the Southern Christian Leadership Conference, organized the student conference in Raleigh, North Carolina, from which SNCC emerged. She encouraged the student leaders attending the Raleigh conference to create their own organization where they would be free to work "to rid America of the scourge of racial segregation and discrimination—not only at lunch counters, but in every aspect of life."

From "Statement of Purpose" by Rev. James Lawson as it appeared in *The Student Voice*, June 1960.

Baker's ideas about leadership and community organizing were adopted by SNCC and they are presented in Ella J. Baker, "Bigger Than A Hamburger," Southern Patriot (June 1960): 1.

Raleigh, N.C.—The Student Leadership Conference made it crystal clear that current sit-ins and other demonstrations are concerned with something bigger than a hamburger or even a giant-sized Coke.

Whatever may be the difference in approach to their goal, the Negro and white students, North and South, are seeking to rid America of the scourge of racial segregation and discrimination—not only at lunch counters, but in every aspect of life.

In reports, casual conversations, discussion groups, and speeches, the sense and spirit of the following statement that appeared in the initial newsletter of the students at Barer-Scotia College, concord, N.C., were re-echoed time and again:

⌈We want the world to know that we no longer accept the inferior position of second-class citizenship. We are willing to go to jail, be ridiculed, spat upon and even suffer physical violence to obtain First Class Citizenship. ⌋

By and large, this feeling that they have a destined date with freedom, was not limited to a drive for personal freedom for the Negro in the South. Repeatedly it was emphasized that the movement was concerned with the moral implications of racial discrimination for the "whole world" and the "Human Race."

"This universality of approach was linked with a perceptive recognition that "it is important to keep the movement democratic and to avoid struggles for personal leadership."

It was further evident that desire for supportive cooperation from adult leaders and the adult community was also tempered by apprehension that adults might try to "capture" the student movement. The students showed willingness to be met on the basis of equality, but were intolerant of anything that smacked of manipulation or domination.

This inclination toward group-centered leadership, rather than toward a leader-centered group pattern of organization, was refreshing indeed to those of the older group who bear the scars of

---

From "Bigger Than A Hamburger" by Ella J. Baker as it appeared in *The Southern Patriot*, June 1960.

the battle, the frustrations and the disillúsionment that come when the prophetic leader turns out to have heavy feet of clay.

However hopeful might be the signs in the direction of group-centeredness, the fact that many schools and communities, especially in the South, have not provided adequate experience for young Negroes to assume the initiative and think and act independently accentuated the need for guarding the student movement against well-meaning, but nevertheless unhealthy, overprotectiveness.

Here is an opportunity for adult and youth to work together and provide genuine leadership—the development of the individual to his highest potential for the benefit of the group. . . .

In Jail in Greenwood, Mississippi

James Forman provides the following glimpse of life for SNCC activists in the Greenwood, Mississippi jail in his book The Making of Black Revolutionaries: A Personal Account *(New York, 1972), 299-301.*

April 2, 1963: We have been in jail one week today. Our morale is good, although there are serious undertones of a desire to be free among some members of the group. . . .

The cell in which we are being held is not so bad so far as American prisons go. (The entire penal system needs reforming.) We are eight in a cell with six bunks. We have two mattresses on the floor. There is an open shower, a sink, a stool. It took us two days to get a broom and five days to get some salt for our food. The inner cell in which we are "contained" is approximately 15' x 12'. Not much room is there? . . .

We are also improving our minds. We have been allowed to keep our books and we have sufficient cigarettes. I even have my pipe and some tobacco. Personally, I have tried to organize our lives. Do you expect anything else of me? We have occasional classes. Moses gave us an excellent math lecture the other day. I gave one lesson in writing and English. Guyot has delivered several in biology. We are always having discussions. Sometimes one of us will read a passage from a book and then we will discuss the meaning of it. We have had several stimulating conversations on Thoreau's essay on Civil Disobedience and Nkrumah's thoughts on Positive Action. . . .

My personal opinion as to the significance of our staying in jail follows: I am convinced that all the people connected with SNCC are busily engaged in protesting our unjust imprisonment. This is as it should be. I am also convinced that others sympathetic to the cause of Freedom are also alarmed at this travesty of justice. Only our bodies are confined to this cell. Our minds are free to think what we wish and we know our stay here will also pass away. Our imprisonment serves to dramatize to the nation and to the world that the black man does not even have the right to *try* to be an American citizen in some parts of our so-called democracy. Our jail-without-bail may also serve to remind others in the movement of the need for some of us to stay in jail to dramatize the situation.

On a local and state level it is important that we stay in jail, for people are remembered more by what they do than by what they say. We have been telling Mississippians that we must prepare to die. We have encouraged them to accept our beliefs. Thus it follows that we must lead by example rather than by words.

Letter from the Birmingham City Jail

King presents his ideas on the use of nonviolence and reminds the white clergymen that he is in Birmingham because "injustice anywhere is a threat to justice everywhere." This version of his famous letter is in Martin Luther King, Jr., "Letter from Birmingham Jail," in Why We Can't Wait *(New York, 1963), 77–83, 98–100.*

April 16, 1963

My Dear Fellow Clergymen:
    While confined here in the Birmingham city jail, I came across your recent statement calling my present activities "unwise and

untimely." Seldom do I pause to answer criticism of my work and ideas. If I sought to answer all the criticisms that cross my desk, my secretaries would have little time for anything other than such correspondence in the course of the day, and I would have no time for constructive work. But since I feel that you are men of genuine good will and that your criticisms are sincerely set forth, I want to try to answer your statement in what I hope will be patient and reasonable terms.

I think I should indicate why I am here in Birmingham, since you have been influenced by the view which argues against "outsiders coming in." . . . Several months ago the [local SCLC] affiliate here in Birmingham asked us to be on call to engage in a nonviolent direct-action program if such were deemed necessary. We readily consented, and when the hour came we lived up to our promise. So I, along with several members of my staff, am here because I was invited here. I am here because I have organizational ties here.

But more basically, I am in Birmingham because injustice is here. . . .

Moreover, I am cognizant of the interrelatedness of all communities and states. I cannot sit idly by in Atlanta and not be concerned about what happens in Birmingham. Injustice anywhere is a threat to justice everywhere. We are caught in an inescapable network of mutuality, tied in a single garment of destiny. Whatever affects one directly, affects all indirectly. Never again can we afford to live with the narrow, provincial "outside agitator" idea. Anyone who lives inside the United States can never be considered an outsider anywhere within its bounds.

You deplore the demonstrations taking place in Birmingham. But your statement, I am sorry to say, fails to express a similar concern for the conditions that brought about the demonstrations. . . .

In any nonviolent campaign there are four basic steps: collection of the facts to determine whether injustices exist; negotiation; self-purification; and direct action. We have gone through all these steps in Birmingham. There can be no gainsaying the fact that racial injustice engulfs this community. Birmingham is probably the most thoroughly segregated city in the United States. Its ugly record of brutality is widely known. Negroes have experienced grossly unjust treatment in the courts. There have been more unsolved bombings of Negro homes and churches in Birmingham than in any other city in the nation. These are the hard, brutal facts of the case. On the basis of these conditions, Negro leaders sought to negotiate with the city fathers. But the latter consistently refused to engage in good-faith negotiation. . . .

You may well ask: "Why direct action? Why sit-ins, marches and so forth? Isn't negotiation a better path?" You are quite right in calling for negotiation. Indeed, this is the very purpose of direct action. Nonviolent direct action seeks to create such a crisis and foster such a tension that a community which has constantly refused to negotiate is forced to confront the issue. It seeks so to dramatize the issue that it can no longer be ignored. . . .

. . . My friends, I must say to you that we have not made a single gain in civil rights without determined legal and nonviolent pressure. Lamentably, it is an historical fact that privileged groups seldom give up their privileges voluntarily. . . .

We know through painful experience that freedom is never voluntarily given by the oppressor; it must be demanded by the oppressed. Frankly, I have yet to engage in a direct-action campaign that was "well timed" in the view of those who have not suffered unduly from the disease of segregation. For years now I have heard the word "Wait!" It rings in the ear of every Negro with piercing familiarity. This "Wait" has almost always meant "Never." We must come to see, with one of our distinguished jurists, that "justice too long delayed is justice denied." . . .

Before closing, I feel impelled to mention one other point in your statement that has troubled me profoundly. You warmly commended the Birmingham police force for keeping "order" and "preventing violence." I doubt that you would have so warmly commended the police force if you had seen its dogs sinking their teeth into unarmed, nonviolent Negroes. I doubt that you would so quickly commend the policemen if you were to observe their ugly and inhumane treatment of Negroes here in the city jail; if you were to watch them push and curse old Negro women and young Negro girls; if you were to see them slap and kick old Negro men and young boys; if you were to observe them, as they did on two occasions, refuse to give us food because we wanted to sing our grace together. I cannot join you in your praise of the Birmingham police department. . . .

I wish you had commended the Negro sit-inners and demonstrators of Birmingham for their sublime courage, their willingness to suffer and their amazing discipline in the midst of great provocation. One day the South will recognize its real heroes. They will be the James Merediths, with the noble sense of purpose that enables them to face jeering and hostile mobs, and with the agonizing loneliness that characterizes the life of the pioneer. They will be old, oppressed, battered Negro women, symbolized in a seventy-two-year-old woman in Montgomery, Alabama, who rose up with a sense of dignity and with her people decided not to ride segregated buses, and who responded with ungrammatical profundity to one who inquired about her weariness: "My feets is tired, but my soul is at rest." They will be the young high school and college students, the young ministers of the gospel and a host of their elders, courageously and nonviolently sitting in at lunch counters and willingly going to jail for conscience' sake. One day the South will know that when these disinherited children of God sat down at lunch counters, they were in reality standing up for what is best in the American dream and for the most sacred values in our Judaeo-Christian heritage, thereby bringing our nation back to those great wells of democracy which were dug deep by the founding fathers in their formulation of the Constitution and the Declaration of Independence. . . .

. . . Let us all hope that the dark clouds of racial prejudice will soon pass away and the deep fog of misunderstanding will be lifted from our fear-drenched communities, and in some not too distant tomorrow the radiant stars of love and brotherhood will shine over our great nation with all their scintillating beauty.

Yours for the cause of Peace and Brotherhood,
MARTIN LUTHER KING, JR.

To Mississippi Youth from Malcolm X

Malcolm X, originally Malcolm Little, took the surname X to represent the lost identity of African slaves. Malcolm became the main spokesman for the Nation of Islam during the 1950s. While in the Nation of Islam, he emphasized racial separatism and black self-reliance and was described by some as militant and extremist. He became disillusioned with and left the Nation of Islam in March 1964 and subsequently founded the Organization of Afro-American Unity (OAAU). From his break with the Nation of Islam in 1964 until his assassination in February 1965, he distanced himself from racial separatism and sought solidarity with the civil rights movement. In this excerpt from a speech on 31 December 1964, Malcolm presents his views on nonviolence and the movement in Mississippi.

Excerpted from Malcolm X, "To Mississippi Youth," in George Breitman, ed., Malcolm X Speaks: Selected Speeches and Statements *(New York, 1965), 138, 142-44.*

My experience has been that in many instances where you find Negroes talking about nonviolence, they are not nonviolent with each other, and they're not loving with each other, or forgiving with each other. Usually when they say they're nonviolent, they mean they're nonviolent with somebody else. I think you understand what I mean. They are nonviolent with the enemy. A person can come to your home, and if he's white and wants to heap some kind of brutality on you, you're nonviolent. . . . But if another Negro just stomps his foot, you'll rumble with him in a minute. Which shows you that there's an inconsistency there.

I myself would go for nonviolence if it was consistent, if everybody was going to be nonviolent all the time. I'd say, okay, let's get with it, we'll all be nonviolent. But I don't go along with any kind of nonviolence unless everybody's going to be nonviolent. If they make the Ku Klux Klan nonviolent, I'll be nonviolent. If they make the White Citizens Council nonviolent, I'll be nonviolent. But as long as you've got somebody else not being nonviolent, I don't want anybody coming to me talking any nonviolent talk. . . .

In studying the process of this so-called [racial] progress during the past twenty years, we of the Organization of Afro-American Unity realized that the only time the black man in this country is given any kind of recognition, or even listened to, is when America is afraid of outside pressure, or when she's afraid of her image abroad. . . .

And today you'll find in the United Nations, and it's not an accident, that every time the Congo question or anything on the African continent is being debated, they couple it with what is going on, or what is happening to you and me, in Mississippi and Alabama and these other places. In my opinion, the greatest accomplishment that was made in the struggle of the black man in America in 1964 toward some kind of real progress was the successful linking together of our problem with the African problem, or making our problem a world problem. . . .

So we here in the Organization of Afro-American Unity are with the struggle in Mississippi one thousand per cent. We're with the efforts to register our people in Mississippi to vote one thousand per cent. But we do not go along with anybody telling us to help nonviolently. We think that if the government says that Negroes have a right to vote, and then some Negroes come out to vote, and some kind of Ku Klux Klan is going to put them in the river, and the government doesn't do anything about it, it's time for us to organize and band together and equip ourselves and qualify ourselves to protect ourselves. And once you can protect yourself, you don't have to worry about being hurt. . . .

If you don't have enough people down there to do it, we'll come down there and help you do it. Because we're tired of this old runaround that our people have been given in this country. For a long time they accused me of not getting involved in politics. They should've been glad I didn't get involved in politics, because anything I get in, I'm in it all the way. If they say we don't take part in the Mississippi struggle, we will organize brothers here in New York who know how to handle these kind of affairs, and they'll slip into Mississippi like Jesus slipped into Jerusalem.

Questions

---

1. *How did these people and organizations use nonviolent direct action? Do they have similar ideas about nonviolence?*
2. *What are some of the dangers that activists in the movement faced?*

3. Did King and his allies, members of SNCC, and Malcolm X understand each others' views on nonviolence and activism? Was there any common ground between them?
4. Do these documents suggest that some people were more idealistic in the 1950s and 1960s? Why or why not?
5. Do you think that you could have been an activist like any of these people? What factors would encourage or inhibit you?

FURTHER READING

Race & Democracy: The Civil Rights Struggle in Louisiana, 1915-1972 by Adam Fairclough (Athens, 1995) demonstrates that civil rights struggles began with the twentieth century. Two studies that analyze the indigenous roots of the movement and emphasize the roles of local leaders are Charles M. Payne, *I've Got the Light of Freedom: The Organizing Tradition and the Mississippi Freedom Struggle* (Berkeley, 1995); and John Dittmer, *Local People: The Struggle for Civil Rights in Mississippi* (Urbana, 1994). The best history of SNCC is still Clayborne Carson, *In Struggle: SNCC and the Black Awakening of the 1960s* (Cambridge, 1995); and there is a collection of fascinating interviews with organizers in *A Circle of Trust: Remembering SNCC*, ed. Cheryl Lynn Greenberg (New Brunswick, 1998). *But for Birmingham: The Local and National Movements in the Civil Rights Struggle* by Glenn T. Eskew (Chapel Hill, 1997) examines one of the most important civil rights campaigns of the 1960s. Belinda Robnett's *How Long? How Long? African-American Women in the Struggle for Civil Rights* (New York, 1997) is a long-awaited study of women's activism that provides a theoretical framework for exploring their unique roles in the movement. Biographies have provided some of the best scholarship on the movement, and the second volume of Taylor Branch's biography of King, *Pillar of Fire: America in the King Years, 1963-65* (New York, 1998), is now available. The life of a significant, but overlooked, woman who was responsible for running SNCC is eloquently presented in Cynthia Griggs Fleming, *Soon We Will Not Cry: The Liberation of Ruby Doris Smith Robinson* (Lanham, Maryland, 1998). A thoughtful comparison of the ideas of King and Malcolm X can be found in James H. Cone, *Martin & Malcolm & America: A Dream or a Nightmare* (Maryknoll, New York, 1992).

The Environmental Movement

Austin Kerr and Terence Kehoe

INTRODUCTION

The environmental movement that emerged in the 1960s and early 1970s built upon previous efforts to conserve and protect America's natural resources and to control the harmful health effects of concentrated urban living and various industrial processes. At the end of the nineteenth century, the closing of the American frontier and the legacy of unrestrained development in ravaged areas, such as the depleted forests of the Upper Great Lakes region, inspired some influential public figures to push for an expanded government role in decisions affecting natural resources. Conservationists such as Theodore Roosevelt and Gifford Pinchot, the first head of the U.S. Forest Service, wanted to bring America's resources under the authority of experts in the federal government so that rational planning could ensure the most efficient use and continued benefits of natural resources for all Americans.

During the same period, the steady push of settlement and the increasingly urban character of American life generated a desire among some citizens to preserve as much of the landscape as possible in its natural, unspoiled state. Preservationists such as John Muir, the founder of the Sierra Club, believed that natural areas possessed an intrinsic value and attached a spiritual significance to wilderness. The preservationist attitude clashed with the views of conservationists, who wanted to efficiently exploit natural areas for their economic value. While the two groups sometimes cooperated to achieve common objectives, their different perspectives increasingly brought them into direct conflict with one another. In 1901, Muir and his allies attempted to block efforts to transform the beautiful Hetch-Hetchy Valley in California's

Yosemite Park into a reservoir for the population of San Francisco. In the end, the needs of the city won out over the desire to preserve the majesty of the valley.

The public health movement of the Progressive Era also represented an effort to tame the excesses of industrial capitalism. In this case, public health reformers focused on improving the urban environment. Politicians, physicians, civic organizations, and other groups worked to impose controls on industrial pollution and improve sanitation practices with the goal of eradicating disease and improving the general quality of city life. These activities also included efforts to improve the safety of industrial workers exposed to various toxic and hazardous substances on the job.

The concerns and objectives of the conservationists became institutionalized through the continuing activities of the Forest Service, the Army Corps of Engineers, and other government agencies. The national park system represented the greatest legacy of the preservationists. Public health reformers achieved their greatest successes in improving urban sanitation practices, while having much less of an impact on industrial practices. But in spite of their considerable gains, none of these reform movements could claim anywhere near the popular, sustained support of the later environmental movement.

The environmental movement that bloomed in the 1960s drew support from a much broader cross section of the American public than these earlier movements and prompted many citizens to question deep-rooted assumptions about the benefits of economic growth and humankind's relationship to the natural environment. While the leadership of the organized environmental movement—especially at the national level—remained overwhelmingly white, male, and affluent, poll after poll demonstrated that Americans from all groups shared a broad consensus about the desirability of preserving and protecting the natural environment. The environmental movement achieved significant and lasting political power; in response to popular concerns about the environment and various forms of activism, governments at all levels enacted new laws and created new agencies designed to ensure greater protection of the environment.

Since 1980, the environmental movement has become more diverse. Minority groups and working-class Americans have become more involved in environmental issues as they attempt to protect their communities from the health dangers posed by nearby hazardous waste dumps and industrial plants that generate toxic compounds. In addition, so-called radical environmentalists have criticized mainstream organizations, such as the Sierra Club, for their willingness to compromise with the forces of development and their unwillingness to challenge seriously what the radicals perceive as the inherent flaws of modern industrial society.

THE EMERGENCE AND EVOLUTION OF THE ENVIRONMENTAL MOVEMENT

Historians are often concerned with explaining why things happened. This question is particularly important in understanding significant social movements. In the first reading, Samuel Hays links the emergence of environmentalism to the increasing standard of living in post-1945 America. According to Hays, new "environmental values" were closely linked to the widespread search for a greater quality of life that extended beyond material possessions. Kirkpatrick Sale then describes the splintering of the environmental movement in recent years and the growing diversity of voices within the movement. During the 1980s, community activists and radical environmentalists criticized the major environmental organizations for their failure to address adequately the environmental health concerns of working-class and minority communities and their willingness to accept incremental reform and play by the traditional rules of interest group politics. The critics of mainstream environmentalism eventually founded organizations of their own that attempted to move beyond the limitations of the established environmental groups.

Environmentalism and the Affluent Society

Abridged from Samuel P. Hays, in collaboration with Barbara D. Hays, Beauty, Health, and Permanence: Environmental Politics in the United States, 1955–1985 *(Cambridge, England, 1987), 2–5, 22–28.*

The Transformation of Values

Environmental concerns were rooted in the vast social changes that took place in the United States after World War II. Although some beginnings can be identified in earlier years, only after the war did they become widely shared social phenomena... . The expansion of this interest brought it to the forefront of public life. This began with a rapid growth in outdoor recreation in the 1950s, extended into the wider field of the protection of natural environments, then became infused with attempts to cope with air and water pollution and still later with toxic chemical pollutants. Such activity was hardly extensive prior to World War II; afterward it was a major public concern.

Two observations help to identify the historical timing of the environmental concern. One is the transition from an older stress on efficient development and use of material resources such as water, forests, and soils known as the conservation movement, which took place in the first four decades of the twentieth century. Conservation gave way to environment after World War II amid a rising interest in the quality of life beyond efficiency in production. The two tendencies often came into conflict as resources long thought of as important for their material commodities came to be prized for their aesthetic and amenity uses. Rivers, forests, wetlands, and deserts were seen as valuable in their natural state as part of a modern standard of living; it was maintained that some such areas should be left undeveloped and undisturbed. This preposterous notion was difficult if not impossible to accept to those whose preferences were rooted in an older time. Many clashes between older commodity and newer environmental values occurred in the Environmental Era. World War II is a convenient dividing line between the old and the new values.

Evolving environmental values were closely associated with rising standards of living and levels of education. These changed markedly after the war. Personal real income grew and the percentage of Americans with college education increased. The social context within which environmental values flourished was two-

---

fold: younger people and the more educated. With each level of age from younger to older, environmental interest fell; and with each level of education from elementary school to college degree, it rose. The advancing edge of demographic change included an advancing interest in environmental objectives. Quality of life as an idea and a focus of public action lay at the heart of what was new in American society and politics; environmental affairs were an integral element.

Several aspects of these changes are worth keeping in mind. . . . One is that they can be thought of as part of a history of consumption rather than of the history of production. They arose not out of the way in which people carried out an occupation and earned income, but out of the kind of life that income made possible and the ways in which people chose to express their new standards of living.

At one time income was spent largely to purchase necessities, and in the third decade of the twentieth century that was extended to the capacity to acquire conveniences that lightened the tasks of normal living. But with rising incomes something beyond necessities and conveniences now lay within the reach of many; they can be called amenities. Associated with home and leisure, with recreation and the "good life," these came to involve considerable choice because spending was not dictated by necessity or convenience. A general direction to the new opportunities emerged that came to be described as quality of life. Sales analysts in private business were particularly attuned to such changes as they identified diverse markets to be supplied with new goods and services. Environmental quality was an integral part of this new search for a higher standard of living.

These changes did not come to all sectors of American society in the same degree or at the same time. There were the older and the newer, those adhering to previously dominant values and those searching out more recently emerging ones. Although age was often the dividing line, there were also geographical variations. New England and the Pacific Coast were among the leading sectors of change, whereas the South moved much more slowly. In between were the Mountain West and the Midwest. These regional differences could be identified in many realms of new cultural values from the changing role of women to self-expression to environmental interests.

Several writers have attempted to analyze the social roots of environmental affairs in a more limited fashion. They emphasize factors on the periphery of American society rather than central to it, or the capacity of a few leaders of environmental organizations to manipulate the attitudes of their members or the public so as to create imaginary problems.

All this seems rather complex and contrived; public interest in environmental affairs is far simpler. It stems from a desire to improve personal, family, and community life. The desires are neither ephemeral nor erratic; they are evident in many nations, first in the advanced industrial and consumer societies and then in more recent years in those of middle and even earlier stages of development. They express human wants and needs as surely as do demands for better housing, more satisfying leisure and recreation, improved household furnishings, better health, and a greater sense of well-being. We customarily associate these with human "progress," which normally is accepted as a fundamental concern unnecessary to explain away in other terms. An interest in the environmental quality of life is to be understood simply as an integral part of the drives inherent in persistent human aspiration and achievement. . . .

The Search for Environmental Amenities

The most widespread source of emerging environmental interest was the search for a better life associated with home, community, and leisure. A new emphasis on smaller families developed, allowing parents to invest their limited time and income in fewer children. Child rearing was now oriented toward a more extended period of childhood in order to nurture abilities. Parents sought to provide creative-arts instructions, summer camps, and family vacations so as to foster self-development. Within this context the phrase "environmental quality" would have considerable personal meaning.

It also had meaning for place of residence. Millions of urban Americans desired to live on the fringe of the city where life was less congested, the air cleaner, noise reduced, and there was less concentrated waste from manifold human activities. In the nineteenth century only the well-to-do could afford to live some distance from work. Although streetcars enabled white-collar workers to live in the suburbs and work downtown, blue-collar employees still could not pay the cost of daily transportation. But the automobile largely lifted this limitation, and after World War II blue-collar workers were able to escape the industrial community as a place of residence. Still, by the 1970s as many as one-third of urban Americans wished they could live farther out in the countryside.

The search for a higher quality of living involved a desire for more space both inside and outside the home. Life in the city had been intensely crowded for urban dwellers. Often the street in front of the house had constituted the only available open space. Moving to the suburbs reflected a desire to enjoy a more natural setting, but it also evidenced the search for nature beyond the metropolitan area in the parks and woodlands of the countryside. This desire increased with the ease of access to rural areas by means of the automobile. The state-parks movement of the 1920s expressed the demand by city dwellers for places in which to enjoy the countryside on the weekend or during summer vacations.

There was also the desire to obtain private lands in the countryside so as to enjoy nature not found in the city. In the 1960s and 1970s the market for vacation homesites boomed. Newspaper advertisements abounded with phrases that signaled the important values: "by a sparkling stream," "abundant wildlife," "near the edge of a forest road," "200 feet of lakefront," "on the edge of a state forest."

This pursuit of natural values by city dwellers led to a remarkable turnabout in the attitudes of Americans toward natural environments. These had long been thought of as unused wastelands that could be made valuable only if developed. But after World War II many such areas came to be thought of as valuable only if left in their natural condition. Forested land, once thought of by many as dark, forbidding, and sinister, a place to be avoided because of the dangers lurking within, now was highly esteemed.

Wetlands, formerly known as swamplands, fit only for draining so that they could become productive agricultural land, were valued as natural systems, undisturbed and undeveloped. Similar positive attitudes were expressed for the prairies of the Midwest, the swamps of the South, and the pine barrens of the East. For many years wild animals had been seen as a threat to farmers and others. Little concern had been shown for the sharp decline even in the deer population, let alone among the bear and bobcat. Yet by the 1960s and 1970s predators, as well as deer, small mammals, and wild turkey, had assumed a positive image for many Americans, and special measures were adopted to protect them and increase their numbers.

Close on the heels of these changes in attitude were new views about western deserts. The desert had long been thought of as a forbidding land where human habitation was impossible and travel was dangerous. The desert hardly figured in the debate over the Wilderness Act of 1964. But by the late 1970s this had changed. The increased popularity of nature photography had brought home the desert to the American people as a place of wonder and beauty. By 1976 western deserts had been explored and identified by many Americans as lands that should be protected in their natural condition.

Environmental Health and Well-being

The search for greater health and well-being constituted an equally significant element of the drive for environmental quality. Such concerns had firm roots in the earlier public-health movement, which emphasized the social conditions that gave rise to health problems. Improvements in water quality all but eliminated typhoid fever and other waterborne bacterial ailments while parasitic and viral diseases such as malaria and yellow fever were brought under control by sanitary measures. The discovery and widespread use of antibiotics after World War II limited the adverse effects of secondary infections. Such measures greatly reduced human suffering and prolonged life. But they also emphasized new causes of illness, many of them environmental.

As tuberculosis declined, other lung problems such as emphysema and cancer received more attention. The Tuberculosis Association changed its name to the American Lung Association to reflect the new emphasis; it became especially concerned with smoking as a cause of lung cancer and air pollution as a cause of pulmonary problems. Exposures formerly associated with infectious diseases now were found to be responsible for more deep-seated problems. Asbestos, for example, once had been thought of primarily as a cause of asbestosis, a pulmonary condition. Many lung problems arising from exposure to asbestos could not be treated with antibiotics and were found to be cancer.

Cancer received particular attention, as its incidence seemed to increase. By the late 1970s one-fourth of all living Americans would contract cancer during their lifetime, and two-thirds of these would die from it. The long latency period between exposure and the appearance of cancer created a sense of peril that made the disease more dramatic. At the same time, cancer was identified with either personal habits, such as smoking and diet, or environmental pollutants in air and water.

The new concerns for environmental health also focused on the workplace. Occupational dangers to workers had long been thought of mainly as posed by physical factors such as machinery. Increasingly the workplace was seen as an environment in which the air itself could transmit harmful substances to cause diseases in workers. Recognition of this danger came only slowly. Much of it awaited evidence accumulated from long-term studies of the relationship between occupational exposure and disease.

The concern for environmental health was primarily an urban phenomenon. The incidence of cancer was twice as high in cities as in the rural countryside, a difference attributed to the impact of urban pollution. The chemical products involved in manufacturing, increasing with each passing year after World War II, seemed especially to affect urban people adversely. The extensive use of the automobile in cities also posed continuing pollution threats. And studies of indoor air identified health hazards in offices and households.

Although older waterborne diseases had been controlled through chlorination and disinfection of drinking-water supplies, the rapid accumulation of newer chemical pollutants in the nation's rivers and its underground water generated new health concerns. Synthetic organic compounds, as well as heavy metals from industry, were discovered in many drinking-water sources. The disposal of industrial toxic wastes constituted an even more pervasive concern; they were often injected underground, but just as frequently they were disposed of in landfills from which they leaked into water supplies.

The increasing emphasis on environmental health arose from a rising level of expectations about health and well-being. As life expectancy increased, the average American could look forward to a decade or more of active life after retirement. As the threat of infectious disease decreased, fear of sudden death or disability from polio, secondary infections from simple surgical procedures such as appendectomies, or other dangers declined sharply. All this led to a new focus in health associated more with expectations of well-being than with fear of death. There was a special interest in the quality of life of elderly people. An increasing portion of the population became concerned about preventive health care, showing interest in physical fitness, food and diet, and protection from exposure to environmental pollutants. This marked innovation in ideas about personal health was an important element in the expanding concern for one's environment as a critical element in well-being.

The Ecological Perspective

Ecological objectives—an emphasis on the workings of natural biological and geological systems and the pressures human actions placed on them—were a third element of environmental concern. Whereas amenities involved an aesthetic response to the environment, and environmental health concerned a choice between cleaner and dirtier technologies within the built-up environment, ecological matters dealt with imbalances between developed and natural systems that had both current and long-term implications. These questions, therefore, involved ideas about permanence.

The term "ecology" had long referred to a branch of biology that emphasized study of the interaction of living organisms with their physical and biological environment. Popular ecology in the 1960s and 1970s went beyond that scientific meaning. One heard of the impact of people on "the ecology." Professional ecologists disdained this corruption of the word as they had used it. Popular use involved both a broad meaning, the functioning of the biological and geological world, and a narrower one, the disruption of natural processes by human action, as well as the notion that the two, natural systems and human stress, needed to be brought into a better balance.

The popular ecological perspective was reflected in the ecology centers that arose in urban areas. Initially these grew out of the recycling movement—the collection of paper, glass, and tin cans for reprocessing. These centers drew together people who wished to help solve the litter problem and thus to enhance the aesthetic quality of their communities. But soon the concept of recycling seemed to spill over into larger ideas about natural cycles, a traditional ecological theme, and to human action to foster such processes. Ecology centers often expanded their activities into community organic gardens, nutrition and food for better health, and changing life-styles to reduce the human load on natural resources and natural systems.

An ecological perspective grew from the popularization of knowledge about natural processes. These were ideas significant to the study of ecology, but selected and modified by popular experience rather than as a result of formal study. An increasing number of personal or media encounters with the natural world gave rise to widely shared ideas about the functioning of biological and geological systems and the relationship of human beings to them. Even before World War II, the problem of deer overpopulation on the north rim of the Grand Canyon, or imbalances between the numbers of deer and food in the cutover forestlands of Pennsylvania, Michigan, Wisconsin, and Minnesota, had popularized knowledge about predator-prey and food-population relationships. Overgrazing by cattle and sheep on the western range sparked discussions in the media of the problem of stress in plant communities in which, through overuse, the more vulnerable plants gave way to the hardier, reducing the variety of species. This conveyed the ideas that species diversity had evolved in the process of natural succession, that the number and diversity of species were reduced under population pressures, and that the capacity of ecological systems to sustain human use without major changes were limited.

The threat of toxic chemicals diffused throughout the biological world led to the spread of knowledge in the 1960s about biological and chemical cycles. Transported through the atmosphere, falling into water and on land, chemicals were absorbed by plants, eaten by animals and then by humans. With each step in that food chain they increased in concentration. Media coverage in the late 1950s and early 1960s of radioactive fallout from atomic testing increased awareness of these processes. The most dramatic example was radioactive cesium, which was absorbed by lichens in the Arctic, eaten by reindeer and in turn by Alaskan Eskimos and Laplanders, at each step increasing in concentration in fatty tissues.

The public encounter with pesticides drove home ideas about the accumulation of toxic materials in the food chain. These persistent pesticides found their way into water to be taken up by small fish that were eaten by larger fish, and then by birds to produce weakened eggshells and reduced hatching. Rachel Carson's book *Silent Spring*, published in 1962, spread the word about the problem; even more influential was a widely reported administrative proceeding about DDT in Wisconsin in 1968 and 1969.

New Strands of Environmentalism

Abridged from Kirkpatrick Sale, The Green Revolution: The American Environmental Movement, 1962–1992 *(New York, 1993), 57–68.*

As the environmental majors expanded their Washington operations, a process that would continue for the next decade, two other important dimensions were added to (or became more noteworthy in) the movement: grass-roots activism and radical environmentalism.

Some part of environmentalism had always been primarily local, simply because many of the problems—nuclear plants, waste dumps, factory emissions—were local. But with the eighties, and the growing feeling that official Washington was unresponsive and environmental Washington preoccupied, grass-roots organizations proliferated; Peter Borrelli, editor of . . . *Amicus* magazine, estimated that some 25 million people were involved one way or another at the local level by 1987–88. With the passion of people whose lives were intimately affected and an energy fired by what came to be called the NIMBY (Not in My Backyard) syndrome, these groups made themselves heard by both state and city agencies and local corporations, often with telling effect. "Today the action is bottom-up," Borrelli noted, "since it is at the local level that laws and programs set in place over the last two decades are implemented"—or, just as often, not. It was just such action that led to the passage of Proposition 65 in California in 1985, an anti-toxic initiative against state agricultural and chemical industries, the first successful environmental initiative since 1972.

The grass-roots response was often much tougher and less compromising than those of national organizations, both because the local activists did not have large disparate constituencies to worry about and because they had, literally, to live with the decisions made. "If someone's worried about the health of their children," as one activist put it, "they won't be convinced by appeals to 'political pragmatism.'" Or as Barry Commoner saw it:

The older national environmental organizations in their Washington offices have taken the soft political road of negotiation, compromising with the corporations on the amount of pollution that is acceptable. The people living in the polluted communities have taken the hard political road of confrontation, demanding not that the dumping of hazardous waste be slowed down but that it be stopped.

Grass-roots organizations also had a broader reach and, in usually undeveloped ways, a somewhat deeper perception than the nationals tended to have. Minority groups of all kinds and many blue-collar neighborhoods were drawn to environmental activism out of some local need—particularly because they were often targets of undesirable and dangerous projects that affluent communities resisted—whereas the majors were made up largely of white and more affluent staffs and constituencies. Women, too, were disproportionately represented in both membership and leadership of local groups, often housewives with little previous activism but a number who were veterans of various protests of the sixties. And because such people were in the trenches, as it were, they tended to have much less reverence either for the assurances of officialdom or for the pronouncements of experts, all of which they treated with a healthy distrust, and they were much less inclined to believe in the inevitable worth of economic growth or the unquestioned right of corporations to make decisions affecting local social and environmental affairs.

The most impressive evidence of grass-roots power came with the hottest issue of the decade, toxic waste. Largely at the instigation of Lois Gibbs, a housewife whose effective leadership of the residents of the Love Canal neighborhood brought her national attention, a Citizens' Clearinghouse for Hazardous Wastes was formed in 1981 to coordinate and assist the work of local groups. By the fall of 1986 it had a network of 1,300 groups, two-thirds of them begun after 1984, when news of the evacuation of dioxin-infested Times Beach and the explosion at the chemical plant in Bhopal was prominent in the media; by the end of the decade it reported working with no fewer than 7,000. Organized around such issues as groundwater contamination from landfills, dumping of industrial chemicals and heavy metals, and new incinerators for municipal garbage, such groups energized many people who had been politically inactive and exerted their power with letter-writing campaigns, town meetings, door-to-door canvassing, and even demonstrations and civil disobedience. With encouragement, information, and advice from the Clearinghouse—for example, on up-to-the-minute alternatives for sewage treatment that could win over reluctant town boards—many of the locals were able to gain substantial concessions or outright victories, usually to the surprise of their high-powered antagonists. One indication of the alliance's effect is that since the Love Canal crisis in 1978, no new hazardous-waste dumps have been established in America. "Not because they're illegal," Lois Gibbs is careful to point out, "but because people have lobbied at the grass roots.". . .

The second new dimension of the eighties, radical environmentalism, was similarly decentralized and often emerged in similar reaction to the nationals, but it was usually inspired by people with considerable political experience, much of it tinged by the insights of the sixties and often informed by years of work inside the mainstream movement. Their causes and their tactics, not to mention their styles and rhetoric, grew directly out of opposition to what they saw as the reformism and the "cooptation" of the mainstream at a time when the perils seemed to be multiplying and the national leadership unresponsive. Among the charges that they leveled was that the old organizations were too legalistic ("You should never support a piece of legislation," said Dave Foreman, radicalized after a decade of suit-and-tie lobbying in Washington, "you should always be asking for more"); too professional ("You've got a new group of bureaucratic professionals," asserted Lorna Salzman, a onetime . . . activist in New York, "who are not in it for a cause but because it's a 'public interest' highfalutin *job*"); and too limited ("The reform environmentalists have no program and no vision," argued George Sessions, a professor of philosophy at Sierra College, "they're about on the level of the penal establishment").

The emergence of this new breed and their criticism of the majors were serious enough to prompt Michael McClosky, director of the Sierra Club from 1969 to 1985 and its subsequent chairman, to send a confidential memo to his board of directors in January 1986 warning of the "new, more militant" environmentalists. "They are people who do not hesitate to criticize the main players such as the Sierra Club," he wrote, but their target is larger, to change "the relationship of individuals to society and the ways in which society works." The question they pose to the movement is "whether it is wise to work within the context of the basic social, political, and economic institutions to achieve stepwise progress, or whether prime energies must be directed at changing those institutions." And he added: "They're just utopian. We may be 'reformist' and all, but we know how to work within the context of the institutions of the society—and they're just blowing smoke."

Not quite smoke. The new radicals could sometimes be more vociferous than they were coherent, sometimes let frustrations lead them into actions insufficiently planned, sometimes were trapped into taking positions in public without having done enough homework—in short, showed the failings of any large group of disparate people acting in the public arena against the status quo. But in the decade of the eighties they made their mark.

Despite differences, sometimes substantial, what generally united the radical environmentalists was an underlying criticism of the dominant anthropocentric Western view of the world and a feeling that the transition to an ecological or biocentric view had to be made with all possible speed, with active and dramatic prodding if necessary. Such a sensibility was deeply ecological, in that it understood the true interdependence of species and their habitats (and the necessarily limited role of the human among them), and deeply radical too, in that it demanded a profound change in the values and beliefs of industrial society from the bottom up. Altogether, in the words of philosopher George Sessions, "it shows us that the basic assumptions upon which the modern urban-industrial edifice of Western culture rests are erroneous and highly dangerous. An ecologically harmonious paradigm shift is going to require a *total* reorientation of the thrust of Western culture."

Among the expressions of this new radicalism, four overlapping tendencies stand out.

Bioregionalism, the idea that the earth is to be understood as a series of life territories defined by topography and biota rather than by humans and their legislatures, was the first to take root in America. It imagined human societies organized on the lines of empowered bioregions, expressing such values as conservation and stability rather than exploitation and progress, cooperation and diversity rather than competition and uniformity, and decentralism and division rather than centralization and mono-culture;

as one early formulation put it, "the bioregional movement seeks to re-create a widely shared sense of regional identity founded upon a renewed critical awareness of and respect for the integrity of our natural ecological communities."

The movement itself began in California in the late 1970s and by the mid-1980s it encompassed some sixty local organizations: some were explicit bioregional councils, as in the Ozarks, the Kansas prairie, the Hudson Valley, and the Northwest; some, such as the National Water Center in Arkansas and Friends of the Trees in Washington State, had the specialized interests their names implied; some, including those in Appalachia, the Columbia River valley, the San Francisco Bay area, and Cape Cod, published regular magazines on bioregional themes. The first of a series of biannual continental congresses, designed to set policies on environmental issues and establish movement-wide links, was held in the Ozarks in 1984, since then followed by meetings in Michigan, British Columbia, Maine, and Texas.

Deep ecology, originally formulated by Norwegian philosopher Arne Naess in the seventies, was brought to the United States primarily by George Sessions and sociologist Bill Devall, who co-authored its first popular account in 1984. Standing in contrast to what Naess termed the "shallow environmentalism" of most of the movement, deep ecology stressed such points as: ecological equality, the right of every species to existence and survival and with equal "intrinsic value" regardless of its importance for humans; the diversity and abundance of all life forms, which should not be reduced by humans except "to satisfy vital needs"; the sharp reduction of human population so that other species may not only survive but have sufficient habitat to thrive; the preservation of the wilderness as a pristine habitat valuable in its own right; and the self-realization of humans through lower levels of consumption and resource use. Complicated as they were, such ideas quickly gained a following in the United States—and elsewhere in the world, including Canada, Australia, and Northern Europe—and proved especially influential among both radical activists and academic philosophers, no mean feat. . . .

Ecofeminism, a synergistic blend of sixties-style feminism with eighties-style ecology, placed its emphasis on the connections between the domination and exploitation of women and the domination and exploitation of nature, both seen as products of a male-dominated society. Inspired in part by two books, Susan Griffin's *Woman and Nature* in 1978 and Carolyn Merchant's *The*

Death of Nature in 1980, ecofeminism sought to go beyond the limits of earlier feminist ideologies, particularly by raising issues that set women in a context wider than just the economic. "Why is it that women and nature are associated, and vilified in our culture?" asked one early proponent, Ynestra King. "Does the liberation of one depend on the liberation of the other?" It also sought to go beyond what were seen as the limitations of other radicalisms by raising questions about "androcentrism," the male-focused perspective, as the real heart of the eco-crisis and about patriarchy as the central instrument in understanding the Western domination of nature. Like deep ecology, ecofeminism had a considerable following on the campuses, in women's studies and philosophy departments particularly, and inspired a veritable torrent of books and articles in this decade; several ecofeminist conferences were held in these years as well, the largest and most comprehensive at UCLA in the spring of 1987.

The Gaia hypothesis, formulated by British scientist James Lovelock in a small book in 1979, suggested that because the earth was apparently so regulated as to maintain its temperature, its atmosphere, and its hydrosphere with extraordinary precision for millions of years, it could in fact be thought of as a living organism. Immediately popular among many nonscientists as a useful metaphor for thinking about a biocentric earth, the Gaia idea spawned a number of similar analyses (as well as conferences, T-shirts, study groups, and an oceangoing Viking ship), all supporting positions congenial to the radical perspective. Interestingly, the hypothesis was seen to embody perceptions not very different from those of various early tribal peoples, including the American Indians, whose record as model ecologists was being brought to light at about this time; it was characteristic of most Indian mythologies to think of the earth as a single living being and to derive ways of behavior and thought that would ensure its careful, productive existence.

These expressions of radical environmentalism naturally gave rise to a great many organizations in these years, several of which had national importance. Among them:

- Earth First!, the more or less organized expression of the activist side of the new radicalism, was started by Dave Foreman and a handful of other disillusioned operatives from mainstream environmentalism around a campfire in 1980. Designedly formless, without national staff, bylaws, formal incorporation, or even membership, it was simply dedicated to the principle that "in *any* decision consideration for the health of the earth must come first" and that in carrying this out, it should make "no compromise in defense of Mother Earth." Inspired in part by novelist Edward Abbey's 1975 *The Monkey Wrench Gang,* Earth First!ers stood foursquare in defense of wilderness and its biodiversity and made militance a cardinal part of their tactics, soon including guerrilla theater, media stunts, civil disobedience, and, unofficially, "ecotage" (also called "monkey wrenching"): sabotaging bull-dozers and road-building equipment on public lands, pulling up survey stakes, cutting down billboards, destroying traps, and, famously, "spiking" trees at random to prevent their being cut and milled. No sure way exists of checking such a figure, but an EF! spokesperson has said that the cost to the nation of such ecotage was $20-$25 million a year.

With such forthright militance, EF! succeeded in attracting a considerable following and by the end of the decade had grown to more than seventy-five chapters in twenty-four states (mostly in the Southwest and on the West Coast) and Mexico and Canada. But it paid a penalty for its success: as Foreman put it, "from one side there are concerted efforts to moderate us, mellow us out, and sanitize our vices; from another side have come efforts to make us radical in a traditional leftist sense; and there are ongoing efforts by the powers that be to wipe us out entirely." Such pressures—including FBI infiltration and a trumped-up federal suit against Foreman and others in July 1989 and a car-bombing of two California activists in May 1990—eventually led to Foreman's dropping out and the group's splintering into several rival groups in the early 1990s. . . .

• Sea Shepherd Conservation Society was started by Paul Watson after he was kicked out of Greenpeace for being too militant; it became the method by which he lived out a vision he had had during a Sioux sweat-lodge rite that he was destined to save the mammals of the ocean, especially whales. With a "navy" consisting of a single ship, he and his crew had dedicated themselves to being the police of the seas, eventually incapacitating at least seven vessels illegally hunting whales, confronting ships illegally fishing with gill nets that trap marine mammals and birds, and taking direct action, not excluding ecotage, to prevent seal hunts in Canada, dolphin slaughter in Japanese waters, and whaling in the North Atlantic. The organization, which has some 15,000 support members, has adopted a slogan of "We don't talk about problems, we act," and it has lived up to it.

Questions

1. *What factors explain the rise of the environmental movement, according to Hays? Can you think of other factors that might have played an important role?*
2. *Compare the environmental movement to other reform movements in American history. Is the environmental movement unique in any way?*
3. *Do you believe that the tactics of direct-action environmental groups such as Earth First! are justified?*
4. *How successful has the environmental movement been in the United States?*

Environmentalists as Critics

In the decades following the end of the Second World War, the material prosperity enjoyed by the majority of Americans made the American standard of living the envy of much of the world. By the early 1960s, however, some influential Americans were beginning to call attention to the negative environmental effects of unrestrained industrial expansion and the wasteful excesses of the consumer society. Despite continuing efforts to present a positive alternative vision of a society in harmony with nature, environmentalists in the United States have made their greatest mark in the role of stern critics of our wasteful, destructive society. In this respect, environmentalism is part of the long tradition of dissent in the United States that has challenged the workings of the capitalist system. The selections that follow question in both explicit and implicit fashion some of the core assumptions that guided the development of American society for generations. As you read these selections, be careful to consider the broader implications of the authors' arguments for individual lifestyles and the role of government in the United States.

The Chemical Threat

One historian called Rachel Carson's book Silent Spring *"the Uncle Tom's Cabin of modern environmentalism." Carson's best-selling volume alerted Americans to the dangers of the unrestrained use of pesticides and foreshadowed the environmental movement's obsession with the health dangers of human-made chemicals. Excerpted from Rachel Carson,* Silent Spring *(Boston, 1962), 1–3, 5–9.*

THERE WAS ONCE a town in the heart of America where all life seemed to live in harmony with its surroundings. The town lay in the midst of a checkerboard of prosperous farms, with fields of grain and hillsides of orchards where, in spring, white clouds of bloom drifted above the green fields. In autumn, oak and maple and birch set up a blaze of color that flamed and flickered across a backdrop of pines. Then foxes barked in the hills and deer silently crossed the fields, half hidden in the mists of the fall mornings.

Along the roads, laurel, viburnum and alder, great ferns and wildflowers delighted the traveler's eye through much of the year. Even in winter the roadsides were places of beauty, where countless birds came to feed on the berries and on the seed heads of the dried weeds rising above the snow. The countryside was, in fact, famous for the abundance and variety of its bird life, and when the flood of migrants was pouring through in spring and fall people traveled from great distances to observe them. Others came to fish the streams, which flowed clear and cold out of the hills and contained shady pools where trout lay. So it had been from the days many years ago when the first settlers raised their houses, sank their wells, and built their barns.

Then a strange blight crept over the area and everything began to change. Some evil spell had settled on the community: mysterious maladies swept the flocks of chickens; the cattle and sheep sickened and died. Everywhere was a shadow of death. The farmers spoke of much illness among their families. In the town the doctors had become more and more puzzled by new kinds of sickness appearing among their patients. There had been several sudden and unexplained deaths, not only among adults but even among children, who would be stricken suddenly while at play and die within a few hours.

There was a strange stillness. The birds, for example—where had they gone? Many people spoke of them, puzzled and disturbed. The feeding stations in the backyards were deserted. The few birds seen anywhere were moribund; they trembled violently and could not fly. It was a spring without voices. On the mornings that had once throbbed with the dawn chorus of robins, catbirds, doves, jays, wrens, and scores of other bird voices there was now no sound; only silence lay over the fields and woods and marsh.

On the farms the hens brooded, but no chicks hatched. The farmers complained that they were unable to raise any pigs—the

---

Excerpts from *Silent Spring* by Rachel Carson, published by Houghton Mifflin Company, 1962. Copyright © 1962 by Rachel L. Carson.

litters were small and the young survived only a few days. The apple trees were coming into bloom but no bees droned among the blossoms, so there was no pollination and there would be no fruit.

The roadsides, once so attractive, were now lined with browned and withered vegetation as though swept by fire. These, too, were silent, deserted by all living things. Even the streams were now lifeless. Anglers no longer visited them, for all the fish had died.

In the gutters under the eaves and between the shingles of the roofs, a white granular powder still showed a few patches; some weeks before it had fallen like snow upon the roofs and the lawns, the fields and streams.

No witchcraft, no enemy action had silenced the rebirth of new life in this stricken world. The people had done it themselves.

This town does not actually exist, but it might easily have a thousand counterparts in America or elsewhere in the world. I know of no community that has experienced all the misfortunes I describe. Yet every one of these disasters has actually happened somewhere, and many real communities have already suffered a substantial number of them. A grim specter has crept upon us almost unnoticed, and this imagined tragedy may easily become a stark reality we all shall know.

What has already silenced the voices of spring in countless towns in America? This . . . is an attempt to explain.

The history of life on earth has been a history of interaction between living things and their surroundings. To a large extent, the physical form and the habits of the earth's vegetation and its animal life have been molded by the environment. Considering the whole span of earthly time, the opposite effect, in which life actually modifies its surroundings, has been relatively slight. Only within the moment of time represented by the present century has one species—man—acquired significant power to alter the nature of his world.

During the past quarter century this power has not only increased to one of disturbing magnitude but it has changed in character. The most alarming of all man's assaults upon the environment is the contamination of air, earth, rivers, and sea with dangerous and even lethal materials. This pollution is for the most part irrecoverable; the chain of evil it initiates not only in the world that must support life but in living tissues is for the most part irreversible. In this now universal contamination of the environment, chemicals are the sinister and little-recognized partners of radiation in changing the very nature of the world—the very nature of its life. Strontium 90, released through nuclear explosions into the air, comes to earth in rain or drifts down as fallout, lodges in soil, enters into the grass or corn or wheat grown there, and in time takes up its abode in the bones of a human being, there to remain until his death. Similarly, chemicals sprayed on croplands or forests or gardens lie long in soil, entering into living organisms, passing from one to another in a chain of poisoning and death. Or they pass mysteriously by underground streams until they emerge and, through the alchemy of air and sunlight, combine into new forms that kill vegetation, sicken cattle, and work unknown harm on those who drink from once pure wells. As Albert Schweitzer has said, "Man can hardly even recognize the devils of his own creation."

It took hundreds of millions of years to produce the life that now inhabits the earth—eons of time in which that developing and evolving and diversifying life reached a state of adjustment and balance with its surroundings. The environment, rigorously shaping and directing the life it supported, contained elements that were hostile as well as supporting. Certain rocks gave out dangerous radiation; even within the light of the sun, from which all life draws its energy, there were short-wave radiations with power to injure. Given time—time not in years but in millennia— life adjusts, and a balance has been reached. For time is the essential ingredient; but in the modern world there is no time.

The rapidity of change and the speed with which new situations are created follow the impetuous and heedless pace of man rather than the deliberate pace of nature. Radiation is no longer merely the background radiation of rocks, the bombardment of cosmic rays, the ultraviolet of the sun that have existed before there was any life on earth; radiation is now the unnatural creation of man's tampering with the atom. The chemicals to which life is asked to make its adjustment are no longer merely the calcium and silica and copper and all the rest of the minerals washed out of the rocks and carried in rivers to the sea; they are the synthetic creations of man's inventive mind, brewed in his laboratories, and having no counterparts in nature.

To adjust to these chemicals would require time on the scale that is nature's; it would require not merely the years of a man's life but the life of generations. And even this, were it by some miracle possible, would be futile, for the new chemicals come from our laboratories in an endless stream; almost five hundred annually find their way into actual use in the United States alone. The figure is staggering and its implications are not easily grasped—500 new chemicals to which the bodies of men and animals are required somehow to adapt each year, chemicals totally outside the limits of biologic experience.

Among them are many that are used in man's war against nature. Since the mid-1940s over 200 basic chemicals have been created for use in killing insects, weeds, rodents, and other organisms described in the modern vernacular as "pests"; and they are sold under several thousand different brand names.

These sprays, dusts, and aerosols are now applied almost universally to farms, gardens, forests, and homes—nonselective chemicals that have the power to kill every insect, the "good" and the "bad," to still the song of birds and the leaping of fish in the streams, to coat the leaves with a deadly film, and to linger on in soil—all this though the intended target may be only a few weeds or insects. Can anyone believe it is possible to lay down such a barrage of poisons on the surface of the earth without making it unfit for all life? They should not be called "insecticides," but "biocides."

The whole process of spraying seems caught up in an endless spiral. Since DDT was released for civilian use, a process of escalation has been going on in which ever more toxic materials must be found. This has happened because insects, in a triumphant vindication of Darwin's principle of the survival of the fittest, have evolved super races immune to the particular insecticide used, hence a deadlier one has always to be developed—and then a deadlier one than that. It has happened also because . . . destructive insects often undergo a "flareback," or resurgence, after spraying, in numbers greater than before. Thus the chemical war is never won, and all life is caught in its violent crossfire.

Along with the possibility of the extinction of mankind by nuclear war, the central problem of our age has therefore become the contamination of man's total environment with such substances of incredible potential for harm—substances that accumulate in the tissues of plants and animals and even penetrate the germ cells to shatter or alter the very material of heredity upon which the shape of the future depends.

Some would-be architects of our future look toward a time when it will be possible to alter the human germ plasm by design. But we may easily be doing so now by inadvertence, for many chemicals, like radiation, bring about gene mutations. It is ironic to think that man might determine his own future by something so seemingly trivial as the choice of an insect spray.

All this has been risked—for what? Future historians may well be amazed by our distorted sense of proportion. How could intelligent beings seek to control a few unwanted species by a method that contaminated the entire environment and brought the threat of disease and death even to their own kind? Yet this is precisely what we have done. We have done it, moreover, for reasons that collapse the moment we examine them. We are told that the enormous and expanding use of pesticides is necessary to maintain farm production. Yet is our real problem not one of *overproduction*? Our farms, despite measures to remove acreage from production and to pay farmers *not* to produce, have yielded such a staggering excess of crops that the American taxpayer in 1962 is paying out more than one billion dollars a year as the total carrying cost of the surplus-food storage program. And is the situation helped when one branch of the Agriculture Department tries to reduce production while another states, as it did in 1958, "It is believed generally that reduction of crop acreages under provisions of the Soil Bank will stimulate interest in use of chemicals to obtain maximum production on the land retained in crops."

All this is not to say there is no insect problem and no need of control. I am saying, rather, that control must be geared to realities, not to mythical situations, and that the methods employed must be such that they do not destroy us along with the insects.

Questioning the Affluent Society

Stewart Udall served as secretary of the interior under Presidents Kennedy and Johnson and played a major role in shaping national environmental policy during the seminal decade of the 1960s. Excerpted from Stewart L. Udall, The Quiet Crisis *(New York, 1963), vii–viii.*

ONE WEEK last fall two events came to my attention which seemed to sum up the plight of modern man: the first was a press report which indicated the T. S. Eliot, the poet, was a victim of London's latest "killer fog" and lay gravely ill; the second was a call from a preservation-minded citizen of New Hampshire who informed me that Robert Frost's old farm—fixed for all time in memory by the poem "West-running Brook"—was now an auto junk yard.

The coincidence of these two events raised questions in my mind: Is a society a success if it creates conditions that impair its finest minds and make a wasteland of its finest landscapes? What does material abundance avail if we create an environment in which man's highest and most specifically human attributes cannot be fulfilled?

Each generation has its own rendezvous with the land, for despite our fee titles and claims of ownership, we are all brief tenants on this planet. By choice, or by default, we will carve out a land legacy for our heirs. We can misuse the land and diminish the usefulness of resources, or we can create a world in which physical affluence and affluence of the spirit go hand in hand.

History tells us that earlier civilizations have declined because they did not learn to live in harmony with the land. Our successes in space and our triumphs of technology hold a hidden danger: as modern man increasingly arrogates to himself dominion over the physical environment, there is the risk that his false pride will cause him to take the resources of the earth for granted—and to lose all reverence for the land.

America today stands poised on a pinnacle of wealth and power, yet we live in a land of vanishing beauty, of increasing ugliness, of shrinking open space, and of an overall environment that is diminished daily by pollution and noise and blight.

This, in brief, is the quiet conservation crisis of the 1960s.

Attacking Corporate America

During the 1960s, the deteriorating conditions of the Great Lakes became a national symbol of unchecked pollution and environmental degradation. Under the leadership of Walter Reuther, the United Auto Workers (UAW) took a prominent role in calling for greater efforts to halt the decline of the Great Lakes. Taken from a public statement by Robert Johnston, regional director of the UAW, submitted to a federal conference on the pollution of Lake Michigan in February 1968, U.S. Department of the Interior, Federal Water Pollution Control Administration, Proceedings of the Conference in the Matter of Pollution of Lake Michigan and its Tributary Basin *(Washington, 1968), 1333–38.*

The UAW wishes to associate itself at this conference with those who believe that we are in danger of being too late with too little if we are to save Lake Michigan. Fifty years of indifference and inaction about Lake Michigan and the Great Lakes has created a problem that can't be solved by old techniques that are comparable to trying to bail out pollution with a bucket. Reliance on such techniques will only result in creating another Dead Sea along the industrial and urban waterfronts of Lake Michigan.

The formula for saving Lake Michigan and the Great Lakes is simple enough. All that is needed is higher anti-pollution standards and the realization of these standards by faster action and rigid enforcement. We believe that the present Federal and State laws are inadequate to secure the enforcement of the anti-pollution measures that are needed. We believe that the present Federal funds, reduced in the proposed new budget, are inadequate to assist cities and States in pure water projects. . . .

The corporations responsible for turning the lakefront into an industrial cesspool reads like a Blue Book of big profit companies in America. United States Steel, Ford Motor Company, Standard Oil, International Harvester, Inland Steel, Republic Steel, Sinclair Refining Company. The Who's Who of Big Business have helped themselves to billions in profits by using the lake water and dumping back pollutants. These same corporations are protesting

Excerpts from *Proceedings of the Conference on Pollution of Lake Michigan and Its Tributary Basin*, published by the U.S. Department of the Interior, Federal Water Pollution Control Administration, 1968.

adequate anti-pollution standards, and dragging their feet under the inadequate enforcement provisions. . . .

The labor movement deserves to be criticized for leaving the corporation polluters alone too long. It isn't enough for a union to get sufficient drinking fountains and hot showers in an auto plant or a steel mill and ignore the fact that the companies are helping kill a great natural resource like Lake Michigan. The lake belongs to union dues payers and the rest of the public, and not to corporations. The labor movement therefore has an obligation to also fight to save the lake. . . .

The corporations certainly can plead poverty about our grievance over Lake Michigan. Corporations in the industrial complex along the lake make several billion in profits annually. They have invested hundreds of millions in the most modern automated equipment and new plants while delaying the installation of effective anti-pollutant systems.

The UAW has welcomed recently the signs of an awakening social conscience on the part of some corporations on such national problems as hard-core unemployment, open housing, and low-cost housing developments. The corporations should also expand their moral obligation to cleaning up Lake Michigan. All these problems have a relationship. Behind the big profit plants on the polluted lake are the poor neighborhoods and the slums enveloped in polluted air and all the increasing social problems of the urban centers. We are either going to clean up Lake Michigan and the slums behind them or the indifference of corporate neglect and public apathy will fan some social firestorms that all the polluted water in the Great Lakes can't put out.

The final solution to pure water, the new sewerage and sanitation systems needed by the cities and the cleaning up of the rivers that dump into Lake Michigan and the Great Lakes, depends upon putting a proper high national and State priority on this crucial problem and allocating adequate funds to solve the problem.

We in the UAW believe that our Nation must remain strong, not only in military hardware, but in social progress. As President Walter Reuther pointed out at our National Pure Water Conference, "We must find a way to spend as much on such basic necessities of life as water and fresh air and social welfare as we do on defense and armaments."

Protecting Working-Class Communities

In 1978, the community of Love Canal near Niagara Falls, New York, received national attention when local citizens and public health authorities connected area health problems to a nearby toxic waste dump. The tactics used by Lois Gibbs and her neighbors to combat this local threat and force government action became the model for other communities across the nation faced with similar problems. The following excerpt is taken from a speech by Gibbs in 1980. Abridged from "'It Does Affect You:' Women at Love Canal and Three Mile Island," ed. Celeste Wesson, Radical America *17 (March-June 1983): 29–32.*

The women of Love Canal are much like myself—housewives, mothers. Most have a high school education. We are lower-middle-class families with our biggest investment our home, and our most precious asset our children. The majority did not work but remained home tending to houses, gardens and growing children. Since the Love Canal exposure, this way of life has changed. Women are no longer at home, because it is unsafe; we're not allowed to go near our gardens. The decisions have changed too, from normal everyday questions such as: What are we going to have for dinner? Where are we going on vacation? What color shall we paint the walls? Now the decisions are: How can we afford a new home? Will my baby have leukemia? Will my daughter ever have a normal baby? What will we do with our sick child? We can't move and we can't stay here.

Women prior to the Love Canal disaster were very sort of square, I guess. Women who at one time looked down on people picketing, being arrested and acting somewhat radical are now doing those very things. Now women who would never have volunteered for anything have given up two years of their lives to try to save their families, working in our office, conducting phone surveys, going from door to door. . . .

Many women, especially the active ones, have been faced with another major problem—their marriages. Most of them were

---

Excerpts reprinted from "'It Does Affect You:' Women at Love Canal and Three Mile Island," a speech by Lois Gibbs, as it appeared in *Radical America*, Vol. 17, No. 2–3, March–June 1983. Reprinted by permission of Lois Gibbs.[1]

homemakers. Dinner was ready at five, laundry was done, and children were properly cared for. Now, in many households, dinner is not ready at five, laundry is not quite done, and the neighbor is taxiing the children around. The husbands are forced to do these things—to be satisfied with hamburgers at McDonald's three times a week, with taking care of the children more. The husbands feel helpless because they cannot protect their families and are also jealous because their wives are now working with other men in the office. The result of all this is stress, which leads to arguments and in many cases divorce. Among families who relocated in August 1978, approximately 40% have ended in separation or divorce. There are pressures and decisions that no normal marriage is subjected to: Will we walk away from our homes and our savings to protect our children? It's easy for you sitting in the audience to say, of course. But think about it. Think about packing the clothes in your closet and walking away to start all over again with nothing—no savings, no furniture, no money, children who are always hungry and ten thousand dollars a year.

The first thing we learned when we started organizing was how valuable the media can be. We learned what would get us national attention, like our survey on women who became pregnant during the construction of the containment system on the canal proper. During this period there was additional air contamination from open trenches. There were 15 pregnancies during this time. Of the 15, only one normal baby was born. All the rest ended in miscarriages, birth defects or diseased children.

We organized rallies and protests around times when coverage was slow throughout most of the state. We found that numbers, long chemical names and statistics confused people, so we arranged a series—a horror story of the day. One family, in their home, would tell of their problems: a mother would explain how her baby died or had three major birth defects, or a family would reveal that state officials told them not to go into their basement, their son's bedroom or their kitchen because of chemical readings—and then the state would publicly announce there was no problem there. This was very successful and we received a large response. Readers became furious with the government for allowing this to continue.

We also found the media very helpful in pushing the government to do what is right. In August 1979, Governor Carey was running for reelection. We held a public meeting and asked: Where is the Governor? Is he campaigning instead of taking care of the emergency situation in his state? What are his priorities? Two days later Governor Carey visited Love Canal, stood on stage in front of hundreds of people who were screaming "Murderer, help our children," with both men and women crying. Cameras rolled. The whole state watched, so he told everyone that the state would buy their homes at fair market value. Now he was a hero. He was reelected. We found that one thing government cannot stand is a confrontation of men, women and children out in the street protesting and pleading for help in front of the press. . . .

Although Love Canal may be the first, it is definitely not the only real toxic waste problem. Because we have received national media coverage, citizens call us from all over the country. Many of them tell us of wastes buried in their backyards and health problems they believe are not normal. The whole toxic waste issue affects everyone. There are thousands of known poisonous dump sites across the country and many unknown ones. These dump sites are invading our land, air and drinking water, and they must be cleaned up. Because of the cost involved to clean and monitor each site, both government and industry would like to ignore them. Meanwhile, innocent people are being hurt and profits are being made by industry.

The only way to clean up the sites properly and to avoid new Love Canals being built is for people to force the government to implement laws to stop careless disposal of toxic wastes and force industries to clean up their own dumps. We, the taxpayers, should not bear the costs of clean up while the responsible party is sitting back making a profit. The one thing you must understand is that *it does affect you*—you, the taxpayer; you, the consumer; or you, the victim! Unless you have thoroughly checked out your backyard and your drinking water, you are not safe. We never knew about Love Canal when we moved in eight years ago. Your children may move into an unsafe area as we did, unaware and innocent, only to suffer.

Basic Principles of Deep Ecology

Those who adhere to the ideals of deep ecology reject the moderation of "reform environmentalism" and call instead for a complete reorientation of the way in which Western society relates to the natural world. George Sessions and Bill Devall are two of the leading proponents of deep ecology in the United States. Taken from Bill Devall and George Sessions, Deep Ecology: Living as If Nature Mattered *(Salt Lake City, 1985), 65–66, 70.*

Ecological consciousness and deep ecology are in sharp contrast with the dominant worldview of technocratic-industrial societies which regards humans as isolated and fundamentally separate from the rest of Nature, as superior to, and in charge of, the rest of creation. But the view of humans as separate and superior to the rest of Nature is only part of larger cultural patterns. For thousands of years, Western culture has become increasingly obsessed with the idea of *dominance:* with dominance of humans over nonhuman Nature, masculine over the feminine, wealthy and powerful over the poor, with the dominance of the West over non-Western cultures. Deep ecological consciousness allows us to see through these erroneous and dangerous illusions. . . .

Basic Principles

1. The well-being and flourishing of human and nonhuman Life on Earth have value in themselves (synonyms: intrinsic value, inherent value). These values are independent of the usefulness of the nonhuman world for human purposes.
2. Richness and diversity of life forms contribute to the realization of these values and are also values in themselves.
3. Humans have no right to reduce this richness and diversity except to satisfy vital needs.

---

4. The flourishing of human life and cultures is compatible with a substantial decrease of the human population. The flourishing of nonhuman life requires such a decrease.
5. Present human interference with the nonhuman world is excessive, and the situation is rapidly worsening.
6. Policies must therefore be changed. These policies affect basic economic, technological, and ideological structures. The resulting state of affairs will be deeply different from the present.
7. The ideological change is mainly that of appreciating life quality (dwelling in situations of inherent value) rather than adhering to an increasingly higher standard of living. There will be a profound awareness of the difference between big and great.
8. Those who subscribe to the foregoing points have an obligation directly or indirectly to try to implement the necessary changes.

Notes

[1]Lois Gibbs began her 16 years of environmental activism as President of the Love Canal Homeowners Association in 1978. Since then, she has spoken at thousands of conferences and seminars, been featured in hundreds of newspapers, magazines and textbooks, appeared on hundreds of television and radio shows, and been the recipient of numerous awards. Among her many honors are the 1990 Goldman Environmental Prize, *Outsider Magazine's* "Top Ten Who Made a Difference" Honor Roll in 1991, and an honorary Ph.D. from the State University of New York, Cortland College.

Lois has struggled alongside thousands of communities to win environmental justice. As Executive Director, Lois has led CCHW's efforts to provide organizing, training, research, educational and technical assistance services to communities in environmental crisis across the country for the past 13 years.

Questions

1. Why did Silent Spring *become such a popular and influential book?*

2. *What tactics do Carson and Gibbs use to appeal to people's emotions? Do these methods get in the way of good public policy or do they promote it?*

3. *How does deep ecology differ from mainstream environmentalism? Can you identify principles of deep ecology in the first four selections? Which of the first four authors is most in tune with the philosophy of deep ecology?*

FURTHER READING

Stephen Fox, John Muir and His Legacy: The American Conservation Movement *(Boston, 1981), places the environmental movement in historical perspective, while John McCormick,* Reclaiming Paradise: The Global Environmental Movement *(Bloomington, Indiana, 1989), surveys the international scene.* American Environmentalism: The U.S. Environmental Movement, 1970–1990, *ed. Riley E. Dunlap and Angela G. Mertig (Philadelphia, 1992), is an excellent source for recent developments. A major new work by Robert Gottlieb,* Forcing the Spring: The Transformation of the American Environmental Movement *(Washington, 1993), offers a useful corrective to much of the scholarship in this field by giving equal attention to urban-industrial health and pollution concerns.*

The Rise of the Gay and Lesbian Movement

Leila J. Rupp

INTRODUCTION

On the night of 27 June 1969, the New York City police descended on the Stonewall Inn, a Greenwich Village gay bar, for what should have been a routine raid. Gay men and lesbians had learned to live with the regular intrusion of police ever since establishments catering to the gay trade had opened in the early years of the twentieth century. But this night was different. Rather than submitting peacefully to arrest, the patrons of the Stonewall Inn—a young, racially mixed crowd—fought back. Soon a full-fledged riot erupted, lasting into the next night. This dramatic resistance to police harassment marked the birth of the modern gay and lesbian movement.

But "Stonewall," as this event has come to be known, did not occur in a vacuum. In order to understand the significance of the Stonewall riot and the subsequent formation of gay liberation groups around the country, it is important to consider both the history of gay and lesbian communities in the period before 1969 and the impact on these communities of the other social movements of the 1960s.

There have always been individuals who loved and desired people of the same sex, but it was not until the late nineteenth century that such individuals began to identify themselves as "homosexuals"—the term itself was first introduced in 1869—and to form communities in urban areas. At first largely male, such communities became more gender-mixed by the early twentieth century as women gained greater access to economic independence and to the public world of the streets. In Paris, where American expatriates gathered, in Greenwich Village, in Chicago,

*and in Harlem, lesbian and gay subcultures flourished in the
1920s.*

*The growth of subcultures paved the way for the emergence of
a social movement focused on the place of lesbian and gay people in
American society. The earliest homosexual rights organization,
the Chicago Society for Human Rights, was founded in 1924 by
Henry Gerber who, as part of the military occupation force in
Germany after the First World War, had come in contact with the
German homosexual rights movement, the earliest and most advanced in the world. But the Society for Human Rights did not
survive long; only after the Second World War did an enduring
gay and lesbian movement begin.*

*The war itself helped to stimulate the growth of gay and
lesbian subcultures. Widespread mobilization of men and women
into both the military and the labor force brought individuals with
sometimes unexpressed desires for same-sex sexual contacts into
sex-segregated worlds far from the confines of small-town life.
Men inducted into the armed forces encountered frank and potentially consciousness-raising questions about their sexual activities
and desires, and women in the new female branches found a high
proportion of lesbians among their colleagues. As a result, gay and
lesbian subcultures boomed, especially in San Francisco, port of
departure for and arrival from the Pacific theater. Even the postwar crackdown on "homosexual perversion," linked by Senator
Joseph McCarthy to Communist subversion, did not destroy the
existing subcultures and may even have spread word of their
existence.*

*In this context, the first phase of gay and lesbian organizing,
known as the homophile movement, emerged. The Mattachine
Society, formed in Los Angeles in 1950, welcomed both men and
women but had a predominantly male membership; the Daughters
of Bilitis, founded in San Francisco in 1955, organized only
women. Both sponsored discussion groups, published magazines,
and sought to change attitudes toward homosexuality. Their major line was assimilationist: they argued that what they called the
"sex variant" was no different from anyone else except in the
choice of a sex partner, and they sought acceptance by the main-*

stream of American society. In contrast, some participants in the subculture—men who wore drag and women who adopted the "butch" and "fem" styles that prevailed in working-class bars—implicitly challenged such an assimilationist stance and thus contributed in a different way to the development of "gay pride" that emerged in the wake of the Stonewall rebellion. Although the homophile organizations took a cautious approach to political organizing and were never able to mobilize large numbers of supporters in the hostile climate of the 1950s, they nevertheless paved the way for the gay and lesbian movement that took off in the 1970s.

The other social movements of the 1960s also helped to shape the development of gay and lesbian activism. Even before June of 1969, the ferment of the 1960s had begun to radicalize the homophile movement. The civil rights struggle contributed the ideology of equal rights for minorities, direct-action protest tactics, and grassroots organizing. The call for a total transformation of society, the linking of personal and political change, and pride in a gay or lesbian identity echoed the Black Power phase of the civil rights movement, the New Left and the counterculture, and the women's liberation movement.

The years since 1969 have witnessed both phenomenal progress in organizing, community-building, and consciousness-raising, and vigorous and often successful efforts to resist the changes favored by the gay and lesbian movement. Stonewall marks not a beginning, but rather an important milestone in the long history of an often-neglected minority group in American society.

THE CASE OF SAN FRANCISCO

San Francisco has played a leading role in the history of the gay and lesbian community and movement since the 1940s. One important theme that emerges from the history of the city is the relationship between gay/lesbian culture and political organizing.

In the second half of the 1970s, gay and lesbian San Franciscans became a real political force, electing a gay man, Harvey Milk, as a city supervisor in 1977, defeating statewide anti-gay legislation, and passing a municipal gay rights ordinance in 1978. But the community also faced the 1978 murders of Harvey Milk and pro-gay mayor George Moscone by a disgruntled former city supervisor and the devastation of the AIDS crisis in the 1980s. As on the national level, the case of San Francisco shows mobilization and progress since 1969, but daunting challenges still to face.

Gay Politics and Community in San Francisco since World War II

This article, originally published in somewhat different form in Socialist Review 55 *(January–February 1981), 77–104, is reprinted, in an edited version, from* Hidden From History: Reclaiming the Gay and Lesbian Past, *ed. Martin Bauml Duberman, Martha Vicinus and George Chauncey, Jr. (New York, 1989), 456, 458–68, 473.*

The gay community in San Francisco and its politics have been a long time in the making. Surveying its history can tell us much not just about one city, but about the emergence of sexual minorities generally, about shifting forms of oppression, and changing political strategies. . . .

Postwar San Francisco

The slow, gradual evolution of a gay identity and of urban gay subcultures was immeasurably hastened by the intervention of World War II. The social disruption of the war years allowed the almost imperceptible changes of several generations to coalesce into a qualitatively new shape. World War II was something of a nationwide coming-out experi-

A drag queen camping it up while under arrest, 1941. Drag queens were often targeted by the police, and they often resisted with humor.

ence. It properly marks the beginning of the nation's, and San Francisco's, modern gay history.

The war uprooted tens of millions of American men and women, plucking them from families, small towns, and the ethnic neighborhoods of large cities and depositing them in a variety of sex-segregated, nonfamilial environments. . . . For some it simply confirmed a way of living and loving they had already chosen. For others, it gave meaning to little-understood desires, introduced them to men and women with similar feelings, and thus allowed them to "come out." For still others, the sexual underside of the war years provided experiences they otherwise would not have had and that they left behind when the war ended.

If the war years allowed large numbers of lesbians and gay men to discover their sexuality and each other, repression in the postwar decade heightened consciousness of belonging to a

"Gay Politics and Community in San Francisco Since World War II" by John D'Emilio from *Hidden from History: Reclaiming the Gay and Lesbian Past,* edited by Martin Bauml Duberman, George Chauncey, Jr., and Martha Vicinus, Penguin USA, 1989. Reprinted by permission of the author.

400

group. . . . Homosexuals and lesbians found themselves under virulent attack: purges from the armed forces; congressional investigations into government employment of "perverts"; disbarment from federal jobs; widespread FBI surveillance; state sexual psychopath laws; stepped-up harassment from urban police forces; and inflammatory headlines warning readers of the sex "deviates" in their midst. The tightening web of oppression in McCarthy's America helped to create the minority it was meant to isolate.

These events also decisively shaped the gay history of San Francisco, initiating a process that has made it a unique place for lesbians and gay men. As a major port of departure and return for servicemen and women destined for the Pacific theater (and, later, for the postwar occupation of Japan and the fighting in Korea), and as an important center of war industry, the Bay Area's charm and physical beauty were exposed to large numbers of young, mobile Americans. Many stayed after demobilization; others later returned. Between 1940 and 1950 the population of San Francisco, which had declined during the 1930s, grew by over 125,000.

The growth included a disproportionate number of lesbians and gay men. The sporadic, unpredictable purges from the armed forces in the Pacific deposited lesbians and homosexuals, sometimes hundreds at a time, in San Francisco with dishonorable discharges. Unable or unwilling to return home in disgrace to family and friends, they stayed to carve out a new gay life. California, moreover, was the one state whose courts upheld the right of homosexuals to congregate in bars and other public establishments. Though the police found ways around the decision and continued to harass gay bars, the ruling gave to bars in San Francisco a tiny measure of security lacking elsewhere. By the late 1950s about thirty gay male and lesbian bars existed in the city. Such small advantages were significant, and over the years created a qualitative difference in the shape of gay life. Census statistics hint at the degree to which San Francisco was attracting a gay populace. From 1950 to 1960 the number of single-person households doubled, accounting for 38 percent of the city's residence units.

Under the combined impact of the war, the publication of the Kinsey studies [on male and female sexuality], the persecutions of the McCarthy era, and the wide currency that a growing civil rights movement was giving to the concept of minority group status, some gay men and lesbians began building a political movement of their own. In 1950, a small group of male homosexuals who were members of the Communist Party or fellow-travelers formed the Mattachine Society in Los Angeles. Initially a secret underground organization, it developed a radical analysis of homosexuals as an oppressed minority and sought to build a mass movement of homosexuals working for their own emancipation. Though the founders were eventually purged and the philosophy and goals of the group transformed, the Mattachine did, at least, survive. In 1953 a branch was formed in San Francisco. Three years later, the organization's national office moved there and its monthly magazine, *Mattachine Review,* was published out of San Francisco. In 1955 in San Francisco, several lesbians founded the Daughters of Bilitis, a lesbian political group. DOB also published a monthly magazine, *The Ladder,* and tried, with limited success, to set up chapters in other cities.

Throughout the 1950s, the "homophile" movement remained small and fragile. The combined membership of DOB and Mattachine in San Francisco probably never exceeded two hundred, yet no other American city reached even that number. Hos-

The Mattachine Society, founded in 1950, was an early homophile movement organization. This advertisement from 1966 promotes equality and rights for homosexuals.

tile as the social climate of the 1950s was to a gay movement, and notwithstanding the personal courage that involvement required, the feeble size of the movement stemmed in no small part from the political choices made by homophile leaders. Mattachine and DOB reflected (after its radical founders were purged) the accommodationist, conformist spirit of the Eisenhower era. They assiduously cultivated an image of middle-class respectability and denied that they were organizations of homosexuals, instead claiming that they were concerned with the problem of the "variant." They expected social change to come through the good offices of professionals. They saw their task primarily as one of educating the professionals who influenced public opinion and only secondarily as one of organizing lesbians and gay men. Moreover, in defining prejudice and misinformation as the problem, both DOB and Mattachine often found themselves blaming the victim. DOB regularly counseled lesbians to grow their hair long and wear dresses, and Mattachine firmly dissociated itself from the stereotypical promiscuous sexuality of male homosexuals, in one instance even applauding police for rounding up gay men who cruised a railroad terminal. Neither organization had kind words for the milieu of the gay bars, though they would have done well to consider why the bars were packed while their membership rolls remained tiny.

Despite these limitations, one cannot dismiss the work of DOB and Mattachine in making San Francisco what it is today. More copies of *The Ladder* and *Mattachine Review* were distributed in San Francisco than elsewhere. The city had more women and men doing gay "political" work than any other. They made contact with a significant number of professionals and initiated a dialogue that was a crucial step in changing antigay attitudes. As the national headquarters of both organizations, San Francisco attracted gay men and lesbians.

Though a militant, grass-roots nationwide liberation movement of lesbians and gay men did not emerge until the end of the 1960s, San Francisco alone witnessed the beginnings of militancy and a mass politics several years earlier. San Francisco was the first city to see the barrier between the movement and the gay subculture break down. The impetus for this pre-Stonewall wave of gay politics emerged not from homophile leaders but from the bar subculture, and resulted from a set of circumstances unique to San Francisco.

one

AUGUST 1958
FIFTY CENTS

THE HOMOSEXUAL VIEWPOINT

I am glad I am homo-sexual

This August 1958 cover of One *magazine shows an early illustration of gay pride.*

San Francisco in the 1940s and 1950s was the setting for an underground literary movement of poets and writers who dissented from the dominant ethos of Cold War America, and who expressed through verse their opposition to the conformity and consumerism of the postwar era. By the mid-1950s, the bohemian literary scene in North Beach began attracting beat writers like Allen Ginsberg. Word of what was happening spread, and the San Francisco poets slowly reached a wider audience.

After 1957, however, what began as a small, underground movement was suddenly transmuted by the media into a nationwide generational rebellion against everything that America held sacred. The summer of 1958 witnessed the trial of Lawrence Ferlinghetti, the owner of City Lights bookstore, on charges of selling obscene literature (Ginsberg's *Howl*). . . . Over the next two years the media turned a spotlight on the beat rebellion and on North Beach, the setting of the most visible, concentrated beat subculture. The sensationalistic portrayal of them quickly overshadowed the reality. . . .

The visibility of the beat subculture in North Beach had a major impact upon gay consciousness in San Francisco. Many of the central figures of the literary renaissance in San Francisco were, in fact, gay men—Robert Duncan, Jack Spicer, Robin Blaser, and, of course, Ginsberg—and through their work they carved out a male homosexual cultural space. Ginsberg's *Howl*, a local bestseller, openly acknowledged male homosexuality. In describing gay male sex as joyous, delightful, and even holy, Ginsberg did in fact turn American values inside out. The geography of the two subcultures, moreover, overlapped considerably. Most importantly, the philosophy behind the beat protest resonated with the experience of gays in the 1950s. The beats were rebelling against the "straight" ethos of Cold War society—career, home and family, suburban life—an ethos that excluded lesbians and gay men. The beats provided a different lens through which homosexuals and lesbians could view their lives—as a form of protest against a stultifying lifestyle and set of values.

Whil[e] the beats exerted their subtle influence upon the self-image of the city's gay population, two homosexual-related scandals rocked the city. In the midst of the 1959 mayoral campaign, one of the candidates accused the incumbent mayor and his chief of police of allowing San Francisco to become "the national headquarters of the organized homosexuals in the United States." The charges, based on the fact that Mattachine and DOB were located in San Francisco, made front-page headlines for several days. Political figures and the local press vigorously denied the charges but the affair made the entire city aware of the homophile organizations in its midst.

The following spring, the city was treated to another extensive discussion of the gay presence in San Francisco when a "gayola" scandal hit the police department. Several gay bar owners reported to the district attorney a long history of extortion by the police. One detective and state liquor department investigator were caught with marked money and pleaded guilty. Several other indicted officers opted for a jury trial that dragged on throughout the summer. All of them were acquitted, but the scandal seriously embarrassed the police department and the city administration.

Taken together, the beat phenomenon and the homosexual scandals were giving San Francisco an unwelcome reputation as the home for the nation's "deviates" and "rebels." By 1959, the police had increased their patrols in North Beach and were systematically harassing beat gathering places and individuals. The following year, immediately after the conclusion of the gayola trials, the police, with the support and encouragement of the mayor, shifted their attention to the city's gay population. Felony convictions of gay men, which stood at zero in the first half of 1960, rose to twenty-nine in the next six months and jumped to seventy-six in the first six months of 1961. Misdemeanor charges against gay women and men stemming from sweeps of the bars ran at an estimated forty to sixty per week during 1961. By October the state alcoholic beverage control department had revoked the licenses of twelve of the city's thirty gay bars and had initiated proceedings against another fifteen. Every one of the bars that testified against the police department during the gayola inquiry was shut down. The police, backed by the city's press, also intensified surveillance of gay male cruising areas. Vice squad officers raided theaters showing male homosexual porn films and confiscated thousands of volumes of gay male and lesbian pulp fiction.

Police harassment of gay bars was not new. In the 1950s, it was endemic to the gay male and lesbian subculture of American cities. What was novel about the San Francisco police crackdown was the social context in which it took place. The scandals of 1959 and 1960 led to an unprecedented degree of public discussion of homosexuality. Just as important, the stepped-up harassment followed upon the growing awareness of the beat rebellion and its subtle impact on gay consciousness in San Francisco. Thus, the conditions were present to encourage a political response to the antigay campaign.

Both DOB and Mattachine were too enmeshed in the accommodationist politics of the 1950s to resist attacks on aspects of gay life that both organizations deplored as unseemly. Instead, the first wave of rebellion emerged directly out of the bar subculture and out of the one bar, the Black Cat, where gay men, bohemian nonconformity, and police harassment most clearly converged. Located on Montgomery Street a few blocks from the center of North Beach, the Black Cat had a long history as a bohemian meeting place. In the 1940s the character of the bar began to change and it became more clearly a gay male bar. But it retained a special flavor. Allen Ginsberg described it as "the greatest gay bar in America . . . totally open, bohemian. . . . All the gay screaming queens would come, the heterosexual gray flannel suit types, longshoremen. All the poets went there." For over fifteen years, beginning in the late 1940s, its owner Sol Stoumen steadfastly engaged in a court fight against the state liquor board to stay open, spending over thirty-eight thousand dollars to finance his protracted court battle.

During the 1950s, the Black Cat had a drag entertainer, José Sarria, who staged satirical operas on Sunday afternoons that drew an overflow crowd. Sarria took a traditional, sometimes self-deprecating, form of gay male humor—camp and drag—and transformed it into political theater. Outrageously dressed in female attire, he would perform Carmen, but Carmen as a homosexual hiding in the bushes trying to avoid capture by the vice squad. For years, Sarria ended his show without satire. As George Mendenhall, a pre-Stonewall activist, recalled it, "José would make these political comments about our rights as homosexuals and at the end . . . of every concert, he would have everybody in the room stand, and we would put our arms around each other and sing, 'God Save Us Nelly Queens.' It sounds silly, but if you lived at that time and had the oppression coming down from the police department and from society, . . . to be able to put your arms around other gay men and sing 'God Save Us Nelly Queens' . . . We were not really saying 'God Save Us Nelly Queens.' We were saying, 'We have our rights too.'"

In 1961, at the height of the police crackdown, Sarria decided to run for city supervisor. He had no chance of winning, but victory wasn't his goal. "I was trying to prove to my gay audience," he recalled, "that I had the right, being as notorious and gay as I was, to run for public office, because people in those days didn't believe you had rights." Sarria's operas made him the best-known gay man in San Francisco; his reputation extended to the entire bar-going population. Though he collected only six thousand votes, his candidacy was the hot topic in the bars that fall, forcing patrons to think about their lives and their sexual orientation in political terms.

Sarria's candidacy set in motion developments that fed lesbian and gay political activity in San Francisco throughout the 1960s. During his campaign, a group of gay men began publishing a biweekly newspaper that they distributed in the bars. Financed by advertising from gay tavern owners, the League for Civil Education *News* used a muckraking style to expose gay oppression. Headlines such as "SFPD ATTACKS HOMOS" and "WE MUST FIGHT NOW!" fueled an ongoing discussion of police abuses among bar patrons. LCE News encouraged gays to vote as a bloc and sponsored registration drives. By 1963 candidates for public office were taking ads in the paper. In 1962 several gay bar owners formed the Tavern Guild as a defense organization to resist attacks from the state. In 1964 some members of the Tavern Guild and a few other friends founded the Society for Individual Rights. SIR was virtually alone among pre-Stonewall gay male homophile organizations in legitimating the social needs of homosexuals. In addition to voter registration, candidates' nights during election time, public picketing, and other "political" activity, SIR sponsored dances, bridge clubs, and picnics, provided VD testing, and opened a community center. Its meetings often attracted more than two hundred people, and by 1968 it had a membership of almost a thousand, making it far and away the largest male homophile organization in the country. . .

Unlike the Stonewall Riot of 1969, the impact of Sarria's symbolic candidacy remained confined to San Francisco. The city's situation was too unique, gay men and lesbians in the rest of the country still too isolated and invisible, for it to have anything more than a local effect. At the end of the 1960s, news of a gay riot in New York could spread rapidly through the networks of communication created by the mass movements of the decade. In 1961, with the exception of the southern civil rights movement, those movements and those channels for disseminating information did not exist. And the absence of a nationwide gay movement placed limits in turn on how far gay politics in San Francisco could develop. . . .

Homophile politics in San Francisco remained within the limits of reformism during the 1960s and actively involved only a small fraction of its potential constituency. At most, two thousand men and women had organizational affiliation and of these only a few dozen could be considered hard-core activists. Yet the movement had achieved a level of visibility unmatched elsewhere. By the late 1960s mass magazines were referring to San Francisco as the gay capital of the United States. When the Stonewall Riot sparked a gay liberation movement, San Francisco's lesbian and gay male community could assume a leading role.

The Growth of the Gay Liberation Movement

Stonewall initiated a qualitatively different phase of gay and lesbian politics. Two aspects deserve emphasis. One is the notion of "coming out," which served both as a goal and a strategy. Coming out became a profoundly political step that an individual could take. It promised an immediate improvement in one's life, a huge step forward in shedding the self-hatred and internalized oppression imposed by a homophobic society. Coming out also became the key strategy for building a mass movement. Gay

Gay Pride Day in New York City's Central Park, 1970.

women and men who came out crossed a critical dividing line. They relinquished invisibility, made themselves vulnerable to attack, and became invested in the success of the movement. Visible lesbians and gay men, moreover, served as magnets that drew others to them.

Coming out quickly captured the imagination of tens of thousands, perhaps hundreds of thousands, of lesbians and gay men. A mass movement was born almost overnight. On the eve of Stonewall, after almost twenty years of homophile politics, fewer than fifty organizations existed. By 1973, there were more than eight hundred lesbian and gay male groups scattered across the country. The largest pre-Stonewall homophile demonstrations attracted only a few dozen people. In June 1970 five thousand women and men marched in New York to commemorate the Stonewall Rebellion. By the mid-1970s, the yearly marches in several cities were larger than any other political demonstrations since the decline of the civil rights and antiwar movements. Lesbians and gay men created publications and independent presses, record companies, coffeehouses, community centers, counseling services, health clinics, and professional associations.

A second critical feature of the post-Stonewall era was the emergence of a lesbian movement. Lesbians were but a small fraction of the tiny homophile movement. The almost simultaneous birth of women's liberation and gay liberation propelled large numbers of lesbians into liberation politics. Lesbians were active both in early gay liberation groups and in feminist organizations. . . .

Only a minority of lesbians and gay men joined organizations, but that minority decisively affected the lives of a much larger number. Through coming out and its example of gay pride, through the vastly increased flow of information that an activist minority stimulated, and especially through the inhibitions on police harassment that militancy imposed, lesbian and gay liberation transformed the self-image of many and offered the hope of a better life even to those who had never attended a meeting or participated in a demonstration.

In concrete terms a better life often translated into a decision to move to one of the handful of large cities known to have a well-developed gay subculture. America in the 1970s saw a massive sexual migration set in motion by the lesbian and gay movements. Here, San Francisco had a running start on every other city. Homophile groups were already getting attention from liberal politicians and had already limited police harassment of bars. Magazines played up San Francisco's reputation as a city that tolerated gays. The 1960s, moreover, established the Bay Area as an enclave of radical and lifestyle politics. The women's movement in the Bay Area, though not free of gay-straight conflict, was noticeably more hospitable to lesbians than elsewhere. While New York NOW [National Organization for Women], for instance, was purging lesbians from its ranks, San Francisco NOW was pushing for a lesbian rights resolution at the organization's 1971 national convention.

By the mid-1970s San Francisco had become, in comparison to the rest of the country, a liberated zone for lesbians and gay men. It had the largest number and widest variety of organizations and institutions. An enormous in-migration had created a new social phenomenon, residential areas that were visibly gay in composition: Duboce Triangle, Noe Valley, and the Upper Mission for lesbians; the Haight, Folsom, and above all the Castro for gay men. Geographic concentration offered the opportunity for local political power that invisibility precluded. . . .

. . . [T]he previous few decades had witnessed a profound and lasting change in San Francisco (and in the nation at large). What was once a secret, despised identity had become the basis for an urban community, sharing many of the characteristics of more traditional ethnic groupings. And the community had, in turn, spawned a vigorous politics that gave it unusual national influence and served as a beacon of hope for others.

Questions

1. *What factors explain the rise of the homophile movement in the 1950s?*
2. *How did the homophile movement differ from the gay and lesbian movement as it developed after Stonewall?*
3. *How does the gay and lesbian movement compare to the other social movements of the 1960s?*

THE HOMOPHILE MOVEMENT

The history of the homophile movement is tied up with the existence of other social movements. The early Mattachine Society copied the cell-like secretive structure of the Communist Party and echoed some of the party's rhetoric in its call for political action on behalf of "one of the largest minorities in America today, . . . victimized daily as a result of our oppression." Like both the labor and civil rights movements in the 1950s, the homophile movement came under attack by anti-Communists and reacted defensively, adopting a more conservative tone after 1953.

The homophile movement was also affected by the civil rights struggle. Gay and lesbian individuals committed to basic civil rights for African Americans brought a consciousness of oppression, a style of organizing, and a set of tactics and strategies to the later homophile and especially the early gay liberation movement.

Feminism, too, played a role within the homophile movement. Even before the "second wave" of the women's movement, lesbians began to demand equality within the mixed-gender homophile movement and attention to the problems that lesbians experienced as women.

Finally, the New Left, Black Power, and radical counterculture left their imprint on the developing Gay Liberation movement. Taken together, the documents in this section reveal how much the rise of the gay and lesbian movement is a part of the history of social movements in the 1960s and 1970s.

Interviews with Harry Hay

Harry Hay, a founder of the Mattachine Society, belonged to the Communist Party for eighteen years and used both his connections within the party and his experience as an organizer to recruit members for a gay organization. In this interview, conducted by Jonathan Katz in 1974, Hay tells of his first attempts to organize gay people. Excerpted from Jonathan Katz, Gay American History: Lesbians and Gay Men in the U.S.A., revised edition (New York, 1992), 407-8.

H.H.: . . .[I]n the fall of 1930, I went to Stanford University. In the fall of 1931, I decided, on the basis of not a great deal of information and not too much experience, that I didn't want to live the life of a lie, so I declared myself on campus to all the people that I knew: to the eating club I belonged to, to the fraternities who were rushing me—

J.K.: You declared yourself as Gay?

H.H.: Yes. I said I would understand perfectly if they all felt they had to stay away for their own security and position—and most of the people I knew did stay away, but the people I loved best said, "Okay, what else is new?"

I first conceived of a Gay group in August 1948, in Los Angeles. What happened was this: I went to a beer bust at the University of Southern California, run by some Gay guys I knew. Half the people there were students—one or two were theology students, some legal students—and we got to talking about the Henry Wallace presidential campaign. Wallace was running on the Progressive party ticket. I came up with the idea that we should start a group called "Bachelors for Wallace." With the help of a couple of quarts of beer, we worked up quite a case for what the Bachelors for Wallace would do, what we would ask for— constitutional amendments, etc. It sounded like a great idea.

J.K.: This was to be an openly Gay group?

H.H.: Yes. We didn't have the words in those years, but that was what we were going to be. I went home and was all excited and sat up all night, writing out the original prospectus for the group. The next day I called up the guy who had given the party and asked for the addresses and telephone numbers of all the people there. I called up all these guys and said, "Look, we can get this whole thing going." They said, "What thing?" I found out that the only one who remembered anything except his hangover was me.

Well, I thought it was too good an idea to drop, so I started putting it in some kind of order. I said, "Let's see, to get started I'll get in touch with all the other homosexuals I can." They said, "You're mad! You're out of your mind! We can't do anything like this!" Then I said, "Wait a minute. Supposing we got some really influential people, like ministers and sympathetic sociologists, and psychologists to condone it, to sponsor it. Then what?" "Well," they said, "well—yes, it's possible. Get 'em, and we'll think about it."

So I went around to a couple of ministers I knew—Unitarians—and some sociologists from UCLA, and a couple of psychologists who were around the progressive movement who were sort of open-minded. One minister, one sociologist, and one psychologist said, "That's not bad; that might be a very useful new idea. You get one of these groups started, and we'll come and visit it. If it's going in the right direction, we'll consider offering our names." This went on for quite a while.

J.K.: Can you say why you conceived of a Gay organization at the time you did?

H.H.: The anti-Communist witch-hunts were very much in operation; the House Un-American Activities Committee had investigated Communist "subversion" in Hollywood. The purge of homosexuals from the State Department took place. The country, it seemed to me, was beginning to move toward fascism and McCarthyism; the Jews wouldn't be used as a scapegoat this time—the painful example of Germany was still too clear to us. The Black organizations were already pretty successfully looking out for their interests. It was obvious McCarthy was setting up the pattern for a new scapegoat, and it was going to be us—Gays. We had to organize, we had to move, we had to get started.

More Comments from Harry Hay

Hay picks up the story of the Mattachine Society in this excerpt from Andrea Weiss and Greta Schiller, Before Stonewall: The Making of a Gay and Lesbian Community *(Tallahassee, 1988), 40–41, a volume that accompanies a documentary film by the same name.*

I wasn't thinking in terms of gay rights yet; that was much later. My thinking was that what we have to do right now is to find out who we are, where we've been, what kind of contribution can be made [to society at large], and what are we for? For the next two years, I searched for people to join me [to start the organization, the Mattachine Society]. Ultimately there were five of us, and then seven, in the original group. We were all terrified of the police, so we made all decisions by unanimous consent, and kept the leadership small. We thought if we all positively agreed on it, we couldn't make a mistake. One of our first ideas was to hold discussion groups; we would sit around and talk about being gay, and within a very short time, we had a whole series of discussion groups going. We had an initiation ceremony—we'd all hold hands and we had ritualistic things that we said, something like, "No gay person coming into the world will ever again have to feel alone and unwanted and rejected."

To the straight public, the word homosexual meant willful, perverse, defiant, sick young heterosexuals who are performing unnatural and therefore criminal acts. So we realized in order to get them to see us as people, we had to break through this madness. There was this total conspiracy of silence, and we knew that if we ever broke through and got into the newspapers, we had to call ourselves something they didn't know, so they'd have to ask us. I spent hours going through the Greek lexicon and found the word homophile, which means lover of same. Our very first public victory was winning the case of entrapment against Dale Jennings [Jennings's arrest in 1952 sparked a Mattachine campaign against police harassment]. We thought this was really significant, so we sent information out to all the newspapers. But not one paper or radio station covered it. Total silence. Not even the leftist papers covered it.

The magazine [Mattachine Review] was started in 1951, and our first Constitutional Convention was held in 1953. By then the organization was growing by leaps and bounds, and we needed some kind of organization to contain it. We drew up a constitution, and so did the people from San Francisco—all these conservative guys who had voted for Nixon and Eisenhower—and they were worried about all these accusations that the leadership was leftist. We realized we were losing. We felt very strongly that the organization had to stay liberal, those were our roots. That is

when we resigned from the organization, and [the more conservative members] took over.

The first national homophile conference was in Kansas City in
1965. By this time the east coast people are very concerned with
the image of the homosexual . . . But here on the west coast, we
had passed a resolution that began, "Whereas the homosexual has
no image to lose . . . ," which was totally rejected on the east coast.
Our feeling was that we weren't interested in respectability, we
were interested in self respect, a very different thing. John
[Burnside, his long-time lover/partner] and I were involved in the
anti-war movement by now, and the counterculture.

Along Telegraph Avenue in Berkeley there were open political forums, and we would go up there and be part of the counterculture and anti-war movements . . . One night a young woman
started asking John and me about our lives together. We told her
about ourselves, about the gay movement, about how we were
involved in the peace movement as gay men, and all of a sudden
we're talking to 100 to 150 people sitting around us. They're all
saying, "hey, we've never heard anyone talk about gay lifestyles
as a positive lifestyle. We hope you guys come back and keep
talking about this."

Articles about the gay lifestyle began to appear in the underground press here. We began to challenge them openly, [arguing
that] if they were going to get rid of the prejudices their parents
had, they should get rid of their prejudices vis-a-vis homosexuals
as well . . . When Stonewall began a new movement here, one of
the first big activities was a "Gay In" in 1970. You see what was
happening here, what's really important, is that we were laying a
powder train. And when Stonewall comes, all of a sudden that
powder train takes off.

The Daughters of Bilitis

---

*This statement of purpose of the Daughters of Bilitis comes from the first
issue of the organization's magazine,* The Ladder, *October 1956, 4.*

Daughters of Bilitis—Purpose

1. Education of the variant, with particular emphasis on the psychological and sociological aspects, to enable her to understand herself and make her adjustment to society in all its social, civic and economic implications by establishing and maintaining a library of both fiction and nonfiction on the sex deviant theme; by sponsoring public discussions on pertinent subjects to be conducted by leading members of the legal, psychiatric, religious and other professions; by advocating a mode of behaviour and dress acceptable to society.
2. Education of the public through acceptance first of the individual, leading to an eventual breakdown of erroneous conceptions, taboos and prejudices; through public discussion meetings; through dissemination of educational literature on the homosexual theme.
3. Participation in research projects by duly authorized and responsible psychology, sociology and other such experts directed towards further knowledge of the homosecual [homosexual].
4. Investigation of the penal code as it pertains to the homosexual, proposal of changes to provide an equitable handling of cases involving this minority group, and promotion of these changes through due process of law in the state legislatures.

The Daughters of Bilitis is not now, and never has been, affiliated with any other organization, political, social or otherwise.

Letter from Lorraine Hansberry

This letter from Lorraine Hansberry, renowned African American writer, appeared in The Ladder, *May 1957, 26–28.*

Reprinted from *The Ladder*, Vol. 1, No. 1, October 1956, a publication of The Daughters of Bilitis.

"Please find enclosed a money order for $2.00. I should like to receive as many of your back issues as that amount will cover. In the event $2.00 is in excess of the cost of six issues—well, fine. Those few cents may stand as a mere downpayment toward sizeable (for me, that is) donations I know already that I shall be sending to you.

I hope you are somewhat interested in off-the-top-of-the-head reactions from across the country because I would like to offer a few by way of the following:

(1) I'm glad as heck that you exist. You are obviously serious people and I feel that women, without wishing to foster any strict *separatist* notions, homo or hetero, indeed have a need for their own publications and organizations. Our problems, our experiences as women are profoundly unique as compared to the other half of the human race. Women, like other oppressed groups or one kind or another, have particularly had to pay a price for the intellectual impoverishment that the second class status imposed on us for centuries created and sustained. Thus, I feel that THE LADDER is a fine, elementary step in a rewarding direction.

(2) Rightly or wrongly (in view of some of the thought provoking discussions I have seen elsewhere in a homosexual publication) I could not help but be encouraged and relieved by one of the almost subsidiary points under Point I of your declaration of purpose, '(to advocate) a mode of behaviour and dress acceptable to society'. As one raised in a cultural experience (I am a Negro) where those within were and are forever lecturing to their fellows about how to appear acceptable to the dominant social group, I know something about the shallowness of such a view as an end in itself.

The most splendid argument is simple and to the point, Ralph Bunche, with all his clean fingernails, degrees, and, of course, undeniable service to the human race, could still be insulted, denied a hotel room or meal in many parts of our country. (Not to mention the possibility of being lynched on a lonely Georgia road for perhaps having demanded a glass of water in the wrong place.)

What ought to be clear is that one is oppressed or discriminated against because one is different, not 'wrong' or 'bad' some-

Reprinted from *The Ladder*, Vol. 1, No. 8, May 1957, a publication of The Daughters of Bilitis.

how. This is perhaps the bitterest of the entire pill. HOWEVER, as a matter of facility, of expediency, one has to take a critical view of revolutionary attitudes which in spite of the BASIC truth I have mentioned above, may tend to aggravate the problems of a group.

I have long since passed that period when I felt personal discomfort at the sight of an ill-dressed or illiterate Negro. Social awareness has taught me where to lay the blame. Someday, I expect, the 'discreet' Lesbian will not turn her head on the streets at the sight of the 'butch' strolling hand in hand with her friend in their trousers and definitive haircuts. But for the moment, it still disturbs. It creates an impossible area for discussion with one's most enlightened (to use a hopeful term) heterosexual friends. Thus, I agree with the inclusion of that point in your declaration to the degree of wanting to comment on it.

(3) I am impressed by the general tone of your articles. The most serious fault being at this juncture that there simply is too little.

(4) Would it be presumptuous or far-fetched to suggest that you try for some overseas communications? One hears so much of publications and organizations devoted to homosexuality and homosexuals in Europe; but as far as I can gather these seem to lean heavily toward male questions and interests.

Just a little afterthought: considering Mattachine; Bilitis, ONE [gay publication]; all seem to be cropping up on the West Coast rather than here where a vigorous and active gay set almost bump one another off the streets—what is it in the air out there? Pioneers still? Or a tougher circumstance which inspires battle? Would like to hear speculation, light-hearted or otherwise."

L.H.N., New York, N.Y.

Interview with Audre Lorde and Maua Adele Ajanaku

In the 1950s, the late Audre Lorde, a famous poet and scholar, and Maua Adele Ajanaku were young African American women living in New York City. This interview comes from Andrea Weiss and Greta Schiller, Before Stonewall: The Making of a Gay and Lesbian Community *(Tallahassee, 1988), 54–55.*

A: I used to go to the bars too often, because they were the only place I went to meet people [lesbians].

M: And going into bars in the Village was going into white women's bars. The bouncers ostensibly were there to keep the johns out, but because I was Black, I was also an undesirable. . . . And I knew that someday this was going to have to be my strength and my power but I also knew that, hey, we're all supposed to be the same.

A: In the Fifties if you were different, you were just as suspicious within the gay community as you were in America. You have to remember that the gay girls (that's what we were called then), were a reflection of what was going on around us . . . The women I ran with, we knew we were outsiders, we knew we were outside the pale. We lived in the Village, we were dykes, a lot of us were artists. We hated typing; we didn't want straight jobs. And this of course was the Fifties. We were like the gay girls version of the beatniks. And even within that group there were divisions; we divided [ourselves] into the blue jeans and the bermuda shorts set . . . And then there were those of us who straddled it and wore things like riding pants. A lot of this thing [was] symbolized by dress.

M: It was like a social group: groups of people who spent most of their time together—to the clubs together, to the parties, to the beach. I have to always [clarify between] the bars uptown and the bars downtown. Down here in the Village, if I wanted to go to Bagatelle, Swing Rendezvous, Danny's, The Seven Steps, whatever, the thugs who were on the door decided if I went in or not.

A: But the parties, white women's parties never had food! They had little potato chips and dip; well, Black parties always had food. The parties I went to were given by a group of Black lesbians who were a little older than I was. They had cars, some of them were performers, like in Porgy and Bess; they were professional, or semi-professional, women. They were all Black, except for the women who were going with white girls—they'd bring them along.

A: In the Sixties, my identity as a gay girl became less so, because I was involved in the civil rights movement, and I was married, having kids. My consciousness of myself as a lesbian was there, but at that particular moment, I was involved in living

421

another life . . . The civil rights movement didn't develop as a conflict for me in terms of being gay. Because in the Fifties, that conflict was already there. Even when I was down in the Village, I was also at college; I was a closet student, I was a closet politico, I was involved in progressive movements, but—it was not cool to be homosexual there. The saying then was it made us vulnerable to the FBI, but really it was homophobia. What you had to present to the world was a front, that was impeccable and perfect according to how they defined it. To take the position that, hey, I'm who I am, I don't want to hide—it was the refusal to hide that became questionable and revolutionary.

M: That's equivalent to when Black Americans said, "no more!" They refused to hide . . . We said "no good!" And then everybody got the feeling that, whatever their oppression was, "well maybe I don't have to take this either."

A: The Black power and the civil rights movement of the late 50's and early 60's was the prototype of every single liberation movement in this country that we are still dealing with today.

Del Martin's Feminist Protest

This magazine piece reports on Del Martin's comments to the Mattachine Society with regard to the role of women within the homophile movement. Martin, along with her partner, Phyllis Lyon, founded the Daughters of Bilitis. Taken from The Ladder, *October 1959, 19.*

Of particular interest to readers of THE LADDER may be Del's introductory remarks: "Last night when I received the award of honorary membership in the Mattachine Society, I replied that we are often accused of competing with Mattachine and that I was glad to see that you people recognized the fact that we were not. Perhaps to some of you the remark needs further clarification. But at every one of these conventions I attend, year after year, I find I must defend the Daughters of Bilitis as a separate and distinct

Reprinted from *The Ladder*, Vol. 4, No. 1, October 1959, a publication of The Daughters of Bilitis.

women's organization. First of all, what do you men know about Lesbians? In all of your programs and your 'Review' you speak of the male homosexual and follow this with—oh, yes, and incidentally there are some female homosexuals too and because they are homosexual all this should apply to them as well. ONE has done little better. For years they have relegated the Lesbian interest to the column called 'Feminine Viewpoint'. So it would appear to me that quite obviously neither organization has recognized the fact that Lesbians are *women* and that this 20th century is the era of emancipation of woman. Lesbians are not satisfied to be auxiliary members or second class homosexuals. So if you people do wish to put DOB out of business, you are going to have to learn something about the Lesbian, and today I'd like to give you your first lesson."

After giving the summary of background and behaviour of 157 Lesbians in the DOB sampling, Del concluded: "One of Mattachine's aims is that of sexual equality. May I suggest that you start with the Lesbian? This would certainly be a 'new frontier in acceptance of the homophile'."

Gay Power Comes to Sheridan Square

Lucian Truscott IV's report on the Stonewall riot appeared in the progressive New York City newspaper, The Village Voice. *Although Stonewall has come to play a central role in the history of the gay and lesbian movement, most newspapers gave the incident little attention at the time. The Voice, as the paper is known, was unusual in this respect. Excerpted from* The Village Voice, *3 July 1969, 1, 18.*

Sheridan Square this weekend looked like something from a William Burroughs novel as the sudden specter of "gay power" erected its brazen head and spat out a fairy tale the likes of which the area has never seen.

The forces of faggotry, spurred by a Friday night raid on one of the city's largest, most popular, and longest lived gay bars, the Stonewall Inn, rallied Saturday night in an unprecedented protest

---

"Gay Power Comes to Sheridan Square," by Lucian Truscott IV, reprinted from *The Village Voice*, July 3, 1969.

against the raid and continued Sunday night to assert presence, possibility, and pride until the early hours of Monday morning. "I'm a faggot, and I'm proud of it!" "Gay Power!" "I like boys!"— these and many other slogans were heard all three nights as the show of force by the city's finery met the force of the city's finest. The result was a kind of liberation, as the gay brigade emerged from the bars, back rooms, and bedrooms of the Village and became street people.

Cops entered the Stonewall for the second time in a week just before midnight on Friday. It began as a small raid—only two patrolmen, two detectives, and two policewomen were involved. But as the patrons trapped inside were released one by one, a crowd started to gather on the street. It was initially a festive gathering, composed mostly of Stonewall boys who were waiting around for friends still inside or to see what was going to happen. Cheers would go up as favorites would emerge from the door, strike a pose, and swish by the detective with a "Hello there, fella." The stars were in their element. Wrists were limp, hair was primped, and reactions to the applause were classic. "I gave them the gay power bit, and they loved it, girls." "Have you seen Maxine? Where *is* my wife—I told her not to go far."

Suddenly the paddywagon arrived and the mood of the crowd changed. Three of the more blatant queens—in full drag— were loaded inside, along with the bartender and doorman, to a chorus of catcalls and boos from the crowd. A cry went up to push the paddywagon over, but it drove away before anything could happen. With its exit, the action waned momentarily. The next person to come out was a dyke, and she put up a struggle—from car to door to car again. It was at that moment that the scene became explosive. Limp wrists were forgotten. Beer cans and bottles were heaved at the windows, and a rain of coins descended on the cops. At the height of the action, a bearded figure was plucked from the crowd and dragged inside. It was Dave Van Ronk [a blues guitarist], who had come from the Lion's Head to see what was going on. He was later charged with having thrown an object at the police.

Three cops were necessary to get Van Ronk away from the crowd and into the Stonewall. The exit left no cops on the street, and almost by signal the crowd erupted into cobblestone and bottle heaving. The reaction was solid; they were pissed. The trashcan I was standing on was nearly yanked out from under me as a kid tried to grab it for use in the windowsmashing melee. From nowhere came an uprooted parking meter—used as a battering ram on the Stonewall door. I heard several cries of "Let's get some gas," but the blaze of flame which soon appeared in the window of the Stonewall was still a shock. As the wood barrier behind the glass was beaten open, the cops inside turned a firehose on the crowd. Several kids took the opportunity to cavort in the spray, and their momentary glee served to stave off what was rapidly becoming a full-scale attack. By the time the fags were able to regroup forces and come up with another assault, several carloads of police reinforcements had arrived, and in minutes the streets were clear.

A visit to the Sixth Precinct revealed the fact that 13 persons had been arrested on charges which ranged from Van Ronk's felonious assault of a police officer to the owners' illegal sale and storage of alcoholic beverages without a license. Two police officers had been injured in the battle with the crowd. By the time the last cop was off the street Saturday morning, a sign was going up announcing that the Stonewall would reopen that night. It did.

Protest set the tone for "gay power" activities on Saturday. The afternoon was spent boarding up the windows of the Stonewall and chalking them with signs of the new revolution: "We are Open," "There is all college boys and girls in here," "Support Gay Power—C'mon in, girls," "Insp. Smyth looted our: money, jukebox, cigarette mach, telephones, safe, cash register, and the boys tips." Among the slogans were two carefully clipped and bordered copies of the Daily News story about the previous night's events, which was anything but kind to the gay cause.

The real action Saturday was that night in the street. Friday night's crowd had returned and was being led in "gay power" cheers by a group of gay cheerleaders. "We are the Stonewall girls/ We wear our hair in curls/ We have no underwear/ We show our pubic hairs!" The crowd was gathered across the street from the Stonewall and was growing with additions of onlookers, Eastsiders, and rough street people who saw a chance for a little action. Though dress had changed from Friday night's gayery to Saturday night street clothes, the scene was a command performance for queers. If Friday night had been pick-up night, Saturday was date night. Hand-holding, kissing, and posing accented each of the cheers with a homosexual liberation that had appeared only fleetingly on the street before. One-liners were as practiced as if they had been used for years. "I just want you all to know," quipped a platinum blond with obvious glee, "that sometimes being homosexual is a big pain in the ass." Another allowed as how he had become a "left-deviationist." And on and on.

The quasi-political tone of the street scene was looked upon with disdain by some, for radio news announcements about the previous night's "gay power" chaos had brought half of Fire Island's Cherry Grove running back to home base to see what they had left behind. The generation gap existed even here. Older boys had strained looks on their faces and talked in concerned whispers as they watched the up-and-coming generation take being gay and flaunt it before the masses.

As the "gay power" chants on the street rose in frequency and volume, the crowd grew restless. The front of the Stonewall was losing its attraction, despite efforts by the owners to talk the crowd back into the club. "C'mon in and see what da pigs done to us," they growled. "We're honest businessmen here. We're American-born boys. We run a legitimate joint here. There ain't nuttin bein' done wrong in dis place. Everybody come and see."

The people on the street were not to be coerced. "Let's go down the street and see what's happening, girls," someone yelled. And down the street went the crowd, smack into the Tactical Patrol Force, who had been called earlier to disperse the crowd and were walking west on Christopher from Sixth Avenue. Formed in a line, the TPF swept the crowd back to the corner of Waverly Place, where they stopped. A stagnant situation there brought on some gay tomfoolery in the form of a chorus line facing the line of helmeted and club-carrying cops. Just as the line got into a full kick routine, the TPF advanced again and cleared the crowd of screaming gay powerites down Christopher to Seventh Avenue. The street and park were then held from both ends, and no one was allowed to enter—naturally causing a fall-off in normal Saturday night business, even at the straight Lion's Head and 55. The TPF positions in and around the square were held with only minor incident—one busted head and a number of scattered arrest—while the cops amused themselves by arbitrarily breaking up small groups of people up and down the avenue. The crowd finally dispersed around 3.30 a.m. The TPF had come and they had conquered, but Sunday was already there, and it was to be another story.

Sunday night was a time for watching and rapping. Gone were the "gay power" chants of Saturday, but not the new and open brand of exhibitionism. Steps, curbs, and the park provided props for what amounted to the Sunday fag follies as returning stars from the previous night's performances stopped by to close the show for the weekend.

It was slow going. Around 1 a.m. a non-helmeted version of the TPF arrived and made a controlled and very cool sweep of the area, getting everyone moving and out of the park. That put a damper on posing and primping, and as the last buses were leaving Jerseyward, the crowd grew thin. Allen Ginsberg . . . walked by to see what was happening and . . . [was] filled in on the previous evenings' activities by some of the gay activists. "Gay power! Isn't that great!" Allen said. "We're one of the largest minorities in the country—10 per cent, you know. It's about time we did something to assert ourselves."

Ginsberg expressed a desire to visit the Stonewall—"You know, I've never been in there"—and ambled on down the street, flashing peace signs and helloing the TPF. It was a relief and a kind of joy to see him on the street. He lent an extra umbrella of serenity of the scene with his laughter and quiet commentary on consciousness, "gay power" as a new movement, and the various implications of what had happened. I followed him into the Stonewall, where rock music blared from speakers all around a room that might have come right from a Hollywood set of a gay bar. He was immediately bouncing and dancing wherever he moved.

He left, and I walked east with him. Along the way, he described how things used to be. "You know, the guys there were so beautiful—they've lost that wounded look that fags all had 10 years ago." It was the first time I had heard that crowd described as beautiful.

We reached Cooper Square, and as Ginsberg turned to head toward home, he waved and yelled, "Defend the fairies! . . ." and bounced on across the square. He enjoyed the prospect of "gay power" and is probably working on a manifesto for the movement right now. Watch out. The liberation is under way.

Questions

1. *What were the basic assumptions and goals of the homophile movement of the 1950s?*
2. *In what ways did the homophile movement conform to, and in what ways did it react against, the conformist atmosphere of the 1950s?*
3. *In what ways can the Stonewall riot be seen as both growing out of and reacting against the homophile movement of the 1950s?*

FURTHER READING

The definitive study of the homophile movement is John D'Emilio, Sexual Politics, Sexual Communities: The Making of a Homosexual Minority in the United States, 1940–1970 *(Chicago, 1983).* Lillian Faderman, Odd Girls and Twilight Lovers: A History of Lesbian Life in Twentieth-Century America *(New York, 1991) provides a comprehensive history of lesbians, and Elizabeth Lapovsky Kennedy and Madeline D. Davis,* Boots of Leather, Slippers of Gold: The History of a Lesbian Community *(New York, 1993), details the history of the working-class lesbian bar community in Buffalo, New York, in the 1940s and 1950s. Jonathan Katz's two documentary histories,* Gay American History: Lesbians and Gay Men in the U.S.A., A Documentary *(New York, 1976) and* Gay/Lesbian Almanac: A New Documentary . . . *(New York, 1983), provide valuable material on gay and lesbian life since colonial times.*